Attributed to George Barrett, 'Bridge under construction over the River Dargle, Co. Wicklow' (private collection).

The Building Site in Eighteenth-Century Ireland

Arthur Gibney

Livia Hurley & Edward McParland
EDITORS

FOUR COURTS PRESS

Typeset in 10.5 pt on 13 pt Ehrhardt by
Carrigboy Typesetting Services for
FOUR COURTS PRESS LTD
7 Malpas Street, Dublin 8, Ireland
www.fourcourtspress.ie
and in North America for
FOUR COURTS PRESS
c/o ISBS, 920 NE 58th Avenue, Suite 300, Portland, OR 97213.

© Arthur Gibney, the editors and Four Courts Press 2017

A catalogue record for this title is available
from the British Library.

ISBN 978-1-84682-638-2

All rights reserved.
Without limiting the rights under copyright
reserved alone, no part of this publication may be
reproduced, stored in or introduced into a retrieval system,
or transmitted, in any form or by any means (electronic, mechanical,
photocopying, recording or otherwise), without the prior
written permission of both the copyright owner and
publisher of this book.

THE PUBLISHER AND EDITORS WOULD LIKE TO ACKNOWLEDGE THE GENEROUS
FINANCIAL ASSISTANCE OF THE FOLLOWING:

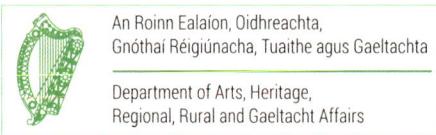

Printed in Spain
by Castuera, Pamplona.

Contents

LIST OF ABBREVIATIONS		6
LIST OF ILLUSTRATIONS		7
GLOSSARY		11
EDITORS' PREFACE		13
Introduction		15
1	Organization and management	18
2	Eighteenth-century building contracts	38
3	Carpentry	57
4	Joinery	86
5	The timber trade	101
6	Wall construction	124
7	The introduction of brickwork	140
8	Stone: its acquisition and use	159
9	The roofing trades: the work of the slater and the plumber	181
10	The glazier and the development of eighteenth-century window patterns	208
11	Plastering and stuccowork	234
12	Painting	252
Epilogue		265
SELECT BIBLIOGRAPHY		273
INDEX		281

Abbreviations

BIGS	*(Quarterly) Bulletin of the Irish Georgian Society* (1958–97) continued as *Irish Architectural and Decorative Studies (IADS)*
BL	British Library
CARD	*Calendar of ancient records of the city of Dublin*, J.T. & R.M. Gilbert (eds) 19 vols (Dublin, 1889–1944)
Commons Journal	*Journals of the House of Commons of the kingdom of Ireland*, 19 vols (Dublin, 1796–1800); index, 2 vols (Dublin, 1802)
DCLA	Dublin City Library and Archive
GSR	*Georgian Society records of domestic architecture and decoration in Dublin*, 5 vols (Dublin, 1909–13; reprint Shannon, 1969)
HMC	Historical Manuscripts Commission
IAA	Irish Architectural Archive
IGS	Irish Georgian Society
JRSAI	*Journal of the Royal Society of Antiquaries of Ireland*
MUBC	Master in Urban and Building Conservation
NAI	National Archives of Ireland
NLI	National Library of Ireland
PRONI	Public Record Office of Northern Ireland
RHK	Royal Hospital Kilmainham
RIA	Royal Irish Academy
RIAI	Royal Institute of the Architects of Ireland
RIBA	Royal Institute of British Architects
TCD	Trinity College Dublin
TNA	The National Archives (formerly PRO, Kew)
UAHS	Ulster Architectural Heritage Society
UCD	University College Dublin
Wren Soc. Vols	*The Wren Society*, 20 vols (Oxford, 1923–43)

Illustrations

Denis Diderot, 'Architecture, Maçonnerie' [Stonemasons' tools] *Encyclopédie*, 35 vols (1751–72), xvii, plates 11 and 13. *Endpapers*

Attributed to George Barrett, 'Bridge under construction over the River Dargle, Co. Wicklow'. 2

1.1	Arms of the Dublin guilds, Charles Brooking, *A map of the city and suburbs of Dublin*, 1728.	19
1.2	A building committee in session; John Trotter, detail of a meeting traditionally said to concern the planning of the Blue Coat School in Dublin, 1772/3.	21
1.3	Allegory of a building site; 'Dawson Grove, the seat of the Rt. Honble Lord Dartrey in the County of Monaghan, Ireland', after Paul Sandby, 1780.	25
1.4	Old Parliament House, Dublin, royal arms in pediment carved by John Houghton, *c*.1730.	29
1.5	George Wilkinson, 'Slate quarry at Killaloe, Co. Clare'.	31
1.6	Building labourers' wages in Dublin, 1660–1910.	36
2.1	Office of Richard Castle, 'An Estimate of the Expense of the Printing House …', 1733.	41
3.1	Proposed Public Offices, Dublin, 1758, section, George Semple.	61
3.2	Royal Hospital Kilmainham, *c*.1685, section.	62
3.3	Kilmacurragh, Co. Wicklow, *c*.1700, section.	62
3.4	Dr Steevens's Hospital, Dublin, 1720s, section.	63
3.5	Dr Clark's School, Drogheda, 1728, section, Michael Wills.	63
3.6	Palazzo Porto, Vicenza, 1540s, section, and Temple of Jupiter, Rome, section, Andrea Palladio, *I quattro libri*.	64
3.7	Multiple-post trusses in bridge construction, Andrea Palladio, *I quattro libri*.	65
3.8	All Souls College, Oxford, truss proposed by Nicholas Hawksmoor, 1716.	67
3.9	Parliament House, Dublin, *c*.1728, section and ceiling plan, Edward Lovett Pearce.	68
3.10	Parliament House, Dublin, *c*.1728, section, Edward Lovett Pearce.	69
3.11	No. 10 South Frederick Street, Dublin, mid-eighteenth century, section.	70
3.12	No. 10 South Frederick Street, Dublin, mid-eighteenth century, top-floor ceiling plan.	71
3.13	No. 10 South Frederick Street, Dublin, mid-eighteenth century, roof structure.	71
3.14	Roof structure of a typical Irish provincial town house; masonry gables and purlins avoided the need for trusses.	72
3.15	Francis Price, *The British carpenter* (London, 5th ed., 1765), plate C & D.	73

3.16	Trussed girders: William Pain, *Carpentry and building, the practical house carpenter*, new ed. (London, 1860/1), plate 10; and Francis Price, *A supplement to the British carpenter* (London, 1735), plate B.	74
3.17	Charlemont House, Dublin, 1763, trussed partitions.	75
3.18	Plan and section showing common floor joists with herring-bone strut.	76
3.19	Plan and section showing common floor joists and binder joists.	76
3.20	Plan and section showing common floor joists and binder joists, with timber girders.	77
3.21	Kilmacurragh, Co. Wicklow, c.1700, floor framing.	77
3.22	James Gandon, 'Proposal for floor framing'.	78
3.23	No. 42 Upper O'Connell Street, Dublin, 1752, floor construction.	79
3.24	No. 40 Lower Dominick Street, Dublin, c.1760, floor construction.	79
3.25	Nos. 13 and 14 Henrietta Street, Dublin, c.1750, floor construction.	80
4.1	Joseph Moxon, *Mechanick exercises* (London, 3rd ed., 1703), plate 4.	89
4.2	System for designing domes and skylights, William Pain, *The carpenter's and joiner's repository* (London, 1778), Plate LIII.	91
4.3	Wooden dentil cornice from 42–43 St Stephen's Green, Dublin, 1745/6.	93
4.4	'Prospect of the Library of Trinity College Dublin', print after Joseph Tudor, c.1753.	97
5.1	James Gandon, 'Plan & Elevation of a Machine for Raising Timber &c'.	102
5.2	Designs for timber centerings for spans of up to 92 feet, George Semple, *A treatise on building in water* (Dublin, 1776), plate 17.	109
5.3	*The book of trades; or, Library of useful arts* (London, 1815), part 1, 'Sawyer'.	111
5.4	Dr Steevens's Hospital, Dublin, 1720s, Pool and Cash, *Views of the most remarkable public buildings … in Dublin* (Dublin, 1780).	116
5.5	James Malton, 'The Four Courts, Dublin', watercolour, 1793, detail showing the floating of timber downstream.	119
5.6	James Malton, 'The Marine School, Dublin', watercolour, 1796, detail showing the landing of timber at Sir John Rogerson's Quay.	119
6.1	Custom House, Dublin, section of stores, by James Gandon, 1795; showing the tripartite construction of the masonry walls.	125
6.2	Goresgrove, Co. Kilkenny, brick reveals to openings and linings to limestone walls.	126
6.3	Castle Durrow, Co. Laois, 1714–18, irregular coursed ashlar.	133
6.4	Entrance front of the Bishop's Palace, Limerick.	133
6.5	George Miller, 'Mr Colles's Marble Mills, Millmount, Co. Kilkenny', early nineteenth-century watercolour.	137
6.6	George Darley, design for a neoclassical chimney-piece, pen and watercolour, c.1775.	138
7.1	Mountjoy Fort, Co. Tyrone, 1601–5.	142
7.2	Jigginstown House, Co. Kildare, 1636.	142
7.3	No. 5 Henrietta Street, Dublin, c.1740, ground-floor window with gauged and rubbed bricks in lintel.	144
7.4	Francis Wheatley, 'Brickmakers', print after oil painting exhibited in 1786.	145

7.5	John Rocque, 'An Exact Survey of the City and Suburbs of Dublin', 1756, detail, 'Old Brick Field' to the west of Sackville Mall.	146
7.6	Marsh's Library, Dublin, *c.*1700, ground-floor window with gauged and rubbed bricks in lintel.	149
7.7	Charles Fort, Kinsale, Co. Cork, joist pockets of brick within stone walls.	152
7.8	James Malton, 'The Tholsel, Skinners Row, Dublin', watercolour, 1792, detail showing Malton's rendering of the texture of brickwork and pointing.	154
7.9	Beaulieu, Co. Louth, 1720s, brick detail.	155
8.1	Thomas Roberts, 'Lucan House and Demesne with Figures Quarrying Stone, County Dublin', *c.*1773–5.	160
8.2	George Wilkinson, 'Black marble quarry, Co. Galway …'	168
8.3	St Anne's Church, Shandon, Cork, 1726.	169
8.4	Kilshannig, Co. Cork, 1760s, detail of entrance front.	170
8.5	St Matthew's Church, Ringsend, Dublin, 1704, detail of entrance front.	172
8.6	St Werburgh's Church, Dublin, 1715–19.	175
8.7	Thomas Cooley, the Royal Exchange, 1770s and Thomas Ivory, Newcomen's Bank, 1780s, Dublin.	177
8.8	John Nixon, 'Quarries at Portland', 1789.	178
8.9	James Malton, 'The West Front of St Patrick's Cathedral, Dublin', watercolour, 1793, detail showing a man with a hod used for carrying brick, stone or mortar.	179
9.1	Slate-hung bow-fronts on the Grand Parade, Cork.	182
9.2	*The book of trades; or, Library of useful arts* (London, 1815), part 1, 'Plumber'.	183
9.3	Hand-forged nails, all (except that on top left) from Palace Street, Dublin, 1760s.	189
9.4	Roof truss designs, B[atty] L[angley], *The city and country builder's and workman's treasury of designs* (London, 1770), appendix, plate 13.	191
9.5	George Wilkinson, 'Roofing slate quarry at Valentia, Co. Kerry'.	199
9.6	General Wade's house, London, garden front, 1723, Colen Campbell, *Vitruvius Britannicus*, 3 (London, 1725), plate 10.	204
9.7	The Provost's House, Trinity College Dublin, 1760s, Robert Pool and John Cash, *Views of the most remarkable public buildings … in Dublin* (Dublin, 1780).	205
9.8	'Front to the Inns Quay of Design for the Publick Offices', Thomas Cooley, 1776.	205
10.1	Advertisement for Benjamin Edwards's glasshouse, Belfast, 8 January 1781.	209
10.2	John Rocque, 'An Exact Survey of the City and Suburbs of Dublin', 1756, detail, glasshouses on the North Wall and Marlborough Green.	211
10.3	Lord Mark Kerr, 'View of Ballycastle', Co. Antrim, with glasshouse, early nineteenth century.	212
10.4	Denis Diderot, 'Verrerie Angloise' [English glasshouse] *Encyclopédie* (1751–72), plate III of Verrerie Angloise.	213

10.5	Trinity College Dublin, Parliament Square, 1750s, example of crown glass.	215
10.6	James Malton, 'The Tholsel, Skinners Row, Dublin', watercolour, 1792, detail showing two mullioned windows with casement opening in the Tholsel.	220
10.7	Trinity College Dublin, Old Library, ground-floor window in the west pavilion.	224
10.8	Tyrone House, Dublin, 1740, Pool and Cash, *Views of the most remarkable public buildings … in Dublin* (Dublin, 1780).	226
10.9	James Malton, 'Leinster House, Dublin', aquatint, 1792, detail of fenestration.	227
10.10	James Malton, 'The West Front of St Patrick's Cathedral, Dublin', watercolour, 1793, detail showing open butchers' stalls.	230
10.11	'A Prospect of the Parliament House in College Green, Dublin …', *c.*1753, print after J. Tudor, detail.	231
10.12	James Malton, 'Royal Exchange, Dublin', watercolour, 1795, detail showing curved shop windows on Cork Hill.	232
10.13	'Front to Astons Quay', watercolour, 1800, showing shop fronts proposed by the Wide Streets Commissioners.	233
11.1	Florence Court, Co. Fermanagh, 1760s, lantern and plasterwork (no longer surviving).	239
11.2	No. 20 Lower Dominick Street, Dublin, built by Robert West, 1758–60, detail of plasterwork in staircase hall.	241
11.3	Plaster ornaments in the shape of urns with metal armatures, from South Frederick Street, Dublin, mid-eighteenth century.	245
11.4	Castletown Cox, Co. Kilkenny, entrance hall, *c.*1767, plasterwork by Patrick Osborne.	246
11.5	Castletown Cox, Co. Kilkenny, staircase hall, *c.*1767, detail of plasterwork by Patrick Osborne.	247
11.6	Kilshannig, Co. Cork, detail of plasterwork in library ceiling attributed to Filippo Lafranchini, 1760s.	249
11.7	Staircase hall and landing, Powerscourt House, Dublin, plasterwork by James McCullagh with Michael Reynolds, 1774.	250

Glossary

adze: a tool similar to an axe, with a curved blade at right angles to the handle, used for cutting or shaping large pieces of wood.
argillaceous: having the nature of clay.
ashlar: type of masonry consisting of blocks with cleanly dressed, smooth faces and squared edges.
bond timber: timber worked into a wall to tie or strengthen it longitudinally.
brazier: one who works in brass.
calp: a limestone found in Co. Dublin.
cames: the lead strips within a leaded window which hold the individual panes in place.
coffer-dam: a watertight enclosure used for obtaining a dry foundation for bridges, piers, etc.; usually constructed of two rows of piles with clay packed between them, extending above high-water mark, the water being pumped out so as to leave the enclosure dry.
cogged joint: a carpentry joint formed by two crossed structural members, each of which is notched at the place where they cross.
collar-beam: a horizontal beam connecting a pair of rafters which prevents them from spreading or sagging; it is attached about the middle of the rafters as distinguished from a tie-beam which is at the feet of the rafters.
cordwainer: a worker in cordwain or cordovan leather; a shoemaker.
cotter-pin: a folded pin with a loop at one end designed to have the other end bent to hold it in place.
countersunk pin: a pin with its head level with, or below, the surface to which the pin is attached, with a flat or oval head.
cutler: one who makes, deals in, or repairs knives and similar cutting utensils.
distemper: a paint using glue or size instead of an oil base.
gauged (as of brickwork): brickwork that is rubbed, or smoothed, and cut to special forms.
hardwood: the wood of broadleaved or dicotyledonous trees (such as oak, ash or teak), which is typically hard, as distinguished from that of conifers (such as pine), which is typically softer.
hydraulic lime: hydraulic lime sets by hydrolysis (i.e., under water), as distinguished from non-hydraulic lime which sets by carbonation.
journeyman: one who having served his apprenticeship to a handicraft or trade, is qualified to work at it for a day's wage, and works at it not on his own account but as the servant or employee of another.
kerf: the cut made by a saw.
king-post: an upright post in the centre of a roof-truss, extending from the ridge to the tie-beam.

laths: thin narrow strips of wood used to form a groundwork upon which to fasten the slates or tiles of a roof, or the plaster of a wall or ceiling.

latten-worker: a worker in brass, lead or tin, which was often made into sheets of alloy.

mitre joint: a carpentry joint made by bevelling each of the two parts to be joined, usually at a 45° angle, to form a corner, usually a 90° angle.

mortise and tenon joint: a carpentry joint whereby a mortise, which is a cavity cut into one timber, receives a tenon, which is a projection on a second timber, to form a secure joint. A tenon is usually of rectangular section.

mullion: a vertical member, dividing a window into two or more lights.

perch: originally a rod of a definite length used for measuring land, etc. Later, a measure of length used for land, fences, walls, etc., varying locally but now standardized at 5½ yards, i.e., 16½ feet (approx. 5.03m).

purlin: a horizontal beam which runs along the length of a roof, resting upon the principal rafters at right angles and supporting the ordinary rafters or boards of the roof.

quarrey: A small, diamond-shaped (or occas. square) pane of glass often held in place with lead cames (qv); also occasionally a small round pane of glass.

queen-post: either of two upright posts in a roof-truss, which extend from the principal rafters down to the tie beam at points equidistant from its middle or ends.

scantlings: both dimensions of timber and dimensioned pieces of timber (or stone). As applied to timber, the word usually denotes the sectional dimensions (thickness and breadth) of a beam etc., in contradistinction to the length.

shale: an argillaceous fissile rock, the laminae of which are usually fragile and uneven, and mostly parallel to the bedding.

softwood: wood which is relatively soft or easily cut; especially coniferous trees like pine.

spawl: a stone fragment broken during cutting and having at least one flat edge.

square: an area of surface 10ft by 10ft, i.e., 100 square feet.

strut: a bar, rod, or built-up member, of wood, iron, etc., designed to resist pressure or thrust in a framework; e.g., a diagonal timber which acts as a brace to support a principal rafter.

tie-beam: a piece of timber connecting the feet of the principal rafters in order to prevent them from spreading.

transom: a horizontal member, usually of stone, across the width of a window.

voussoir: a wedge-shaped block, usually of stone, helping to form an arch and rising to the keystone.

wainscotter: a timber panel maker

wall-plate: a timber placed horizontally on or in a wall, to form a support for joists and rafters.

Editors' preface

THE HOPE OF AN AUTHOR OF A doctoral thesis is that the work will satisfy just two people (the examiners); a published book must be aimed at a larger audience. The conversion of a thesis into a book, therefore, can be a laborious task, particularly if carried out by others than the original author. As editors, forced to work without the guidance and wisdom of our good friend Arthur, we have converted his thesis into this book.

Arthur Gibney was awarded his doctorate from the University of Dublin for 'Studies in eighteenth-century building history', the thesis on which this book – with the new title of *The building site in eighteenth-century Ireland* – is based. His death in 2006 prevented him from effecting his ambition to publish the work, as his obituary in the *Irish Times* (27 May 2006) reminds us. This was a great pity because it had been much consulted in its unpublished form in the library of Trinity College Dublin by architects, architectural historians and scholars. As Gibney says in his own Introduction, the published literature on the techniques and materials of eighteenth-century building in Ireland is not extensive. His experience, both on the building site and in archives and libraries, made his thesis an unparalleled contribution to the subject.

While Gibney was a very distinguished watercolourist he is best known as an architect. After completing his degree in the School of Architecture in Bolton Street, he formed a practice with his fellow student Sam Stephenson and together they won the competition in 1961 for the ESB buildings in Lower Fitzwilliam Street. In 1974 he was awarded the RIAI Triennial Gold Medal for his Irish Management Institute in Sandyford. He was much involved in the institutional life of the arts in Ireland. He served on the Arts Council of Ireland and as President of the Royal Institute of the Architects of Ireland in its 150th anniversary year in 1980. He was President of the Royal Hibernian Academy for nine years to 2005.

The ideas, research, speculations and conclusions in this book are Gibney's and the responsibilities for these are his. We have corrected a few minor errors in the original (while being not at all sure that we have avoided introducing a few new errors ourselves); we have simplified the apparatus of footnotes; occasionally we have moved paragraphs around to make the argument run a little more fluently; we have omitted some illustrations and commissioned the redrawing of others; and where the 1997 text has been superseded by later research we have not rewritten Gibney, but have indicated in footnotes the existence of more recent work. In other words we have, throughout, respected the original text as an enduringly valuable presentation of the professional and academic experience of a distinguished architect. All photographs are by the editors unless otherwise indicated.

The publication of this volume has been supported by the Department of Arts, Heritage, Regional, Rural and Gaeltacht Affairs; the Office of Public Works; the Irish Georgian Society; the Royal Institute of the Architects of Ireland; Arthur Gibney & Partners Architecture; and the Primrose Trust. We are also very grateful for the support of McCullough Mulvin Architects, Piaras Beaumont, P.J. Hanna, Brian O'Connell, Toal Ó'Muiré and Emer O'Siochru. Sincere thanks to Conor Rochford our draughtsman, Elizabeth Mayes our copyeditor, Julitta Clancy our indexer, and Martin Fanning and all at Four Courts Press. Our gratitude goes to the Dublin City Library & Archive; the Irish Architectural Archive; the National Archives of Ireland; the National Inventory of Architectural Heritage; the National Library of Ireland; the libraries of Trinity College Dublin, University College Dublin and the Royal Irish Academy, and to all who gave permission to quote or reproduce (these are credited fully in the footnotes and illustration captions). Many friends and colleagues have assisted us in the preparation of this book: special mention should be made of Wendy Barrett; John, 8th Earl Belmore; Carla Briggs; Donough Cahill; Christine Casey; Martin Colreavy; Willie Cumming; Adam D'Arcy; Fergus D'Arcy; David and Edwin Davison; Charles Duggan; Lisa Edden; Sophie Evans; Siobhán Fitzpatrick; Phyllis Gibney; Fernando Girbal Piñero; Nicola Gordon Bowe; John Graby; Brendan Grimes; Jacqueline Hill; Orla Kelly; William Laffan; Conor Lucey; Robin Mandal; Eve McAulay; Patricia McCarthy; Niall McCullough; Jason McElligott; John Montague; Andrew Muldowney; Kevin Mulligan; Patrick Murphy; Ciaran O'Connor; Gregory O'Connor; Freddie O'Dwyer; Colum O'Riordan; Peter Pearson; Carole Pollard; Nessa Roche; Ellen Rowley; Robert Towers; and Primrose Wilson.

LIVIA HURLEY & EDWARD MCPARLAND

Introduction

THIS STUDY OF EIGHTEENTH-CENTURY building history examines the development of Irish building practice from the last quarter of the seventeenth century until the beginning of the nineteenth. As such, it covers the great age of classical building in Ireland, opening with the construction of the Royal Hospital Kilmainham in the 1680s and closing with the completion of Gandon's Four Courts in the 1790s. It thus coincides with one of the most cohesive periods in Irish history from the re-establishment of the viceregal court after the Restoration until the enactment of parliamentary union with England at the end of the eighteenth century. This period commenced with the reorganization of the medieval craft guilds in the 1670s and ended with the beginning of industrialized building processes and the emergence of the general building contractor in the early 1800s.

The choice of this subject comes, first, from my own interest in historic building structures, and also from the perceived need for research into a field that could benefit architectural restoration and refurbishment of historic buildings. Building history is a relatively new field of study in Ireland and, except for a few works such as Maurice Craig's *Classic Irish houses of the middle size* and E.M. Jope's essays on sixteenth- and seventeenth-century structures, there is little published information available on its patterns and practice. [An important resource, much enlarged since Gibney wrote, is provided by the theses in the library of the School of Architecture in UCD presented for the MUBC degree.]

The main documentary sources used for research have been artisans' building accounts and receipts for payments; records of state expenditure on public building programmes; correspondence of merchants and owners of country estates; and seventeenth- and eighteenth-century English publications on buildings, such as measurers' and carpenters' manuals. The scarcity of reliable information on the building guilds, with the exception of the painters' Guild of St Luke, has inhibited a full examination of this subject.

Evidence from documentary research has been augmented by information gleaned from investigations and site surveys of historic buildings. The many restoration programmes undertaken in recent years on important Irish classical buildings have provided invaluable opportunities for close inspection of exposed structural fabric. These include public buildings in Dublin such as the Royal Hospital Kilmainham, the Custom House, Dublin Castle and Leinster House; privately owned urban houses in Dublin such as 13 Henrietta Street, 35 North Great George's Street and Mornington House and, in the provinces, classical mansions such as Castletown Cox, Co. Kilkenny and Castletown, Co. Kildare. The ruins of country houses such as

Tudenham, Co. Westmeath, Tyrone House, Co. Galway and Wardstown, Co. Donegal afforded similar opportunities. I found that the experience gained from my own architectural responsibilities for the refurbishment of parts of the Old Library in Trinity College, and for work on Dr Steevens's Hospital in Dublin, on Avondale, Co. Wicklow and on urban houses such as 25 Eustace Street Dublin, was of valuable assistance in assessing the structural characteristics of other eighteenth-century buildings.

The method of presentation used here divides the material into separate chapters to describe the activities of individual trades. Each trade is treated as a discrete entity, but congruous trades such as carpentry and joinery, or masonry and brickwork, are grouped together.

The decision to include an introductory section with two chapters covering organizational patterns and building contracts was felt to be a necessary addition to the individual trade descriptions. This provides an opportunity to discuss the control of contracts, methods of payment, the provision of building plant, the role of supervisors, measurers and professional architects, and the involvement of the surveyor general's office in building commissions. The description of the different contractual forms used, their advantages and disadvantages, helps explain the change from individual trade contracts to general (all-trade) contracting in the early decades of the nineteenth century.

The conclusions reached are thus supported by evidence from historic records and surveys of surviving eighteenth-century construction. In some cases where documentary evidence was unavailable, or site surveys unobtainable, conclusions have been reached by speculation on constructional practices. A good example of a well-documented conclusion is the comparison of English and Irish floor framing, which is based on both evidence from building manuals and drawings of floor structures. A typical speculative conclusion can be found in the claim for the frequent use of gypsum plaster in Irish stucco work. This is based on close observation, personal experience in casting and modelling plaster, and informed discussions with present-day craftsmen such as Thomas Leyden and Séamus Ó hEocha. The considerable range of the subject matter and the need to confine the discussion within reasonable limits have restricted the examination of each trade to its general characteristics and working practices. However, this broad comparison of the operational patterns of all the building trades should provide a valuable resource for more comprehensive research into individual trade activities.

This study provides new information on the construction of early classical architecture in Ireland. It evaluates the technical response of the building trades to the introduction of new architectural ideals and how the performance of building materials influenced design concepts. It examines regional variations in building patterns and particularly the considerable divergence between Irish and English building practices. It clarifies the role played by innovative classical designers such as

Edward Lovett Pearce and Richard Castle in the introduction of new architectural ideals and the technical advances which accompanied their work. And it throws new light on the craftsmen who built important historical buildings, their contribution to both the fabrication and design of these buildings and their part in the development of the emerging architectural profession.

CHAPTER ONE

Organization and management

THE EIGHTEENTH CENTURY WAS a period of transition between the feudal practices of the building guilds and the emergence of a highly capitalized building industry in the early decades of the nineteenth century. In England, change was already apparent in the seventeenth century with the introduction (in 1667) of stringent building regulations after the fire of London, in the ascendancy of the professional architect as a principal influence on the rebuilding of the capital city, and in the demand for special skills to support the importation of new architectural ideals from the European mainland.

The gradual erosion of the guild monopolies began during this period. The urgency and scale of reconstruction in London forced a relaxation of guild control to allow *forrens* (artisans from outside the city who were not freemen) to work in the metropolitan area.[1] The rapid urbanization of seventeenth-century suburbs such as Bloomsbury, St James's and St Martin's Fields (through the development of speculative housing estates) gave suburban artisans the same benefits as the liverymen of the city companies, without the equivalent costs. The advent of the urban house builder (an artisan who employed artisans from other trades) in the speculative development of housing estates promoted new trade relationships and helped to break the traditional divisions between members of the building guilds. The reconstruction of London introduced new materials and constructional methods. The emphasis on incombustible materials in the building regulations promoted the use of brick masonry in place of the traditional timber cage structures, and introduced significant demand for bricklayers, bricks and brickmaking facilities. The shortage of materials caused by the great scale of reconstruction encouraged the increased use of Norwegian and Baltic softwoods instead of traditional English oak.

The heavy investment by the crown and city institutions encouraged the development of building designers who were capable of giving their full attention to the task of organizing large contractual operations. Important commissions such as St Paul's Cathedral, the city churches and the new royal palaces provided architects such as Wren and Hawksmoor with unprecedented opportunities to develop their formal talents, but they also presented formidable problems in the control and management of building standards and building costs. The records of Wren's leadership of the Office of Works in the construction of the royal palaces, and of

---

Material in this chapter should be supplemented with work by Fergus D'Arcy and Conor Lucey: see Select Bibliography.   1 Linda Clarke, *Building capitalism* (London, 1992), p. 46.

Organization and management

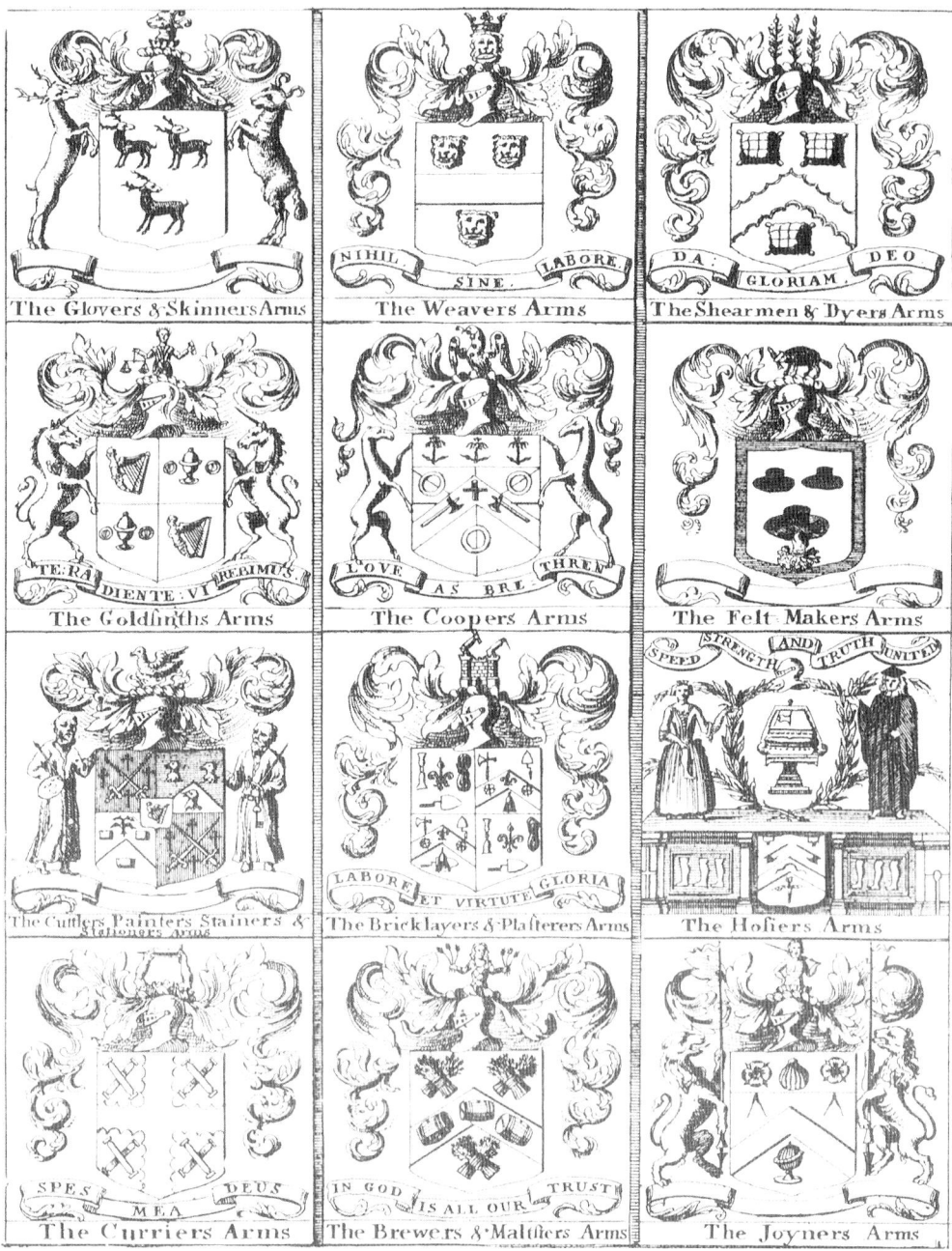

1.1 Arms of the Dublin guilds, Charles Brooking, *A map of the city and suburbs of Dublin*, 1728.

his role in the city churches, shows a rigorous concentration on standards of workmanship, and an intervention in the production and purchasing of materials to control their quality and cost.

In Ireland, the new century brought with it most of the patterns of change experienced in English building practices after the London fire. By the end of the seventeenth century the country was no longer a major producer of commercial hardwood, and Irish builders were forced to rely on suppliers of timber from Norway and the Baltic ports. Irish oak, that was used unsparingly in the structure and finishes of the Royal Hospital Kilmainham in the 1680s, was more reserved in early eighteenth-century buildings such as Burgh's Library in Trinity College Dublin and Pearce's Parliament House for roof framing and decorative joinery fittings. By the mid-century oak was too scarce and expensive for use in most Irish roofs. The change from timber-frame construction to masonry structures would not have been as noticeable in Ireland, as timber-frame structures had been common only in cities such as Dublin, Waterford and Cork, and plantation towns in Ulster, such as Derry and Lisburn.

The indigenous tradition of stone masonry prevailed everywhere in Ireland throughout the eighteenth century, but the convenience of brickwork for interior walls and window dressings (already recognized in some seventeenth-century structures) greatly increased its use in urban buildings and country houses. The establishment of the Dublin bricklayers' guild (by royal patent) in 1670 anticipated a new migratory influx of Protestant artisans who were encouraged to settle in Irish communities because of the scarcity of competent native craftsmen.[2] They brought with them new masonry and carpentry practices, and Irish building methods developed under their influence from the last decades of the seventeenth century until the 1730s. The tradition of brick urban houses, common in Dublin and other coastal cities, dates from this period, as does the use of roofing tiles, king-post roof trusses, sliding sash windows, timber panelling and the use of timber bonds in masonry walls.

The emergence of the professional architect and the importation of new architectural ideals brought demands for special skills and for people who could interpret a new language of classical ornament. The importation of new masonry materials, such as white limestone from the Isle of Portland, and facing bricks from Holland and the south of England, developed rapidly from the early decades of the century. The foundation of a separate guild of joiners, wainscotters and ceylers (ceiling-makers) in Dublin in 1700 is evidence of a particular interest in interior architecture based on the introduction of classical forms.[3]

The craft guilds were mostly of medieval origin, established by royal patent, to regulate entry into the trades and to control the quality of workmanship. Over the centuries weaker guilds were forced to affiliate with stronger guilds and their representation became remarkably varied. In Dublin, for instance, the Corporation

---

2 DCLA, Gilbert Collection, Charter of Dublin Guild of Bricklayers and Plasterers, MS 81.   3 Henry Guinness, 'Dublin trade gilds', *JRSAI*, 52 (1922), 162.

1.2 A building committee in session; John Trotter, detail of a meeting traditionally said to concern the planning of the Blue Coat School in Dublin, 1772/3. Reproduced with permission of the Law Society. Photograph by David Davison.

of Carpenters was an amalgamation of three earlier federations: the house carpenters, the ship's carpenters and the millers. By 1508, under a new charter, it represented carpenters, millers, masons and heliers (roofers). It also represented plumbers, joiners (before 1700) and bricklayers and plasterers (before 1670).[4] In 1670, the bricklayers and the plasterers formed a new association and, as we have already seen, in 1700 the guild for joiners, wainscotters and ceylers received its charter. The painter-stainers shared the Guild of St Luke with the stationers and (in an unlikely fellowship) with the cutlers. Each guild was governed by a master and two wardens who were elected annually. Entry was gained by serving an apprenticeship for seven years with a master craftsman who undertook the apprentice's education. After the apprentice had completed his seven years of service, he became a journeyman and eligible to become a full member of the guild and also a freeman of the city. The latter entitled him to vote in parliamentary elections; the former enabled him to employ other journeymen and contract them for work.

4 Mary Clark & Raymond Refaussé, *Directory of historic Dublin guilds* (Dublin, 1993), p. 17.

The guilds in the provincial cities also represented a variety of trade interests. Clonmel, the capital of Ormonde's palatinate, had three eighteenth-century guilds catering for merchants, cordwainers and brewers, and building artisans may well have been accommodated in any one of them.[5] Cork, the largest city outside Dublin, had twenty-four guilds, but in the first decade of the eighteenth century they had difficulty in maintaining a monopoly against the encroachment of local Catholic artisans.[6] The Company of Goldsmiths (founded in 1657) represented plumbers, tinsmiths, founders, latten-workers, braziers, upholsterers, saddlers and bridlemakers. A carpenters' guild was founded in 1667, a masons' guild in 1696 and a guild for painters, sawyers and brogue makers in 1787.[7] Ferrar's *Directory* lists fifteen guilds operating in Limerick in 1769. One of these federations specifically represented the local carpenters, but the masons' and bricklayers' guild also accepted slaters, plasterers, painters, paviers and limeburners. Guild monopolies (for Protestant freemen) were never as firmly established in Cork and Limerick as they were in Dublin. In 1761, a parliamentary committee, presided over by Edmund Sexton Pery, decided that the Limerick guilds had no legal authority to prevent Catholic artisans coming inside the city walls to practise their trade.[8]

Membership of the guilds was restricted to people who were eligible to receive the freedom of the city where the guild was founded, and in Ireland this franchise was normally restricted to members of the Protestant faith. In 1671, the Dublin bricklayers' and plasterers' charter offered membership 'to all Protestant strangers and foreigners of the aforesaid Arts or mysteries, that shall transport their families into the kingdom, [who] shall be admitted free on paying 20s'.[9] Membership was especially open to the sons of Protestant artisans who had served an apprenticeship with their fathers. However, by the mid-eighteenth century access to the guilds was being increasingly sought by aspiring politicians seeking office in parliament or the city assemblies, on the basis of the voting power of the guild fraternities. A considerable number of these political candidates had no direct connection with the crafts represented by their guild, and some were not even tradesmen.

For instance, in mid-century Limerick, the Guild of Masons, Bricklayers, Slaters, Plasterers, Painters, Paviers and Lime-burners admitted Mitchell Bennis, a saddler, and Edward Keatten, a breeches maker, and others not obviously connected with the building trades.[10] In Dublin in 1749, the famous attempt of the political agitators Charles Lucas and James Digges La Touche to manipulate freemen's votes for their election as MPs for the city led to a parliamentary censure, disgrace for Lucas and the stripping of a parliamentary seat from La Touche. Twelve years later, in 1761, Lucas

---

5 Constantia Maxwell, *Country and town in Ireland under the Georges* (Dundalk, 1949), p. 270. **6** Richard Caulfield (ed.), *The council book of the corporation of the city of Cork* (Guildford, 1876), pp 311, 319. **7** J. Windele, *Historical and descriptive notices of the city of Cork* (Cork, 1839), p. 98. **8** Robert Herbert, 'The trade guilds of Limerick', *North Munster Antiquarian Journal*, 2:3 (spring, 1941), 95. **9** DCLA, Gilbert Collection, Charter of Dublin Guild of Bricklayers and Plasterers, MS 81. **10** The Jim Kemmy Municipal Museum, Limerick, minutes of the Limerick Guild of Masons, Bricklayers, Slaters, Plasterers, Painters, Paviours, and Lime-burners, 27 June 1747; 20 Oct. 1749; 3 Oct. 1750; MS LM 1989: 65.

(on his return from exile) was to win his parliamentary seat on foot of his popularity with the Dublin freemen.

The decline of the guilds in the second half of the eighteenth century can be attributed to several factors. One was the dilution of their purpose by the admission of unsuitable members (such as the political opportunists) who had no specific involvement with the trade represented by the guild. Another was the strong opposition to their trading monopolies by groups of Catholic artisans who enjoyed a new political status in the last decades of the century. The third was the increasing friction between master artisans and their journeymen employees caused by the demand for better wages (to cope with the increased cost of living) during the period of rapid financial inflation from the 1770s until well into the nineteenth century.

Although trade monopolies were to remain in the control of the guilds until the end of the eighteenth century, one important aspect of their powers had declined well before this time. This was the guild fraternity's intervention in building works to monitor or adjudicate on cost and workmanship. A good example of this practice (and, perhaps, of its decline) is recorded in a visit to Trinity College in March 1681 by four members of the Dublin Guild of Carpenters to certify a value of £103 14s. 0d. for work completed by the carpenter Patrick Stenton.[11] In April 1700, William Sherriff, a member of the Guild of St Luke, was fined by the guild for poor workmanship on a house in York Street and in 1704 complaints were received by the guild about the heraldic painter Aaron Crossley.[12] However, as the century advanced, this form of guild intervention appears to have ceased.

One reason for the lack of trade intervention into quality control was the increasing involvement of architects such as Richard Castle and Hugh Darley in the design, supervision and certification of buildings. The change in practice from self-regulation by trade federations to direct control by building owners and their agents was apparent in London early in the century. Yeomans illustrates this in the case of the Company of Bricklayers and Tilers who complained of their declining control to the commissioners of the Queen Anne churches in 1714.[13] The eighteenth-century preference for measured contracts based on predetermined rates, and the use of professional measurers to quantify the value of workmanship, minimized disputes about cost and made the form of guild intervention used in the college in 1680 unnecessary.

The mid-century minute books of the Limerick Guild of Masons, Bricklayers, etc. record judgments issued on the condition of buildings (e.g., the city gaol is unsafe and should be demolished), on liability for party walls and encroachments and on disputes about payment for work done.[14] However, there is one well-known record of this guild's intervention into a major building dispute in 1748, when they were called

11 TCD, Patrick Stenton's accounts, MUN/P2/1/34. 12 Charles T. Keatinge, 'The Guild of Cutlers, Painter-Stainers and Stationers', *JRSAI*, 30 (1900), 139. 13 David T. Yeomans, 'Managing eighteenth-century buildings', *Construction History*, 4 (1988), 16–17. 14 Kemmy Museum, Limerick, minutes, 19 Feb. 1750; 26 Feb. 1751; 25 Nov. 1754; 2 Oct. 1756; MS LM 1989: 65.

as witnesses by the Dublin carpenter Pierce Archbold to testify to the fitness of the construction and cost of a barracks built by him in Limerick.[15] This endorsement by the Limerick guild fraternity was one of several testimonies submitted to parliamentary enquiry (in 1752) into the propriety of a programme of sixty-five building contracts for provincial barracks, but none of the other sworn testimonials concerning barracks in other parts of the country were obtained from guild corporations. The contractor's reliance on the Limerick guild (who represented most of the local building trades) was undoubtedly influenced by the fact that most of the work on this barracks was subcontracted to members of this guild. On the other hand, Samuel Cardy, the contractor for the Navan and Drogheda barracks, who was a warden of the Dublin Corporation of Carpenters, Millers, Masons, Heylers, Tinners and Plumbers during this period, sought no intervention or support from his fraternity.[16]

Many of the master artisans working in cities such as Dublin, Waterford, Cork and Limerick were of English origin, being part of a continuous influx of Protestant craftsmen introduced into Irish urban communities during the seventeenth century. This migration was to continue into the early years of the eighteenth century, and the construction of urban housing during this period was especially influenced by their presence. Bricklayers John Herne from Dorchester and Richard Mills from Gloucestershire became freemen of Dublin in 1670 and 1671.[17] The carpenters Benjamin Rudd from Cumberland and Job Ensor from Warwickshire arrived in the city between the 1710 and the 1720s, but the long economic recession from that period until the mid-century undoubtedly broke this migratory pattern.[18]

In Dublin we find the names of the same building families recurring from generation to generation. The Darleys, for instance, who first claim our attention as the stonecutters on Trinity College Library and Dr Steevens's Hospital, were continuously engaged on important stone cutting contracts until the end of the century. They became prominent also as suppliers of limestone from Ardbraccan, Co. Meath, Sheephouse, Co. Louth and of granite from Golden Hill, Co. Wicklow. Other notable families include the Balls, who operated as carpenters and joiners and, by the mid-century, became timber merchants and suppliers of joinery to other contracting artisans; the Semples, who were masons, bricklayers, plasterers and occasionally architects; the Walls, who were plasterers, painters and stuccodores; and the Ensors, who started their careers as carpenters and developed into master builders, with responsibility for both the architectural design and construction of entire building projects. These eighteenth-century master artisans were independent craftsmen who had considerable control over their own destinies through the guild system and its privileged position within the city oligarchies. They are distinguished from their nineteenth-century successors by their freedom to choose their own standards of

---

15 *Commons Journal*, 5, lxxv.   **16** Ibid., 5, lxxvii.   **17** DCLA, typescript, 'Roll of the freemen of Dublin city'.   **18** Mary Amelia Rudd, *Records of the Rudd family* (Bristol, 1920), p. 203; E. Estyn Evans (ed.), *Harvest home* (Armagh, 1975), p. 141.

1.3 Allegory of a building site; 'Dawson Grove, the seat of the Rt. Honble Lord Dartrey in the County of Monaghan, Ireland', after Paul Sandby, 1780, NLI, ET/C380. Reproduced with permission of the National Library of Ireland.

workmanship, by their broad theoretical knowledge and by their social mobility among the merchant community.

The realization of imported architectural ideals was, to a great extent, left in the hands of these craftsmen. Artisans such as carpenters, joiners, stonecutters and stuccodores were the interpreters of stylistic ensembles of space and ornamentation. Carpenters' manuals and pattern books of the time were more concerned with the canons of architectural form than with the assembly of building components. An artisan architect such as George Semple, who admitted to little or no formal schooling, could rationally discuss the works of Alberti, Palladio, Scamozzi and Serlio, and in 1776 publish a learned treatise on bridge building based on the most advanced methods used in France by the Ecole des Ponts et Chaussées.[19] A manuscript translation of Vitruvius belonging to Semple's contemporary, the carpenter-architect Michael Wills, still survives in the Chester Beatty Library in Dublin. James Rudd, a son of the Dublin carpenter and master builder Benjamin Rudd, opened a bookshop in Dame Street in 1755, and became the most ambitious stockist of architectural books in the city. His stock ranged from practical manuals such as William Pain's *The builder's companion* to theoretical works such as Robert Morris's *Architectural remembrancer*. As Casey points out, Rudd's background as a member of a prominent building family influenced his specialization in architectural publications and made him aware of the demand for such works.[20]

Social and political advancement was a possibility for ambitious tradesmen. The notorious John Magill, whose critics accused him of buying a parliamentary seat for the borough of Rathcormac, began his career as a journeyman carpenter in the 1720s. During the 1730s he worked his way upwards as a building supervisor under Pearce at the Parliament House. He was appointed Commissioner and Overseer of the Barracks in 1759. Charles Thorpe, the stuccodore and house builder, provides us with a good example of the upwardly mobile guildsman; he is listed as a representative of his guild (bricklayers and plasterers) on the common council of the city in 1787, as a city sheriff in 1790, in the position of a city alderman from September 1792 and as lord mayor of Dublin in 1800.[21] Many Dublin building tradesmen were wealthy men. Baron Ferrard, the builder of Beaulieu, Co. Louth, records a meeting with such an artisan: 'I spoke to one Mr Quin [probably Francis Quinn] a master builder in Dublin and very rich'.[22] Benjamin Rudd, the expatriate Cumbrian carpenter, owned houses in Clarendon Street, Grafton Street, Molesworth Street, Frederick Street, Henry Street and Bachelor's Walk at the time of his death in 1756.[23] Robert Ball, who sold timber to other artisans and who built houses in Sackville Mall and Rutland Square in the 1750s, obviously prospered, as his family's merchant bank dates from this period. The stuccodores Michael Stapleton and Charles Thorpe both owned substantial properties in Mountjoy Square in the 1790s. Two members of the carpenters' guild, George and John Ensor, were continuously engaged as architects and master builders from 1749 onwards, in both speculative housing in Dublin and in institutional buildings in the provinces. George evidently prospered, as he ended his days as the owner of a country house and a large estate in Armagh.[24]

Most eighteenth-century building operations in Ireland (with the exception of some speculative housing developments) followed the English practice of separate building contracts for each individual trade engaged on a building. This pattern of contracting was an undoubted legacy from traditional divisions of the trades into

---

19 George Semple, *A treatise on building in water* (Dublin, 1776). **20** Christine Casey, 'Books and builders: a bibliographical approach to Irish eighteenth-century architecture' (PhD, University of Dublin, Trinity College, 1991), p. 15. **21** *CARD*, 14, pp 287; 441–2; 544. **22** NLI, Lord Ferrard to Lord Molesworth, 4 Sept. 1722 (in file 'Letters to or from 1st Viscount Molesworth'), microfilm, p. 3753. **23** Casey, 'Books and builders', p. 16. **24** Evans (ed.), *Harvest home*, p. 142.

separate guilds and the discreet nature of guild control over the crafts they represented. The use of separate agreements for masons, stonecutters, carpenters, joiners, slaters, plumbers, glaziers, plasterers and painters meant that, although the workforce on a building site could be large, the number of artisans employed by any one trade contractor could be quite small.

This reduced the contractor's responsibility to the control and management of his own sector of the building work and enabled him to operate with modest capital outlays. On large masonry contracts such as the Library in Trinity College between April and September 1718, the masonry contractor Francis Quinn employed nine different artisans and seven labourers at different times (not more than five in all in any one week), and he was financed by regular interim payments as the work proceeded.[25] On the Parliament House site (c.1730) we find the extensive stonecutting contract divided between four separate contractors which enabled them to cope with a fast building programme without undue pressure on their resources.[26] Many eighteenth-century trade contractors were family workshops consisting of a master artisan and his sons contributing to the work, with journeymen and labourers hired on a casual basis as the workload demanded.

Thus, most artisans worked within the well-established system of separate agreements (with each trade) based on predetermined prices and subject to measurement of quantities of completed work at the contract's completion. These measured contracts allowed tradesmen reasonable profits, provided that they were allowed to work at a productive pace without delays or interruptions. Building accounts of the period provide us with a clear picture of the building process, the trades and suppliers involved and the cost of work and materials.

* * *

Masonry and bricklaying contracts had to be agreed before work could begin on site to enable foundations to be built, but contracts for finishes such as plastering, painting and interior joinery could be settled at any convenient time during the building process. Each trade provided its own unskilled labour to attend the skilled craftsmen, but general labour for earth excavation, scaffolding and clearing site rubbish was usually provided by the building owner. Building rates made provision for either the owner or the trade contractor to provide building materials, and in the early part of the century, institutions and the owners of large country estates themselves often provided expensive materials such as facing stone and framing timber.

When considering masonry we should remember that Irish building accounts distinguish between the work of walling contractors like Francis Quinn, who built structural masonry with random-sized local stone, and on the other hand stonecutters like Moses Darley or Nathaniel Whinrey, who applied precise stone facings to walls.

25 TCD, Francis Quinn's accounts, MUN/P2/37/64.   26 *Commons Journal*, 4, xxxii; xxxiii.

The main material of Quinn, and his like in Dublin, was roughly squared local limestone or calp, quarried within the vicinity of the building site. Darley, on the other hand, used dressed stone blocks from selected quarries such as Portland and – characteristically in the neighbourhood of Dublin – limestone from Ardbraccan, Co. Meath and Palmerstown, Co. Dublin, or granite from Golden Hill, Co. Wicklow. These two trades are distinguished in the eighteenth century as those of (rough) mason and stonecutter.

In all this the work of the bricklayer occupies an ambiguous place. Bricklayers in Dublin were originally accommodated in the carpenters' guild.[27] The formation there of a bricklayers' and plasterers' guild in 1670, and the survival at Jigginstown, Co. Kildare (c.1637) of fine brickwork, indicates an established and no doubt independent trade in the seventeenth century. Bonded brick masonry, however, was unusual in Ireland outside the large coastal cities and its use (in Dublin, Cork and Limerick) was usually confined to speculative houses. The most common use of brickwork was as a component in stone masonry walls, as dressings to form the regular outline of door and window openings in rough masonry, or as a slender brick lining on the inside face of exterior structural walls.

In Trinity College Dublin, bricklayers such as William Caldebeck and Francis Quinn, who worked under Burgh, James Morris and Gilbert Plummer in the 1730s and 1740s, and John Semple in the 1760s, contracted for both stone and brick masonry and employed both masons and bricklayers to build structural walls.[28] In provincial towns and in rural areas too, local masons handled both stonework and the rough brick dressings and linings that were normally used in Irish masonry. Owen McGinnis from Galway described himself as a mason, bricklayer and slater in the parliamentary inquiry into barrack building in 1752.[29] Thomas Humphreys writing of provincial building practices in 1813 confirms such an overlap of trades: 'in every part of Ireland except Dublin and its vicinity, stone masons and bricklayers slate'.[30]

It is necessary also to distinguish between the work of carpenters and joiners in eighteenth-century buildings, as their labour sometimes overlapped. Moxon notes that carpenters worked with larger timbers than joiners, but that joiners 'observe the Rules more exactly than carpenters need do'.[31] The fashionable demand at the beginning of the eighteenth century for moulded panelling, timber cornices, ramped handrails (in lieu of newel posts on stairs) and sliding sash windows promoted the joiner's trade and provided a new market in building work.

The joiner's usual responsibilities were the production of components in a workshop, which were fitted by carpenters into structural masonry on the building site. This included – but was not limited to – the making of doors, windows,

---

27 Clark & Refaussé, *Directory*, pp 16–17.   **28** TCD, William Caldebeck's accounts, MUN/P2/2/22/4–6; Francis Quinn's accounts MUN/P2/ 36/19; James Morris's accounts MUN/P2/65/2; Gilbert Plummer's accounts MUN/P2/65/21; John Semple's accounts MUN/P2/137/2.   **29** *Commons Journal*, 5, cxxviii, cxxx.   **30** Thomas Humphreys, *The Irish builder's guide* (Dublin, 1813), p. 169.   **31** Joseph Moxon, *Mechanick exercises* (London, 1703), p. 118.

1.4 Old Parliament House, Dublin, royal arms in pediment carved by John Houghton, *c*.1730.

wainscots, architraves, skirtings and staircase sections. The carpenter was responsible for the framing of roofs and floors, and the fitting of doors, windows, staircases and other components (produced by the joiner) into the building structure. In practice, however, the work of these two artisans had a considerable overlap. John Sisson's joinery accounts for work in Trinity College included site time for the fitting of components he had made, while Isaac Wills's carpentry accounts for the same period include the production of joinery items such as doors and windows.[32] Robert Ball was a carpenter who built up a considerable business in the production of joinery fittings for use by other artisans in housing contracts.

32 TCD, John Sisson's accounts, MUN/P2/19/26, 27, MUN/P2/24/20; Isaac Wills's accounts, MUN/P2/38/43, 44.

The sawyer was another craftsman who dealt exclusively with timber. Sawyers worked in pairs (a top man and a pit man) as an itinerant team, moving from building site to building site and in joinery workshops. Their specific task was the conversion of timber baulk into scantlings for uses such as rafters, joists and flooring boards for carpenters, and planks for joiners. Although some sculptural and decorative carving commissions were undertaken by expatriates from Europe such as Willem De Keyser and James Tabary, the eighteenth century witnessed the foundation of a strong school of Irish carvers in both timber and stone. Isaac Wills, John Kelly, John Houghton, Thomas and Richard Cranfield operated as competent, and at times brilliant, wood carvers in Dublin between the 1720s and the 1780s. Carvers such as Houghton worked successfully in both wood and stone. He was responsible for carving the Ionic capitals and the royal arms on the Parliament House in the 1730s (fig. 1.4), and in the 1740s he collaborated with John Kelly in carving the arms on the front of Carton, Co. Kildare. Michael Shanahan, the architect and stonecutter, owned a marble workshop in Cork and supplied carved chimney-pieces and stone leopards (for the entrance gate) in his contract at Downhill, Co. Londonderry in the 1780s. Edward Smyth (who trained as a stonecutter with Henry Darley) emerged in the 1780s (through his work on James Gandon's Custom House) as the most gifted architectural sculptor of the eighteenth century in Ireland.

Eighteenth-century plumbers, as their name suggests, worked almost exclusively in lead and lead-tin solder. They made cisterns for water supply and pipes for its distribution; they also cast lead sheet in a variety of thicknesses from (mostly imported) lead ingots and scrap lead taken from local buildings. Sheet lead was used to cover domes, cupolas, pediment pitched roofs (such as on the Parliament House), platform (flat) roofs and for gutters and flashings. Plumbers worked closely with other artisans, such as stonecutters, in the provision of molten lead fixings for iron cramps in facing stone, and with carpenters in the construction of valley and parapet gutters. The high frequency of failure in lead roofs and gutters in Ireland, particularly in the first half of the century, kept plumbers busy in repair and maintenance work. At the end of the century, copper was introduced as a roofing material. Vincent Waldré's plea in 1804 to replace lead on the roof of the Royal Hospital with copper reflects the problems experienced with Irish roofs.[33]

The slater's work followed that of the plumber's in a sequence of impervious roof coverings over timber roof members. Slaters worked with slates of different sizes and with clay roofing tiles. They provided slating (or tiling) laths, mortar beddings and renderings of lime and sand on the underside of slated or tiled roof membranes. Imported tiles were used extensively in the main coastal cities during the first half of the century – for example, during the building of Castle's Dining Hall at Trinity College in the 1740s, the college accepted delivery of 9,860 'best glazed Holland Pantiles'.[34] Dublin slaters used slates brought by sea from quarries in Co. Down; Cork slaters depended on

---

[33] NAI, Royal Hospital Kilmainham minutes, 7, 31 Oct. 1804, RHK 1/1/7, p. 432. [34] TCD, Richard Castle's accounts MUN/P2/85/10.

1.5 George Wilkinson, 'Slate quarry at Killaloe, Co. Clare', G. Wilkinson, *Practical geology and ancient architecture of Ireland* (London, 1845), p. 30.

local quarries in Kinsale; and Limerick slaters on quarries at Killaloe (fig. 1.5). But as the efficiency of the Welsh quarries increased by the mid-century, slates from Caernarvon and Bangor replaced other imported tiles and the products of local quarries. Slaters, like plumbers, were continuously engaged in the repair of defective roofs, and institutions like the Royal Hospital and Trinity College were often forced to engage artisans in maintenance contracts which were paid for on an annual basis.

Glaziers' accounts in the records of Trinity College reveal the unexpected use of lead glazing with square and diamond shaped panes (quarries) up to the mid-1730s. (These accounts may have covered the repair of casements in older buildings dating from the turn of the century.) The earliest indication we find of references to sash windows was in the rebuilding of the Duke of Ormonde's apartments in Kilkenny

Castle in 1679/80.[35] The first appearance of sashes in Dublin may have been in Marsh's Library in 1700–3. French glass was used extensively for glazing early Irish classical buildings. It was used in the Dublin Tholsel in c.1680 and in Trinity College in 1712/13.[36] Crown glass from London and Bristol was used extensively through the eighteenth century in Ireland, although Irish crown glass was available intermittently from the 1760s onwards. Hodgson records comparative prices of window glass in 1793, with Irish glass at 7 to 8 pence per sq ft, common Bristol glass 8 to 10 pence per sq ft, Scotch crown glass at 13 pence and best London crown glass at 32 pence per ft.[37]

Plasterers worked on both the exterior and interior of buildings, in the application of plaster coats to cover the external surfaces of rubble masonry and internal wall surfaces and ceilings. Both exterior and interior wall surfaces were rendered with a mixture of sand and lime, but interior work was finished with an additional coat of smooth lime putty. Ceilings were formed on timber laths with lime plaster but quick-setting plaster of Paris was also used in decorative stucco work. Cornices were moulded in situ in wet plaster, but complex mouldings such as modillions and egg-and-dart profiles were cast in bench moulds and applied to the cornice in sections. The bricklayers' and plasterers' guild accommodated both plain plasterers such as George Spike and Edward Semple as well as stuccodores with specialist skills such as Robert West and Charles Thorpe. Accounts of Nathaniel Spencer between 1707 and 1714, of George Spike between 1716 and 1734, and of the Wall family between 1733 and 1765, show charges for painting work as well as plastering.[38] Problems between the painters and plasterers in Dublin surfaced in 1677, when the painters' Guild of St Luke drafted a petition to the city assembly seeking to restrict plasterers from painting in colours other than 'whiteing, blacking, red lead, red and yellow ochre, and russet, mixed with size only, and not with oyle'.[39] This in effect meant that they could paint with earth pigments bound with water and glue into a distemper, which limited the range and quality of colours obtainable, and the use of these paints to plaster surfaces.

Many of the combined painting and plastering accounts in Trinity College may relate to plaster surfaces painted with distemper, but several plastering contractors' accounts record the painting of sashes and window frames, rain-trunks and gutters, doors and architraves, posts, rail and palisades, which all required oil paint. It is evident from Irish building records that several prominent plasterers such as Isaac Chalke, George Spike and William Wall operated fully as both plastering and painting contractors on important contracts in Dublin. This overlap did not infringe the regulations of the city council or the guilds, as in most cases the artisans involved held joint membership of both the plasterers' and painters' guilds.

---

35 HMC, *Ormonde*, NS, 5, p. 292.   **36** *CARD*, 5, p. 310; TCD, George Delane's accounts, MUN/P2/24/10–12.   **37** P. Levi Hodgson, *The modern measurer* (Dublin, 1793), pp 104–5.   **38** TCD, Nathaniel Spencer's accounts, MUN/P2/16/21, MUN/P2/26/24; George Spike's accounts, MUN/P2/32/25, MUN/P2/66/17; William and John Wall's accounts, MUN/P2/64/21, P2/139.   **39** *CARD*, 5, pp 145–6.

These trade divisions and the system of separate trade contracts placed considerable responsibility on individuals and institutions who commissioned building projects and on their appointed architects or managerial agents. The tasks of coordinating eight or nine separate contracts and the problems of keeping final building costs close to predetermined estimates were firmly placed in their hands. On government work, managerial teams consisting of trade supervisors, clerks of works, inspectors and measurers worked under the control of the surveyor general until that office was suppressed in 1762.

The position of the professional architect was firmly established on government contracts from the end of the seventeenth century by successive surveyors general who were prominent themselves as architects, or who employed assistants with architectural and building experience. William Robinson (surveyor general 1670–1700), Thomas Burgh (surveyor general 1700–30/1), and Edward Lovett Pearce (surveyor general 1730/1–33) designed important civic buildings as part of their appointed duties, but they also engaged in private commissions with institutions such as the church, Trinity College and with private clients. As surveyors general, Arthur Dobbs (1734–43), Arthur Jones Nevill (1745–52) and Thomas Eyre (1752–62) apparently designed buildings but designs were also made by people in their employ such as George Ensor, Joseph Jarratt and Thomas Jarratt. After 1762, when most of the surveyor general's duties had been taken over by the Barrack Board and the Board of Works, the design and management of state contracts continued in the hands of trained professionals such as Thomas Cooley, Christopher Myers and Vincent Waldré.

An indication of the management structure adopted by Robinson in the 1680s can be found in the records of the Royal Hospital Kilmainham. Apart from the surveyor general's own inspections of the work in progress, two overseers and a clerk of works were in full-time attendance on the building site.[40] The principal overseer was expected to coordinate the work 'to give all manner of Directions for composing and carrying on the building according to the Model agreed on … and to superintend the whole work.' The second overseer, a senior tradesman 'whose business must be to inspect several operations and to choose out proper and fit materials according to the respective Places where they were to be used', supervised the quality of workmanship. The clerk of works was appointed to keep accounts of workmen employed by the day and to measure completed workmanship for the principal overseer's certification.

This management model may have been used on successive government contracts, as it is similar to the arrangements used by Thomas Eyre on Charles Fort, Kinsale, Co. Cork in 1756.[41] On private contracts, where managerial resources were more limited, the work of an overseer might be combined with that of a clerk of works or a measurer. Thomas Hand was used in the capacity of an overseer and paymaster

---

40 Richard Colley, *An account of the foundation of the Royal Hospital of King Charles II* (Dublin, 1725), pp 14–15. **41** IAA, Thomas Eyre's letter books, letter to Captain Vallancey, 2 Aug. 1756, accession no. 81/88.

(under Burgh) on Dr Steevens's Hospital in the 1720s and George Wheeler acted as measurer; Benjamin Crawley was the overseer and measurer on the construction of Castle Durrow from 1715; and Benjamin Ball combined the functions of overseer, clerk of works and paymaster (in his capacity as a master builder) on Lady Hume's house in Dominick Street in the 1730s.[42]

We have no records of how Robinson communicated with contractors or controlled costs, but accounts of building in Trinity College and Dr Steevens's Hospital from 1712 to the 1730s show that Burgh managed his many responsibilities with a minimum of written instructions or certificates. George Wheeler's accounts for measuring plasterwork at Dr Steevens's Hospital in 1729 refer to a charge of 10s. a day 'which Capt Tho Burgh allways allowed me'; in 1722 the mason Quinn was being paid 2s. a day.[43] Among the fairly full documentation, the scarcity of certificates signed by Burgh for the hospital and for the Library in Trinity College is another indication of his casual management style.

How far these unbusinesslike arrangements depended on close personal relationships between Burgh and his favoured contractors is difficult to assess. His predecessor Robinson is known to have been close to Edward Miller, a carpenter whom he recommended as an overseer on the Royal Hospital in 1702 and whose name, with that of another carpenter's (Abraham Hawksworth's) widow, occurs as beneficiary in his will.[44] Burgh, for his part, was named as executor of the will of Francis Quinn, the masonry contractor who worked under his control on Chichester House, Dublin Castle, Trinity College Library and Dr Steevens's Hospital.[45] Burgh consistently used the carpenter Isaac Wills for contracts such as the Laboratory (1710/11), the Kitchen (1719/20) and the Library in Trinity College and in the early phases of the construction of Dr Steevens's Hospital in the 1720s. The appointment of Michael Wills (Isaac's son) as overseer and paymaster on the hospital, and his subsequent career as an architect, may have been due to Burgh's influence and encouragement. By contrast, the management style employed by Pearce and Castle appears to be highly formalized and carefully regulated. Castle's introduction of competitive proposals from different artisans in Trinity College is reminiscent of Wren's attempts to control prices in London.[46] His recorded orders for the purchase of materials, the certification of costs and his intervention in the valuation of accounts, established a professional management structure in the college. Pearce's use of four separate contractors on the Portland stone cladding of the Parliament House also recalls the London practices of Wren and Hawksmoor.[47] This introduced several advantages. It permitted the architect to reduce costs through competitive bargaining

---

[42] TCD, folder 'Mrs Grizell Steevens' Charity – Financial Accounts', f. 1, MS 3508/1; NLI, Flower MSS 11455 (1–3); NAI, Ball, MS Dublin, 43. [43] TCD, folder 'Steevens' Hospital Building Accounts', f. 36, MS 3508/1; TCD, folder 'Mrs Grizell Steevens' Charity – Financial Accounts', f. 1, MS 3508/1. [44] Rolf Loeber, *A biographical dictionary of architects in Ireland* (London, 1981), p. 71; TNA, wills of William Robinson, DEL. 1. 357, pp 104–13, ff 37–49. [45] Loeber, *A biographical dictionary*, p. 33. [46] TCD, Proposals for building a Printing House, MUN/P2/65/1–4. [47] *Commons Journal*, 4, xxxii; xxxiii.

and to reduce building time through the use of multiple resources. It also promoted higher qualities of craftsmanship in the complex stone-facing contract by continuous comparison of the different contractors' standards of workmanship.

By any standards of the period, the construction of a building of the scale and quality of the Parliament House without marked increases in predetermined costs, and within a short building time of less than three years, must be seen as a managerial triumph. How much Pearce's and Castle's experience (through Vanbrugh's office) of London practice contributed to the success of this achievement is difficult to say. Meticulous cost records combined with carefully detailed constructional drawings bespeak a professionalism that was new in Ireland at this time. Castle's later career and his extensive practice in institutions such as Trinity College and in private commissions for estate owners must have been a big influence in the development of contractual management in Dublin and the Irish provinces.

Although the eighteenth-century surveyors general, or most of them, were professional architects in terms of their full-time engagement on design and control of building contracts, their remuneration did not entirely depend on their state salary of £300 per annum and a contribution towards staff and office expenses.[48] The advantage of their office was their freedom to benefit from the contractual process and from artisans working on contracts under their control. Apart from state gratuities (such as the £2,000 granted by parliament to Edward Lovett Pearce for his work on the Parliament House) they were entitled to receive 5 per cent from the contracting artisans' accounts they supervised. This was a profitable process. William Molyneux, who shared William Robinson's patent in the 1680s, benefited sufficiently over his short period (eighteen months) in office to finance the exile of himself and his family in Chester for nearly two years. These attractive conditions of engagement, however, were curtailed in 1744 on the appointment of Nevill, who was disappointed by the new restrictions preventing the receipt of commission from contracting artisans. Thomas Eyre, Nevill's successor in 1752, and the last surveyor general, received £200 compensation for the abolition of his office added to his new salary of £365 per annum as Chief Engineer of the Ordnance. The combined salary of £565 per annum was considerably lower than the earnings of some of his predecessors.

Earlier surveyors general such as Burgh and Pearce must have enjoyed even more lucrative benefits than William Molyneux. Active as architects in commissions for private houses and for institutions such as Trinity College, they had fees from their clients and presumably gratuities from artisans. In 1738, Castle was paid 5 per cent of building costs by Trinity College for 'surveying sundry works'.[49] It is interesting to compare these high levels of remuneration with the earnings of artisan contractors and other operatives engaged in the building process. However, we must bear in mind that the surveyor general's remuneration was seen as a return on investment.

---

[48] For this paragraph see: Edward McParland, 'The office of the surveyor general in Ireland in the eighteenth century', *Architectural History*, 38, (1995), 97–9. [49] TCD, Richard Castle's accounts, MUN/P2/68/4.

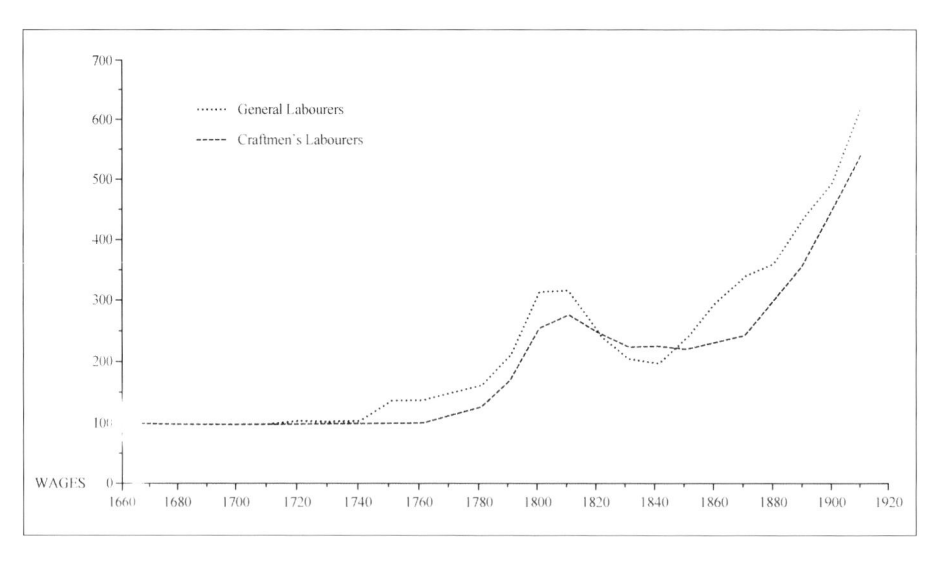

1.6 Building labourers' wages in Dublin, 1660–1910, Fergus D'Arcy, 'Wages of labourers in the Dublin building industry, 1667–1918', *Saothar*, 14 (1989), 29.

Molyneux bought his share of Robinson's patent for £250; it cost Nevill £3,300 to secure his position in 1745.[50]

Daywork (time and material) accounts in Dublin indicate a remarkable stability in labour charges (and presumably wages) from the 1670s to the mid-1760s (fig. 1.6). The consistent contractual rate of 2*s*. per day for skilled artisans and 1*s*. per day for attendant labourers over a long period of ninety years suggests steady and unvarying levels of profit and a considerable measure of agreement between the building guilds (through the city council) on fixed levels of remuneration.[51] Contractual rates in provincial areas were lower and more variable than Dublin rates. Accounts for the Dungarvan aqueduct in 1759 show labourers paid 6½*d*. per day, paviers and 'country masons' 1*s*. 1*d*. and 'carpenters' and 'masons' between 1*s*. 3*d*. and 1*s*. 6*d*.[52] These rates were not net wage payments. They included a percentage of cost to supplement the contractor's profits. Benjamin Ball's accounts establish actual wage payments to journeymen carpenters of 1*s*. 2*d*. to 1*s*. 4*d*. per day in 1734.[53] In Trinity College *c*.1700, the contractor charged the college at the rate of 1*s*. a day for labourers, while those paid directly by the college received from 8 to 10*d*.[54] In the provinces labourers earned 6½*d*. per day on the Newry Canal in 1731 and on the Shannon Navigation works in 1758 but Thomas Eyre paid wages of 8*d*. per day to building labourers

50 McParland, 'The office of the surveyor general', 97.   **51** TCD, cf. agreement with Richard Mills, 1672, MUN/P2/1/27 and J. Rooney's accounts, 1765, MUN/P2/138/13–37. By this time some contractors in the college were paying labourers 1*s*. 2*d*. per day, e.g., Richard Plummer's accounts, MUN/P2/135/4 and John Semple's accounts, MUN/P2/137/2.   **52** *Commons Journal*, 6, ccxxxiv–ccxlii.   **53** NAI, Ball, MS Dublin, 43.   **54** TCD, cf. John Rayman's accounts MUN/P2/8/28 and working on fortifications in Cork in 1757.[55] Eyre's records also provide us with information on wages paid to experienced provincial artisans acting as foremen. Referring to a level of wage expected by a foreman mason at Duncannon, Co. Waterford in 1756, he expressed the view that '9/- to 10/- per week [was] the best price even in Dublin'; this would indicate a daily wage of 1s. 6d. to 1s. 8d. per day for chargehands in Dublin.[56]

The surveyor general's clerks or assistants such as George Ensor had a salary of £40 per year in the 1740s but of course this is only part of the story.[57] The accounts of building the fortifications at Cobh, Co. Cork in 1750–1 reveal Ensor's presence there as supervisor and paymaster, at the remarkably high rate of 5s. 9d. per day.[58] His earnings for 341 days over a two-year period brought him £92 2s. in addition to his salary. Ensor was not in his Dublin office for the remainder of this two-year period. He was busily engaged as a contractor on three barrack buildings at Mallow, Co. Cork and at Cappoquin and Tallow, both in Co. Waterford. Thomas Jarratt, who worked in the same capacity as Ensor (under Eyre) on the Charles Fort contract in Kinsale in 1756, had a lower payment of 4s. per day.[59] The records of the last four decades of the century reveal patterns of continuous increases in contractual rates and, surprisingly, a marked differential between rates paid to different trades. Stonecutters and masons, for instance, had rates of 2s. 6d. per day in the late 1760s, while plumber rates were still only 2s. per day.[60] In the late 1790s stonecutters' rates rose to 4s. per day, slaters were paid 3s. 3d. per day and plumbers a mere 2s. 6d. per day.[61] The sustained rise in rates was a direct result of increases in living costs. The fluctuations in prices paid to different trades can be attributed to the aggressive demands of journeymen's combinations in some trades and to the individual bargains obtained. These unstable fluctuations were to continue into the nineteenth century for over two decades.

tradesmen's bills MUN/P2/8/37 and Nat Hall's accounts MUN/P2/14/8. **55** *Commons Journal*, 6, ccxxv; IAA, Thomas Eyre's letter book, Eyre to Clarke, 28 Sept. 1756, accession no. 81/88. **56** IAA, Thomas Eyre's letter book, Eyre to Clarke, 28 Sept. 1756, accession no. 81/88. **57** *Commons Journal*, 5, xcix. **58** Ibid., 5, ccxlii, ccxliv and ccxlv (where 'travelling to' is included in the 5s. 5d. per day). **59** IAA, Thomas Eyre's letter book, Eyre to Vallancey, 12 Mar. 1757, accession no. 81/88. **60** TCD, George Darley's accounts, MUN/P2/145/3; John Reed's accounts, MUN/P2/144/11. **61** TCD, George Darley's accounts, MUN/P2/173/1; M. and J. Elliot's accounts, MUN/P2/173/9; William Pike and sons' accounts, MUN/P2/173/33.

CHAPTER TWO

Eighteenth-century building contracts

ALTHOUGH THE USE OF DIRECT LABOUR for large engineering works such as the Newry Canal and the fortifications at Kinsale, Co. Cork was common in the eighteenth century, most buildings were constructed on foot of formal contracts between the building owner and the contracting artisans. On large estates such as Castletown, Co. Kildare or Baronscourt, Co. Tyrone unskilled agricultural labour was often employed (on a seasonal basis) to quarry stone, to make bricks, or to dig foundations, but the important task of the main building work was entrusted to craftsmen, often brought long distances from cities such as Cork or Dublin for the value of their specific skills.

Building contracts were of three different types. The measured contract paid each trade separately for measured quantities of work based on agreed rates. The dayworks contract paid artisans on the basis of time spent on the work and the materials used. The contract in-gross paid a contractor a fixed sum based on a predetermined estimate for an entire building, or a specific part of a building. On public contracts, those contracts in-gross were sometimes regulated by measurement of the work to assure their value. The following discusses the way these contractual forms were used and their particular advantages in use. The measured contract was the most common form of agreement used throughout the century for state and institutional buildings. It involved separate agreements with each trade for payments (based on predetermined rates) for standard units of workmanship. For instance, in Richard Castle's preparatory estimates for the Trinity College Printing House (*c.*1733) we find proposals from the mason James Morris for 18-inch stone walls at 5*s.* per perch and from the carpenter Joseph McCleery for timber floors at 2*s.* 6*d.* per square.[1] (The slater's trade also priced their measured contracts by the square, i.e., 100 square feet, but other trades like plasterers, painters and stonecutters used units such as the square yard or the linear foot.)

This system of measured contracts for separate trades treated main building tasks such as masonry, carpentry or roofing as separate and discrete operations. Contractual terms were agreed between each trade and the building owner, but no formal agreements were made between the different trades to cover the coordination of building operations or the handling of common resources. The rate agreed by a

---

Material in this chapter should be supplemented with work by Fergus D'Arcy and Conor Lucey: see Select Bibliography.   1 TCD, James Morris's accounts, MUN/P2/65/2; Joseph McCleery's accounts, MUN/P2/65/3.

mason for a perch of brickwork, or by a carpenter for a square of flooring, covered workmanship and materials, but it made no allowances for the provision of scaffolding, or lifting equipment, or the time spent in the coordination of collective tasks such as fitting timber members into masonry walls.

The Trinity College accounts have numerous records of the use of unskilled casual labourers (hired by the day) for general building tasks. The accounts for the Library, for example, specifically refer to payments to labourers for hoisting beams for the floors; for the carriage of materials to the site, and for the provision of equipment such as scaffolding poles and wheelbarrows for the masons. It is evident from these accounts that the general organization of the site and the provision of building plant is clearly the responsibility of the college or its agent and not the contractors. Burgh, the architect for the Library, or supervisors under his control, obviously intervened between the trades to coordinate building tasks and to settle disputes between individual artisans.

It is not possible to tell how far this policy of providing building plant and attendance on the artisans was carried in later contracts in the college. However, items in the accounts of the Royal Hospital Kilmainham (1680s), where the main contractors worked with measured contracts, include large sums for day labourers, supervisors and the provision of tools.[2] An estimate of Arthur Jones Nevill for rebuilding part of Dublin Castle (c.1750) has costs for attendance on masons and bricklayers and the provision of scaffolding and centering for arches.[3] Clearly, the measured rates in the contract made no allowances for collective building tasks or contributed in any way to the general organization of work. Valuations of work were measured at intervals during the course of the contract to enable interim payments to be made to the contractors, but full payment was subject to a final measurement at the completion of the building work. Thus we find the mason William Caldebeck in receipt of sums of £100 on three occasions (April, June and November) in 1714 for work on the Library, but his total account of £900 12s. 0d. was settled by the payment from the college of an outstanding balance of £236 8s. 9d. (paid to Francis Quinn and others) in February 1722.[4]

Cost by unit of measurement such as the mason's perch, or the carpenter's square, usually included the cost of workmanship and materials, but contracts were also agreed on the basis of workmanship only, with the materials supplied by the building owner. This was often the case in agreements made for the construction of country houses such as Castle Durrow (1715), Cashel Palace (1729) or Baronscourt in Co. Tyrone (1770) where timber, stone and bricks were provided by the respective owners.[5] We can also find instances of timber and masonry materials being separately supplied in Dublin for large early eighteenth-century contracts such as the Library

---

2 Richard Colley, *An account of the foundation of the Royal Hospital of King Charles II* (Dublin, 1725), p. 23. 3 TNA, Estimate for rebuilding Dublin Castle, T1/337/96. 4 TCD, William Caldebeck's accounts, MUN/P2/27/2, 3, 4; Francis Quinn's and William Caldebeck's accounts, MUN/P2/48/1. 5 NLI, Flower papers, MS 11455 (1–3); PRONI, Dean Hearn to Archbishop of Cashel, D562/458;

in the college, the Parliament House or Dr Steevens's Hospital. This must have significantly reduced the amount of capital invested by the contractors involved. The provision of a sum of £24 7s. 0d. for the 'diet' of the carpenters, bricklayers and stonecutters working on Cashel Palace from 1728 to 1729 was another aspect of rural contracts that obviously affected the rates agreed for workmanship.[6]

The use of measured contracts as the main method of commissioning buildings introduced the role of the measurer who became an important figure in the management of the eighteenth-century building process. On state contracts such as Dublin Castle, the Parliament House, or in institutions like Trinity College, measurers made interim valuations under the direction of architects such as Burgh, Pearce, Castle and Hugh Darley, and presented them with measured and priced bills of work for their approval and certification. In the building of Castle Durrow (c.1715) the various contracting artisans' work was measured by the overseer Benjamin Crawley, who was also responsible for settling the terms of their contracts.[7] Although contractors could also employ a measurer to act on their behalf and agree final valuations of cost, there are few instances of the use of measurers by contracting artisans in eighteenth-century accounts. This is not surprising. Artisans were obliged to take careful measurements of their materials in the performance of their tasks; they were capable of providing accurate measurements on their own behalf, and the cost of a measurer's services was considerable.

Measurers were commonly chosen from among the ranks of master artisans who were capable of acting as supervisors or clerks of work. Jack Magill, the ambitious carpenter who was to become a commissioner of the Board of Works, measured work for Castle in Trinity College in the 1730s. The remuneration of 10s. per day, paid to the measurer George Wheeler (under Burgh's direction) on Dr Steevens's Hospital, suggests a very high level of competence, but an even larger sum of 16s. 3d. per day was allowed to measurers working for the surveyor general's office in the 1740s.[8] Contracts in England were frequently measured by the superintending architect, while there are several instances in the college records of Castle's assistant, John Ensor, acting in this capacity during the 1740s.[9] After the mid-century, however, the College measurers were specialists such as Richard King, William Purfield and Bryan Bolger and the comprehensive quality of the accounts reflect the increased professionalism of the times.

The second contractual system we find in use, by the state and large institutions throughout the century, is the dayworks contract based on payments for time and materials. This was exclusively used for small contracts and jobbing work such as the maintenance and repair of existing buildings. It, too, involved separate agreements

PRONI, Abercorn papers, D623/C/3/1. 6 PRONI, Dean Hearn to Archbishop of Cashel, D562/458. 7 NLI, Flower papers, MS 11455 (1). 8 TCD, folder 'Steevens' Hospital Building Accounts', transcript, MS 3508/1, f. 12; PRONI, Wilmot papers, Neville to Weston, 15 Apr. 1749, T/3019/1317. 9 Malcolm Burrows, 'Measurers of architecture 1750–1850', *Chartered Quantity Surveyor* (Dec. 1980), 23; TCD, George Plummer's accounts, MUN/P2/85/13; Thomas Heatley's accounts, MUN/P2/84/5, MUN/P2/85/11.

2.1 Office of Richard Castle, 'An Estimate of the Expense of the Printing House …', 1733, TCD, MUN/P2/65. Reproduced with permission of the Board of Trinity College Dublin.

with each individual trade and separate payments to each trade contractor. Payments were made on the basis of predetermined daily rates for journeymen, unskilled labourers and master artisans (if they participated in the work) and of agreed prices for materials used. A typical jobbing account of William Caldebeck's in 1709 for masonry work in the college included time payments for bricklayers at 2s. per day, and for labourers at 1s. per day.[10] The cost of materials included 2 hogsheads of lime costing 2s.; 1 load of sand costing 1s. and 2 loads of bricks costing 3s. 3d.

The third form of agreement is the contract in-gross, in which a contractor legally bound himself to provide a specific amount of work for a fixed lump-sum payment. This could involve an undertaking to provide the carpentry, or the masonry, or, in many cases, the entire building structure for a predetermined amount of money. These all-trades agreements, in which one single tradesman employed all the other trades, were common in the speculative housing market in Ireland and England. Their use in England on public works was usually accompanied by after-measurement, at prices certified for each locality by reputable local builders.[11] Local artisans were used to certify the value of a series of lump-sum contracts, that is, contracts in-gross, for provincial barracks in Ireland in 1749.

This type of agreement was used extensively in medieval times and there are two well-known instances of its use in the late seventeenth century, in Archbishop Boyle's house at Blessington, Co. Wicklow (1671) and in Burton House, Co. Cork (1670). We can find no evidence of its use on any of the principal eighteenth-century buildings in Dublin, or any of the larger country houses designed by well-known architects; however, small contracts in-gross, based on lump-sum agreements, for rebuilding barracks at Belturbet, Co. Cavan, Kinsale, Co. Cork and Belfast had been commissioned by the surveyor general Arthur Dobbs in 1739. The only reference to contracts of this type in the extensive building records in Trinity College are two accounts for the carpenter Charles Brooking in 1723, which include a proposal for a structure costing £435.[12] Such contracts were undoubtedly used on buildings built without architects (such as urban housing) or in provincial areas where builder-architects such as John Coltsman (in Cork) and George Ensor (in Athlone, Roscommon and Armagh) built buildings to their own architectural designs. Thomas Cooley's proposals for the church at Kells, Co. Meath in 1778 were based on his involvement as a lump-sum contractor.[13]

Although lump-sum contracting was not used on public works in Dublin, its use was widespread enough to make it unpopular with the enlightened *cognoscenti* of the late 1760s who were intent on the introduction of new architectural ideals to the city. In 1769, the year of the Royal Exchange architectural competition, an anonymous correspondent in the *Freeman's Journal* published the following commentary on contractual abuses:

---

[10] TCD, William Caldebeck's accounts MUN/P2/19/1–2.   [11] Linda Clarke, *Building capitalism* (London, 1992), p. 82.   [12] TCD, Charles Brooking's accounts MUN/P2/49/1.   [13] NLI, Kells church accounts, MS 25304.

It will not be inconsistent with our Design to take some Notice of the Causes which principally obstruct the progress of good Architecture. One in particular (of which severe and repeated Complaints have been made by several ingenuous Writers) is the Custom of what is called building by Contract, and employing a general contractor. When it is considered what Numbers at present both here and in London are engaged in this Business, the ample Fortunes they have raised by it, the Variety of Opportunities for Profit, and perhaps too frequently for Imposition, that is afforded, to the Person who has the Supply of every Material, and the absolute Command of the Workmen in every Department, it ceases to be a Doubt that the Profession is very lucrative.[14]

Our specific interest in this contractual form lies firstly in the instance of its use in 1749 for a programme of provincial barrack building that provoked a parliamentary inquiry, and particularly in the evidence recorded, which throws considerable light on building conditions during this period. The other reason is the assumption that its frequent use by master builders such as John and George Ensor, Samuel Sproule or Robert West (during the second half of the century) anticipated the advent of the nineteenth-century general contractor, and provided the basis for the development of the contractual form used in England and Ireland from the first decade of that century onwards.

* * *

We must now examine each of these contractual forms in the context of their use, to look at their advantages, and how these advantages were implemented by building owners, architects and contractors. This is a simple task in the case of the measure and value contract, because of its well recorded use in public works through the century. Our main difficulty in discussing the lump-sum contract is a lack of records of the speculative house transactions where it was mostly employed. The principal advantage of the measure and value system was its impartial fairness to both the owner and contractor, in that payments were precisely related to performance. It satisfied individual contracting artisans, as their responsibility was limited to performance within their own specialized field, as their capital investment was limited to the cost of their own materials, and in the certainty of a fixed profit margin on their work. The use of separate individual contracts for each trade also suited the guild system as it helped maintain trade divisions within the building crafts.

In England, the measured contract was preferred by architects like Christopher Wren because the fixed profit system discouraged artisans from reducing the quality of their work to increase their earnings, and because the cost of ad hoc changes in

---

[14] *Freeman's Journal*, 27–31 Dec. 1769.

design could be accommodated easily by the valuation process. There is no doubt that, under the ideal management conditions of strong architectural supervision, the system could produce buildings of superb craftsmanship like Wren's Hampton Court, Pearce's Parliament House or Cooley's Royal Exchange. The measured system was supported through much of the century by an amazing stability in prices and unit rates for each trade. Although the price of a perch of stone or brickwork might vary considerably between Antrim, Dublin and Kerry, local prices remained stable: the 5s. 6d. paid to the mason Mills for a perch of walling for Ringsend church in Dublin in 1713 would still purchase a perch of walling in the same city in 1764.[15] This lack of inflation was an important consideration at a time when large building contracts (like Trinity College Library or Dr Steevens's Hospital) could be prolonged for many years.

The system had disadvantages. One of these was the difficulty in predicting final cost which, in contracts lasting three or four years, could well exceed all expectations, and while the predetermined unit rates were proof against loss of profits and unfair charges, the problem of evaluating the total cost of large projects from undeveloped architectural drawings remained. The changes in design and the consequent delays in Burgh's Custom House in Dublin (c.1705) more than doubled its estimated cost; the prolonged contract for his College Library saw its cost rise to over £20,000 on an original costing of £7,000; and even the relatively short contract for Nevill's additions to Dublin Castle (1746/7) ended in heavy increases over his original estimate.[16] Although payments for variations in design were easily accommodated by the system of measurement, variations were usually accompanied by contractual delays which were at the contractor's expense, as payments were on the basis of work completed and not of the time spent on construction.

The system's use of separate trade contractors, each with their own responsibilities, and their own labour force and building materials, was inefficient in the deployment of labour, the purchase of materials and the need for coordination between contractual tasks. For instance, in the construction of a building such as the Library, the divided responsibilities between stonecutters on the face of the exterior wall, masons and bricklayers building the structural core of the wall, and plumbers fixing metal cramps (in cut-stone facings), could lead to costly delays if one trade was tardy in attendance, or if their materials were not supplied at the correct time. On such contracts the coordination of building tasks was obviously in the hands of the building owner or his agents, with architects, clerks of works and supervisors active in the purchase and supply of timber, bricks and stone. This worked well on large state contracts, but it is not surprising to find private house owners like Lady Hume using the services of one trade (the master carpenter Benjamin Ball) to supervise the work of the other trades and to provide materials for the construction of her house in Dominick Street, in the 1730s.[17]

---

15 *CARD*, 6, p. 477; TCD, John Semple's accounts, MUN/P2/137/2. 16 Rolf Loeber, *A biographical dictionary of architects in Ireland* (London, 1981), p. 35; Edward McParland, *Public architecture in Ireland, 1680–1760* (New Haven & London, 2001), p. 147; *Commons Journal*, 5, cclxxv. 17 NAI, Ball, MS Dublin, 43.

Post-contractual measurement of work was based on previous rates for work and materials and, as long as normal profits were assured (by measuring quantities of work), fixed material prices were more or less acceptable. Clarke records the sudden drop in the cost of building materials that followed the repeal of the mercantile laws in England in 1814, and the common acceptance of competitive lump-sum contracts which followed.[18] The contractual reliance on unit rates for work and materials, rather than the discipline of a fixed sum, provided insufficient incentive for architects to produce developed constructional drawings, resulting in costly design alterations during the course of the contract. Even an architect with considerable managerial skills such as Castle could be careless about pre-contractual design decisions. In his revision of estimates for the Dining Hall at Trinity College he records that 'The roof of the Hall has eight pairs of Principals, which I supposed but five … the timber cost 55/- per tun, which I computed at 50/- … The oak I computed at £4.10 which cost £5'.[19]

The additional timber costs might be easily explained, but Castle's error in the calculation of the number of roof trusses is surprising. What is more surprising is his lack of embarrassment in an unqualified admission of such an error in a document intended for his employer's perusal. It suggests that expensive variations, arising from the development of designs after contracts had started, were a common and acceptable practice at the time.

The dayworks (time and materials) contract had certain advantages for contractors, as they were ensured the net cost of materials and a profit margin on the cost of time. It also provided an added advantage (over the measured system) in that delays (caused by architects, building owners or contractual incompetence) were fully paid for, as time, and not the measured quantity of completed work, was the basis of payment. It had disadvantages for building owners as the contractor had no incentive to control productivity (particularly if he was short of work) and it could lead to abuses if the contractual programme was delayed for any reason. Its advantage to building owners was its flexibility in dealing with small repairs (such as broken window panes) that did not justify the use of a measurer. It was an ideal formula for agreeing costs on maintenance work, such as roofs and gutters, which could not be measured, as the amount of new materials used might be negligible. The surveyor general Thomas Eyre, in a memorial to the House of Commons in 1756, excused the use of time costs at Charles Fort, Co. Cork on the grounds that the unpredictable amount of rock in excavated ground could not be computed on the basis of fixed task rates.[20] The unpredictable nature of the repairs to the crossing piers in the crypt of St Paul's was Wren's justification for dayworks payments in 1713.[21] Although it was consistently used in Trinity College for jobbing and maintenance work, its use was less frequent in the second half of the eighteenth century under the stewardship of Hugh Darley and Christopher Myers. Castle refused to accept a slater's dayworks

---

18 Clarke, *Building capitalism*, p. 82.   **19** TCD, Richard Castle's accounts, MUN/P2/80.   **20** *Commons Journal*, 6, xlii.   **21** *Wren Society Vols*, 16, 166n, p. 167.

accounts in 1743 on the grounds that the value of the work should be measured.[22] The attempts by both the college and the Royal Hospital Kilmainham to negotiate roof maintenance contracts on the basis of a fixed annual fee were obvious attempts to avoid the uncertainties of the time and material contract.

The principal advantage of contracts in-gross to building owners was the legal obligation on the contractor to provide a building, or part of a building, for a predetermined sum. This was obviously an attraction to most people involved in the commission of building projects, and it must have been particularly attractive in the later part of the century, when rising costs of wages and materials inflated building budgets and increased the need for cost control. Why then was it unpopular with architects and institutions throughout the century? It had a bad reputation among architects because of the opportunities it offered to contractors to skimp on materials and workmanship in order to ensure profit margins. As the English architect Jeffrey Wyattville explained in 1814: 'Common London houses, like so many boxes in a row, may be built by contract in the gross with little chance of ruin; but ... public works ought to be conducted upon such fair terms that every tradesman should be certain of some gain and the Public be sure of good and lasting work'.[23]

The most important advantage claimed for the contract in-gross was better management of cost control and a predictable final cost. Unfortunately, because of the specific conditions under which buildings were commissioned during this period, these objectives were not easily achieved. These conditions relate to the ability of architects to describe their intentions properly, to the ability of building owners to anticipate their own requirements and to the contractor's ability to control the process of building production.

The operation of the contract in-gross or lump-sum contract required three conditions for success. The first was the prior provision of information on the full extent of building and its complexity to enable accurate estimates of cost to be made. The second was the avoidance of delays in the building programme (due to the architect's or the owner's intervention) which would increase labour costs beyond those estimated in the contract sum. The third was the need for stable conditions in the price of labour and materials, for the duration of the contract.

Most surviving drawings produced by Irish architects between the early 1700s and the 1780s provided very little information about the constructional organization of the buildings they described. There are some exceptions of course, such as the dramatic cross-section (by Pearce or Castle) of the new Parliament House c.1730, the drawings for the construction of Oakfield, Co. Donegal in 1739, the working drawings for Dromoland, Co. Limerick (attributed to John Aheron) in the 1740s, and Joseph Jarratt's design for the monumental base under the statue of George II in 1756. The arrival of highly trained architects such as Cooley and Gandon in Dublin (in the 1770s and 1780s) introduced a more professional approach to the production of

[22] TCD, Thomas Heatley's accounts, MUN/P2/85/13.   [23] Clarke, *Building capitalism*, p. 82.

building information, and early nineteenth-century drawings such as those for Francis Johnston's Cash Office in the Bank of Ireland in Dublin in 1802 show how well this professionalism had been assimilated by native architects in the intervening twenty years.

Contract (or working) drawings were obviously not seen as an important requirement in Ireland until the later decades of the eighteenth century. Prices for work and materials were fixed and unchanging up to the beginning of the 1770s, and contracts were not commissioned essentially on the basis of competitive rates. The high increases in building costs towards the end of the century brought new demands for competition among contractors and for cheaper procurement of building materials. It became apparent by that period that competitive bids for work could only be successfully organized on the basis of fully developed building information.

One of the main problems with contracts in-gross was additional cost arising from variations in design. These variations could result in disputes between building owners and builders over the responsibility for the variation and the increased cost involved. It is interesting to look at how variations in design affected the cost of two late seventeenth-century in-gross contracts. In May 1669, the builder-architect Captain William Kenn signed a contract to build a substantial house at Burton, Co. Cork for Sir Philip Perceval.[24] The contract sum of £700 sterling was mostly for workmanship, as brick, stone, lime and timber were to be supplied by Perceval's estate. Over a year later, in September 1670, Kenn signed a revised contract for a slightly larger house with a more substantial specification, for a contract sum of £1,030 sterling.[25] By September 1672, with the house almost finished, Perceval had paid Kenn and his son Benjamin a figure of £1,387 13s. 6d.[26] The additional cost over the contract figure was apparently well justified by variations in the design (probably at Perceval's request) as the contract proceeded. A similar contract between Archbishop Boyle and the Dublin mason Thomas Brown was signed in February 1672. The agreement committed Brown to build a house of certain specific dimensions at Blessington, Co. Wicklow for £600.[27] Unlike the Burton House agreement, this contract ended in dispute, with Boyle complaining of smoking chimneys, and Brown claiming £76 5s. 0d. for additional work not specified in the contract. There is no record of the dispute being settled, but there is evidence of additional expenditure over the next two years, and the final cost indicated was the considerable sum of £2,323 10s. 10d.

The contract in-gross was particularly unsuitable for the construction of great eighteenth-century private houses where the inclinations and ambitions of prospective owners needed deliberation and debate. In the building of houses such as Castletown or Carton (both in Co. Kildare), the detailed development of the design

---

24 BL., Egmont papers, Add. MSS 46946A, ff 140–1. **25** Ibid., Add. MSS 46947B, ff 50–. **26** Ibid., Add. MSS 46949, ff 150–. **27** IAA, Boyle papers, Blessington Manor (photocopies), RPD 118; see Brian de Breffny, 'The building of the mansion at Blessington, 1672', *The GPA Irish Arts Review Yearbook* (Belfast, 1988), 73–7.

became a serial part of the building (and rebuilding) process. The complexity of houses such as Baronscourt, Co. Tyrone, or Charlemont's Casino at Marino in Dublin, could not have been reduced to rational calculation in a prior estimate of cost. Who could anticipate the realization of a house such as Castlecoole, Co. Fermanagh, which took ten years to build and cost its owner £54,000 instead of the £30,000 he had set as a budget figure? On the other hand, some eighteenth-century buildings were well suited to the lump-sum or in-gross contractual system. Although Burgh's drawings for Dr Steevens's Hospital (1720s) were probably no more than sketches, the lack of complex architectural features and the simplicity of the construction and finishes used would have made cost control an easy matter. The Schoolmaster's House at Drogheda, Co. Louth (*c.*1730) had sufficient information even in the surviving drawings and bill of scantlings to anticipate its cost and building programme. Semple's drawings for St Patrick's Hospital, Dublin (1749) and his highly descriptive specification would have provided ample information to construct this rational building and accurately project its final cost.

The most suitable opportunities provided for lump-sum or in-gross contracting were in the construction of the speculative terraced houses of the urban estates in Dublin and other Irish cities. These house designs provided all the basic conditions necessary for the economic management of building programmes. The repetitive nature of the designs, the identical constructional patterns and the lack of interference from prospective owners (or tenants) during the building process made costs predictable. The considerable numbers of prominent Dublin artisans who became speculative housing developers is indicative of the profitability of such ventures. In-gross contracts were also used in the construction of important buildings in provincial towns. George Ensor worked with such contracts for the Sessions House in Roscommon, charity schools in Athlone and Roscommon and the Armagh hospital in the 1760s. Roger Mulholland acted in a similar capacity (as architect, carpenter, builder) in Belfast in the 1780s on buildings such as the Presbyterian church in Rosemary Street. There is also evidence of an extensive use of in-gross contracts in one major state building programme in 1749, which tells us a considerable amount about the contractual process.

The strange affair of the parliamentary inquiry of 1752 into the surveyor general's handling of a barracks building programme costing £40,000 (1748–50) records the testimony of contractors, supervisors, artisans, barrack masters and military personnel. The parliamentary report of the enquiry (*Commons Journal*, 5, appendix lxv to ccxlvi), on which the following is based, is a rich source of information surrounding the case. The surveyor general Nevill was accused of accepting work of inferior quality and of encouraging extravagant prices from contractors engaged in the programme. The charges against him were that many of the rebuilt and repaired barracks were 'extremely ill-executed, unfit for the reception, and dangerous to the Health of his Majesty's troops'. The consequences of the enquiry contributed to Nevill's dismissal from office in 1753 and the loss of his parliamentary seat. The evidence given throws considerable light on the management of the office during this period and of the contracting artisan's view of the building process. The most surprising aspect of the inquiry is the clear testimony that the agreements were not separate trade contracts of the type formerly used by the office for state buildings, or in institutions such as Trinity College. A few of them were signed by two artisans (such as a carpenter and a bricklayer) but most of them were signed by one tradesman who subcontracted the work to the other trades.

The inquiry into the barrack contracts was part of an ongoing political attempt to discredit the surveyor general's patrons, the lord lieutenant and Primate George Stone. However, it revealed defects which were more serious than mismanagement and poor administrative practices. It provided evidence of Nevill's approval of inflated building costs, of his willing acceptance of inferior building standards, and of his encouragement of bribes from contractors to officials engaged in the inspection and commissioning of the contracts. The inquiry did not explicitly charge the surveyor general with accepting payments from contractors. However, it is clear from the proceedings that the only explanation for Nevill's conduct was his personal profit. His encouragement of high prices and his attempts to increase rates in the bill of measurement were obviously done in his own interest. So also were his payments to contractors for buildings that were uncompleted or badly finished. The evidence presented clearly shows that he was in collusion with his clerk George Ensor and a number of Dublin-based contractors for his and their mutual gain. Ensor, as the inquiry proved, made considerable profits through gratuities from contracting artisans, quite apart from the profits he might have himself received as a contractor.

Nevill had been appointed as surveyor general in 1743 and he was responsible between 1746 and 1748 for important extensions to Dublin Castle. He was disappointed in the financial conditions of his appointment, which were considerably less lucrative than those enjoyed by his predecessors in office.[28] In 1749, he made representations seeking a commission of 5 per cent of the cost of building work under his control, on the basis that this percentage of costs had been traditionally deducted by his predecessors from payments to artisans engaged on public works.[29]

The advent of such a large building programme as that of the barracks, involving an expenditure of over £40,000 in a period of less than two years, was a considerable challenge to the organizational capacity of the surveyor general's office and a tempting opportunity for Nevill to profit as his predecessors had done from such a venture. His main problems were his lack of authorization under the terms of his employment to charge such commissions and the inadequacy of the form of his contracts in concealing such commissions from public scrutiny.[30] Although much of the evidence deals with the testimony of measurers and bills of measurement (suggesting a series of normal measured contracts), there can be no doubt that the agreements used were

---

[28] Edward McParland, 'The office of the surveyor general in Ireland in the eighteenth century', *Architectural History*, 38 (1995), 98. [29] Ibid., 98. [30] Ibid., 98.

contracts in-gross. This requires some explanation. The typical uses of the in-gross agreement – such as in the building of speculative terraced houses – did not need the services of a measurer, or bills of measurement. These agreements were related to fixed sums of money and not to unpredictable quantities of building work. However, as stated earlier, in-gross agreements were not normally used for public projects. In England, if they were considered for such purposes, they were usually measured and valued and, as an additional precaution, certified by sworn testimony from independent artisans.[31] In his choice of in-gross agreements for buildings involving such considerable state expenditure, Nevill was obviously obliged to follow English practice.

The evidence that in-gross contracts were used for the barrack programme is clear from evidence given during the enquiry. The contractual sums quoted appear to have been precisely calculated to the nearest penny and not round approximations based on unit rates. The contract sum for the Galway barracks, for instance, was a figure of £5,328 2s. 11d. and the contract sum for Carlow barracks was a figure of £2,778 11s. 11d. In Richard Reilly's testimony that 'when he received his contract [for Loughrea barracks], he looked upon it as an Absolute one upon the Estimate annexed to his Contract, and did not expect the work to be measured again', there is the clear perception that the contract sum was a fixed figure and not subject to measurement. George Ensor in his evidence claimed that he also 'made an absolute Agreement with the Surveyor General upon the Contract'. John Chambers, in reply to a comment about the final payment under his contract, stated that 'he had received his Money in Gross, as before.' Some contractors in their evidence described themselves as master builders, a term normally associated with in-gross contractual agreements.

This ambitious building programme, starting in 1748 and finishing in 1750, involved sixty-five separate provincial sites and many different artisan-contractors. However, a large percentage of the programme was under the control of a small group of Dublin contractors who were closely involved with the surveyor general. These were Pierce Archbold, John Chambers and the brothers George and John Ensor. Chambers and Archbold were the main carpenter-contractors working on Dublin Castle during Nevill's term of office, and in 1747 Chambers received the lion's share (£2,927 12s. 1d.) of a total contract of £7,143 19s. 11d. for rebuilding the castle's principal entrance. John Ensor was a former assistant of Richard Castle and his recent experience of the in-gross contracting system gained on the Gardiner estate might have been of assistance to Nevill. George Ensor's presence in the list of contractors is somewhat surprising, as he was Nevill's clerk/assistant. As such, he was responsible for the preparation of the contract documents (plans and bills of scantling), and he also negotiated building prices with the various contractors based on prior estimates prepared by him. Thus, he was acting in the extraordinary roll of contractor, estimator, supervisor and architect for the programme. He was also given the

---

31 Clarke, *Building capitalism*, p. 82.

responsibilities, as the evidence of the inquiry revealed, for the settlement of prices in the measurement of the contractor's final accounts.

The division of contractual responsibilities for the building programme was undoubtedly determined by Nevill in consultation with Ensor, Archbold and Chambers. Chambers took responsibility for four barracks (at Galway, Gort, Headford and Athenry) at a total contractual figure of £7,750 5s. 0d. Archbold undertook contracts (at Limerick, Carlow, Clarecastle and Carrick-on-Suir) valued at £6,567 10s. 2d. George Ensor's responsibilities (for Mallow, Tallow and Cappoquin) were valued at £2,811 6s. 9d. His brother John contracted for Carrick-on-Shannon barracks for the sum of £832 14s. 7d. This brought the total value of contracts under the control of this group to nearly £18,000 or about 45 per cent of the entire budget for the building programme. George Ensor also introduced another group of Dublin artisans into the programme: Richard Reilly, Edward Byrne and Patrick Gernon, who were variously the contractors for Loughrea, Portumna, Roscommon, Clonmel, Kilkenny and Cashel. In the case of Carlow, the contractual conditions for the programme contained a startling proviso in that the contractor Archbold was to receive an advance payment of two-thirds of the contract sums on acceptance of the contractual agreements. In 1748, Nevill noted that normal practice would be that the builder would execute a bond as security for his certified performance. So, in the autumn of 1749, we find the government engaged in a programme of considerable expenditure on contracts based on the unusual use of in-gross agreements and the disbursement of substantial advance contractual payments. The government's acceptance of such unusual conditions might be explained by historic problems experienced in building and maintaining barracks in Ireland. The bulk of public expenditure in Ireland was accounted for by the army, and poor management of a vast investment in fortifications and military buildings occasioned continuous changes in the administrative structures responsible.[32] The problems experienced in the late 1740s were particularly acute, due to the inadequate condition of existing premises and the fear of foreign invasion.

The unusual receipt of such a large percentage of contractual funds before work commenced must have been a massive incentive to prospective contractors, particularly as the buildings proposed were relatively simple in construction and finishes. It must have been particularly attractive to an assistant such as George Ensor whose normal income as Nevill's clerk was a mere £40 per year. The disadvantages of the conditions to contractors were the requirement of sworn testimony from independent local artisans (such as masons, carpenters and slaters) and also, as it emerged from evidence given in the inquiry, the need to satisfy the measurer Laurence Purfield and a barracks inspector called Robert Lawe.

The process of measurement, as it emerged, did not unduly worry the contractors. Purfield, on his own admission, was new to this kind of work, and

---

32 McParland, 'The office of the surveyor general', 91–101.

although the surveyor general instructed him to estimate certain costs and 'to note what is not done in a workmanlike manner', he failed to do more than measure. The parliamentary inquiry censored him for this, notwithstanding his claim that 'it is not the Business of a Measurer to observe whether the work is well or ill done, or to affix Prices'. It also became apparent that Nevill had limited the measurer's customary role. In Purfield's testimony he states 'Ensor put the Prices to the several Articles in the Measurement, and particularly those prices that were higher charged in the Bills of Measurement than in the Estimate.' He also stated that Ensor 'informed him at the same Time, that he, the said Ensor, affixed these prices to the said Bill of Measurement, by direction of the Surveyor-General.' There were other serious shortcomings in Nevill's control of the contractual process. Considerable payments were made to contractors based on certificates presented to Nevill, with affidavits from carpenters, masons and slaters endorsing the quality of the finished buildings. These certificates were challenged later by the parliamentary committee on the grounds that many of the certifying artisans were employed by the contractors involved. Archbold, for instance, had used artisans employed by them on the barracks construction to certify the work. The report on Rosscarbery barracks (in Co. Cork) stated 'that the two Men who made the Affidavit of the Sufficiency of this Work, the one a Mason, the other a Carpenter, were both employed under Reilly, the Contractor, in this Building'.

The difficulty of satisfying Robert Lawe, the barracks inspector, on the quality of materials and workmanship was clearly anticipated by the contractors, as he gave evidence 'that he had been offered money by all, or most of the Contractors, except George Ensor'. It is clear that under normal circumstances this inducement might have influenced his judgment, but the evidence revealed that he had been warned by a 'Person of Experience' of the impending parliamentary inquiry. His report was critical of the materials and workmanship in many of the barracks contracts.

Bribes such as those offered to Lawe were apparently a common practice in public contracts. Ensor admitted to receiving the 'several following Sums of Money, that is to say from Roberts £12; from Byrne eleven Guineas, from Reilly £10; from Gernon £10; from Mr Nesbit five Guineas; from one Wilson 10/; from Mr Parker twenty Guineas; from Cardiff [Cardy] five Guineas; and a Promise from the contractor of Doneraile of twenty Guineas which he never had received'. Gernon's payment was made on the basis 'that Ensor told him he believed he could get him a Barrack [contract]'. Lawe had to admit that he accepted money from contractors (Chambers, Byrne and others) but he had prudently returned most of these payments after an interval of a few months. He also testified that contractors had offered him these gratuities on the insistence of the surveyor general. None of the contractors, however, admitted to making payments to the surveyor general himself. Burke, the Galway barrack master, testified that Chambers told him 'he was to allow £5 per Cent to the Surveyor-General upon his Work, and that it was allowed to him all over the Kingdom'.

The most critical indictment of Nevill was contained in statements made by Samuel Cardy, the contractor at Navan. Lawe's testimony claimed that Cardy, after unsuccessfully attempting to bribe the inspector, 'swore a great Oath he would not suffer any Man, but would declare the Truth, that he had got, or was to get but either £150 or £200 for these repairs out of a total contract sum of £388 17s. 0d.' Cardy, however, was unavailable for questioning by the parliamentary committee. Fearing, possibly, the outcome of Lawe's report on the poor execution of his contract, he had emigrated to South Carolina where he subsequently had a successful career as an architect and master builder.[33] Lawe's report on the constructional standards he found in the barracks varied considerably. He found Archbold's work at Carlow[34] executed in a workmanlike manner and in George Ensor's Tallow 'the Workmanship ... appeared to be well executed'. Chambers' work at Galway and Headford was found to be acceptable but at Athenry was badly executed. The inspector, who was critical of Gernon's work at Kilkenny and Samuel Cardy's work at Navan, was, however, much more tolerant in his views than most of the later military reports which were highly critical of many of the buildings they occupied.

Whatever about the certainty of Nevill's mismanagement of the contracts, or of his ambitions to share in the contractors' profits, we can have no doubts about the motives of Ensor, Archbold or Chambers in entering into contracts that could bring them high profits without significant risks. Chambers and Archbold were involved in substantial building operations in the Dublin market. Why would they become involved in diverse contracts in places like Gort, Headford, Limerick and Carlow? Why would Ensor, Nevill's assistant, become a contractor and take contractual risks in places as distant as Mallow, Tallow and Cappoquin? The reason, of course, was that no risks were involved until an unexpected parliamentary inquiry was engineered by the surveyor general's political enemies. Ensor was the architect of these barrack designs; he had drawn up the contractual conditions, he had advised the other contractors on prices, and he had adjusted the prices in the bill of measurement. He was fully aware of the minimal risks involved and of the state's lack of supervisory controls during the contractual process. Lawe, the barracks inspector, was not expected to be difficult, but after he was warned about the inquiry he duly returned gratuities he had received from contractors and refused to accept money from others who offered it to him.

Many of the advantages and disadvantages of the in-gross contractual agreement are apparent from the evidence given at the inquiry. Its main advantage – the predictability of final cost – was accomplished. In spite of increases of rates in the bills of measurement, Nevill managed to produce a final contractual account which had 'an Exceeding to [the] Publick, between the Contracts and Bill of Measurement' of £481 14s. 1½d. Given the massive cost increase of Burgh's contract for the Dublin

---

33 Kenneth Severens, *Charleston, antebellum architecture and civic destiny* (Knoxville, TN, 1988), p. 10.
34 *Commons Journal*, 5, lxxvii; the text says 'Limerick' but it is probable that 'Carlow' is meant.

barracks in 1707, this was no mean achievement in the handling of a contractual budget of £41,741 12s. 10d. From a management viewpoint, the use of in-gross agreements for this large building programme was a sound choice. It had the benefit that it placed the entire responsibility for the performance of all trades engaged in any particular contract on one general contractor. Given the urgency and scale of the programme – the repair and construction of sixty-five barracks in different provincial centres – it was probably the only choice available. The surveyor general's office did not have the administrative capacity to organize and monitor individual trade contracts on sixty-five remote sites.

The 1748 barrack programme was ideally suited to the use of in-gross agreements. The buildings were simple basic structures without complex decorative features. They were well described by drawings and bills of scantling, which could be accurately measured and priced without difficulty. Costly contractual delays due to variations in design were unlikely. The contractual terms offered in the programme were obviously attractive to the contractors. Most of the gratuities paid to Ensor (like the payments of Gernon and Reilly) were for introductions to the surveyor general and involvement in the contractual process. The contract sums were calculated on the basis of rates which were comfortably high and, as an additional comfort, the contractors received two-thirds of their contract price at the commencement of the work. No wonder Archbold, Chambers and George Ensor were happy to take such a large share of the building programme at such a distance from their operational base.

However, the distance from operational bases caused considerable difficulties for some contractors. John Ensor had serious problems in the supervision of his contract at Carrick-on-Shannon. He subcontracted the workmanship to local artisans and Nesbit, the local barrack master, reported that 'Ensor did not often attend the Building'. Hugh Wilson also tried to manage the contract at Tullamore from Dublin with disastrous results. Richard Nary and Edward Cooke were the contractors at Granard barracks, though 'neither was concerned in the Execution of the Work', which was carried out by the barrack master. Richard Reilly and Edward Byrne testified that they had no knowledge of local prices at Loughrea. The contracts at Carrick-on-Shannon, Tullamore and Loughrea were severely criticized during the inquiry for poor standards of workmanship.

The most common fault reported in many contracts was the persistent eighteenth-century problem of leaking roofs. Evident also was a characteristic defect of the in-gross contractual system in the attempts by contractors to increase profit margins by skimping on materials. There was criticism of the use of unseasoned timber in contracts such as Kilkenny and Galway. Lawe reported on an important deviation from the contractual agreements found in all the barracks, the substitution of white deal for the more expensive red deal flooring boards.

The contractors most criticized for bad workmanship and materials were John Ensor, Cardy, Gernon, Wilson, Byrne and Reilly, all from Dublin and all involved in payments of gratuities to George Ensor. Ensor's own contractual performance largely appears to have satisfied the inspector, as did most of the work undertaken by the experienced Dublin master builders Archbold and Chambers. Archbold seems to have emerged from this debacle unscathed, as he was continuously employed by the surveyor general's office in the 1750s under the control of Nevill's successor Thomas Eyre.[35] George Ensor evidently found the career of a master builder engaged in lump-sum contracting profitable and fulfilling, as he continued to work in this capacity in succeeding years. Ensor's talents combined architectural skills with entrepreneurial ambition. In 1762, he acted as architect and builder (with his brother John) for the Sessions House in Roscommon; from 1763 until 1766 he was involved in the design and construction of schools for the Ranelagh charity in Athlone and Roscommon; and from 1767 until 1770 he designed and built the public hospital in Armagh.[36] In 1780, we find him back in Dublin engaged in the speculative development of two houses in Merrion Square.[37] These contracts may have been lucrative, as by this time he was the owner of Ardress House and its estate in Co. Armagh.

The two factors that combined to develop the use of in-gross contracts were the continuous expansion of the speculative housing market and the unprecedented rise in building prices after the 1770s. The organizational methods used by master builders in the construction of town houses provided the experience needed in the coordination of different trades, the bulk purchasing of materials and the handling of capital finance. The repetitive design patterns allowed the precise calculation of costs without the need of drawings and descriptive specifications. Builders such as Samuel Sproule working in Merrion Square, or Charles Thorpe working in Mountjoy Square, were their own architects, and were totally in control of the building process. Thorpe's houses were nearly identical to their neighbours with the exception of their stuccoed ceilings, but he had full control over the execution and cost of the stucco work, and the total house cost could be easily established before building commenced.

The need by both the state and private building owners to respond to the rapid inflation of building costs at the end of the century forced them to favour fixed price agreements and the rationalization of contract documentation. The high quality of construction drawings prepared during this period by architects such as Francis Johnston reflects this demand for predictable estimates which remained unaltered by design variations during the building contract. As Thompson in his history of quantity surveying explains:

> As long as the system of separate-trades contracting persisted it was certainly possible to make an advance estimate of building cost, for the illumination or dejection of the prospective owner, but it was not possible to use such an estimate to bind the hands of builders. Hence advance estimating remained in the hands of architects, performed from sketchy calculations and guess

---

35 IAA, 'The General Accompt of Thomas Eyre', Accession Nr 86/149, pp 24, 27, 28, 36, 46, 54, 64, 72. 36 See www.dia.ie, 'George Ensor'. 37 *GSR*, 4, p. 81.

work to propriate their clients, until the revolution in contracting in the early nineteenth century, which produced the all-trades contract and the single building contractor undertaking to carry it out.[38]

The scarcity of building materials during the French Wars (1793–1815) and their escalating costs destabilized the traditional basis of the measured contract system. Clarke, in *Building capitalism*, describes this process:

> Though rates were relatively stable up until the 1770s, after this time the system became more and more unworkable because, in the first place, it was impossible to know what price tradesmen had paid for materials or how much material had been bought for a given price and, in the second place, different methods of measurement were used.[39]

The demand for the control of building costs and the need to make contracting more competitive promoted a shift away from the traditional sources for the supply of building materials. This pattern had already been established earlier in the eighteenth century by house builders like Robert Ball, who also became a timber merchant and supplied joinery, bricks and sand to other builders. In the 1760s, both Pierce Archbold and John Chambers (the barrack builders) are listed as timber merchants in the Dublin directories, and Chambers, during this period, was building speculative houses in Merrion Square.[40] By the nineteenth century, the capital investment by builders in building plant and equipment grew considerably: Thomas Cubitt, for instance, in London, owned a joinery shop, a marble shop, scaffolding stores, a plaster shop, an engineering workshop and a steam-powered sawmill by 1820.[41]

This marked the end of the measured system, the trade divisions and the close associations with the building guilds. Tradesmen no longer owed allegiance to a master artisan or his workshop; they became skilled building workers under the direction of experienced foremen. The general builder was now in full control of the process of building, and he took responsibility for the coordination of building tasks and the supervision of workmanship. The architect relinquished his role as coordinator and supervisor, and he became, instead, an inspector and a certifier of quality. The in-gross contract became general, though not without objections from architects such as Decimus Burton and Robert Smirke, who echoed the same complaints voiced over a century earlier, by Christopher Wren, and reiterated by the anonymous architectural critic of the *Freeman's Journal*, in Dublin in 1769.[42]

---

38 F.M.L. Thompson, *Chartered surveyors, the growth of a profession* (London, 1968), p. 81.   39 Clarke, *Building capitalism*, p. 81.   40 *GSR*, 4, p. 81.   41 Clarke, *Building capitalism*, pp 82–3.   42 Ibid., p. 83.

CHAPTER THREE

Carpentry

THE IMPORTANT PART PLAYED by timber in ensuring the stability of eighteenth-century masonry structures promoted the carpenter's central role in regulating the activities of many other artisans employed on building sites. The introduction of masonry casings as a common building method (in lieu of timber-cage structures) in the second half of the seventeenth century reduced the carpenter's involvement in the building fabric, but his responsibilities were still considerable. Robert Campbell's description of the London carpenter in 1747 explains the importance of these responsibilities:

> The Carpenter is employed in the Wooden-Work, from the Foundation to the Top. In Works where the Foundation is supposed soft, the Carpenter drives Piles down to support the Edifice. In Brick-Works he places Bearers, where the chief Weight of the Building lies: he lays the Joists, Girders, and Rafters in Flooring, and when the outward Case is built, he puts on the Roof and prepares it for the Slater.[1]

Carpenters had other duties in fitting timber components into the structural carcase. They installed windows in exterior walls, and they balanced sliding sashes with iron weights. They hung doors, and provided wooden partitions and framework supports for decorative plaster. They installed the elaborately moulded timber casings used as door-frames, window-cases, skirtings, cornices, wainscots and panelling. Thus they were involved in the determination of the structural performance of buildings, their functional operation and their decorative characteristics. Francis Price, in his introduction to *The British carpenter* in 1753, insists that 'Carpentry naturally comes in among the essential heads of *architecture*', because of its characteristics of 'strength, use *and* beauty'.[2]

The carpenter's training in the processing of timber for structural and decorative work was obtained through the guild system and apprenticeship with a master carpenter. This involved the apprentice in the practical exercise of his craft in workshops and building sites, under the supervision of the master and his assistant journeymen for a period of seven years. That the perceived need for the addition of a broader theoretical knowledge was necessary in contemporary practice is evident from

---

[1] Robert Campbell, *The London tradesman* (London, 1747), p. 160. [2] Francis Price, *The British carpenter; or, A treatise on carpentry* (London, 3rd ed., 1753), introduction.

the considerable number of building manuals published during the eighteenth century, and from the activities of training establishments such as the Dublin Society schools.

The Dublin Society provided financial subsidies for Robert West's drawing school in George's Lane in the 1740s, and by 1750 they had opened 'an Academy for Drawing and Design' in Shaw's Court in Dame Street.[3] The schools' activities included tuition in the arts and crafts, and the promotion of art and architecture, through a series of annual awards. Some of its pupils included Francis Sandys, Robert Pool, John Cash, Richard Morrison and James Hoban. The schools' awards list records premiums to the sculptor John Houghton for carving in 1742, to George Ensor (a former carpenter) for the design of a house in 1745, and to Thomas Cranfield for carving in 1769.[4] The architect Thomas Ivory (a former carpenter) took control of the newly established school of architectural drawing in 1764, and his successor from 1787 was Gandon's pupil Henry Aaron Baker. The tuition offered by Ivory and Baker to young craftsmen contributed significantly to the fine quality of architectural ornament visible in the façades and interiors of Dublin buildings in the neoclassical period.

An examination of the better-known eighteenth-century building publications provides us with an insight into contemporary constructional theory and the practical requirements of artisans such as carpenters in meeting the demands of new architectural ideals. These books covered a wide variety of subjects dealing with both contractual practices and the application of architectural principles to buildings. They dealt with methods of measuring and pricing workmanship, the setting out of basic geometric figures, calculations for timber structural members, systems for framing roofs and floors, and descriptions of the proper use of the classical orders of architecture and their application to doors, windows, fireplaces and elevational profiles, from the cornice to skirting and plinth levels.

Although this material was intended for the use of many artisans engaged in building activities, it is easier to measure its general characteristics in a discussion on carpentry because of the carpenter's central role in the building process. In a review of historic literature dealing with building practices from 1592 to 1820, Yeomans expressed the belief that building manuals were principally addressed to carpenters.[5] His view is based on the carpenter's predominance as the central figure in building operations and his involvement in the coordination of other artisans' tasks. This is supported by the considerable amount of published material dealing specifically with carpentry.

Apart from the great folios such as *Vitruvius Britannicus*, building literature in its most basic form can be classified under three headings. First, we have measurers' manuals dealing with mathematical information on the mensuration of workmanship.

---

[3] John Turpin, *A school of art in Dublin since the eighteenth century* (Dublin, 1995), p. 8; Anne Crookshank and the Knight of Glin, *Ireland's painters* (New Haven & London, 2002), p. 85.   [4] Turpin, *A school of art in Dublin*, pp 12, 19.   [5] David T. Yeomans, 'Early carpenters' manuals, 1592–1820', *Construction History*, 2 (1986), 13.

Second, we have technical manuals showing the design of roofs, floors and other components with guidance on the dimensions of structural members. Under the third heading, we have pattern books, which guided artisans in the choice and application of stylistic embellishment. As the century progressed, authors began to combine aspects of all these classifications in their publications to increase their saleability. Although the amount of material published was extensive, the information produced was highly repetitive and its quality varied considerably from book to book.

* * *

The earliest books to appear were the measurers' manuals. Many seventeenth-century publications were still in use in the eighteenth century and, as Yeomans has pointed out, most of the subsequent building literature was influenced by these surveyors' manuals.[6] Essentially, the manuals dealt with the reduction of quantities of materials into units of measure (such as a perch of masonry or a cubic foot of timber) that enabled artisans to calculate the cost of their work. Edward Hoppus's *Practical measuring now made easy* was probably the most useful and widely read example of its type. Published in London in 1736, it provided a series of tables that were easier to read and more comprehensive than other contemporary manuals. The success of Hoppus's tables can be judged by the many editions printed in the eighteenth century, the appearance of a New York edition in 1846, and a further London edition in 1870. In Ireland, William Hawney's *The complete measurer* was obviously successful, as the Dublin edition of 1730 was reprinted in *c*.1740 and in 1767, and a Cork edition appeared in 1768. It was overtaken, however, by Philip Levi Hodgson's *The modern measurer*, which appeared first in the 1760s (as an adaptation of Hoppus) and remained in continuous demand until its tenth edition in 1801.

What do these measurers' manuals tell us about the eighteenth-century carpenter and his work? Hawney's *The complete measurer* could only have been welcomed as a mathematical primer, as over half its contents were devoted to the principles of decimal arithmetic, multiplication, division and the extraction of square and cube roots. The remainder showed, by a series of examples, how these principles could be applied in practice to the measurement of workmanship. The only inference we can draw from this material is the view that artisans received little or no training in basic mathematics before or during their apprenticeships. This is supported by the inclusion of sections dealing with mathematics and elementary geometry in publications by Batty Langley and Francis Price.

Hoppus's *Practical measuring now made easy* provided a simpler answer. His tables were comprehensive enough to provide carpenters with the solid content (in cubic feet) of scantlings of a wide variety of sectional sizes, and from 1ft to 50ft in length, without any calculations. His fifth edition, published in 1759, went further. It displayed 'a New Set of Tables, Which Shew, at sight, the Solid Content of any Piece of Timber

[6] Ibid.

at any Price from 1/6, 2/-, 2/6, 3/- per foot cube', thus providing a ready reckoner of both quantities and cost.[7] This was the format adopted by Levi Hodgson in Dublin and by most English manuals in the second half of the century. The rapidly rising cost of materials after the 1770s promoted the demand for updated cost information and the need for newer and newer editions. Hodgson's ninth edition (in 1793) is a good example of how far the demand for guidance on costs had developed by the end of the century. As well as the tables borrowed from Hoppus and typical advice on girthing regular, irregular and tapering timber, Hodgson included prices for sawyers' work with different timbers, the cost of labour at various rates for a six-day week, and a comprehensive analysis of prices for framing (floors, roofs and stairs) and fitting (skirtings, doors and wainscot) in a typical building. Although his background as a measurer was in the timber trade, Hodgson provided similar costs for the work of bricklayers, stonecutters, plasterers and slaters.

* * *

Technical manuals dealing with the design of structural components such as roofs and floors and the construction of circular and elliptical framing for stairs, vaults and domes are particularly important, as they illustrate problems faced by carpenters in the interpretation of the new stylistic ideals introduced by classicism. They also allow us to discuss the widening gap between carpentry practices in England and Ireland which became evident in the eighteenth century. The earliest and most authoritative book to appear in the first half of the century was Francis Price's *The British carpenter; or, A treatise on carpentry*, which was introduced in London in 1733, with a sixth edition published in Dublin in 1768. Price's work carried on its title page the imprimatur of James Gibbs, Nicholas Hawksmoor and John James, a master carpenter who had a considerable reputation as an architect in the London area. Price's first chapter ranged from simple propositions in basic geometry, such as the erection of a perpendicular on a horizontal line, to the sophisticated setting out of intersecting elliptical vaults. These geometric exercises reflect the carpenter's traditional responsibility for setting out the entire building structure, as well as timber centerings to facilitate the construction of masonry arches and vaults.

Price's descriptions of roof trusses show a clear understanding of the structural efficiency of truss members (such as struts and ties) and the joints used to assemble them. His adaptations of king- and queen-post trusses to accommodate attics and plaster barrel vaults, and as M-profile roofs with lower ridge heights, provided his readers with valuable guidance on flexibility in the choice of roof structures. His illustrations of the framing of hipped roofs reflect one of the problems faced by carpenters at this time. Palladian classicism brought with it a preference for low tiled roofs with hipped ends, which allowed the use of a continuous cornice. British and Irish carpenters – accustomed to finishing their high ridged roofs against masonry

---

7 Edward Hoppus, *Practical measuring now made easy* (London, 1759), p. iv.

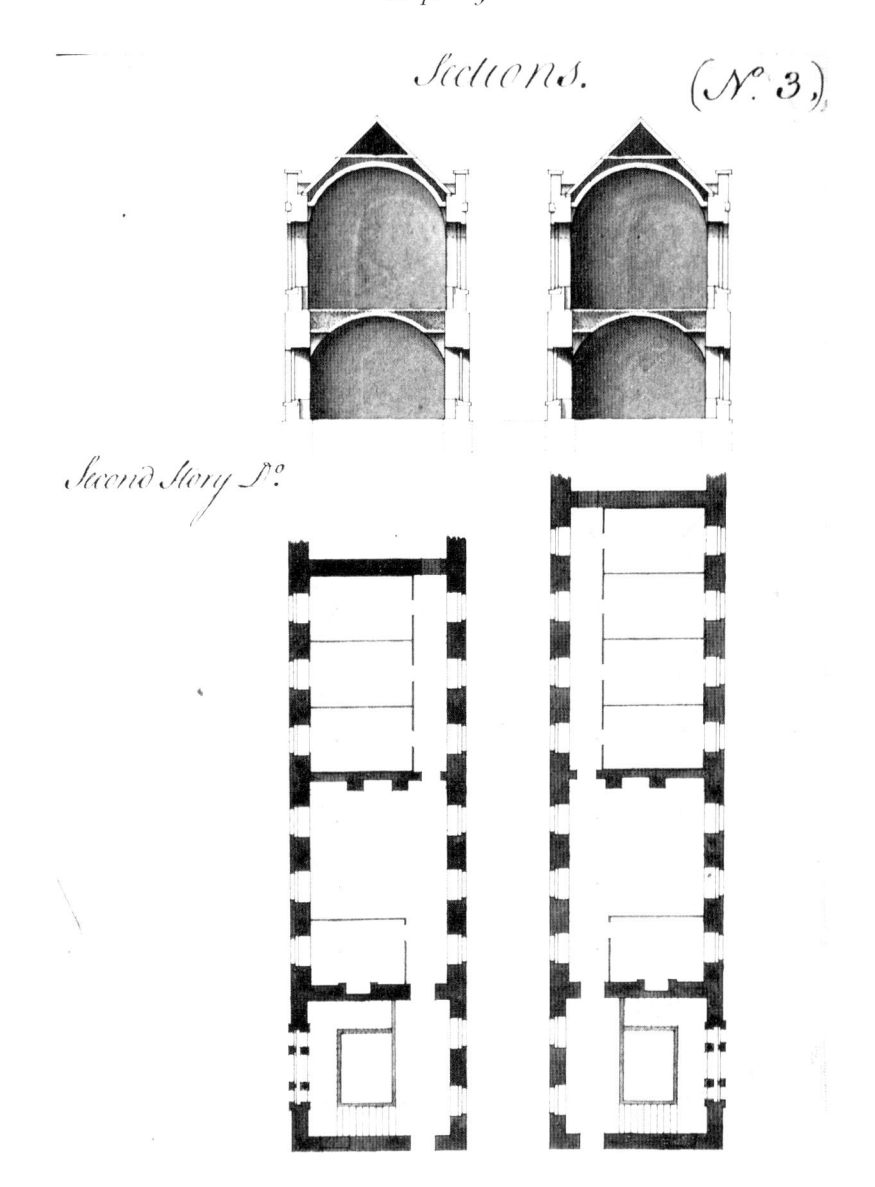

3.1 Proposed Public Offices, Dublin, 1758, section, George Semple, King's Inns Library, MS H1/1–1. Reproduced with permission of the King's Inns.

gables – found the geometry of the diagonal hip trusses difficult, and particularly so when buildings were not perfectly rectangular. Price's layout of 'bevel roofs' with hips shows how the length of hip rafters could be calculated.

Casey's critical view of the unprogressive nature of building practices in Ireland is supported by the persistence of seventeenth-century roof framing methods in the

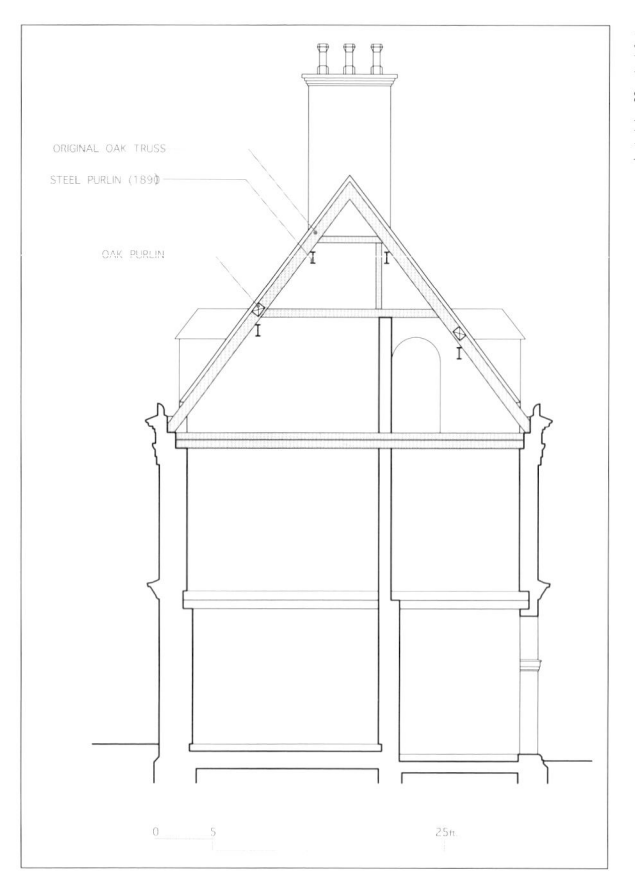

3.2 Royal Hospital Kilmainham, *c.*1685, section, Conor Rochford from original by Joseph McCullough & Partners.

3.3 Kilmacurragh, Co. Wicklow, *c.*1700, section, Conor Rochford from original by Charles Lyons.

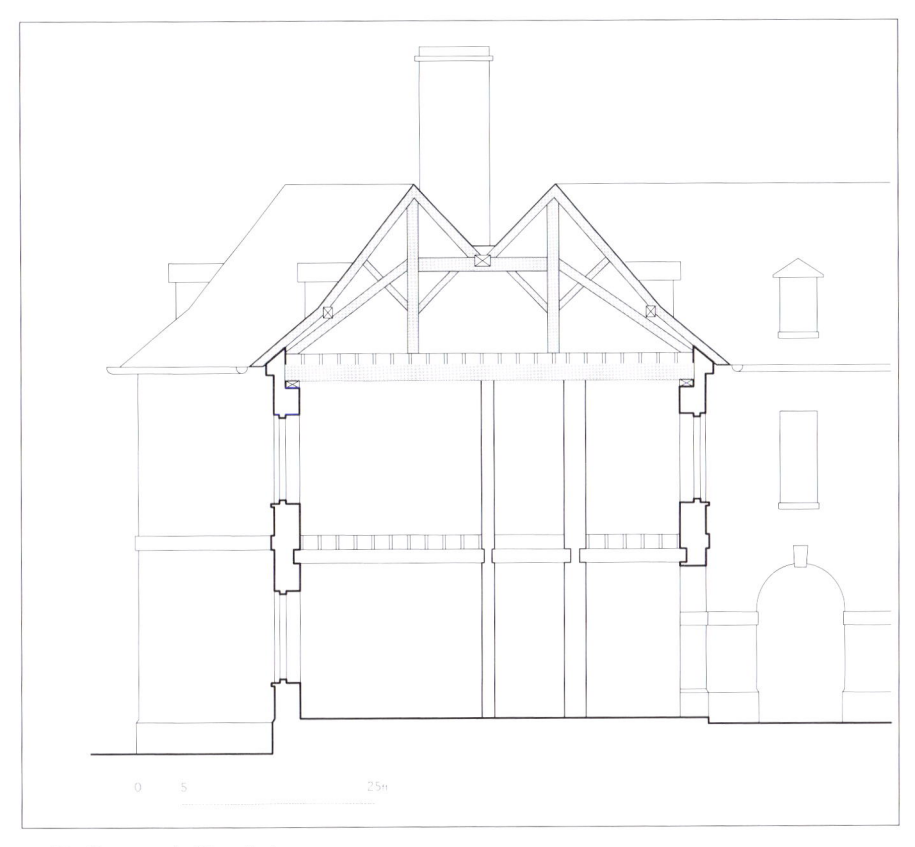

3.4 Dr Steevens's Hospital, Dublin, 1720s, section, Conor Rochford from original by Arthur Gibney & Partners.

3.5 Dr Clark's School, Drogheda, 1728, section, Michael Wills, IAA, 92/24. Courtesy of the Irish Architectural Archive.

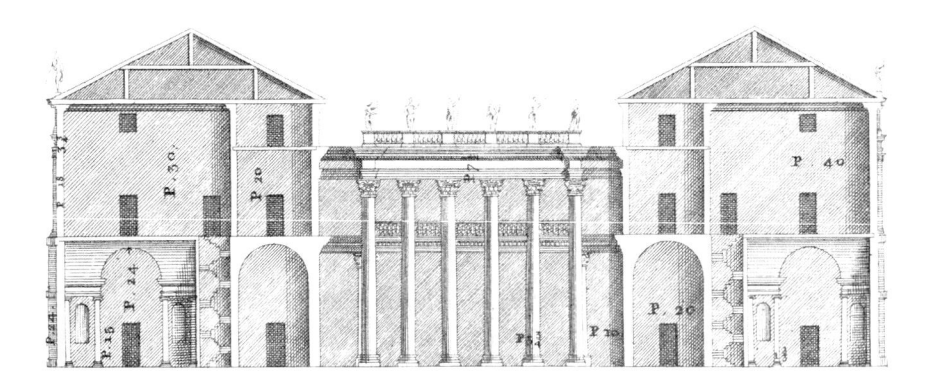

3.6 Palazzo Porto, Vicenza, 1540s, section (upper) and Temple of Jupiter, Rome, section (lower), Andrea Palladio, *I quattro libri*, book 2, plate 4 and book 4, plate 27.

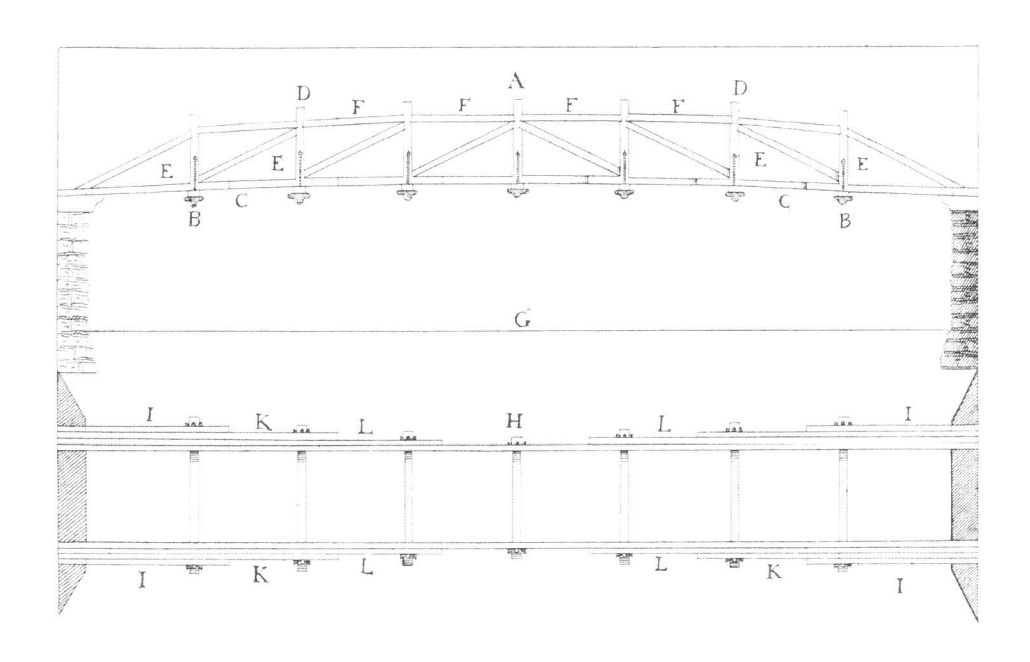

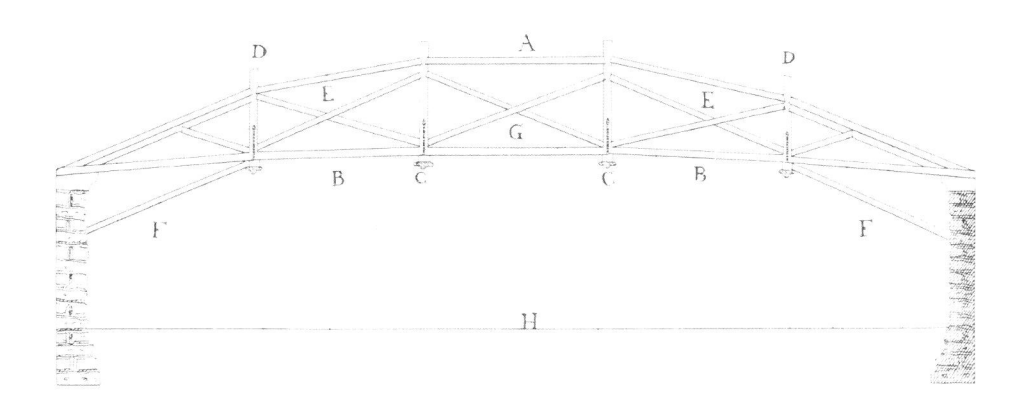

3.7 Multiple-post trusses in bridge construction; these influenced Wren's trusses in the Sheldonian Theatre, Oxford, in the 1660s, Andrea Palladio, *I quattro libri*, book 3, plate 4.

eighteenth century.[8] Most of the generation of buildings that followed the Royal Hospital Kilmainham in the first three decades of the next century used the same steeply pitched roofs and similar roof structures to those employed in the 1680s. The use of classical king-post framing started in England before the 1650s, but it was to await its full development in the hands of designers such as Wren, Gibbs and Hawksmoor, between the 1670s and the 1720s. Price's work was the first attempt to publicize the proper design of classical roof framing, and it was probably the first sight many carpenters or architects outside London had of this system, apart from the illustrations in Barbaro's *Vitruvius*, or Palladio's *Quattro libri*.

The design of classical roof profiles was to become one of the most important influences on changing constructional practice in England and Ireland and one which (in England) clearly separates the seventeenth from the eighteenth century. The stylistic demand from Palladian builders for low Italianate roofs coupled with the need for longer roof spans influenced the choice of roofing materials and produced radical changes in the structural framing of roof timbers. Early classical roof structures in Ireland used common rafters, supported on purlins spanning between framed principal rafters (or roof trusses). The most basic form of truss was an A-frame of principal rafters connected by a collar beam at a level between the wall-plate and the apex of the roof. This form of roof framing derived from medieval practice. The essential basis of the collar truss used in the late-fifteenth-century Dunsoghly Castle was still employed in the eighteenth century but only for short spans (fig. 3.1). A more advanced form of roof framing (found in the Royal Hospital in 1685 (fig. 3.2), Kilmacurragh, Co. Wicklow, *c*.1700 (fig. 3.3), Molyneux House, Dublin, *c*.1711, Dr Steevens's Hospital, 1720s (fig. 3.4) and the Drogheda Schoolmaster's House, 1720s (fig. 3.5)) used tie-beams at wall-plate level to resist the outward thrust of the roof and collar-beams as structural braces at a higher level. Some frames used diagonal struts to help distribute the load of the roof.

This early (pre-Palladian) roof framing had certain limitations, as Yeomans has noted.[9] It impeded the development of lower roof profiles, as it was only effective when used in high pitched roofs. The use of the collar, for instance, had little effect on principal rafters at pitches as low as 30 degrees. The transmission of structural loads onto the lower tie-beam (through posts and struts) necessitated the use of single baulks of timber, thereby limiting its capacity for longer spans. The problems were overcome in the late seventeenth century in England by the adoption of the classical roof truss, illustrated by Palladio and visible in such structures as the octastyle portico of the Roman Pantheon. The advantages of this truss were fully exploited in the shallow lead-covered roof of Wren's Sheldonian Theatre in 1669. This spanned 70ft using a tie-beam fabricated from several individual timber members, joined together to resist the tensile forces at the base of the roof.

---

8 Christine Casey, 'Books and builders; a bibliographical approach to Irish eighteenth-century architecture' (PhD, University of Dublin, Trinity College, 1991), pp 185–6. **9** David T. Yeomans, *The architect and the carpenter* (London, 1992), pp 25–6.

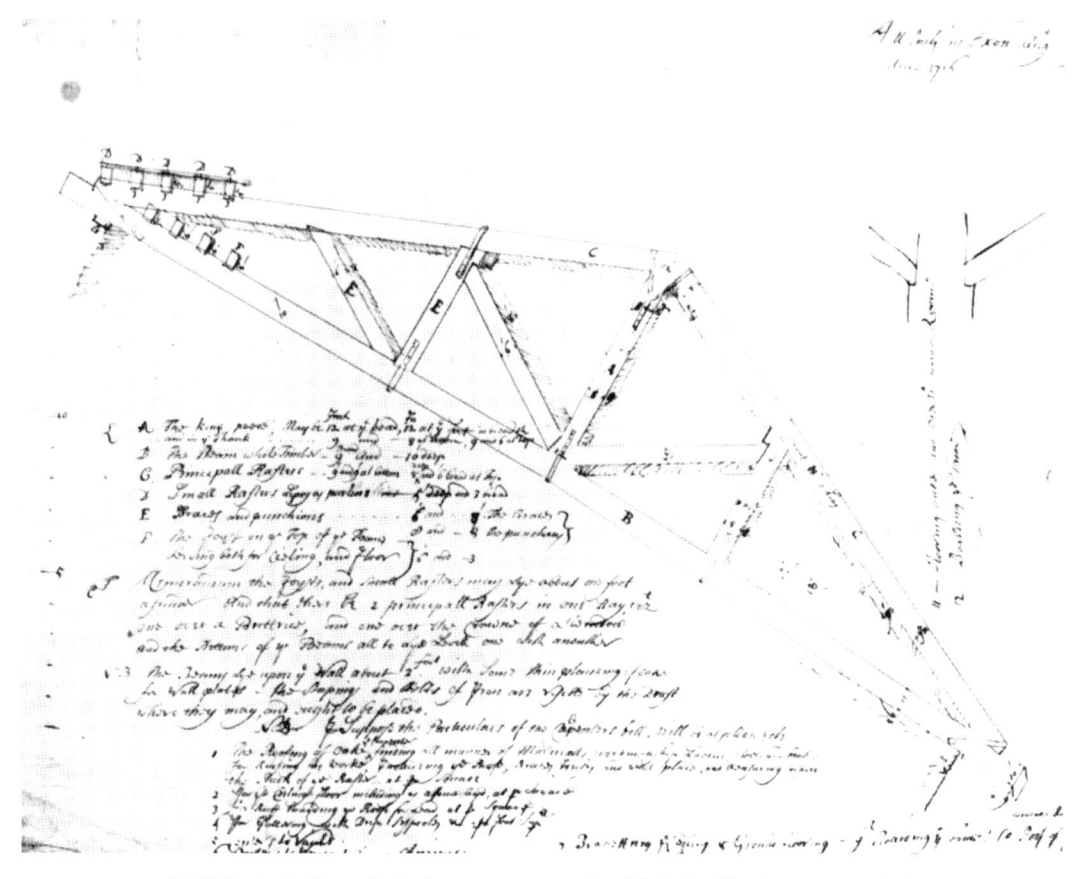

3.8 All Souls College, Oxford, truss proposed by Nicholas Hawksmoor, 1716, from David Yeomans, *The architect and the carpenter* (London, 1992), p. 48. Reproduced with permission of the Provost and Fellows of Worcester College, Oxford.

Palladio illustrated the use of various framing arrangements to suit different spans and structural conditions. These ranged from a truss with a single (central) vertical post and two diagonal struts over short spans, to multiple post and strut arrangements used for the construction of timber bridges (figs. 3.6 & 3.7). These trusses formed the basis for the design of eighteenth-century king-post and queen-post roof structures. Wren's triple-post truss for the Sheldonian was influenced by Palladio's design for a bridge with laminated tie-beams. He was also undoubtedly influenced by Palladio's comments on the structural efficiency of the framing methods advocated and on his use of iron cramps or stirrups.

The structural efficiency of the Palladian truss depended on the cohesive action of all framing members working in equilibrium and the use of vertical posts (as ties) to carry the tie-beam at the base of the truss. This required considerable care in the fabrication of the joints connecting structural members together especially at the terminal points of the truss (apex and wall junctions) and the junction of king-post

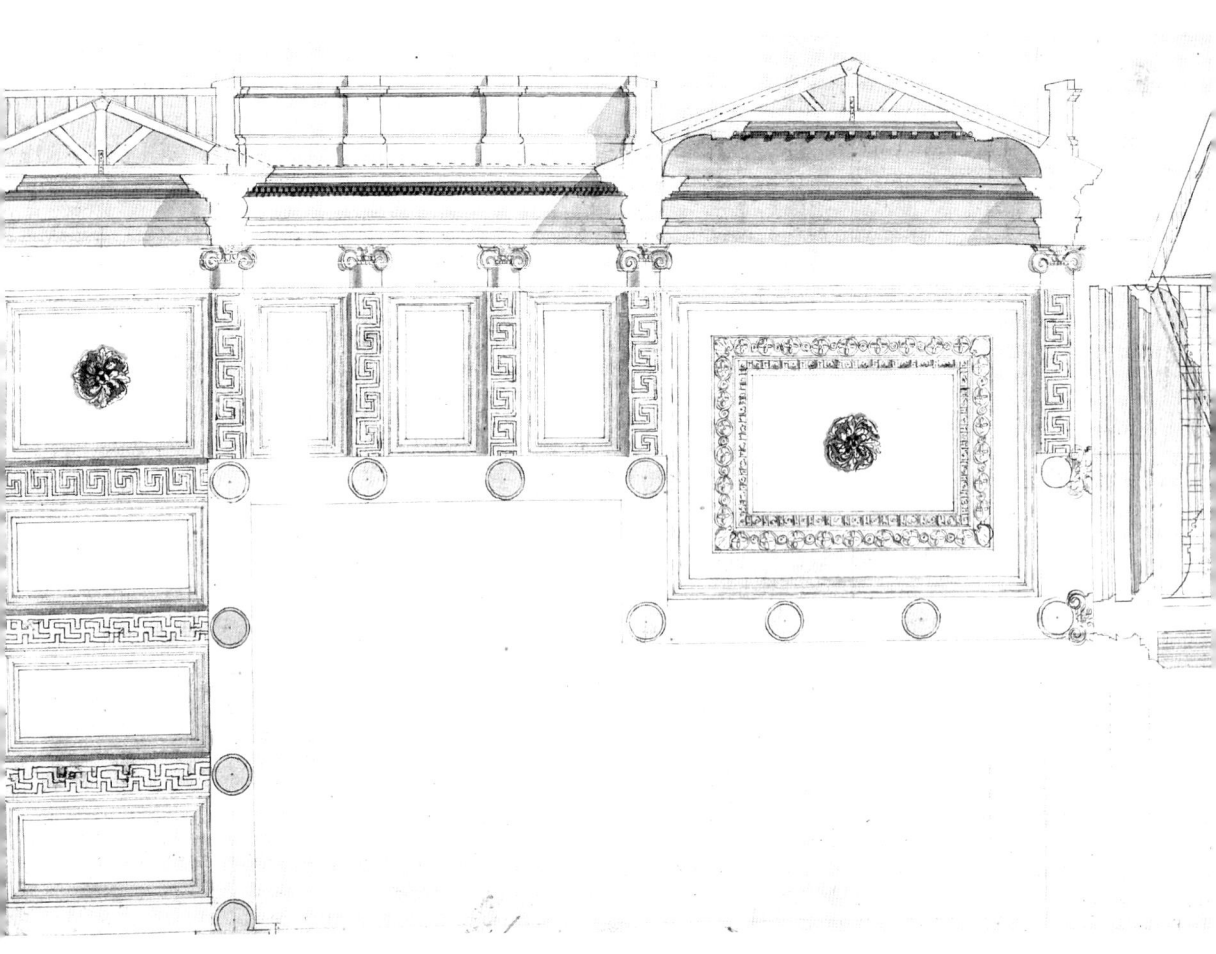

3.9 Parliament House, Dublin, *c.*1728, section and ceiling plan, Edward Lovett Pearce, V&A Drawings Collection, E2124:184–1992, © Victoria and Albert Museum, London.

and tie-beam. The use of iron stirrups and cotter pins to strengthen these junctions became common in the eighteenth century. A drawing of Hawksmoor's truss design for All Souls College, Oxford, in 1716 (fig. 3.8), shows the proper use of such iron straps and the careful handling of junctions between structural members.

By 1733, the publication date of Price's *British carpenter*, the situation in Ireland had already changed considerably. Edward Lovett Pearce's appointment to build a new Parliament House in 1728, and his decision to employ Richard Castle as his assistant, marked a new direction in Irish architecture and a corresponding change in technical standards. The triumphant introduction of Palladianism into Ireland in a work of such quality was, of course, due to Pearce's brilliance and personal ambitions. The execution of a building of this magnitude in such a short building period was also a managerial triumph which could not have been achieved without considerable organizational resources. Pearce's high opinion of Castle – 'as I know nobody in this

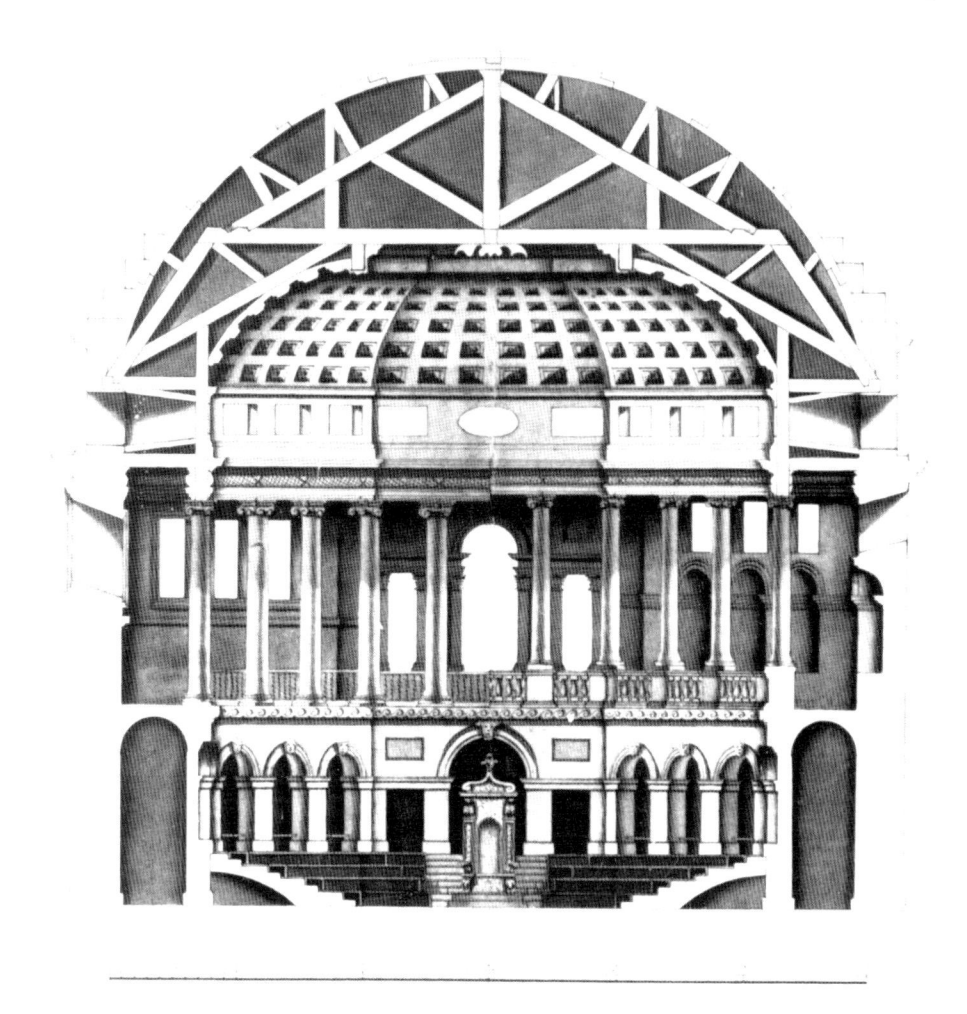

3.10 Parliament House, Dublin, c.1728, section, Edward Lovett Pearce, V&A Drawings Collection, E2124:1–1992, © Victoria and Albert Museum, London.

town whom I could employ capable of drawing fair designs of this nature but one person' – confirms his assistance in the execution of the work, but it does not clarify the extent of his role.[10] As such, it is difficult to know if Pearce relied on Castle's technical experience in the development of the structural design of the building.

It is clear from drawings of the colonnaded portico that the use of the Palladian truss in low (pediment pitched) roofs was fully understood (fig. 3.9). What is more

10 Quoted in Edward McParland, 'Edward Lovett Pearce and the Parliament House in Dublin', *Burlington Magazine*, 131:1031 (Feb. 1989), 99–100.

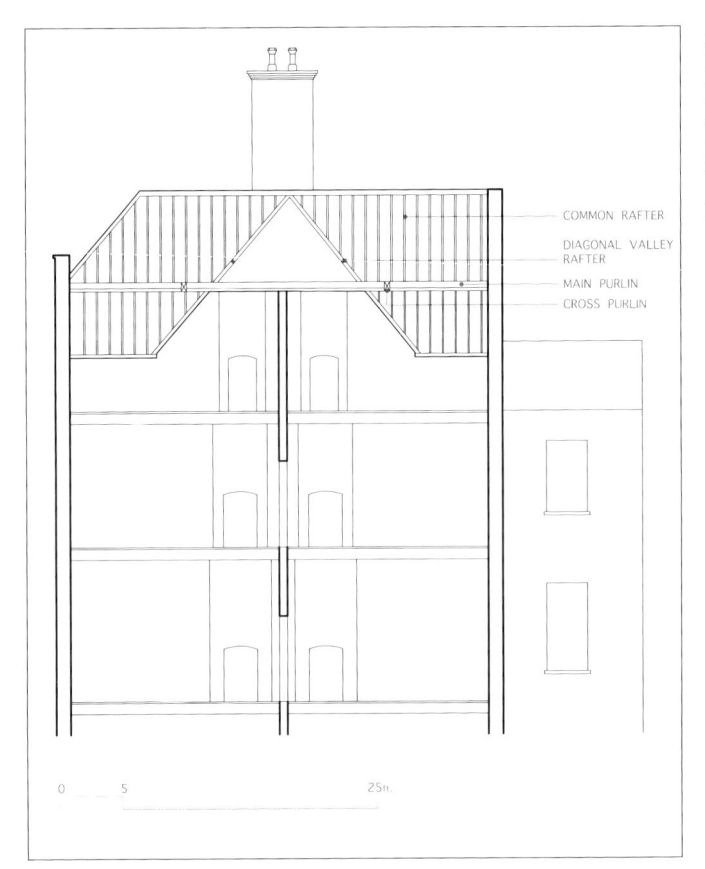

3.11 No. 10 South Frederick Street, Dublin, mid-eighteenth century, section, Conor Rochford from original by Arthur Gibney & Partners.

notable, and completely unexpected, is the daring use of a series of trussed timber arches to roof the high central Commons chamber with an octagonal dome (fig. 3.10). This use of the king-post in a series of linked trusses is highly innovative and, like the architectural refinements of the entire building, unusual for its time.

Ireland was not to experience architecture of the quality of the Parliament House again for another fifty years, but Castle's professionalism remained. The spread of Palladian designs through the country promoted rationalized roof framing, helped, no doubt, by the publications of such writers as Price and Langley. By the 1740s, well-designed trusses were in common use in Dublin and provincial areas. George Semple's drawings of St Patrick's Hospital in 1749 show an example of a carefully considered king-post truss with iron stirrup straps. *Faulkner's Dublin Journal* published a notice in 1752, seeking tenders from carpenters for roof framing for St Mark's Church: the bill of scantling reveals a comprehensive knowledge of long-spanning truss construction.[11]

While this use of the king-post truss represents a convergence of a sort with English practice, it is from Castle's time that an equally significant divergence

11 George Faulkner, *The Dublin Journal*, 22–25 Aug. 1752.

Carpentry 71

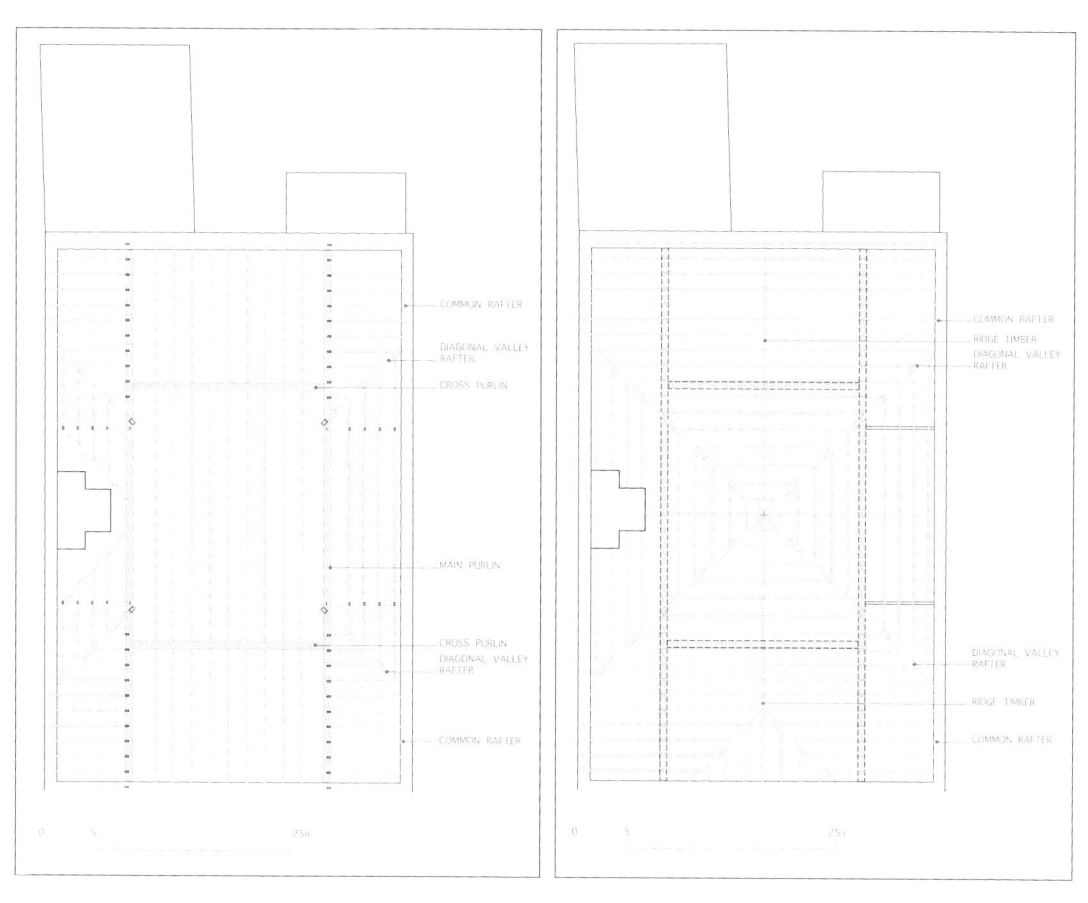

3.12 (*left*) No. 10 South Frederick Street, Dublin, mid-eighteenth century, top-floor ceiling plan showing use of purlins between gables, Conor Rochford from original by Arthur Gibney & Partners.   **3.13** (*right*) No. 10 South Frederick Street, Dublin, mid-eighteenth century, roof structure, Conor Rochford from original by Arthur Gibney & Partners.

between English and Irish carpentry patterns becomes noticeable. It is certainly evident by the 1740s in the construction of country houses such as Tudenham, Co. Westmeath and Ledwithstown, Co. Longford, and in Dublin in palatial mansions such as Leinster House, Doneraile House and the terraced houses of Henrietta Street. Castle's links with the designs of this generation of buildings are clear, but what may be difficult to establish is how much he influenced the balance between existing traditions and new carpentry practices in Ireland.

A division between Irish and English carpentry traditions was already apparent from the earliest part of the century. This can be seen in the roofs of the Dublin gabled houses that formed extensive suburbs in the Meath and Aungier estates, and in succeeding generations of early brick houses on St Stephen's Green and in the Molesworth estate. These houses, known as Dutch Billies, were also visible in the

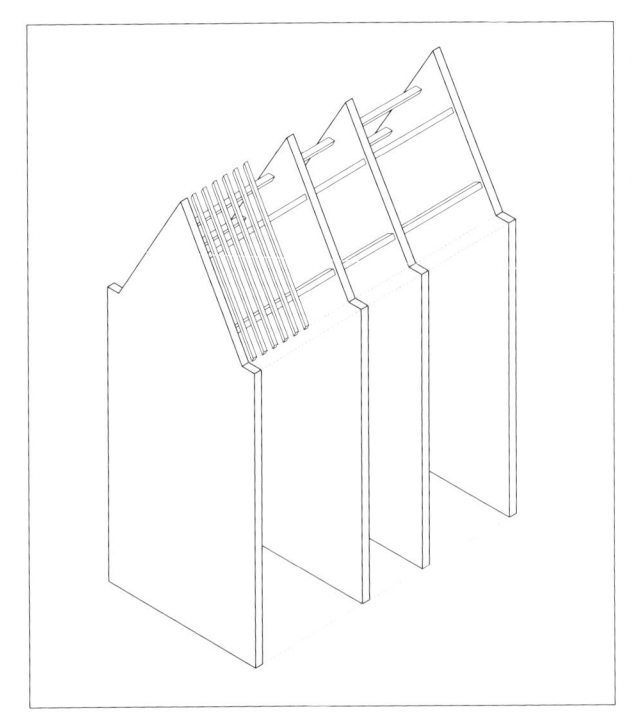

3.14 Roof structure of a typical Irish provincial town house; masonry gables and purlins avoided the need for trusses, Conor Rochford from original by Arthur Gibney & Partners.

streetscapes of port cities such as Limerick, Cork and Waterford. The house type appears to have come to Ireland with the influx of artisans from the south of England in the late seventeenth century, but its origins were undoubtedly Dutch. Holland was known to have the most progressive urban housing in Europe in the early part of the seventeenth century, and the importation of Dutch bricklaying techniques into England at this period anticipated the change from timber to brick housing, which started after the London fire of 1666.

Dublin gabled houses have roof structures which are very different from foreign examples. These roofs were built with a primary structure of timber purlins spanning between masonry gables and supporting in turn a secondary structure of common rafters (figs. 3.11 to 3.13). The main difference between this construction, and methods used in similar houses in England and Holland, was the substitution of masonry supports for timber trusses (fig. 3.14). The efficiency and economy of this system encouraged its use, and we find it employed in later houses in Dublin and Cork. These roofs were to become unfashionable in Dublin after the 1740s, but the technical objectives which developed them were to have a powerful influence on Irish carpentry over the entire eighteenth century. Essentially, these objectives were the avoidance of massive timber members and complicated mortise joints and a reliance, where feasible, on the use of masonry rather than wooden supports.

The framing systems for floors, trussed girders and trussed partitions proposed by Price were an integral part of the English carpentry tradition (fig. 3.15). The trussed girder relied on the insertion of cambered scantlings (or sometimes metal

3.15 Francis Price, *The British carpenter* (London, 5th ed., 1765), plate C & D.

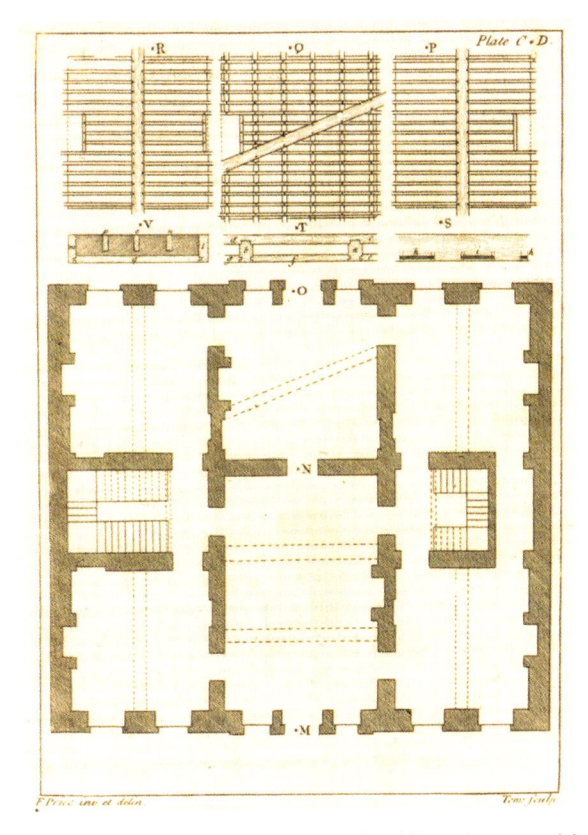

straps) into the sides of heavy beams (providing additional stiffness) to avoid deflection over long spans (fig. 3.16). The only known example of the use of such girders in Ireland was by William Chambers in the floors of Charlemont House in Dublin. Chambers also used the trussed partition here which was an adaptation of the roof truss to provide a partition that, while not bearing on a wall beneath, could support floor loadings (fig. 3.17). It provided remarkable flexibility in planning, particularly in the alignment of rooms in London's terraced houses. However, its advantages were ignored by the builders of Dublin's terraced houses and only Gandon's drawings for Carrigglas and Roslyn Park suggest their use elsewhere.[12]

Price sums up the main principles of English floor framing practices in the introduction to *The British carpenter* (3rd ed., 1753):

> Also observe, that all case-bays, either in floors or roofs, do not exceed twelve feet if possible; that is, do not let your joists in floors, your purlins in roofs, &c. exceed twelve feet in their length, or bearing; but rather let the bearing be eight, nine, or ten feet; which should be observ'd in forming a plan.[13]

12 For Gandon's drawings see Edward McParland, *James Gandon* (London, 1985), pp 129, 139.
13 Price, *The British carpenter*, p. ii.

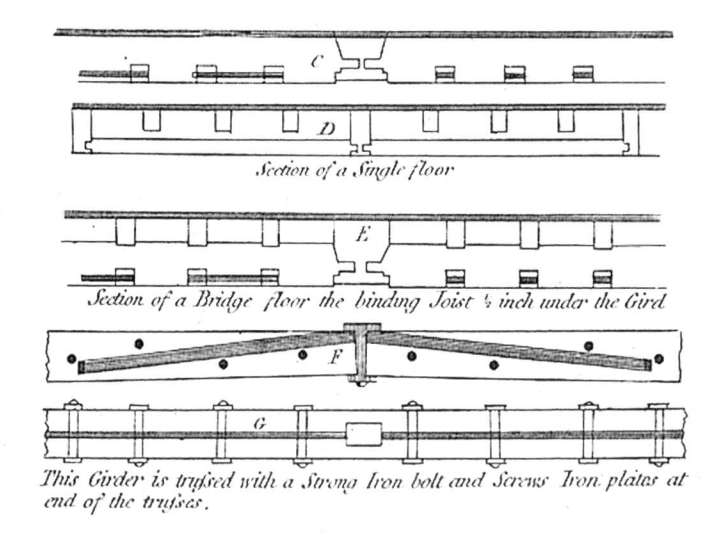

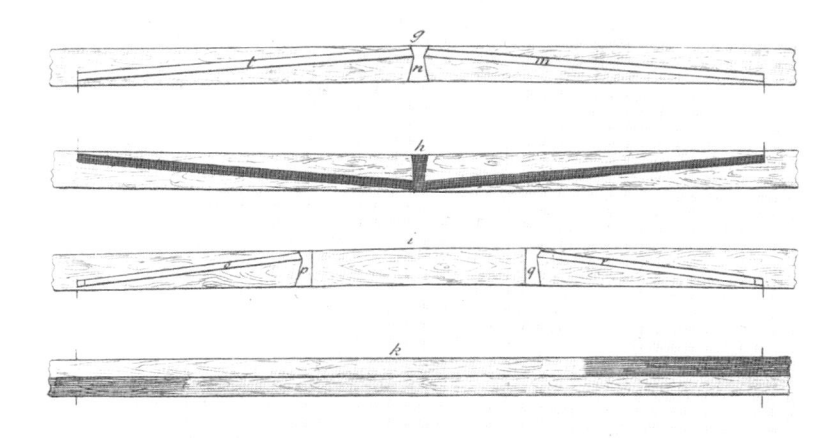

3.16 Trussed girders; (top) William Pain, *Carpentry and building, the practical house carpenter*, new ed. (London, 1860/1), plate 10; (bottom) Francis Price, *A supplement to the British carpenter* (London, 1735), plate B.

These general principles were already enshrined in the London building regulations, and they were endorsed by most eighteenth-century manuals. The effect of these regulations meant that, even in the most economically designed buildings, two structural members supported the floor: a girder and a floor joist. It was necessary in the simpler system to use a separate set of ceiling joists if a level ceiling (without beams) was required (figs. 3.18 & 3.19). In better quality work, a more complex

3.17 Charlemont House, Dublin, 1763, trussed partitions. Photograph by Arthur Gibney.

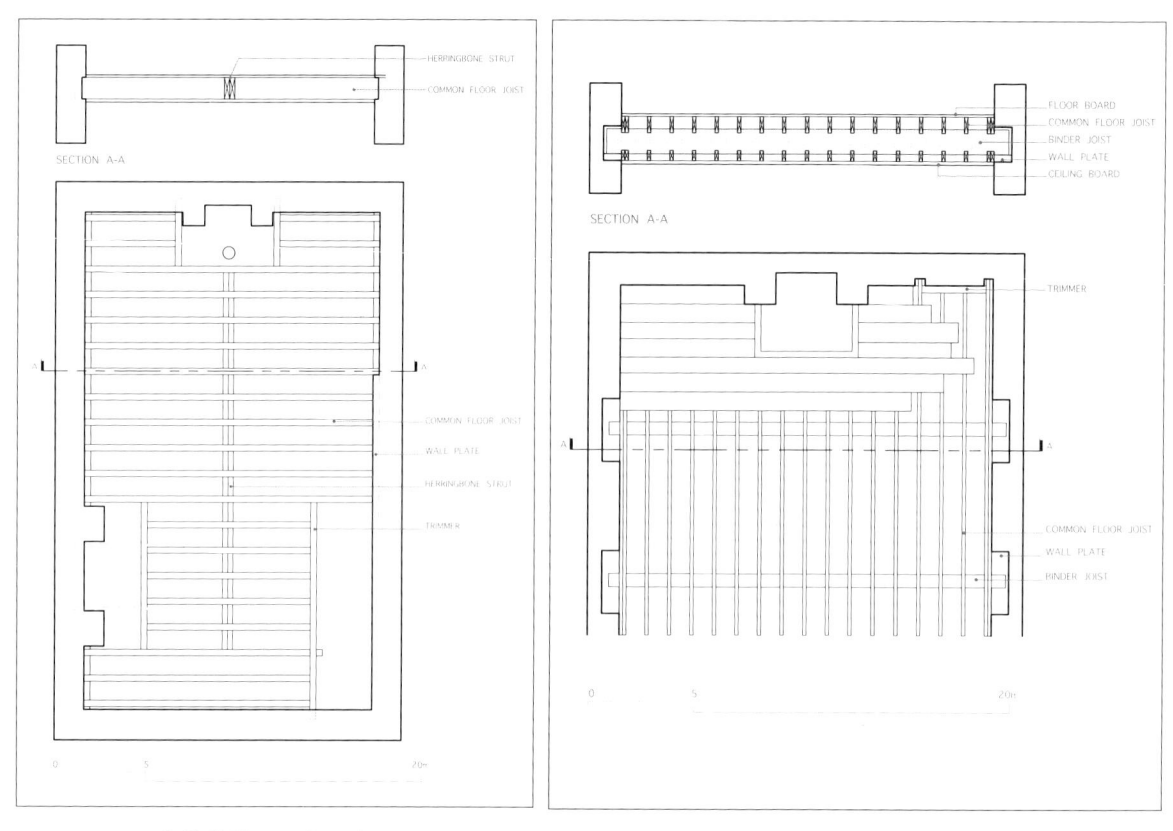

3.18 (*left*) Plan and section showing common floor joists with herring-bone strut, Conor Rochford.
3.19 (*right*) Plan and section showing common floor joists and binder joists, Conor Rochford.

system of three structural members was used: girders, binder joists and common floor joists (fig. 3.20). In the more complex system, ceiling joists were also often used to avoid sagging or deflection. All of these members, floor joists, binders, ceiling joists and girders were joined together by mortises, tenons and cogged joints. The simpler form of these floor systems (beams and joists) can be found in Kilmacurragh, Co. Wicklow (fig. 3.21), Marsh's Library, Trinity College Library, Dr Steevens's Hospital, and most Irish buildings built before the 1740s. As far as we know, the more complex system has only occurred in Ireland in the work of Chambers and his former pupil Gandon (fig. 3.22). The system must have been well known here, however, as it was well illustrated in the Irish editions of Price's and Langley's publications and in most English manuals.

From the late 1730s onwards, a decisive change in the design of Irish floor construction marked a fundamental departure from English practice and the stringent provisions of the London building regulations. By the 1740s, Irish carpenters had abandoned the use of framed floors entirely and put their trust in the use of one single structural member – the long spanning joist – running in clear spans

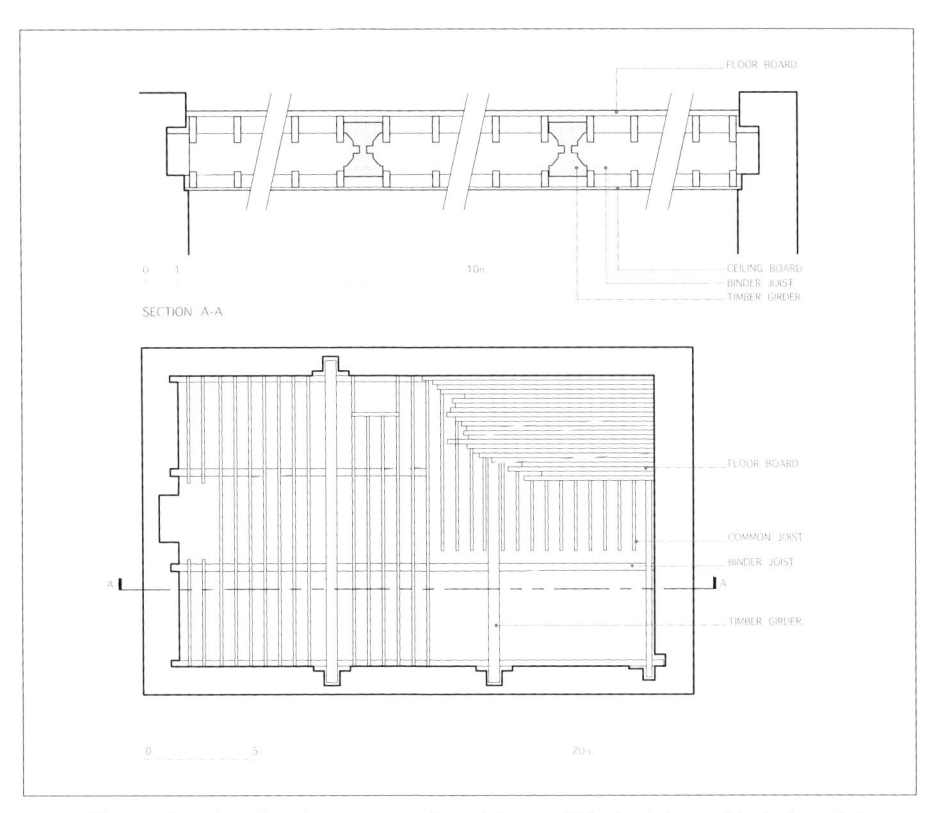

3.20 Plan and section showing common floor joists and binder joists, with timber girders, Conor Rochford.

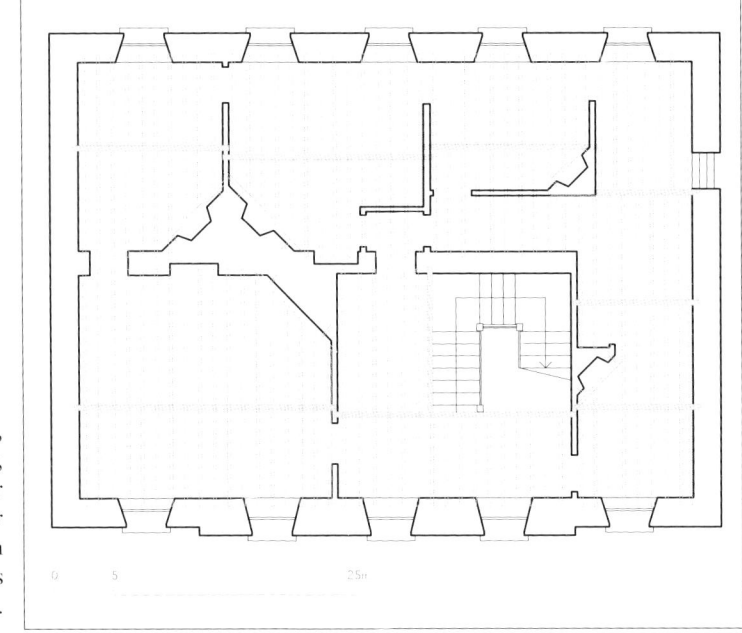

3.21 Kilmacurragh, Co. Wicklow, c.1700, floor framing, Conor Rochford from survey by Charles Lyons.

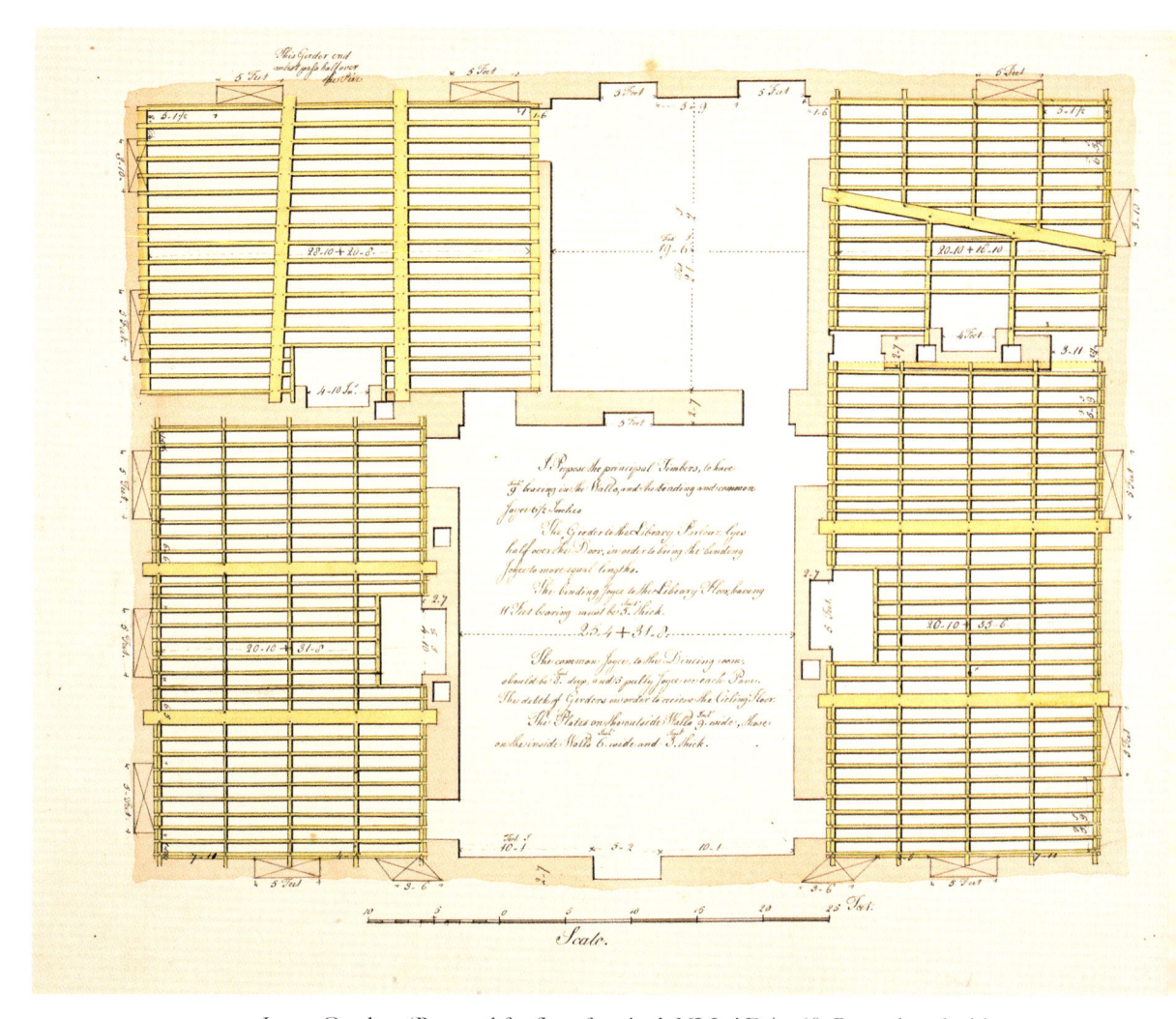

3.22 James Gandon, 'Proposal for floor framing', NLI, AD/3268. Reproduced with permission of the National Library of Ireland.

between structural walls (figs. 3.23 & 3.24). This difference in the structural expectations of the joist is clearly expressed in the building manuals. Both Price (London, 1753) and Pain (London, 1794) recommend maximum lengths of 12ft.[14] Langley (Dublin, 1729) recommends 11½ft but Hodgson in his Irish manual gives dimensions of joists spanning 20ft.[15] In practice, Irish carpenters using joisted floors exceeded this span. The advantages Irish carpenters saw in the use of the clear spanning joist were, like the qualities they sought in the gabled roof system, an economy and simplicity in construction. It avoided the expense and the complications

14 Ibid., p. 51; William Pain, *The practical house carpenter* (London, 1794), p. v. **15** Batty Langley, *The builder's vade-mecum* (Dublin, 1729), p. 68; P. Levi Hodgson, *The modern measurer* (Dublin, 1793), p. 91.

Carpentry

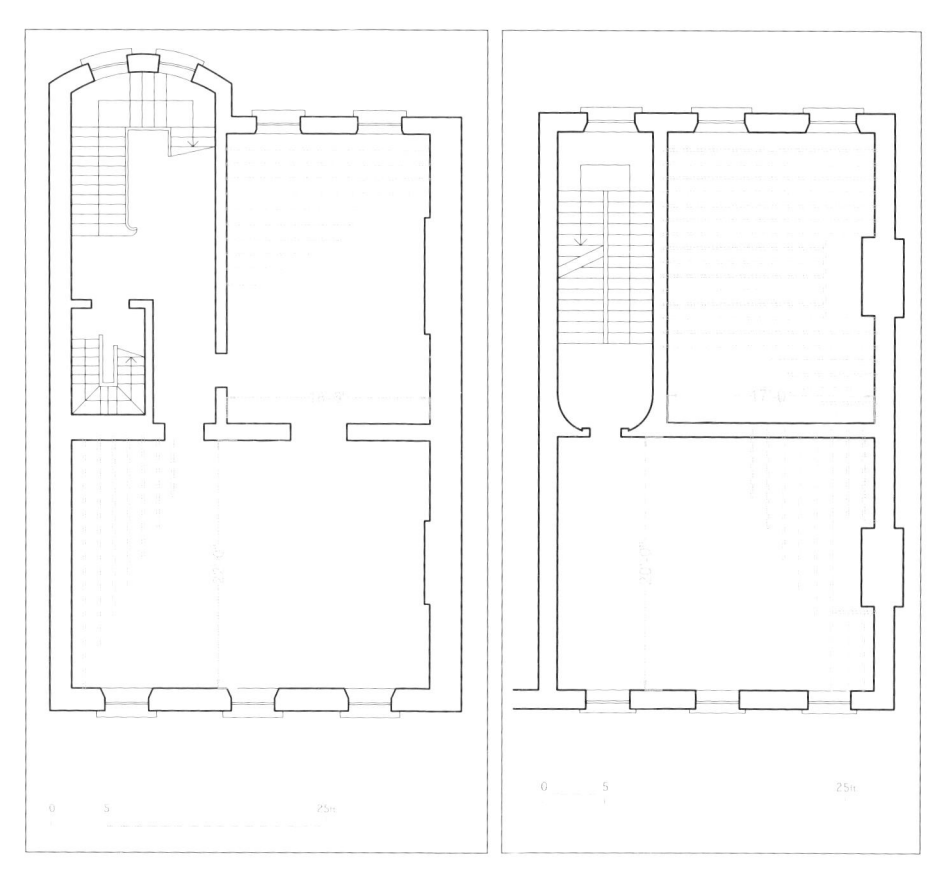

3.23 *(left)* No. 42 Upper O'Connell Street, Dublin, 1752, floor construction, Conor Rochford from original by Arthur Gibney & Partners.   **3.24** *(right)* No. 40 Lower Dominick Street, Dublin, *c*.1760, floor construction, Conor Rochford from original by Arthur Gibney & Partners.

of heavy girders that could not be manipulated easily by hand; it removed the laborious process of cutting tenons, mortises and cog joints and their considerable cost. In addition it required no ceiling joists, as the ceiling laths could be simply applied to the undersides of the floor joists.

The most significant advantage of English floor construction was the additional stiffness provided by the use of heavy primary timbers and short joists. This avoided deflection and consequent damage to the ceiling plaster. In its most complex form (of joists, binders and girders), it was particularly adaptable to the use of coffers, or compartmented ceilings; in its simplest form, however, (of joists and girders) the protrusion of the girders below ceiling level (as in the Worth Library at Dr Steevens's Hospital) could have a disturbing effect on the interior. Another disadvantage, that could become apparent with time, was the effects of shrinkage on the bearing ends of the structural joints that may have reduced the stiffness and structural continuity of the floor. In this, the Irish long joist flooring, acting as a continuous tie between the structural walls, was particularly efficient.

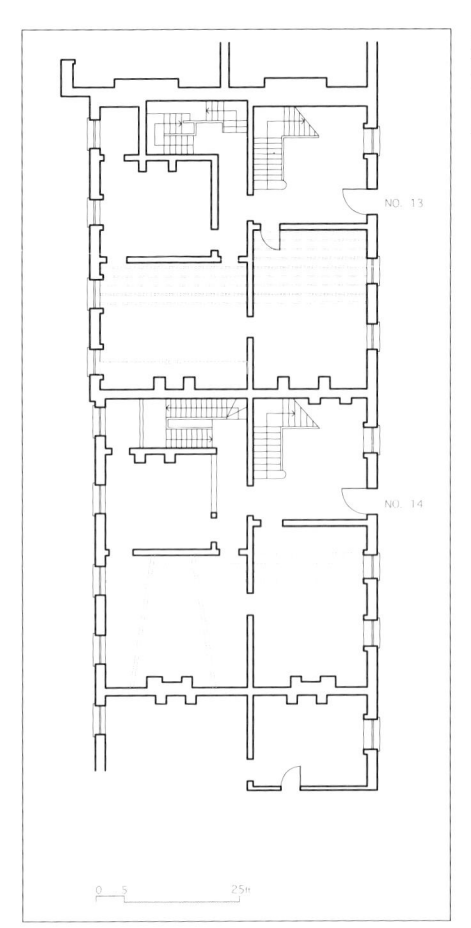

3.25 Nos. 13 and 14 Henrietta Street, Dublin, *c.*1750, floor construction, Conor Rochford from original by Arthur Gibney & Partners.

Richard Castle's part in this change from framed floor structures to long joists is difficult to define, but the use of the new flooring method in Palladian buildings associated with him cannot be discounted. Nor can we ignore the influence of the carpenters themselves and the same spirit of economic rationalism that produced the unique roof structure of the Irish gabled house. Many carpenters of the era (such as Benjamin Ball, Benjamin Rudd and George Ensor) were involved as master builders and architects, and it was from this source that the pressure to simplify the building process probably stemmed. One of the most likely places to look for the emergence of the flooring method is in Henrietta Street, where houses (such as numbers 13 and 15), built in the 1740s, used long joists on spans of up to 26ft (fig. 3.25). This span was probably seldom repeated, but by the mid-century the use of the long joist in clear spans was common practice and, with a few exceptions, it was to remain so for the entire century. But it was Castle's imprimatur that promoted its use in buildings of quality, where its obvious economy was not the first consideration. Palazzi like Leinster House, or Tudenham, with four façades in cut-stone and ornate interiors, were buildings where cost cutting was inappropriate; Castle's decision to use long-joisted floors in both buildings clearly indicates their proven efficiency in use.

The conclusion we must draw from the independence shown by Irish carpentry construction is that artisans were largely uninfluenced by the structural methods described in imported technical manuals. This was not the result of unprogressive practices, but part of a process designed to suit rational preferences and local conditions. The complex carpentry of eighteenth-century English architecture had as its roots the medieval craftsmanship of York Minster, Westminster Hall and the great tithe-barns of the countryside. No parallel tradition existed in Ireland, and its absence encouraged experimentation and change. It is true, of course, that many Irish carpenters had English roots – the Rudds came from Northumbria and the Ensors from Warwickshire – but the economic recession of the first three decades of the eighteenth century disrupted the migratory pattern of English artisans into Ireland, and influences which might have been strong at the beginning of the century may not have prevailed for long.

* * *

The third influence on carpentry practices was the pattern books. Most of these, as Wittkower points out, were intended as guides to the correct use of the architectural orders.[16] In this they were remarkably successful. The significant gap between the outmoded buildings depicted by Joseph Moxon in 1703 and in Langley's Palladian copperplates in 1729 reflects a revolution in architectural taste and a demand for stylistic guidance. Wittkower saw the publications of writers such as Halfpenny, Langley and Salmon as vulgarizations of the Palladian model, intended principally for artisans, but he also stressed their importance, as part of a publishing craze associated with the rise of neo-Palladianism.[17]

Langley's *The builder's vade-mecum*, which appeared in 1729, was one of the first publications to cover the correct use of the orders, as part of a series of practical lectures intended for artisans. The reprinting of this work (in 1729) in Dublin, less than a year after its appearance in London, is significant; it coincided with the organization of a large team of craftsmen, brought together to build Pearce's design for the new Irish Parliament House in College Green. This was probably the first occasion on which most of the artisans had encountered Palladian work. Job Ensor, the master carpenter entrusted with the framing of the low hipped roofs and the complex construction of the dome, had come to Dublin from rural Warwickshire. Nathaniel Whinrey, a Dublin mason employed on the cut-stone exterior, had trained under his father, who had worked extensively with Thomas Burgh. Immigrant stonecutters – Borrowdale, Simpson and Gilbert – worked alongside Whinrey. The sophistication of the stone colonnade and demands made on the carpenters (in setting

---

16 Rudolf Wittkower, *Palladio and English Palladianism* (New York, 1974), pp 105–7.   **17** Ibid., pp 103–8.

out the innovative design of the dome and roofs) must have raised considerable speculation among the Dublin artisan community at this time.

By the second half of the century, when the basic relationships of classical proportions were more familiar, authors began to devote more attention to the application of typical designs. Some of the fruits of this can be seen in the doorcases of many Irish terraced houses (such as numbers 14 to 17 St Stephen's Green, Dublin) which show an obvious debt to William Pain's *The builder's companion*, published in London in 1758.[18] Pain's designs, following London practice, were intended for timber construction, but the Dublin doorcases were commonly made of stone. Pain, who described himself (on different occasions) as a carpenter, a joiner and an architect, published plans of houses, and designs for the interiors of dining rooms, libraries and churches in works such as *The carpenter and joiner's repository* (1778) and *The practical house carpenter* (5th ed., 1794). The books were an important influence on the popular promotion of neoclassicism, in the same way as the works of earlier authors popularized the Palladian style.

The implications of Pain's publications are clear. They were addressed to carpenters who clearly saw their responsibilities as covering both the design and the construction of buildings. Pain, as Yeomans suggests, was probably a master builder, and his experience would have been gained from contracts where he undertook the carpentry and joinery himself, and employed the other trades as subcontractors. His varying descriptions of himself as carpenter and architect, and joiner, raises an important matter as it relates to the dual role that many master artisans regarded as normal practice. Severens refers to this aspect of practice in a description of the rebuilding of St Werburgh's Church after a fire in 1754.[19] He describes the submission of plans and estimates by a number of prominent carpenters and builders for roofing and repairing the church, and the subsequent appointment of William Goodwin as contractor. Joseph Jarratt, the surveyor general's assistant, who was one of the advisers to the building committee, acted as a supervisor, but his involvement was 'sporadic' and, apparently, unpaid. It was apparent from the contractual records that the artisans who were engaged in the building work were acting in quasi-architectural roles. Severens concludes his description of the contract with the view 'that master carpenters could perform most of the functions usually associated with architects'.

This is an interesting point, which touches both on our perceptions of the full role of eighteenth-century master craftsmen and on the origins of the architectural profession. During the course of their careers, many artisans who served apprenticeships as masons and carpenters became involved as measurers, supervisors, clerks of works, architect's assistants and architects. Michael Wills and George Ensor, who were both members of the guild of carpenters, won premiums offered by the Dublin Society for architectural designs. Like many other carpenters and masons, they worked as architects. Yet it is difficult to say how far trades such as carpentry were perceived as a threshold to a career as a professional architect.

18 William Pain, *The builder's companion* (London, 1758). 19 Kenneth Severens, 'A new perspective on

The employment of eighteenth-century artisans as architects has been seen historically as a necessity, thrust on their employers in the absence of professionally trained designers. By the second half of the century, as craftsmen became more confident in the handling of architectural forms, this situation may have improved, but there is no evidence that artisans saw the development of design skills as stepping stones to vocations as professional architects. Carpenters were the most obvious beneficiaries of the architectural guidance offered by pattern books but, with the exception of Thomas Ivory, none of the Irish carpenters who acted as architects are known to have practised consistently as independent professionals (though in London Thomas Cooley, who started out apprenticed to a carpenter, became a clerk to Robert Mylne and architect of the Royal Exchange in Dublin). It is unlikely that carpenters, or other master artisans, had ambitions to relinquish their trade and become only professional designers.

They may not have had sufficient incentive to do so. Although Richard Castle (as far as we know) appears to have lived solely on fees received from his clients, his was not a common or well-defined career category in Ireland for most of the eighteenth century. The important architects who preceded him (Pearce, Burgh and Robinson) were, as McParland points out, involved financially in the contractual process through their office as surveyors general; Arthur Jones Nevill tells us that payments from contractors were regarded as an important part of remuneration for this position.[20] Robinson was a member of three powerful guilds involved in the building market, and he also traded as a timber merchant. George Esdall was also listed in the *Dublin directory* for 1765 as architect and timber merchant. Thomas Ivory, who did leave his trade as a carpenter to practise architecture, worked as the master of the Dublin Society School of Architectural Drawing from 1764 until his death in 1786.

In Dublin, the carpenter-architects Michael Wills and the Ensor brothers were the most likely candidates to follow the lead established by Castle as professional consultant. Wills may have been active as an independent supervisor in his work under Thomas Burgh in the 1720s, but in the Smock Alley Theatre in 1735, and in his proposals for St Patrick's Hospital in 1749, and for Essex Bridge in 1753, he saw himself as both the architect and the builder. John Ensor, who had the great advantage of working under Castle and inheriting part of his practice, spent most of his subsequent career as a master builder in Rutland [now Parnell] Square in the 1750s, and in the Fitzwilliam estate in the 1760s.[21] George Ensor designed and built the Church of St John the Evangelist in Dublin in 1766–9, but as we saw in chapter 2 he is best remembered as an architect-builder in Athlone and in Co. Roscommon in the 1760s and in Armagh from 1767 to 1770.[22]

The arrival of Thomas Cooley and James Gandon in Ireland in the latter part of the century might have promoted the ideal of professionalism among the architectural

---

Georgian building practice', *BIGS*, 35 (1992–3), 3–16. **20** Edward McParland, 'The office of the surveyor general in Ireland in the eighteenth century', *Architectural History*, 38 (1995), 97–8. **21** See www.dia.ie, 'John Ensor'. **22** See www.dia.ie, 'George Ensor'.

community, but carpenters were still active as designer builders. The carpenter Roger Mulholland (first described as an architect in 1786) provided the supervision and design of the elliptical First Presbyterian church in Rosemary Street Belfast in the 1780s. The earlier Presbyterian church at Dunmurry, Co. Antrim (1779) was probably also designed and built by him.[23] Samuel Sproule, who enjoyed considerable patronage as an architect in Dublin in the 1790s, was still interested in tendering for the construction of the Cork barracks in 1801.[24] There is evidence that even the most established professional architects of the era may have built (as well as designed) some of their own work. Cooley, who started his career in London as a carpenter, made proposals to the Earl of Bective in 1778, which can only be reasonably explained as an offer to build his own design for the new church at Kells, Co. Meath.[25]

The reluctance of artisan architects to pursue careers as professionals may reflect the lack of powerful patronage to sustain these careers during this period. On the other hand, the acquisition of design skills brought significant advantages to craftsmen. A facility for drawing and experience in the management of architectural ensembles liberated the master artisan from the competitive world of fixed rates and continuous interference from supervisory architects. The market for speculative housing attracted artisans from all trades, but it particularly promoted carpenters because of their central role in regulating the work of other trades and their capacity to handle architectural relationships.

Eighteenth-century master artisans enjoyed privileges under the guild system, which were to disappear forever in the nineteenth century. Successful careers in contracting could ensure high living standards and social recognition among the merchant community. The master carpenter John Chambers, for instance, could earn a gross figure of £2,947 12s. 1d. (over an eighteen-month contract) in Dublin Castle rebuilding 'the principal entrance', in 1746/7.[26] If this produced even a small profit of 10 per cent (after he had paid for himself, his workmen and timber), he would have a surplus of over £290 for a year-and-a-half's work. This compares favourably with the salary of £300 per annum granted to the surveyor general (who employed him), the £40 per annum salary of the surveyor's assistant, and the figure of £20 per annum (earned as wages) by the average journeyman carpenter during this period.

Speculative ventures by carpenters working as master builders could be even more rewarding. Michael Wills's charitable services given to Dr Steevens's Hospital, and his apparent retirement in the 1750s, were funded by rents he received from houses his father (Isaac Wills) had developed in the Dawson Street area.[27] Benjamin Rudd, who appears to have spent most of his career as a master builder, owned a number of houses in fashionable streets at the time of his death in 1756.[28] After Robert Ball's death and the sale of his timber yard on the North Strand in 1761, his family had sufficient funds to start a successful merchant bank.[29] Roger Mulholland's

23 C.E.B. Brett, *Roger Mulholland: architect of Belfast, 1740–1818* (Belfast, 1976), pp 4, 8, 12.   24 NLI, Kilmainham papers, MS 1122, p. 88.   25 NLI, Kells church accounts, MS 25304.   26 *Commons Journal*, 5, ccxxxiii.   27 IAA, Michael Wills's ledger 1731–77, accession no. 81/88, 34.   28 Mary Amelia Rudd, *Records of the Rudd family* (Bristol, 1920), pp 206, 208.   29 Eileen McCracken, *The Irish woods*

speculative housing in Belfast's Talbot Street, Dunbar Street, Robert Street, Hills Street and elsewhere in the 1790s undoubtedly contributed to his estate, which was valued at £3,835 17s. 2½d. after his death in 1818.[30]

Although it is uncertain whether building artisans received much formal schooling before their apprenticeships, there is ample evidence of high standards of literacy and cultural development among eighteenth-century Irish craftsmen and their families. The Dublin Society schools made an important contribution to the visual education of apprentices from the 1740s onwards. Carpenters, as we might expect, would have provided a good market for the Dublin reprints of books by Langley and Price, and for London editions of Pain and Halfpenny that appeared in Dublin booksellers' catalogues. But what little we know of the prominent carpentry families such as the Wills, the Rudds and the Sproules points to a more cultivated taste than a basic Palladian grammar, popularized by pattern books.

Understandably, these interests are to be found among the group of carpenters who are known also as architectural designers. Michael Wills spent a considerable part of his life in the translation of the first four books of Vitruvius; his own annotations to the text, as Casey points out, concentrate on the practical modern application of their contents while 'his remarks upon Wotton's *Elements* testify to his keen understanding of antique and modern classics'.[31] After Benjamin Rudd's death, his practice as a house builder was taken over by his son Stephen, who described himself in leases as a master builder. Another son, James Rudd, became well known as the most prominent retailer of architectural books in Dublin from 1755 until his early death in 1758.[32]

Mulholland, who was still describing himself as a carpenter in leases taken in 1789, was a subscriber to Pool and Cash's *Views of the most remarkable public buildings monuments and other edifices in the city of Dublin* in 1780, and among his gifts to the new Linenhall Library in Belfast were his three volumes of *Vitruvius Britannicus*.[33] Samuel Sproule had more advanced and more catholic tastes. He, too, was a subscriber to Pool and Cash, but he also owned the copy of Carlo Fontana's *Templum vaticanum et ipsius origo* now in the James Joyce Library of University College Dublin; his signature also appears on the flyleaf of a copy of Robert Wood's *The ruins of Palmyra*, now in the Irish Architectural Archive.

Wills, Mulholland and Sproule may not have been typical of the average artisan but the eighteenth-century carpenter's deep involvement in the cultural content of his work cannot be ignored. Like other craftsmen such as stuccodores, cabinet makers and ironsmiths, he was committed to an interpretation of stylistic formulas that raised his work above the level of technical skill to the borders of artistic creativity. This encouraged his interest in the visual culture of his age, and promoted his involvement in architectural design.

since Tudor times (Belfast, 1971), p. 130. **30** Brett, *Roger Mulholland*, pp 12–13, 18. **31** Casey, 'Books and builders', pp 154–5. **32** Ibid., p. 15. **33** Brett, *Roger Mulholland*, pp 4–5.

CHAPTER FOUR

Joinery

JOINERS WERE WELL ESTABLISHED in the seventeenth century in Ireland, and they appear to have been conspicuously involved in building contracts during that period. Until the establishment of the Corporation of Joiners, Ceylers and Wainscotters in 1700, in Dublin, they operated as members of the carpenters' guild (of the Blessed Virgin Mary), which represented masons, bricklayers, plasterers and helliers (roofers) as well as a few trades uninvolved in building practice.[1] A surviving roll of this guild's membership in 1656 records the names of 119 artisans.[2] These included 29 carpenters, 23 coopers, 16 joiners, 13 bricklayers and 11 plasterers, as well as helliers, masons, distillers, millers, turners and boxmakers.

In the medieval era the joiner's main tasks were the fabrication of furniture such as tables, chairs and storage presses. His link with building practice was undoubtedly developed through the provision of panelled wainscots, which became remarkably common in the Tudor period. Evidence of joiners working both in Dublin and provincial centres during the seventeenth century has survived. Edmund Tingham, a carver and joiner, was employed by the Earl of Cork to wainscot the gallery of his newly purchased Dublin house in 1631; accounts in Trinity College record charges of Matthew Kessel for joinery in the Library in 1636 and for wainscot panelling in the Hall in 1639; Joseph Turner and Thomas Howell were engaged in the joinery contract for the Dublin Tholsel; their bills were examined in 1685.[3] The contractual accounts for building the Royal Hospital Kilmainham, from 1680 to 1686, record payments to joiners and carvers of £809 12s. 1d.[4]

In Kinsale, Anthony Flemming was articled as an apprentice to a joiner named William Russell in 1656; James Letgeredge was engaged by the second Earl of Cork for joinery work in Lismore Castle in 1663; an account of 'Mr Barthol[omew] Connor Joiner' with Kilkenny Corporation was settled in 1669.[5] In 1680, the installation of sash windows in the duke's apartment in Kilkenny Castle was undertaken by artisans under a supervisor called Massy.[6] This was probably the Dublin joiner Robert Massy (enfranchised 1656) who worked on the contract for the Blue Coat School.

---

1 Mary Clark and Raymond Refaussé, *Directory of historic Dublin guilds* (Dublin, 1993), p. 22.   2 DCLA, Gilbert Collection, Carpenters' guild, roll of members 1656, MS 21.   3 Rolf Loeber, *A biographical dictionary of architects in Ireland, 1600–1720* (London, 1981), p. 108; TCD, Matthew Kessel's accounts, MUN/P2/1/4, 20; *CARD*, 5, pp 372–3.   4 Richard Colley, *An account of the foundation of the Royal Hospital of King Charles II* (Dublin, 1725), p. 23.   5 Richard Caulfield (ed.), *The council book of the corporation of Kinsale from 1652 to 1800* (Guildford, 1879), p. 19; Loeber, *Architects*, p. 68; NLI, MSS Ormonde 'Misc orders for payment', MS 11,048 (44).   6 HMC, *Ormonde*, NS, 5, 292.

Although joinery was clearly established as a separate trade in Ireland, it is difficult at times to distinguish between the responsibilities of the joiner and those of the carpenter. This is not surprising. This occupational overlap is a familiar pattern in Irish eighteenth-century building practice, even with bricklayers and masons, or with plasterers and painters, both groups belonging to separate guilds. Before discussing this overlap, however, let us look more closely at the role of the joiner.

* * *

It is possible to produce a definition of the joiner's role and responsibilities from an examination of contemporary English practice. Our main sources of information are the building manuals, although most authors were uninterested in descriptions of everyday practice, because of the great demand for guidance on more arcane subjects, such as building geometry and stylistic interpretations of the architectural orders. The most comprehensive coverage of artisan's working practices is to be found in Joseph Moxon's *Mechanick exercises* (London, 1st ed., 1677). Moxon, a late seventeenth-century author, specialized in descriptions of tools, machinery and working processes. His publications dealt with building and other trades (such as printing, smithing and turning) and his last edition of *Mechanick exercises* (1703) was expanded to include some simple building designs. These are crude in comparison to the later generation of designs published by Palladians such as Price and Langley, but they are evidence of a demand for guidance on changing constructional patterns at the beginning of the eighteenth century.

Moxon's description of the basis of the joiner's craft as 'an art manual, whereby several Pieces of Wood are so fitted and join'd together by straight-line, Squares, Miters, or any Bevel, that they shall seem one intire Piece', emphasizes the trade's responsibilities for making composite wooden panels (e.g., for doors and wainscots) from smaller pieces of timber.[7] This description of timber joints leaves us in no doubt about the derivation of the word 'joiner' as an apt description for members of the trade. Moxon's sections on joinery describe the making of joints, the use of the timber frame and the fabrication of panelled wainscots; they also describe the use of the workbench, the use of various planes (such as the jointer and the moulding plane), the characteristics of various saws and the making of glue. Joinery fittings were made on workbenches (of the type described by Moxon) and fitted, as assembled or partially assembled components, into the building carcase. In his advice on sawing large timbers, he points out the advantages for joiners of doing so 'at home' in preference to sending the work out to the sawyers.[8] Joiners, in common with many other eighteenth-century craftsmen, undoubtedly had workshops attached to their dwellings.

Another important task he described was the production of timber mouldings. These were made by a moulding plane fitted with a series of different profiled cutting tools. The dimensions of the moulded surface, however, were restricted (particularly

---

7 Joseph Moxon, *Mechanick exercises* (London, 3rd ed., 1703), p. 63. 8 Ibid., p. 99.

in the use of hardwoods) by the difficulties of manually driving the plane through the fibres of the wood. The problem of producing skirtings or architraves of large dimensions was overcome by combining several mouldings together as one unit. The oak glazing bars of the early sash windows in Kilmacurragh, Co. Wicklow, and Marsh's Library, Dublin were made with two separately moulded pieces of timber which were laminated together, although the finished size of the glazing bars did not exceed an inch-and-a-half in any dimension.

Skirtings, cornices, architraves and doorcases often comprised three or four separate timber members, which were fixed together with countersunk pins and glue. Glue was an essential material in workshop practice, when sash frames or wainscot panelling would be assembled together from several individual pieces of timber. It was seldom used on building sites, as carpenters relied on pegs, nails and screws to fix timber components into the masonry fabric and to reinforce mortise joints in framed floors and roofs.

The joiner's participation in the building market was undoubtedly developed through his ability to produce flush jointed panels of considerable size from boards that were reduced to narrow (8 to 9 inch) dimensions to avoid shrinkage. This skill was essential for the production of floor to ceiling panelling, which became a common feature of seventeenth-century architectural interiors. His traditional role as a furniture maker provided the joiner with the required background for this operation. In his guidance on finishing wood with the plane, Moxon refers to the joiner's control of his tools in making flush (close jointed) surfaces from timber boards.[9] Rapid changes in constructional patterns and the introduction of new decorative patterns brought new opportunities in building practice. The expansion of cities such as London and Dublin in the 1680s and 1690s greatly increased the building market. Timber cornices both on exteriors and interiors of buildings, ornate door-surrounds, moulded wainscotting, framed sashes and window casings, were an important requirement of this new market.

* * *

Turning to Moxon's treatment of carpentry, we see that he leaves us in no doubt about the considerable similarities he saw in the work of the carpenter and the joiner:

> the Rules both work by are upon the matter in the same as <u>Sawing</u>, <u>Mortessing</u>, <u>Tenanting</u>, <u>Scribing</u>, <u>Paring</u>, <u>Plaining</u>, <u>Moulding</u>, &c., and likewise the Tools they work with the same, though somewhat stronger for Carpenter's use than need be for Joiners, because Joiners work more curiously, and observe the rules more exactly than carpenters need do.[10]

9 Ibid., p. 63.   10 Ibid., pp 117–18.

Joinery 89

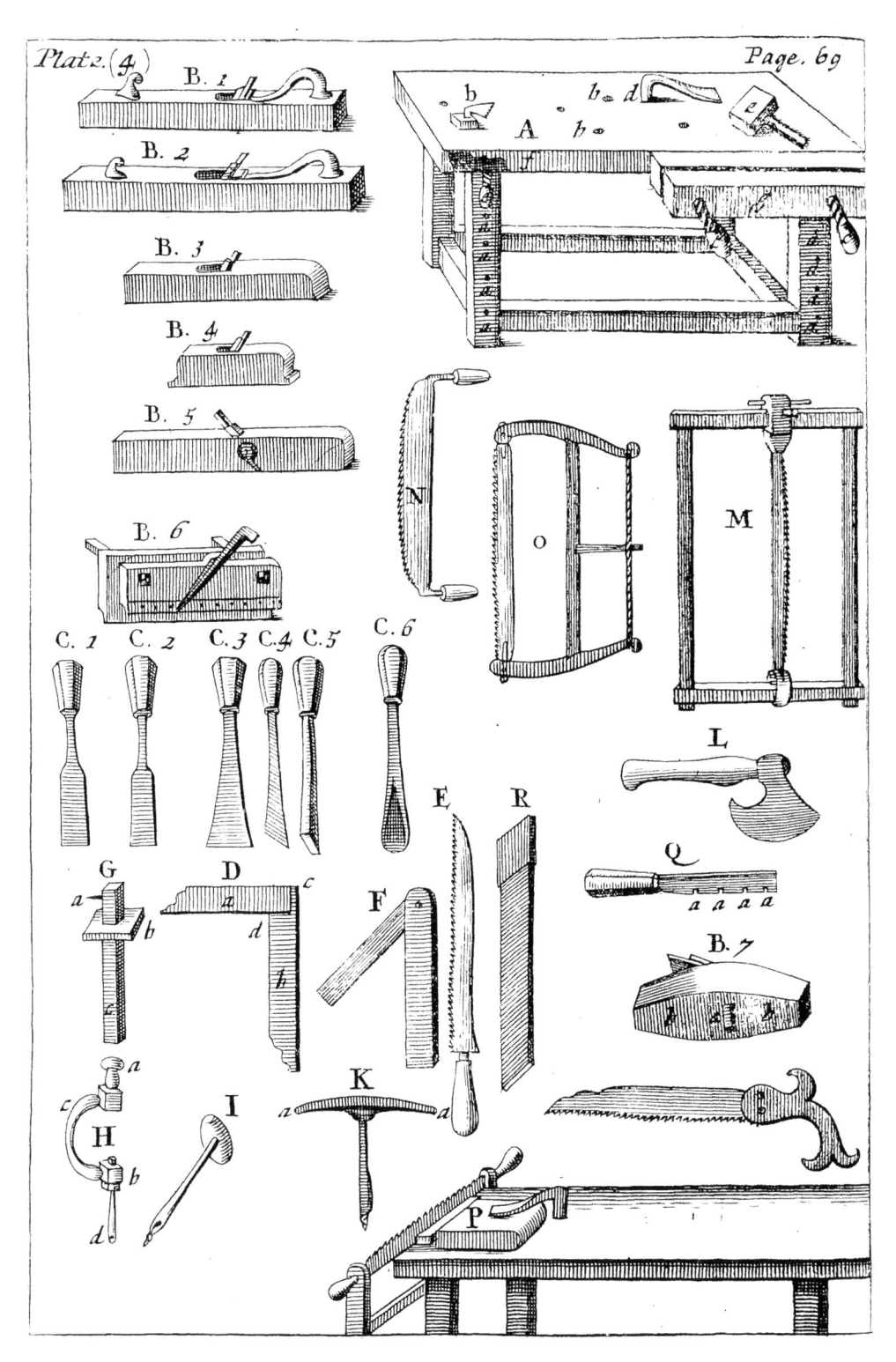

4.1 Joseph Moxon, *Mechanick exercises* (London, 3rd ed., 1703), plate 4.

Moxon's sections on carpentry describe the use of tools such as the axe and the adze, the hammer and the ripping chisel (fig. 4.1). They also advise on the setting out of buildings, making foundations, framing structural floors and roofs, laying floorboards, making staircases and hanging doors and windows. With joiners working (sometimes but, as we will see, not always) in their workshops on smaller timber scantlings, making components such as doors, architraves, skirtings and wainscots, structural timbers of unwrought wood were shaped by carpenters and framed together on building sites to form part of the building carcase.

However, if we examine the matter more carefully we see that this separation of workmanship into carpentry (structural elements hidden from view) and joinery (highly finished components which were part of the decorative design), though convenient and familiar from nineteenth-century practice, is not in fact what Moxon is describing. Such divisions of responsibility were untypical of building practice in eighteenth-century Ireland, and they cannot be reconciled with the patterns we find in contemporary building records. Furthermore, in England, Moxon's and later building manuals combine both non-structural fittings and structural framing as essential parts of the carpenter's work.

Although he encourages us to see the joiner as a specialist in finely wrought fittings and the carpenter as a specialist in structural woodwork, he does not limit the carpenter's role to the operations described under carpentry. His introductory comment, 'that the tools they work with [are] the same', tacitly implies that carpenters produced the same fittings as joiners did. However, his emphasis on the heavy tools used only by carpenters and his comment 'yet there are many Requisites proper to a Carpenter (especially a master carpenter) that a Joiner need take little notice of', unequivocally limits the joiner's role to non-structural fittings.[11]

With this explanation of Moxon's views as guidance, we can make considerably more sense of the patterns of workmanship emerging in eighteenth-century records. Master carpenters undertook the structural framing of buildings as well as the production of decorative fittings that were fixed into the building fabric; joiners concentrated on assembled or partially assembled fittings that were fixed into the building fabric. If we examine some of the most influential English manuals published later in the century, we find sufficient evidence to show that components such as doors, sash windows, wainscot panelling and staircases were commonly made by both carpenters and joiners, and that this pattern persisted up to the end of the century.

Langley's Dublin edition of *The builder's vade-mecum*, published in 1729, has no descriptions of working processes, but under that section dealing with methods of measuring we find a useful description of workmanship associated with both trades. The carpenter's responsibilities listed include structural framing of roofs and floors, as well as other elements such as staircases, rails, balusters, cornices, skirtings, doors and sash windows.[12] The joiner's work listed includes mouldings, window seats, doors, sash windows, window shutters, pilasters, columns, architraves, cornices, and sub bases.[13]

[11] Ibid., p. 118. [12] Batty Langley, *The builder's vade-mecum* (Dublin, 1729), pp 89–90. [13] Ibid., pp 90–1.

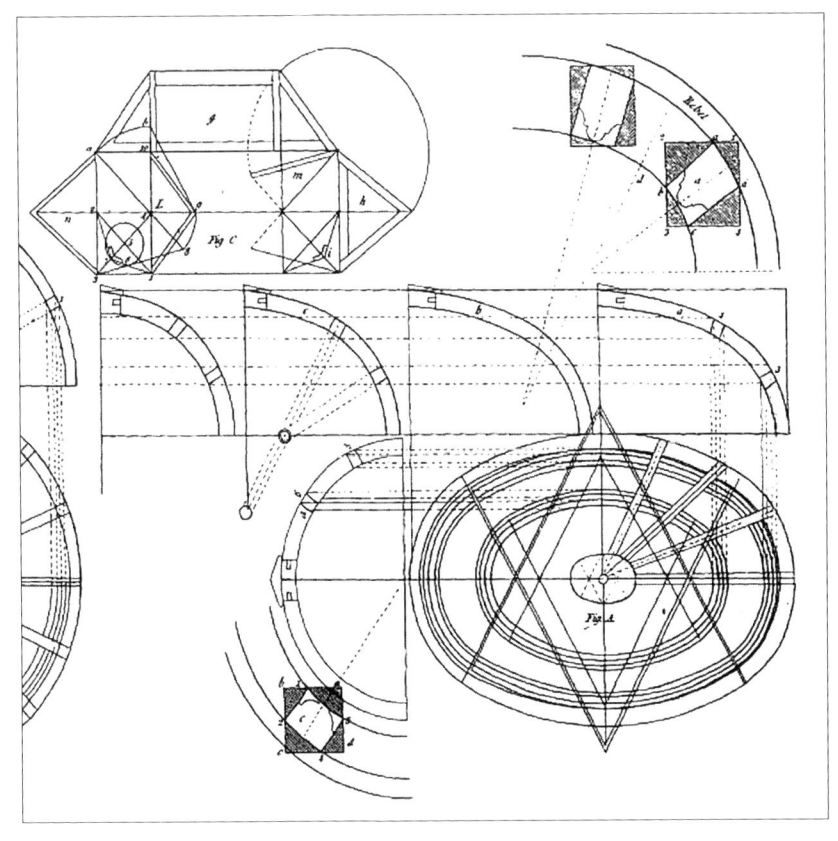

4.2 System for designing domes and skylights, William Pain, *The carpenter's and joiner's repository* (London, 1778), Plate LIII.

William Pain, the most authoritative writer of building manuals in the second half of the century, is a further help in a discussion on timber usage in later eighteenth-century buildings. Pain who, as we have seen, described himself variously in different publications, as architect, carpenter or joiner, typifies the eighteenth-century master craftsman's adaptability in changing roles to suit the challenge presented by expanding building markets.[14] Pain's 1778 edition of *The carpenter's and joiner's repository* (where the author describes himself as an architect and joiner) is obviously a pattern book intended as a guide to the design and layout of architectural interiors. There are no references to structural timbers or the design of floor and roof framing within its contents. Most of the book is taken up with designs of ornate doorcases, windows, chimney-pieces, cornices, circular and elliptical skylights and staircases (fig. 4.2). This work could easily be perceived as a publication devoted to joinery practice, but its title establishes its additional relevance to the work of the carpenter. Pain's intentions are

---

14 William Pain, *The builder's sketch book* (London, 1793); *The carpenter's pocket directory* (London, 1781); *The practical builder* (London, 1774).

clear in his later publication, *The practical house carpenter*, of 1794. Here, wearing his other hat, he introduces himself as an architect and a carpenter, and the contents cover many technical aspects of building. His text and illustrations provide comprehensive guidance on floor framing systems, and his designs for roof trusses anticipate the structural clarity of the nineteenth century. His designs for interior fittings are particularly interesting as they include chimney-pieces, staircases, cornices, panelling, bookcases and other components which were also commonly made by joiners.

The quality of the designs for houses and other structures in *The practical house carpenter* leaves us in no doubt about their author's competence as an architect. Pain is a good example of the considerable number of well-educated and cultured master craftsmen who could have practised as professional architects. Like Irish carpenters such as Roger Mulholland and the Ensor brothers, his working as a master builder was undoubtedly prompted by the financial advantages offered in lump-sum contracts for buildings constructed to his own design.

Irish eighteenth-century building records support the view of respective trade responsibilities expressed by Moxon, Pain and Langley. They record payments to carpenters for structural work such as the construction of floors and roofs, and payments to both joiners and carpenters for building fittings such as windows, doors, stairs and wainscots. However, the pattern of payments in Irish contracts reveals some unusual relationships between the two trades and their share of the building market. Joiners became dominant as the main suppliers of building fittings during the last part of the seventeenth century and the first few decades of the eighteenth century. As the new century progressed, carpenters assumed the responsibility for making most of the fittings used in important civic and institutional buildings, and joiners appear to have lost their share of the market.

* * *

If we look back at the last quarter of the seventeenth century, it is evident that it was advantages such as precise skills and workshop control that gave craftsmen like John Sisson (whom we will consider in some detail below) their predominance in the construction of architectural interiors at this time. The rapid changes in style and construction after the London fire in 1666 introduced new formal patterns, which obliged established trades (such as masons and carpenters) to abandon traditional practices and learn new skills, and to cope with stylistic innovations. This learning process took a considerable amount of time.

These changes in working practices introduced opportunities for craftsmen like the joiner to penetrate markets that the traditional carpenter could no longer control. The joiner's experience in moulding timbers and assembling timber artefacts from smaller timber sections promoted his skills in many diverse fields. In the construction of St Paul's Cathedral, for instance, Wren had a team of joiners continuously employed in the 1680s in making moulds (templates) for use by the stonecutters, both

4.3 Wooden dentil cornice from 42–43 St Stephen's Green, Dublin, 1745/6, Peter Pearson Collection. Photograph by David Davison.

on site and in the Portland quarries in Dorset.[15] (In the eighteenth century, stone-cutters knew enough to make their own templates out of clay and plaster.)

The joiner's skill was particularly useful in the construction of architectural interiors of the type popular in London in the late seventeenth and early eighteenth century. Wren's city churches used lavish quantities of oak wainscot, while royal palaces (such as Kensington or Hampton Court) were fitted with floor-to-ceiling bolection panelling and modillion cornices made of timber. Panelled interiors became a popular feature of domestic architecture during this period and they were widely used in housing developments by speculative builders. Panelling and timber cornices appeared in Dublin before the end of the seventeenth century, in houses such as 96 Bride Street, and panelled walls are recorded in many early eighteenth-century houses in streets such as Dawson Street, Molesworth Street, Jervis Street, Bachelors Walk and Eustace Street (fig. 4.3).

Another important opportunity for joiners arrived in the rapid progression from casement windows (glazed mostly with lead) to sash windows, which started in the 1670s in London. The earliest counterbalanced sashes used in England are recorded as the work of the master joiner Thomas Kinward, at Whitehall Palace in 1669.[16] Wren ensured the popularity of the sash window when he used it on a massive scale

---

[15] *Wren Soc. Vols*, 14, p. 49; 15, p. xix.   [16] H.J. Louw, 'The origin of the sash-window', *Architectural History*, 26 (1983), 63, 65.

in building the new royal palaces between 1685 and 1695. Sash frames required a precise control and craftsmanship which could only be guaranteed in a workshop. Even the smallest of Wren's windows (in the attic) of Hampton Court required twenty halved and scribed joints at the intersections of the glazing bars, and thirty-six mortise joints at the junction of the glazing bars with the sash frames. By the beginning of the eighteenth century, sashes were in use in most important domestic buildings in England, and Wren's accounts for building Winslow Hall in Buckinghamshire *c*.1700 throw light on his different reliance on carpenter and joiner. Matthew Banks, carpenter, provided transom windows; Charles Hopson, joiner, provided '2010 ft of very strong two Inches Sashes and frames', and compass (i.e., arched) sashes in the pediments.[17]

In Dublin during this period, the scarcity of skilled artisans induced the corporation to offer a city franchise to foreign tradesmen (of the Protestant faith) who were willing to settle there and contribute to its future prosperity. Joiners, with carpenters, formed a significant percentage of the trade applicants for freedom of the city, during the years of rapid expansion from 1670 until the end of the century.

Artisans who could combine traditional skills with experience in the interpretation of classical ornament had access to valuable opportunities and powerful patronage. This experience was especially scarce in Ireland. Few artisans outside the London area at this time were fully exposed to classical ideals until the 1720s and the publication of the Palladian manuals. Even as late as 1715 we find the city of Cork building such an important new building as the Green Coat School with a façade full of mullion and transom windows and leaded casements.

The Dublin joiner John Sisson obviously had an established reputation as a craftsman with a capacity to handle important building commissions. He was one of a small group of tradesmen (such as Francis Quinn and John Whinrey) who were closely involved with Thomas Burgh over a lengthy period and engaged on many of his best-known buildings. He was already well established in the city before his relationship with Burgh, as we find him playing a central role in the establishment of the new guild of Joiners, Ceylers and Wainscotters in December 1700. The name of the guild is a good indication of the objectives its members wished to pursue and of the building market at this period. Apart from their interest in joining timber – which covered their traditional role as furniture makers – the specific reference to ceylers (ceiling makers) and wainscotters (panel makers) must relate to timber cornices and interior panelling which were a feature of buildings of this period. The promotion of these skills at the turn of the century in Dublin can be seen in the context of the new demand for classical decoration in Irish interiors.

The following description of the founding membership of the guild is interesting, as it is indicative of the prestige enjoyed by well-established craftsmen at the time and of their considerable influence in the city:

---

17 *Wren Soc. Vols*, 17, p. 68.

John Sisson, joiner, Master; James Robinson and Richard Marplass, Wardens; Robert Rochfort, Esq., Attorney-General; Allen Broderick, Esq., Solicitor-General; William Robinson, Esq., Deputy Receiver of the Revenues in Ireland; William Scriven, senior; Thomas Howell, senior; John Hart, Francis Armstead, James Mitchell, William Asherton, Thomas Armstead, George Hothard, John Littledall, Robert Rudd, George Gibson and Peter Iredall, assistants.[18]

The presence in the list of William Robinson (who until April 1700 had held the position of surveyor general) and important office holders such as Rochfort (the attorney general) and Brodrick (the solicitor general) is a measure of this prestige. The relegation of most of the new guild brothers into a junior category as assistants is particularly interesting. This division probably refers to the freedom of the senior members to train apprentices. A similar division is evident in the listed membership of the carpenters' guild in 1656. This rigid classification of experience within a new guild is indicative of the scarcity of interpretative skills at this time. It also helps to explain the monopoly joiners enjoyed in the manufacture of building components in the early classical period.

By the 1730s, after Burgh's death and the end of Sisson's domination of the market, this was all to change. Under the Palladians such as Castle, interiors used less panelling, timber cornices disappeared and decorative plasterwork became more important. The passage of time allowed carpenters to gain experience in making sash windows and wainscots, and the recession in the building market from the 1710s until the mid-century obviously forced carpenters to expand their activities to obtain enough work.

* * *

Thomas Burgh, who became surveyor general in 1700, used joiners extensively in his buildings. His accounts for work on the Parliament (Chichester) House in 1703 and 1705 show payments for joinery to Thomas Middlebrook and John Sisson.[19] Sisson became a prominent member of the group of artisans closely associated with Burgh, and he was engaged on several important state contracts. He was employed regularly in Trinity College from 1700 until 1731. He worked on Dublin Castle in 1704, and again later on the Barrack Office there in 1720.[20] Some records of his accounts in Trinity College describe the nature of his responsibilities and are worth scrutinizing in some detail.

As we might expect, these include charges for the supply of prefabricated timber fittings such as sash windows and wainscot panelling. He made windows for Burgh's

---

18 Henry Guinness, 'Dublin trade gilds', *JRSAI*, 52 (1922), 162. **19** *Commons Journal*, 2, ccviii. **20** TCD, John Sisson's accounts, between MUN/P2/8/29 and MUN/P2/62/14; Loeber, *Architects*, p. 34; *Commons Journal*, 3, ccxxix.

chemical laboratory in 1709, and he was paid for '40 yards and halfe of new wenscott' and '12 new sash windows ... finding olive wood pullies' for the College Hall in 1710.[21] He was almost continuously involved in Burgh's most prestigious project, the Library, from 1712 until its completion. Those accounts include charges for supplying timber, making windows and for stairs and wainscotting.[22]

Other Sisson accounts are surprising, as they relate to extensive site operations and to the supply of unfabricated timber as well as fabricated fittings. For instance, an account of 1709 for work in the Hall and the Provost's House records time charges (at 2s. per day); a similar account of 1713 for repairs to the wainscot of the Chapel and the Hall includes a charge for artisan's time of 40½ days.[23] These accounts, and later accounts for the Library, show that Sisson supplied fittings (such as windows and wainscot) that were fixed on site by himself, or his assistants. Some accounts, simply described as 'work on new library' or 'joiner's work and materials for new library', give no indication of the nature of the work or responsibilities involved, but they must have been considerable, to judge from the series of payments. He was paid a total of £1,700 between June 1722 and December 1723; £1,500 between February 1724 and December 1728; and £540 14s. 7d. between June 1729 and January 1733.[24] This amounts to a sum of £3,740 14s. 7d. paid mostly in small amounts (£100 to £300) during the contract. His accounts describing 'timber for new library', or 'timber delivered to new library', are more difficult to understand, as they relate only to timber supplied, with no involvement (of Sisson) for workmanship or artisans' time. These payments also amount to a substantial financial sum. He was paid sums totalling £517 5s. 10d. in 1712; £764 2s. 6d. in 1713; £350 in 1714 and £485 1s. 6d. between 1715 and 1716.[25] This amounts to a sum of £2,116 9s. 10d.

Such accounts provide no indications if the timber supplied was cut and finished to specific dimensions, or if it was in the form of unprocessed baulks or planks, but some accounts confirm that the timber referred to was oak. However, the choice of Sisson as a supplier (rather than a timber merchant) suggests that the timber may have been cut to a specification for use in the structural framing of the building, which was under construction during this period. An earlier account of Sisson (from 1712) shows charges for the supply of 12 scantlings of oak, each 9ft long and 4 x 3-inch section, intended for repairs to the roof of the College Hall.[26]

These accounts for the supply (only) of timber members are interesting, as the timber was undoubtedly intended for the use of the Library carpenters, and this introduced a new relationship between joiners and carpenters. The Library accounts support the view that structural timbers were supplied and paid for by the college, as most carpentry accounts covered only the fixing of structural timbers into the masonry carcase. Isaac Wills's account for fixing and securing ceiling joists in 1717,

---

21 TCD, John Sisson's accounts, MUN/P2/19/26; P2/19/27.   22 Ibid., MUN/P2/23/55; P2/25/54–59; P2/59/4–13.   23 Ibid., MUN/P2/19/26; MUN/P2/24/20.   24 Ibid., MUN/P2/48/15–18; P2/52/19–22; P2/54/ 15–23; P2/59/4–13.   25 Ibid., MUN/P2/23/57–59; P2/25/54–60; P2/27/35–38; P2/31/9–15.   26 Ibid., MUN/P2/22/22.

4.4 'Prospect of the Library of Trinity College Dublin', print after Joseph Tudor, c.1753.

for instance, contains no references to the cost of materials; his substantial account for roof framing in 1722 shows measured rates described and priced as workmanship only.[27]

The Library records allow us to look at the scale of the joiner's responsibility and his relationship with the work of the carpenter in the early decades of the century, when the demand for a new architectural language, and skills to support it, were becoming evident. The extent of Sisson's share of the contract is surprising. Out of an overall cost of something over £20,000, payments to him noted above come to almost £6,000, or nearly 30 per cent of the cost of the building. By 1722, when most of the structural masonry was complete, costs of brick and stonework had amounted to slightly more than £6,500 (which included at least some, if not all, of the cost of stone supplied by Moses Darley).[28]

The Library, of course, was an unusual building in its proportion of interior fittings and in its high window-to-wall ratio (fig. 4.4). It is interesting to compare these figures with the cost ratios of the Royal Hospital Kilmainham.[29] In this case, the masonry at £5,423 7s. 4½d. was the largest cost in the contract; the carpentry cost £1,639 2s. 4½d. and carving and joinery cost £809 12s. 1d. The masonry cost, of course, can be explained by the cellular nature of the hospital plan and by the massive

[27] TCD, Isaac Wills's accounts, MUN/P2/31/19; MUN/P2/48/22. [28] TCD, accounts of Caldebeck et al., MUN/P2/48/1, 8. [29] Colley, *Foundation of the Royal Hospital*, p. 23.

scale of the walling. The joinery contract was probably confined to wainscot panelling. The hospital (at this period) was not fitted with sash windows and most of the interior spaces (apart from the Hall and Chapel) were quite frugal.

Joiners were also engaged in building operations outside the Dublin area in the early decades of the century. Records of the construction of Beaulieu near Drogheda refer to joiners and carpenters working alongside each other in 1722; the records of the construction of Durrow Castle from 1715 to 1718 show payments to the joiner John Rudd for wainscotting, window seats, doors, doorcases and two storeys of stairs.[30] Rudd probably worked on the building site as the oak he used was supplied by his employer, Colonel Flower. Surprisingly, there are no references to the supply of windows in his comprehensive account. These may have been made by the carpenters, John Owens and John Coltsman, who were also engaged at Durrow.

Isaac Wills's bill 'for Carpenters Work' in 1720 covers work on a detailed Ionic doorcase for the college Chapel; in 1722, while Sisson worked on the Library, Wills provided sashes and wainscot for a new building adjoining the kitchen; Charles Brooking, carpenter, provided sashes in 1723.[31] It is difficult, in comparing these minor contracts with Sisson's involvement on the Library, to avoid the impression that the important commissions (for non-structural fittings) were entrusted to joiners, and that work on buildings of lesser importance was given to carpenters. However, this pattern appears to have changed by the 1730s. In 1733, estimates submitted by Isaac Wills and Joseph McCleery for the carpentry in Castle's Printing House included costs for all the fittings (doors, windows, stairs and wainscotting) as well as the structural work.[32]

The Printing House contract marks the beginning of a new building policy in the College, which changed the trade relationships used on the Library and other buildings under Burgh's direction. None of the records of buildings built after 1732 indicate payments made to joiners, with the exception of a minor account for repairs to existing buildings in 1756. If joiners were involved in work on such buildings as Regent House, the Provost's House or the Theatre, they could only have been employed as subcontractors to carpenters, as all payments for fitments were to the carpenters' accounts.

This rapid and inexplicable change is also evident in other contemporary contracts in Dublin. It is tempting to see the preference given to Sisson (on plum jobs like the Library) as a mark of respect to the joiners for their extra diligence in, as Moxon puts it, observing 'the rules'. However, in Edward Lovett Pearce's contract from 1728 to 1731 for the new Parliament House – an even grander and more expensive building than the Library – we find the relationships reversed. The total

---

30 NLI, Lord Ferrard to Lord Molesworth, 4 Sept. 1722 in file 'Letters to or from 1st Viscount Molesworth', microfilm, p 3753; NLI, Flower papers, MS 11, 455 (1). **31** TCD, Isaac Wills's accounts, MUN/P2/40/45; MUN/P2/48/22; Charles Brooking's accounts, MUN/P2/53/3–4. **32** TCD, Joseph McCleery's accounts, MUN/P2/65/1, 3; Isaac Wills's accounts P2/65/8.

receipts paid to the carpenters (George Stewart and Job Ensor) amounted to £1,121 17s. 1¾d. in a building contract valued at £19,271 12s. 0d. The only payment certified to the joiner (John Armstead) was a sum of £15 16s. 8d.[33]

By the mid-century, the market for timber fittings (windows, doors, stairs and wainscots) in Dublin was dominated by carpenters, and payments to joiners are rarely encountered. Records of the completion of the Parliament House *c*.1750, under John Magill's direction, show payments for stairs and wainscotting to the carpenters George Stewart and John Sproule.[34] The records of the cost of Doctor Mosse's Lying-in Hospital in Dublin in the early 1750s itemize individual payments made to measurers, carters, paviers and architects, but no payments are recorded for joiners.[35] Although Burgh had used the services of the joiner William Ord in the contract for building St Werburgh's in 1715, the parish rebuilt the church after a fire in 1754 and, after much deliberation, the making of the windows and the supply of the pews, pulpit and reading desk were entrusted to William Goodwin, the carpenter who built the roof and ceiling.[36]

* * *

What accounts for the disappearance of the joinery trade from the building market after the 1730s? What seems to have happened is that joiners continued to produce fittings as subcontractors to the carpentry trade and that these fittings were fixed by the carpenters on site, and included in their accounts without any reference to their origin. References in Benjamin Ball's accounts of 1733 – 'paid Edward Simmons joyner £1.0.0' and 'paid 13 joyners' (for work) – suggests that there are good grounds to support this viewpoint.[37] Ball's son Robert had developed his own workshop to produce fittings by the mid-century.

We already have the precedent of John Sisson acting as a supplier of pre-cut timber sections to Trinity College that were obviously supplied for use by carpenters. Sisson was paid by the college, and the carpenters were paid for their time in using the timber (similar to the policy whereby the college supplied facing stone for stonecutters who were paid only for labour at the Library). After the 1730s, however, most carpentry accounts (and stonemasons' accounts) included gross payments for both the time and material content. There was nothing unusual in a carpenter using a local joiner as a supplier of fabricated (or part-fabricated) fittings: in the 1760s wainscot panels were imported into Ireland from Britain, Holland, Flanders, 'the Plantations' and the 'East Country'.[38]

The production of prefabricated fittings in workshops for delivery to contractors, or building owners, was an established practice by the mid-century in Ireland. In

---

33 *Commons Journal*, 4, xxxii, xxxiii.   34 Ibid., 5, xlvii, l, lx.   35 *The case of Bartholomew Mosse* [Dublin, 1755].   36 Kenneth Severens, 'A new perspective on Georgian building practice: the rebuilding of St Werburgh's Church', *BIGS*, 35 (1992–3), 7–9.   37 NAI, Ball, MS Dublin, 43.   38 NLI, Customs ledgers of exports and imports, MS 353 (1).

September 1722, in the construction of Beaulieu, Co. Louth, the work of joiners and carpenters was interrupted pending the arrival of 'the great staires' which was 'dayly expected from Dublin'; the construction accounts of Castle Forward, Co. Donegal, include a payment of £10 13s. 0d. in 1737 'To the Great Stares made in Dublin'; a stone doorcase, chimney-pieces and other building supplies also came from Dublin.[39]

Robert Ball's records from 1752 to 1754 provide a good description of the operation of workshop practice in the Dublin building market.[40] His accounts refer to the supply of cut scantlings to Robert West, and to doors, doorcases and six storeys of stairs supplied to Henry Darley, obviously intended as fitting for speculative houses in Rutland Square. Ball, of course, was a master carpenter, but the joiners, with their specific skills and well established workshops, would have advantages in the supply of fabricated and part-fabricated fittings to contractors (master builders such as West and Darley) as well as carpenters working on building sites.

Evident from Benjamin Ball's accounts of 1733, in other words, is the probability that carpenters subcontracted the production of timber fittings to joinery workshops, but fixed these fittings on site themselves. The considerable expansion of the market from the 1750s onwards provided opportunities for well-established carpenters (such as Robert Ball) to develop their own timber stores and workshops and to supply the contracting trades. Most of the fittings used on important contracts, in the second half of the century, were undoubtedly made by carpenters (such as Chambers, Archbold, Sproule, Stewart and Goodwin) in their own workshops. The joiner was to remain a minor specialist in the Irish building market, until the era of the general contractor in the nineteenth century.

---

[39] NLI, Lord Ferrard to Lord Molesworth, 4 Sept. 1722, in file 'Letters to or from 1st Viscount Molesworth', microfilm, p 3753; NLI, Castle Forward papers, MS 10,470.   [40] NAI, Ball, MS Dublin, 43.

CHAPTER FIVE

The timber trade

ISAAC WARE, writing about building timber in England in 1756, is unequivocal about the necessity to use only two timbers in the building process: 'Custom has received the two kinds of timber', he wrote, 'oak and fir, in the place of all others … At present we have no medium between the oak and the fir'.[1]

This was also true of Irish building practice. Although references to timbers such as mahogany from Honduras and walnut can be encountered, the majority of building accounts record the consistent use of oak or fir (or a combination of both timbers) in the construction and internal finish of classical building in the eighteenth century. Irish oak was the principal timber used for structural framing and internal joinery in buildings up to the end of the seventeenth century. Its scarcity from the beginning of the eighteenth century introduced an increased reliance on imported northern softwoods from ports in Norway, Sweden and the Baltic coasts of Germany, Poland and Russia. These softwoods were already in common use in England. The rapid redevelopment of the city of London after the Great Fire of 1666 encouraged a growing market for imported timber. While English oak was still available commercially for most of the eighteenth century, its considerable expense curtailed its use in many buildings.

Irish oak was usually purchased as unfelled trees in large estates such as Powerscourt or Shillelagh in Co. Wicklow, or the Earl of Clanrickard's forests at Portumna. It was transported (often by water carriage) as logs to building sites, where it was sawn into building timber. Fir was imported as squared baulks and pre-sawn boards and sold by merchants for immediate use in building contracts. The increasing demand for imported softwood as the eighteenth century advanced encouraged traders to specialize in timber importation and distribution. Prominent timber merchants in Dublin included William Montgomery and Caspar White, who supplied timber for buildings in Trinity College between 1702 and 1740, and floor and roof framing timbers for Pearce's Parliament House. Benjamin Ball and his son Robert operated a timber yard on the North Strand between 1733 and 1760, which supplied timber for speculative houses in Rutland Square and Sackville Mall built by artisan developers such as George Darley, John Ensor and Robert West.[2] Dublin directories list Bridget Moss acting as timber merchant from Golden Lane in the 1760s and 1770s.

Timber was often described in terms of its place of origin, such as Norway or Pomeranian baulk or, in the case of boards, Dram deals or Dronto deals, denoting

---

1 Isaac Ware, *A complete body of architecture* (London, 1756), pp 75–6.   2 NAI, Ball, MS Dublin, 43.

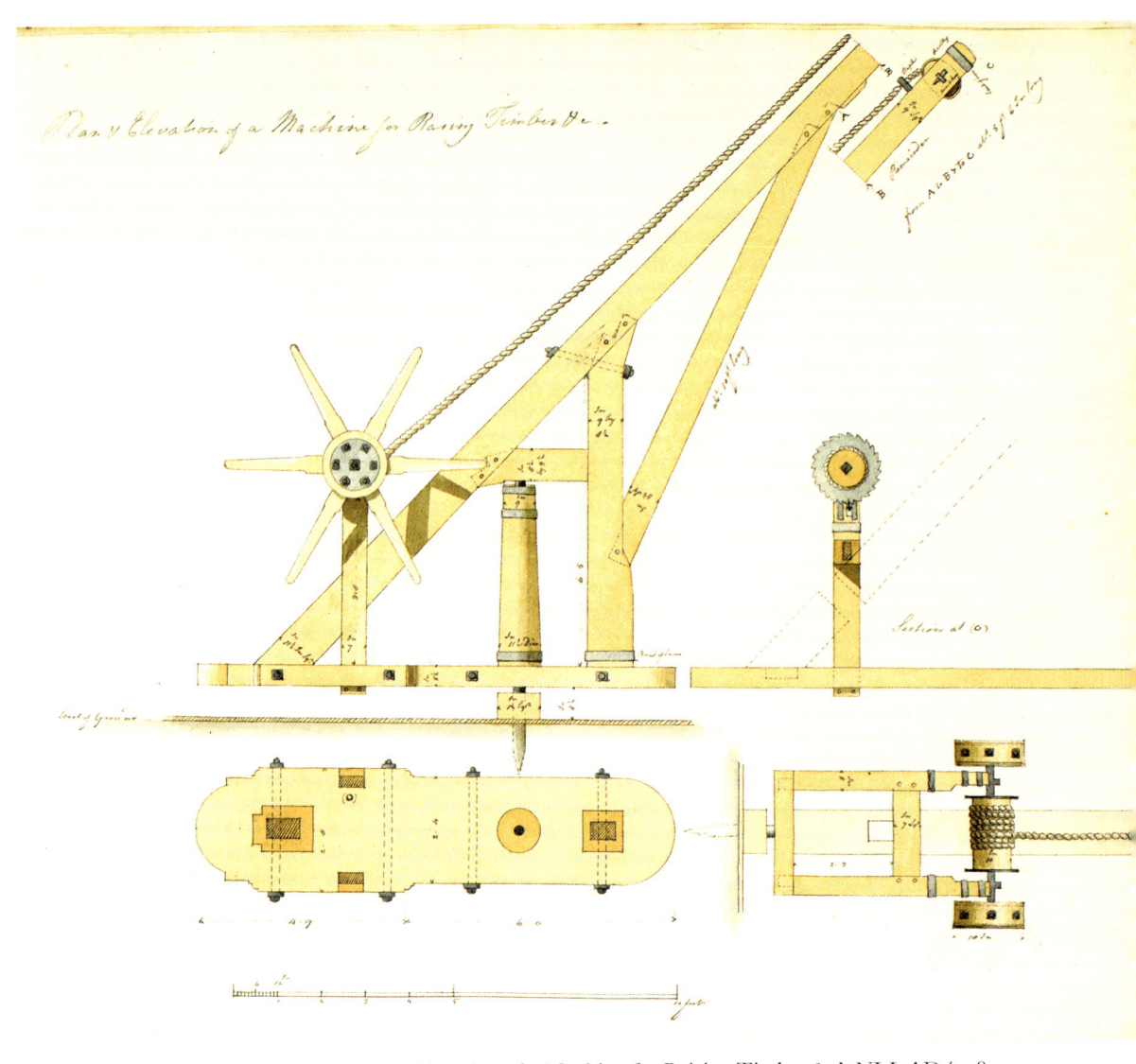

5.1 James Gandon, 'Plan & Elevation of a Machine for Raising Timber &c', NLI, AD/3287. Reproduced with permission of the National Library of Ireland.

their importation from the Norwegian ports of Drammen and Trondheim. Timber accounts frequently made use of obscure and often misleading terminology, and some of these terms need definition before we can fully understand the patterns which emerge from such accounts.

* * *

A close scrutiny of eighteenth-century building accounts indicates that the term 'fir' is broadly used to describe two different species of timber with different characteristics and different market values. In the timber trade, the term 'deal' (or dale) was also widely used to describe these two species of fir, and both terms were obviously interchangeable. The traditional method used by the trade to identify either species was by the colour of its timber, white or red. White deal, the cheaper timber of the two, was sometimes referred to merely as fir, deal or common deal in accounts. Red deal was always fully described because it was charged at a higher rate. In England, eighteenth-century records frequently use the description 'yellow fir' or 'yellow deal' to refer to timber known in Ireland as 'red fir' or 'red deal'. The carpenter's estimate for Wren's St Andrew's Church, Holborn, covered roofing 'boarded with yellow deale'.[3] Also in the eighteenth century, the word 'deal' (or deals) came to be commonly used to describe a fir board of certain dimensions as well as the species of timber from which it was produced.

The different characteristics of these two timbers were well described by the eighteenth-century English surveyor Thomas Miles. In *The concise practical measurer* of 1740 Miles advised that 'Yellow Deals are to be applied for Flooring, Stairs, and all outside Works, the White for Pannells to Wainscotting is better on account of its being clearer of Turpentine, it holds the Glew much better than yellow Stuff.' In a reference to floor framing he points out that 'yellow Christiania deals are most proper for these uses'.[4] (Christiania was a timber port in Norway.) An abbreviated description, 'best Chris' deals, referred to as part of a cargo received by George Steuart at Baronscourt, Co. Tyrone in 1779, may relate to the same port.[5] The red and yellow timber described has been identified as the wood of the *pinus sylvestris* or Scots pine. The use of the term 'fir' to describe this timber in the eighteenth century is quite understandable, as the tree was known colloquially among British foresters as the Scotch fir. Its wood is a pale yellow colour with red annular rings, and it weighs about 36lbs per cubic foot. It contains a resinous substance, which makes it more durable than many hardwoods for use in external doors and windows. Its availability in long lengths and its elasticity made it particularly suitable for the carpenter's use as beams, joists and roof members. It was the main choice in Europe for structural carpentry up to the early decades of the twentieth century. Its common name in the timber trade was red deal. The white timber has been identified as the wood of the *abies excelsa* or Norwegian spruce. This tree was not confined to Norway; it was common among the indigenous Baltic forests and its name links it with Prussia (otherwise known as Spruce). Its wood was white to pale beige in colour with a fine regular grain that promoted its use by joiners in making mouldings, wainscot panels and kitchen furniture. It was neither as strong nor as durable as northern pine, it performed badly in damp conditions, and it weighed about 30lbs per cubic foot.

---

3 *Wren Soc. Vols*, 10, p. 99. 4 Thomas Miles, *The concise practical measurer* (London, 1740), p. 84.
5 PRONI, Abercorn papers, D/623/C/3/1.

Today, under the trade name of white deal, it has replaced red deal as the most commonly used wood for carpentry in Europe.

Fir was usually shipped from the northern timber ports such as Trondheim, Drammen, Riga, Memel and Danzig as baulks, planks and deals. Baulks were squared logs, sold usually by weight in units of the ton. Planks were typically 2 to 6 inches thick, over 9 inches in width, and 9ft and more in length. The Dublin measurer Levi Hodgson published tables in which scantlings thicker than 8½ inches were measured as baulk timber.[6]

Table 5.1: Common timber scantlings

	Thickness (inches)	Width (inches)	Length (feet)
Planks	2–6	9+	9+
Deals	1¼–1½	7–9	9–18
Whole deals	1¼–1½	?	c.12

Deals were usually supplied in smaller dimensions than planks (as we will see, there were exceptions to this). Deals were typically 1¼ to 1½ inches thick (though boards with thicknesses of 2 inches and more are also sometimes described as deals in eighteenth-century records), and 7 to 9 inches wide. These dimensions made deals ideal for use as flooring boards. Hodgson provided costs for 'common dales' of 9ft in length, and for 'long dales' measuring up to 18ft long.[7]

Building accounts in Trinity College make frequent references to the purchase of slit deals for use by carpenters such as Gabriel Price or Isaac Wills. Semple also refers to the use of slit deals in 1749 for window shutters and sheeting on doors in St Patrick's Hospital.[8] Slit deals, as their name suggests, were deal boards sawn along their length into two identical, but thinner scantlings. Thus, a 1¼-inch deal board could be sawn into two slit deals of ½ inch thickness when allowances were made for the kerf of the saw and the use of the plane on the surface of the sawn timber. Slit deals, depending on their thickness, had a variety of uses as wainscot panels, linings, shutters and component parts of box skirtings, box cornices, sash boxes and architraves.

There are frequent references to boards described as 'whole deals' in eighteenth-century building records. The 'whole deal' may have been an archaic term used to describe a unit of measure such as the mason's perch or the slater's square in seventeenth-century practice. However, the term appears to have been loosely used by eighteenth-century carpenters to describe boards about 12ft long and 1¼ to 1½ inches thick. An interesting reference in Irish building records can be found in George Steuart's accounts of timber boards shipped from Norway for use in his

[6] P. Levi Hodgson, *The modern measurer* (Dublin, 1793), p. 11.   [7] Ibid., p. 121.   [8] St Patrick's Hospital, George Semple, 'A further description of the foregoing designs ...', pp 14–15 (xerox copy in IAA, accession no. 2008/44).

contract at Baronscourt, Co. Tyrone in 1779.[9] He described part of this consignment as 'whole deals' with dimensions of 12ft in length and 1¼ inches in thickness. No dimensions of the width of the boards were recorded.

This definition is supported by an eighteenth-century reference in William Pain's *The practical house carpenter*, which describes 'whole deal' as '1¼ inch deal' in 1794.[10] Two nineteenth-century references can be found in D. Boyers's *The builder's companion* published in 1807 and Peter Nicholson's *Builder's dictionary* of 1817. Boyers makes a reference to the proper standard for Russian deals, which he describes as 'twelve feet long, eleven inches broad, and one and a half inches thick'.[11] Nicholson is less specific, but he, like Pain, describes a whole deal as having a thickness of 1¼ inches.[12] That said, it remains true that because of the variety of ways in which the word deal is used, at different times and in different places, it is not possible to pin down its definition in precise terms.

These references, though somewhat inconclusive, provide us with a broad idea of the descriptive terms employed. In practice, as both eighteenth-century records and measurers' manuals reveal, deal boards could vary considerably in length and thickness. The only dimensions referred to in carpenters' accounts in Trinity College relate to lengths. Most of the boards used were in lengths ranging from 9 to 12ft, but 12-inch wide boards, apparently original, up to 30ft long survive on the floor of the gallery of the Library.

Local conditions governing timber production in Scandinavian and Baltic forests may have influenced the qualities and dimensions of timber shipped from various ports. Hodgson's prices refer to 'Swedish Dales, 14 feet long' and 'Dram Dales [from Drammen], 7 feet long', as though these dimensions represented common import patterns at this time.[13] A reference in 1755 to oversized timber is quoted in the correspondence of Nathaniel and Robert Alexander who acted as agents in Londonderry for the Belfast timber importer Daniel Mussenden: 'we do not imagine [this]… timber would sell for more than 32s. per ton if so much, it is verry large and we imagine from his invoice ill squared'.[14] It is apparent from a printed catalogue of prices for deals and planks (see p. 104) that sawmills servicing the port of Trondheim had opted to convert fir into specific dimensional patterns which suited local production facilities as well as certain international markets. The lengths of deals quoted (of 8½ to 9ft) conform with Hodgson's dimensions of 'Common Dales' but the variety of thicknesses from 1½ to 3½ inches is surprising. The only dimensional distinction between planks and deals referred to is one of length, the deals being about 9ft long and the planks 14ft, but the planks were probably wider than the 9-inch deals.

---

9 PRONI, Abercorn papers, D623/C/3/1.   **10** William Pain, *The practical house carpenter* (London, 5th ed., 1794), p. 8.   **11** D. Boyers, *The builder's companion* (Horncastle, 1807), 15, section ix.   **12** Edward Lomax and Thomas Gunyon (eds), *Encyclopaedia of architecture: being a new and improved edition of Nicholson's Dictionary* (London, 1852), p. 228.   **13** Hodgson, *The modern measurer*, p. 121.   **14** PRONI, Mussenden papers, D354/764.

These dimensional patterns may have been peculiar to that part of Norway during the 1750s. Hodgson (as we have seen) refers to 14ft Swedish deals, long deals of 17 to 18ft, and Boyers published tables for deals of up to 20ft in length. Some of Mussenden's correspondence with the Norwegian port of Christiania refers to whitewood planks which were 2 inches in thickness and in lengths of 10 to 12ft.[15] It seems reasonable to conclude from all this information that there were no fixed international definitions for the dimensions of deals and planks, and that ports as far apart as Trondheim, Danzig and Riga could opt for their own dimensional standards to suit local conditions as well as European markets. Another confusing method of measurement that needs clarification is the sale of softwood planks and deals 'by the hundred'. In practice, this was known as the long hundred and it contained 120 planks or boards. For large purchases by timber merchants in northern timber ports the measure of the long thousand or 1,200 was commonly used.

* * *

It is interesting to speculate on the probable use of planks and deals shipped to Ireland during the eighteenth century. Scantlings 2 to 3 inches in thickness were ideal for immediate use as floor joists in Irish buildings and also as common rafters. The depths of joists varied in relation to the floor spans but a gradual reduction in joist thickness (from 2½ or 3 inches to 2 inches) is noticeable over the century.

Table 5.2: Scantlings for individual buildings

	Joists (inches)	Rafters (inches)
School Master's House, Drogheda, 1720s	10 x 2½	5 x 2½
Dr Steevens's Hospital, 1720s	9 x 2½	
Parliament House, 1730	12 x 3	
Leinster House, Library Floor, 1745	11 x 2½	
St Patrick's Hospital, 1749	9 x 2	5 x 2

After the 1760s the use of 10 x 2 inch and 9 x 2 inch planks as joists became very common in the rationalized construction patterns of Dublin's speculative terraced houses. Planks of 2 to 3 inches in thickness were also used to make door frames, door rails, door stiles and sash windows. For St Patrick's Hospital, Dublin, in 1749, George Semple specified that 'the frame of the front door, is to be made of six Inch Oak scantling, Beaded & rabited'.[16] Before framing doors or windows, the unwrought surfaces of the plank were removed with the carpenter's plane, thus reducing its thickness. A 2-inch plank for example, could be reduced to a (wrought) thickness of between 1¾ and 1⅞ inches when planed. The 1¾ inch specified for the sashes (and

15 Ibid., D354/725. 16 Semple, 'A further description', p. 14.

glazing bars) in the bill of scantling in the Drogheda Schoolmaster's House (1720s) was a common thickness for windows derived from the use of 2-inch unwrought deal planks.

Deals of 2 inches and more were also used for doors and sash-framing. William Montgomery was paid in 1708 for deals used by the carpenters in Trinity College to fabricate doors. In 1734, Isaac Wills proposed 'sashes 1¾ [inches] thick of red firr and frames with oak Cills' for the Trinity College Printing House.[17] In St Patrick's Hospital, Semple specified that some cell doors were to be 'of Whole dale ... lined, with three quarter dale'. Elsewhere doorcases were to be of oak 'about 3 by 6 inches' with doors 'of stout ¾ dale ... battened on ye out side with slit dale'.[18]

One of the most common uses for deals was as floorboards. The upper floors in Semple's St Patrick's Hospital in 1749 were 'floor'd with whole dale' laid as 'common Broken Joynt floors', which allowed the use of random length boards as flooring. Semple's reference to whole deal boards probably relates to the thickness of the floorboards rather than to their lengths and widths. Most eighteenth-century deal floorboards were 1⅛ to 1½ inches in thickness, 7½ to 9 inches in width and over 9ft in length. These floorboard dimensions are recorded in Table 5.3.

Table 5.3: Floorboard dimensions for individual Dublin buildings

	Thickness (inches)	Width (inches)	Length (feet)
25 Eustace Street (1720s)	1½	8–9	random
13 Henrietta Street (1743)	1¼–1⅜	7½–8½	29
20–25 Merrion Street (1760s)	1⅛–1¼	random	random

Eighteenth-century floorboards surveyed in these terraced houses (in Eustace Street, Henrietta Street and Upper Merrion Street) had an interesting feature in common. Many of them had a partial reduction in thickness at regular intervals along their length coinciding with the positions of the floor joists. This was achieved by cutting away a shallow trench of up to ⅛ of an inch in depth on the (unwrought) underside of the boards with an adze. It is apparent from this reduction in thickness in so many boards that deals used for flooring were seldom precisely the same thickness, and that small adjustments were necessary to obtain a perfectly level floor surface. The difficulty in converting logs and baulk timber into identical board thicknesses with pit saws is understandable. This helps to explain the variations in thickness in the deals offered to Mussenden from the Trondheim market in 1755.

Fir provided considerable advantages as a structural framing timber. Its availability in large sizes and long lengths (up to 50ft) allowed flexibility in the choice of room dimensions and roof spans. Many early classical architects – such as Wren in

17 TCD, Isaac Wills's accounts, MUN/P2/65/8.   18 Semple, 'A further description', pp 7–8, 14.

the building of St Paul's – must have experienced long delays in finding sources of supply for long oak beams for floors and roof trusses. The elasticity of red deal under bending loads promoted its use in the peculiarly Irish system of the through joist, spanning distances (in Leinster House and houses in Henrietta Street) of more than 20ft. It is unlikely that a material as brittle as Irish oak would have been as effective in joists over such spans without a significant increase in cross-sectional area.

The availability of fir planks and deals in stock sizes, particularly in the 9 x 2 inch to 10 x 2 inch range, promoted the standardization of floor structures so noticeable in Dublin's eighteenth-century terraced houses. Its delivery as pre-sawn scantlings minimized waste and encouraged a more precise control of building costs. It also arrived on building sites ready for immediate constructional use. Thomas Miles, writing in 1740 on the seasoning of building timber, specifies that 'oak should lie for a year in scantlings already cut'.[19] Of fir, he says that 'it may be us'd as soon as it can be converted after it comes to England in large Scantlings; but as to Deals for Flooring and Stairs, and many other Uses, as Deal Wainscotting, etc. these Deals should lay by piled at least a Year'. Fir planks and deals, according to the timber agent Andreas Friedlieb of Trondheim, were seasoned on their long journey (by flotation) down river from forests where they were sawn, to the ports of exportation.[20]

George Semple had strong views on the relative advantages of oak and fir timbers and he criticized the performance of the oak piles used in the construction of the South Bull Wall in Dublin Harbour in 1728.[21] He was impressed with the durability of red fir and specified its use in the fabrication of coffer-dams used in the building of Essex Bridge in 1753. He advocated a treatment (based on Venetian practice) consisting of the application of a mixture of linseed oil and tar spread on the surface of fir scantlings which had been preheated in a fire. He held the opinion that 'Good red Fir prepared after this Manner, will for many Uses last as long, if not longer than Oak Timber, especially in Water'.[22] Semple, of course, was referring to situations where timber was permanently wet (such as its use in piles). In uses such as window cills or gutters (where alternating wet and dry conditions could occur) oak was superior. However, the most pertinent advantage of red fir in construction was its capacity to perform as well as oak under normal conditions at a much reduced cost. Although the transportation cost from Norway and the Baltic ports added considerably to the purchase price of the timber, it was still less expensive to purchase imported fir in Dublin than to have oak delivered from Co. Wicklow. Fir baulks were also an important import from Norway, Sweden and Pomerania. Although hardwoods such as oak and mahogany were supplied in logs of considerable dimensions (sometimes up to 3 and 4ft in diameter), building records and measurers' manuals indicate that softwood (deal) baulk was usually converted from logs of from 9 to 18 inches in diameter. The circular shape of fir trunks produced baulk timbers that were usually square in cross section with chamfered corners to minimize wastage.

19 Miles, *The concise practical measurer*, pp 63, 83.   20 PRONI, Mussenden papers, D354/790.
21 George Semple, *A treatise on building in water* (Dublin, 1776), p. 83.   22 Ibid., 85.

5.2 Designs for timber centerings for spans of up to 92 feet, George Semple, *A treatise on building in water* (Dublin, 1776), plate 17.

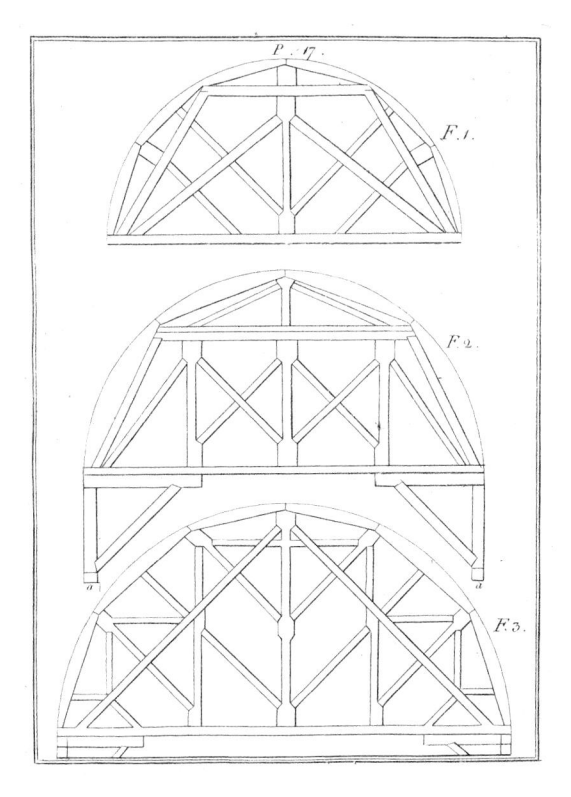

Building accounts of the Earl Bishop of Derry's house at Downhill in Co. Londonderry in 1783 record the purchase of baulks '14 to 17¼ [inches] square' in lengths from 19 to 46ft.[23] A letter from an agent of the Belfast timber importer Daniel Mussenden in 1756 records the following description of baulk timber for sale from Norway:

> Our correspondent Mr Michael Leon of Christiania, Norway desires us to recommend him to our friends in Ireland, if any of your friends have occasion for Timber he could deliver it early next spring in Ireland, good fir logs 14 to 18 feet long & from 9 to 14 Ins. square for 31sh[illings] Irish per ton or 40 feet solid, and white Wood Plank 10 to 12 feet long & 2 In. thick for £6.10.0 per hundred, the Buyer to pay the duty.[24]

23 PRONI, Downhill papers, D1514/1/1/13. 24 PRONI, Mussenden papers, D354/725; the meaning of '31sh Irish per ton or 40 feet solid' is obscure. 40 cubic feet of white or red fir would weigh much less that a ton; this is also true of oak. It may be worth noting that Levi Hodgson (p. 45) gives 'A Table shewing the exact Price, per Foot Solid, of Round Timber at Fifty, or Square at Forty Feet to the Ton. From £8 down to £1 10s. per ton'. Clearly, different kinds of timber are involved here, from expensive (£8) to cheaper (£1 10s. 0d.) per ton. These timbers are of different densities and on arrival will be of different cross section: a ton of oak of 1 square foot section at approx. 45lb per cubic ft, will measure approx. 50ft long. However, the length of a ton of baulk can be easily measured, and perhaps the price then calculated as a percentage of the price quoted per 50 or 40 feet.

Red fir baulk was an essential component in structural framing and particularly in the provision of floor beams. The characteristic eighteenth-century square beam with chamfered corners was in common use in Irish floor construction up to the 1750s. In Dr Steevens's Hospital (1720s) beams 11 inches and 12 inches sq were used over spans of 18 to 22ft. The gallery of Castletown, Co. Kildare (1720s) has beams 12 inches sq supporting its floor. The accounts of the new Parliament House in 1732 record the use of beams 12 inches sq and 21ft in length.[25] Baulk beams 12 inches sq were proposed for the bishop's palace at Elphin in 1747.[26] Robert Ball's accounts describe baulks 11, 12 and 13 inches sq shipped from Danzig for use in Wilson's Hospital, Co. Westmeath in 1755.[27] The bill of scantling for the Drogheda Schoolmaster's House (c.1728) had floor beams 12 x 8 inches revealing a more efficient use of the structural properties of the beam.[28] Roof framing members such as principal rafters, purlins, king-posts and collar beams were also provided by the use of red fir baulk.

* * *

Baulk timber was also purchased in Ireland for division into smaller scantlings on building sites and in local timber yards. This work was undertaken by sawyers, a separate trade who specialized in the conversion of roughly squared lumber into boards and planks for use by carpenters, joiners and some other trades not involved with building activities.

Sawyers worked as itinerant teams (usually in twos) moving from site to site and from yard to yard as the need for their services arose. Although the increased use of imported (pre-sawn) softwood (in lieu of native oak) must have limited their employment after the 1720s, they were employed to saw fir baulks into smaller scantlings, and the considerable expansion of the building market helped to promote their services. They were also not wholly dependent on building work, as they were engaged in many aspects of timber usage. They cut oak to make staves for barrels and casks, and ash for use in carriages, carts and tool handles. They cut oak and beech for upholsterers and a large variety of exotic timbers such as mahogany, walnut, cherry and satinwood for furniture and cabinet-makers.

The manual method commonly used to convert logs and baulks into building timber was by pit sawing. This required the log to be suspended over a sunken pit excavated in the earth for this purpose. Sawyers worked in pairs, a top man and a pit man, to divide the log in parallel cuts with long two-handled saws. The top man – standing astride or on the log at ground level – controlled the precise direction of the cuts; the pitman – standing below ground in the pit – provided motive force from underneath the log (fig. 5.3).

---

25 *Commons Journal*, 4, xxxiii.   26 Marie-Louise Legg (ed.), *The Synge letters* (Dublin, 1996), p. 15.
27 NAI, Ball, MS Dublin, 43.   28 IAA, Drogheda Grammar School folio, accession no. 92/24.1/1–4.

5.3 *The book of trades; or, Library of useful arts* (London, 1815), part 1, 'Sawyer'.

Moxon describes another alternative to the use of pit sawing for converting timber into smaller scantlings.[29] This consisted of a saw frame made with a pair of high timber trestles, which suspended the log 6 or 7ft above ground. This allowed the sawyer underneath the log to work at ground level, as the top man controlled operations from above. Obviously the system was only practical with smaller logs or baulks which could be easily hoisted off the ground. It was probably used more in workshops than building sites, although Robert Ball's accounts refer to the making of a sawpit in his workshops in 1750.[30] Sawyers were paid either on a time basis at fixed daily rates – or more commonly – on the basis of productivity, or piece rates. Payments for time were based on rates normally paid to building artisans during the first half of the eighteenth century. Piece rates varied according to the species of timber they handled, and depended on the hardness of the timber involved. Payments were also based on either the number of sawcuts required, or alternatively, on measurements (in square feet) of the converted timber scantlings.

29 Joseph Moxon, *Mechanick exercises* (London, 1703), p. 100.   30 NAI, Ball, MS Dublin, 43.

Examples of time charges in Trinity College show payments of 2*s*. per day to sawyers converting timber for Burgh's Laboratory in 1710, for his new Library in 1718 and for the 'New Buildings over the Cellars' in 1720 and 1721.[31] All of these charges were relatively small accounts and they were mostly paid out of Nathaniel Hall's (the head porter's) funds. Hall commonly hired casual workers such as labourers and sawyers and was reimbursed for their costs by the college.

An example of the more complicated basis of piece rate payments can be seen in the following sawyer's account for work on the Library in 1714:[32]

	£	*s.*	*d.*
To 1075 [sq] foot of Oak cut to ly in ye walls at 3*s*. p[er] hundred:	1	12	3
To 850 [sq] foot of Firr cut to putlocks and uprights for the windows [at 3*s*. per hundred]:	1	5	6
To 8 Doz. and 4 flat cutts in deals for Braces:		4	2
To 7 cutts in 7 Polls for Ladders:		2	4

This account, and some other accounts of their period, are eccentric in the charge of identical rates (of 3*s*. per hundred square feet) for sawing both oak and fir. Irish oak was much harder to cut than fir, and it needed more time and effort to convert it into building scantlings. It is likely that fir was only being introduced into the college building programmes during this period, and that the rate for converting it was based on the only yardstick available at that time. By the 1730s, Richard Castle was paying sawyers such as Henry Neal or John Scott (working on the Printing House) 2*s*. per hundred square feet for sawing fir and 2*s*. 6*d*. for sawing oak.[33] This differential was to continue through the century.

A clear picture of cost differentials for sawing timbers is given by Levi Hodgson in an index of Dublin rates for the last decade of the century.[34] The cheapest convertible timber, as we might expect, was fir at 2*s*. 6*d*. (prices are per hundred square feet). Riga, Holland and Danzig oak cost 3*s*., and all other oak cost 3*s*. 6*d*. Beech varied between 2*s*. 8*d*. and 5*s*. based on the diameter of the log. Mahogany was the dearest of the common timbers, ranging from 5*s*. for logs under 2ft broad to 7*s*. 6*d*. for logs of 3ft and upward.

The increase in sawing fir and oak over a period from the 1730s until the 1790s was small enough, in the light of considerable increases in building costs from the mid-1760s onwards. Sawyers may have been more vulnerable in the building market than other artisans, as their skills were more limited than those of the carpenters and joiners, and their work could be undertaken by either of these two trades. Moxon, in

---

31 TCD, Nathaniel Hall's accounts, MUN/P2/19/20; MUN/P2/37/56; MUN/P2/42/23–24; MUN/P2/44/7. **32** TCD, John Hall's accounts, MUN/P2/27/27. **33** TCD, Henry Neal's accounts, MUN/P2/68/31; John Scott's accounts, MUN/ P2/68/46–48.   **34** Hodgson, *The modern measurer*, pp 121–2.

his advice to joiners, encourages them to convert timber into smaller scantlings themselves, rather than employ sawyers.[35] In 1711, Sir John Perceval's agent at Burton Manor, Co. Cork, advised him of the services of local carpenters and joiners, as good as ones from England or Dublin, and, he added, 'ye Carpenters undertake the sawing'.[36] In 1776, 'A country sawyer' objected to a recent advertisement offering work in Dublin deal yards to sawyers 'from any Part of Great brittain, or Country Parts of Ireland'.[37] The sawyers claimed that there was no shortage of workmen available in Dublin, and that the merchant's intentions were to reduce the cost of deal cutting by 20 per cent.

* * *

The inclusion in Hodgson's list of imported Riga, Holland and Danzig oak is another reference to the scarcity of native Irish oak, which is evident from the early decades of the eighteenth century. Towards the end of the previous century, Ireland changed from being a primary exporter of timber to a country that needed considerable imports of foreign timber to sustain its trades and industries. The exploitation of the indigenous oak forests by English planters in the seventeenth century was seen, not merely as a source of quick profits from the wood, but as an essential part of the colonization process. Most of the forest grew on rich agricultural land, and the underwood provided shelter for Irish outlaws and woodkerns. Gerard Boate, writing during Cromwell's time, remarked that the woods were fast disappearing:

> But the County of Louth, and far the greatest part of the Countys of Down, Armagh, Monaghan, and Cavan (all in the same Province of Ulster) are almost every where bare, even in places which in the beginning of this present Age, in the War with Tirone, were encumbered with great and thick Forrests.[38]

By the 1720s, the direction of trade was completely reversed and imports of timber greatly exceeded exports. John Bush, discussing the scarcity of woodlands in 1764, remarked that there was as much timber in Kent as in the whole kingdom of Ireland.[39] In 1600, over 12.5 per cent of the country was covered by forests; by the end of the eighteenth century this percentage had been reduced to 2 per cent. Most of the heavy consumption of Irish hardwood had little to do with building. Shipwrights relied on oak for hull construction, but the amount of shipbuilding in Ireland was insignificant, and the admiralty's intentions of transporting large quantities of Irish oak for use in England were never properly realized. The main industries that consumed the forests were tanning (which required great quantities of bark), the manufacture of barrel and cask staves both for the Irish provisions trade and for export to France and Spain and,

---

35 Moxon, *Mechanick exercises*, p. 99.   **36** BL, Egmont papers, Add. MS 46964B, ff 71, 72, 107, 108, 117, 118.   **37** George Faulkner, *Dublin Journal*, 12–15 Oct. 1776.   **38** Gerard Boate, *Irelands naturall history* (London, 1652), pp 122–3.   **39** J[ohn] B[ush], *Hibernia curiosa* (London, 2nd ed., 1782), p. 41.

particularly, the production of charcoal for iron smelting, which was carried on in the vicinity of woodlands in many areas, until the supplies of timber were exhausted. At the beginning of the century most of the accessible forests such as the mature woodlands of the Barrow, Nore and Blackwater valleys had almost disappeared. The most extensive woods remaining lay in the remote north-west and south-west of the country, in the Glens of Antrim, on the north shore of Lough Neagh and on the slopes of the Wicklow and Wexford mountains. Tongues of woodland survived elsewhere in the country, particularly on the lands of well-established estates. These woodlands provided the oak used in most early eighteenth-century buildings. In the second half of the century oak was so scarce in Ireland that it was rarely used for structural purposes. The closure of ironworks in Foxford, Boyle, Drumshambo, Mountmellick, Mountrath and Shillelagh in the 1750s and 1760s signalled the end of the Irish forests.[40]

Although Norwegian and Baltic fir was available in Ireland before the beginning of the century, oak was still in demand. Durrow Castle, built on the banks of the Nore in 1715, used oak for structural framing, which was transported overland from Lord Clanrickard's Portumna estate, about sixty miles away on the west bank of the Shannon.[41] This must have been an expensive purchase, and it is clear evidence of the scarcity of woodlands along the Nore Valley at this early part of the century. However, some local woodlands survived the seventeenth century, as *Faulkner's Dublin Journal* advertised the sale of Raheen woods 'consisting of well grown oak on the banks of the Nore, near Durrow' in February 1743.[42]

The specific preference for the choice of oak rather than fir could only be satisfied on occasions by importing the timber from abroad. In 1726, the Dublin Ballast Board ordered 600 pieces of straight Polish oak from Montgomery and White at £3 5s. 0d. per ton.[43] In piling for the South Wall in Dublin harbour *c*.1720, a shortage of oak had persuaded the City Assembly to allow the Ballast Board to use red fir.[44] But oak was preferred and in 1722 it was decided 'that oak only be made use of in piling'.[45]

The durability of oak especially in damp conditions made it especially valuable as a building timber. Oak was seen traditionally by many early eighteenth-century builders as an essential material in the construction of roofs, gutters and other parts of the building fabric that might be exposed to rain or water penetration. Oak's principal advantage over fir (apart from its great strength) was its durability in rafters, gutter linings and other roof members affected by the poor performance of Irish roofs. After the mid-century, with the advent of larger slates from the Welsh quarries and a better understanding of the fixing of roofing lead, this advantage was not so apparent. Piles used as foundations, joists at ground level (in buildings without basements) and timber cills in sash windows, were components for which oak was also preferred, or considered essential.

40 Eileen McCracken, *The Irish woods since Tudor times* (Newton Abbot, 1971), p. 94.   41 NLI, Flower papers, MS 11455 (3).   42 George Faulkner, *Dublin Journal*, 14 Feb. 1743.   43 *CARD*, 7, p. 365.   44 *CARD*, 6, p. 549; 7, pp 21, 194.   45 *CARD*, 7, p. 200.

This is particularly true of English practice. Oak had been used unsparingly in most seventeenth-century buildings in both England and Ireland. From the beginning of the eighteenth century, the use of fir for framing and fittings had become increasingly common, but the London building regulations, introduced in 1667 and expanded in 1707 and 1709, specifically demanded the use of oak in roofing members such as trusses, rafters and purlins. Throughout the eighteenth century, the consistent references to oak scantlings in English building manuals are indicative of their common, if not exclusive, use. The two most authoritative writers on carpentry practices of their time, Francis Price in the first half of the century, and William Pain in the second half, provide comprehensive tables of preferred dimensions for rafters, beams, joists and other structural timbers in both fir and oak (the building regulations notwithstanding).[46] Christopher Wren's massive queen-post trusses, roofing his Hampton Court palace in the 1690s, had upper members (rafters, principals, purlins) of oak and lower members (beams, posts, struts) of imported fir.[47] Although oak might have been scarce in England in the eighteenth century, it is evident that it was still available for specific use in buildings of high quality.

This tendency to insist, where possible, on the use of oak for certain structural purposes, can also be seen in Ireland in the works of early classical builders. In William Robinson's time, from the 1670s until the 1700s, oak was extensively used for roof construction, windows and other building components where durability under damp conditions was considered important. The Royal Hospital Kilmainham, built in the 1680s, had oak roofs and floor framing, staircases and decorative fittings. Kilmacurragh House in Co. Wicklow, built in the early 1700s, had oak roof members, floor beams and sash windows. Remnants of oak construction dating from 1703–7 survive in Marsh's Library, although a considerable amount of the interior framing dates from the nineteenth century. Thomas Burgh, who succeeded Robinson as surveyor general in 1700, undoubtedly held the same preferences as his predecessor for oak construction, but his surviving buildings are a good indicator of compromises imposed by changing economic patterns in the early eighteenth century. His preferences were fully realized in Trinity College Library, which was brought to structural completion from 1712 to 1723 with roofs framed with oak, on foot of a generous budget provided by government. Dr Steevens's Hospital, built between 1720 and 1733 on a budget less than a third of that of the Library's, indicates a pattern that was to become common practice later in the century (fig. 5.4). It was estimated in 1722 that it would be necessary to purchase 'one hundred and fifty Tunns of Firr timber and two Tunns and a half of oak scantleing, the Firr rated to forty two schill[ing]s per Tunn amounts to £315, the oak at £4 per Tunn amounts to £10'.[48] The order stipulated that Isaac Wills the carpenter would frame the floors and roof

---

[46] Francis Price, *The British carpenter; or, A treatise on carpentry* (London, 1735); William Pain, *The practical house carpenter* (London, 1794), p. v. [47] Huw Jones, 'Wren tests restorers', *New civil engineer*, 27 Oct. 1988, 28–31. [48] T. Percy C. Kirkpatrick, *The history of Dr Steevens' Hospital, Dublin, 1720–1920* (Dublin, 1924), pp 35–6.

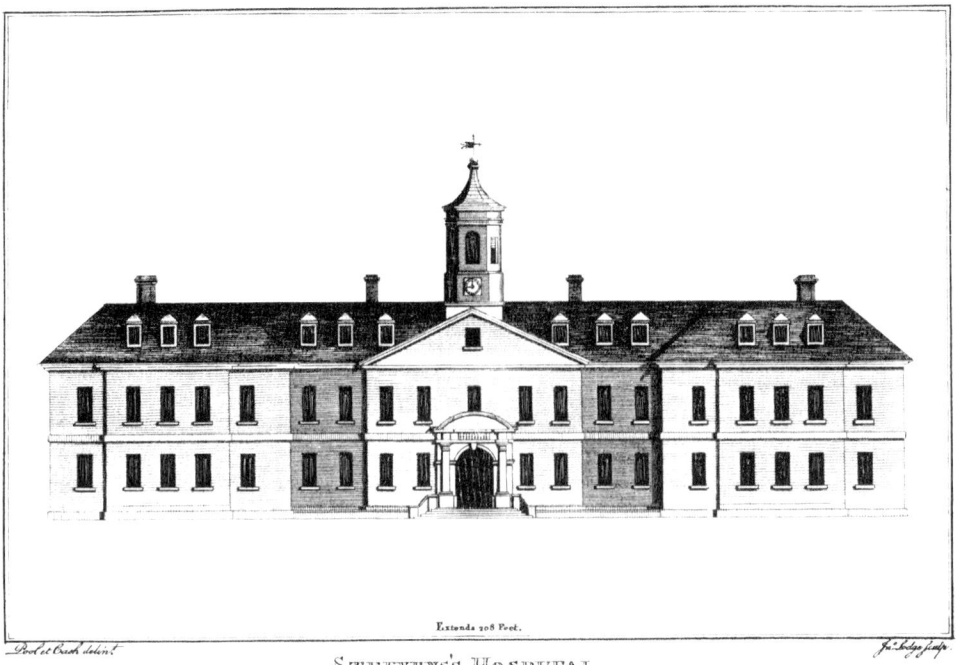

5.4 Dr Steevens's Hospital, Dublin, 1720s, Robert Pool and John Cash, *Views of the most remarkable public buildings … in Dublin* (Dublin, 1780).

with fir and use the oak for 'cills to windows and doors'. Richard Castle, who understood the efficiency of fir joists in floor framing better than anyone of his period, still used oak in roof construction if it was available. Although his Printing House in Trinity College (*c.*1733) had floors and roofs of fir, the roofs of Leinster House in Dublin and Belvedere House in Co. Westmeath (attributed to his hand) are both built with oak.[49]

However, by this period oak was no longer an economic choice in roof construction in most buildings, and its use was probably confined to the functions described in the bill of scantling for Drogheda Grammar School, which dates from the 1720s. This shows the sizes of timbers to be used in floors, roofs, walls, staircases, doors and windows. It specifies the use of oak for timbers (such as lintels, wallplates and dischargers) built into masonry walls, for the cills of windows, for joists used at ground level and for the sleepers (main supports) to staircases.[50] In Dublin, Lady Hume's house in Dominick Street was built by Benjamin Ball *c.*1733, using fir framing for floors and roofs, and oak for window frames and sashes.[51] Irish oak was

[49] TCD, Isaac Wills's accounts, MUN/P2/65/8. [50] IAA, Drogheda Grammar School folio, accession no. 92/24.1/1–4. [51] NAI, Ball, MS Dublin, 43.

much prized as a decorative finish in the first half of the eighteenth century as the interior design of Marsh's Library (1703), Burgh's Trinity College Library in the 1720s (though Danzig oak as well as Irish was used in the Library), and Pearce's Parliament House (1730) reveal. Its scarcity and high cost in 1749 is evident in Edward Synge's comment about a purchase of timber required to construct a bookcase:

> you may order it to be made of Dantzick Oak, since Irish is so hard to be got. The Difference will be only in Colour. Yet I would rather have Irish, if it can be got even on tolerable terms.[52]

* * *

Turning to the question of costs, oak which could be bought in the Dublin market for 45s. per ton at the end of the seventeenth century was becoming expensive by the 1720s.[53] The committee appointed for the erection of a statue of George I recorded a figure of £4 per ton as the 'very lowest price we could engage the same for' in 1721.[54] Wicklow timber, probably Shillelagh oak, delivered for use by the joiner John Sisson in Trinity College, cost a little over £5 per ton in 1721, with carriage at £1 5s. 0d. per ton included.[55] At the Dining Hall in Trinity College in the 1740s, the estimate for oak had to be increased from £4 10s. 0d. to £5 a ton.[56] Transportation costs had a considerable effect on the price of timber delivered to building sites. A breakdown of costs of the Shillelagh oak used in Trinity College in 1721 is revealing: oak which cost £3 15s. 0d. per ton was carried overland to Wicklow harbour for 17s. per ton. Sea freight to Dublin including fees came to approximately 9s. per ton.[57] Shillelagh oak was normally floated down the River Slaney to the port of Wexford for sea transportation, but this was a slow process as the river was not navigable above Enniscorthy. The demand for the timber in Trinity College was obviously urgent enough to justify the cost of bringing it overland to Wicklow.

Daniel Mussenden's correspondence with Andreas Friedlieb, his agent in Trondheim, provides a comprehensive picture of timber exports from that port during the 1750s. A letter from Friedlieb of 27 November 1755 enclosed a printed catalogue of prices for deals and planks, showing prices, in Norway, for boards by the long thousand (i.e., 1,200) with freight to Ireland quoted at 39s. per long hundred (i.e., 120). (The original prices are given in rixdollars, here converted to shillings and pence at the rate of 1 rixdollar = 4s. 6d.):[58]

---

52 Legg, *The Synge letters*, p. 116. 53 McCracken, *The Irish woods since Tudor times*, p. 78. 54 *CARD*, 7, p. 151. 55 TCD, John Sisson's accounts, MUN/P2/44/25. 56 TCD, Richard Castle's accounts, MUN/P2/80. 57 TCD, John Sisson's accounts, MUN/P2/44/25. 58 PRONI, Mussenden papers, D354/779.

Deals (8'6"–9') x (8½"–9") x (1½"–2"):
red	£29 5s. 0d.	to	£30 7s. 6d.
white	£27 0s. 0d.	to	£28 2s. 6d.
undermeasure red	£20 5s. 0d.	to	£21 7s. 6d.
undermeasure white	£18 0s. 0d.	to	£18 11s. 3d.

Planks (14'):
red	£54 0s. 0d.	to	£55 2s. 6d.
white	£47 5s. 0d.	to	£48 7s. 6d.

Deals and Planks (3" to 3½" thick): double price

Half deals (about 6' long):
red	£14 12s. 6d.	to	£15 15s. 0d.
white	£13 10s. 0d.	to	£14 12s. 6d.

Thus, with freight at 39s. we arrive at a cost of importing of about £4 19s. 0d. per 120 redwood boards, with freight from Norway accounting for nearly 40 per cent of the cost. Prices in the Irish market in the 1750s would have provided comfortable profits on such purchases. An account of Dublin timber merchants Montgomery and White in 1734 contain references to 'Common Deals at £5.5.0 per hundred, read Deals at £7 per hundred' to denote whitewood boards and redwood boards respectively.[59] Mussenden's correspondence records the receipt of £5 5s. 0d. per hundred for undermeasure deals in 1755 which were for sale in Norway at about 8 Rixdollars (£1 16s. 0d.) at this period.[60] To this has to be added Friedlieb's freight charges of £1 19s. 0d. and possibly fees for loading, shipping agents and custom house. It is not clear from Mussenden's accounts if the transportation cost included customs duty; the Dublin carpenter and deal merchant George Stewart was paid £6 per hundred for white deals in 1755.[61]

Prices of baulk timber are a little more difficult to pin down since descriptions in the Trinity College muniments of Norway or Pomeranian timber rarely distinguish between red and white fir. Prices in Dublin such as 31s. in 1756 or 35s. in 1734 per ton are unusually low, and may have been for white fir, or for fir of inferior quality; in 1718, the college had paid 45s. per ton for red fir baulk; this price is recorded for Norwegian (red) baulk in the 1720s and also in 1752 when it is quoted as the 'Common Price' in a parliamentary enquiry; in 1753 Robert Ball sold Swedish baulk for 46s. per ton.[62]

* * *

[59] TCD, Montgomery and White's accounts, MUN/P2/ 68/29. [60] PRONI, Mussenden papers, D354/766. [61] TCD, George Stewart's accounts, MUN/P2/105, p. 8; MUN/P2/105 gives prices in the 1750s as follows: whole deals at 14d.–15d. each, 'thin' deals at 10d., 'wrack' deals at 10d.–12d., 'slit' deals at 16d., and half deals at 9d. [62] PRONI, Mussenden papers, D354/725; TCD, MUN/P2/68/29; TCD, MUN/P2/37/85; *Commons Journal*, 5, lxxvii; NAI, Ball, MS Dublin, 43.

5.5 James Malton, 'The Four Courts, Dublin', watercolour, 1793, detail showing the floating of timber downstream, NGI, cat. no. 7713. Reproduced with permission of the National Gallery of Ireland.

5.6 James Malton, 'The Marine School, Dublin', watercolour, 1796, detail showing the landing of timber at Sir John Rogerson's Quay, NGI, cat. no. 2704. Reproduced with permission of the National Gallery of Ireland.

Transportation cost is only one explanation we can offer for the consistent differential between prices of timber imported from Norway and timber from the more easterly sea ports on the Baltic coast. In the 1720s and 1730s Pomeranian (i.e. Baltic) baulk was more expensive than Norwegian. By the 1760s this differential had increased considerably. The list of timber prices compiled for a regional barrack building programme in 1760 clearly indicates this pattern:[63]

Table 5.4: Regional timber prices in 1760 (per ton)

	Carlow	Kilkenny	Clonmel	Wicklow		
Norway	44s.	45s. 6d.	44s. 6d.	43s.		
Danzig	62s. 6d.	62s. 6d.	61s. 6d.	63s.		

	Cork	Tallow	Carrick-on-Suir	Waterford	Ross
Norway	43s. 6d.	42s.	45s.	42s.	43s. 6d.
Danzig	60s.	65s.	65s.	62s.	63s. 6d.

	Navan	Belfast	Derry	Belturbet	Drogheda	Granard
Sweden	80s.	63s.	65s.	95s.	63s.	95s.

	Carrickfergus
Riga fir	60s. to 65s.

The differential in price between Norwegian and Baltic timber in the 1720s and 1730s is reasonably explained by additional carriage costs in the sea journey around the coast of Denmark from the Baltic to the North Sea. The imposition of toll duties by the Danish authorities on ships passing through Helsingor Sound was another expense added on to timber imported from Prussian, Polish or Russian ports. However, the higher cost of Baltic timber in 1760 and the increased differential between it and Norwegian timber in this period cannot be explained by differences in transportation costs alone. This cost difference, ranging from 16s. 6d. (in Cork) to 23s. per ton in Tallow, must relate to variations in the quality of the timbers in question. It is relevant that timber had increased considerably in cost between 1755 and 1760. The price of Baltic timber quoted was probably an accurate expression of market forces. The price of Norwegian baulk (42s. to 43s. per ton) in port cities such as Wicklow and Waterford is remarkably low in such a buoyant market.

By 1760, quality redwood might have become scarce in Norway, and inferior timber may have found its way into the Irish market. Complaints about the quality of

---

63 *Commons Journal*, 6, ccxc onwards.

timber available were not unknown during the mid-century in Ireland. In 1749, Bishop Edward Synge complained bitterly of the quality of timber beams supplied for his new house at Elphin by the Dublin timber merchant Maximilien Bonvillete. Timbers used by artisans in barracks contracts in 1749–50 were subsequently criticized during the 1752 parliamentary inquiry because of their poor quality.[64] The low price of Norwegian timber in the rising market conditions of 1760 reflects a decline in the quality of this timber during that period.

Table 5.4 also provides a good indication of the cost of transporting timber from sea ports to inland centres. The price of timber in inland towns such as Navan, Belturbet and Granard was particularly high, and it reflects a reliance on overland carriage. Edward Synge paid £1. 3s. 3d. per ton for carriage of timber to Elphin from Dublin in 1749, during a period when timber was not expensive.[65] In *Hydrographia Hibernica* (published in 1710), a commentator describes the expense of overland carriage 'I have paid 5ᵈ for carrying a Deal-Board from Dublin to Roscommon, that had been brought but the Week before from Norway to Dublin for Three-half-pence'.[66] This reveals some of the disadvantages of building in remote areas, although the price quoted for carriage from Norway seems to be too low. Mussenden's costs for freight charges between Trondheim and Ireland was 39s. per long hundred (120) boards in 1755. This indicates a charge of just under 4d. per board.

* * *

The 1760s introduced a period of increased building costs in Ireland together with a considerable increase in building activities. The building boom experienced from about 1764 onwards is reflected in the steep rise in imports, the value of which in 1770 is more than double that in 1761; the value of deals imported increased thirteen-fold between 1711 and the 1790s.[67] The relatively small quantities of planks imported over the century helps to explain the continuous employment of sawyers throughout the eighteenth century. Much of the baulk imported was converted locally into planks, especially after the mid-century, when Irish floor framing dispensed with the use of beams.

Import statistics also provide information on foreign hardwoods shipped to Ireland from various countries including the American plantations. New World timber from ports such as Jamaica and New York were mostly hardwoods such as oak and mahogany. Up to 1770, colonial products had to be initially shipped to Britain and re-shipped to Irish ports. Although considerable quantities of mahogany arrived in Ireland, it appears to have been mostly used for furniture. Its cost (at £10 per ton in the 1760s) limited its selection for building purposes but it was used later in the century for joinery components such as internal doors and handrails on internal

64 *Commons Journal*, 5, xciv, civ.   **65** Legg, *The Synge letters*, p. 119.   **66** *Hydrographia Hibernica; or, A view of the considerable rivers of Ireland* (Dublin, 1710), p. 9.   **67** McCracken, *The Irish woods since Tudor times*, pp 113, 115.

staircases. A curious use (in terms of its poor performance in damp conditions) was in sash windows designed by Francis Johnston for Ballynagall, Co. Westmeath in 1808.

Wrought oak wainscot was imported from Holland, America and the Baltic ports throughout the century. Almost the entirety of the £1,521 worth of wainscot shipped to Ireland in 1771 came from the American plantations, but before 1770 most wainscotting came from Holland and Danzig.[68] Danzig oak was used in Ireland from the beginning of the century. It was much softer and easier to work than Irish oak, but it was not as attractive as a decorative surface. Its choice for the carved frontispiece of the chapel door in Trinity College in 1720 (executed by Isaac Wills) was probably on account of its workability.[69] John Sisson's joinery accounts for the Trinity College Library record payments for 455 [sq] yards of Danzig oak wainscot at 6s. per [sq] yard and 181 [sq] yards of Irish oak wainscot at 8s. per [sq] yard in 1731.[70]

On the whole, however, hardwoods (local or imported) were not extensively used in Irish buildings over most of the eighteenth century. Apart from the uses we have described (wainscot, panelled doors and stair rails), they were sometimes used as flooring in expensive buildings such as Chambers's Casino at Marino in the 1760s, and George Steuart's reconstruction of Baronscourt, Co. Tyrone, c.1780.[71] Irish houses and public buildings substantially depended on the imports of the northern European forests for the entire century. The considerable dependence on this source was clearly recognized by Arthur Dobbs in 1729:

> As for our Importation of wood, I am afraid we shall not in a long Time, if ever, save in that Article, even should we plant, to which we seem generally to have so great a Disinclination: For as we encrease and improve, our Demands for it will still be encreasing: and when Norway and the Baltick fail, we must look out for another Market, to buy at greater Expense.[72]

* * *

The growth of timber imports in the second half of the century is reflected in the expansion of the timber trade in Dublin and in some of the main port cities. Mussenden's correspondence of the 1750s records the activities of timber merchants such as John Holmes in Belfast, Isaac Read and Pat Gernon in Dundalk, and Nathaniel and Robert Alexander in Derry.[73] William and John Ogle of Newry were active in the import of colonial timber in the 1760s.[74] In Dublin, many timber merchants combined timber sales with allied operations, the most common combination being timber merchant and carpenter. The *Dublin directory* for 1753 lists

---

[68] TNA, Export-import ledger 1770–1, Cust. 15.   [69] TCD, Isaac Wills's accounts, MUN/P2/40/45.
[70] TCD, John Sisson's accounts, MUN/P2/59/9.   [71] PRONI, Abercorn papers, D623/C/3/1.
[72] Arthur Dobbs, *An essay on the trade and improvement of Ireland* (Dublin, 1729), p. 49.   [73] PRONI, Mussenden papers, D354/762, 764, 788, 848.   [74] Thomas Truxes, *Irish-American trade, 1660–1783* (Cambridge, 1988), pp 218, 394.

John Connell as a timber merchant: a John Connell also acted as carpenter and joiner in the 1730s and 1740s. The carpenters (and master builders) Pierce Archbold and John Chambers (well known for their involvement in the barrack building scandal in 1749) are recorded as timber merchants in the 1760s. George Stewart, a carpenter employed on the Parliament House and in Trinity College, owned a deal yard in the 1760s. George Esdall was listed in the *Dublin directory* for 1765 as both timber merchant and architect. This should not unduly surprise us as the surveyor general William Robinson owned a timber yard.

The Dublin directories from the 1750s indicate the presence of timber merchants in many parts of the city, but most of them tended to be located on the quays, or in streets with easy access to the river. On the south side a high concentration of timber yards were located in Townsend Street, on City Quay, Hawkins Street, Usher's Quay, Golden Lane and Bridgefoot Street. On the north side the main concentrations were in Smithfield, on Arran Quay, Earl Street, Bachelors Walk and the North Strand. There were 10 timber merchants listed in the directory in 1752. A decade later in 1762, their number had increased to 34 and three decades later in 1792, 50 timber traders were recorded. This increase in numbers reflects the considerable expansion of the city by the development of the speculative housing estates, north and south of the river, and the steady growth of timber imports from the 1760s onwards.

CHAPTER SIX

Wall construction

T̲ʜᴇ ᴄᴏɴsᴛʀᴜᴄᴛɪᴏɴ ᴏꜰ ᴄʟᴀssɪᴄᴀʟ ᴀʀᴄʜɪᴛᴇᴄᴛᴜʀᴇ in both the seventeenth and eighteenth centuries had the advantages of an indigenous masonry tradition that had persisted in Ireland since the medieval period, and an abundance of easily obtained local stone. The main differences between wall construction in classical buildings and their medieval counterparts were the introduction (in the seventeenth century) of clay bricks for certain masonry tasks, an increased use of cut-stone ashlar for exterior wall faces and carved masonry mouldings as decorative enrichments.

Although the type of stone chosen and the way masonry materials were used could vary considerably from place to place, three distinct constructional patterns are discernible in Ireland. One system consisted of walls entirely, or substantially, built of stones and mortar. A second system used walls of stone and mortar in conjunction with clay bricks as dressings and facings, to either the interior or exterior wall surfaces. The third system was of walls built entirely, or substantially, of clay brickwork.

The first system was identical in most respects to the medieval walling used in monastic buildings, castles and fortified houses, and it was clearly a continuation of existing local traditions. An important characteristic of these walls was their use of a tripartite construction (fig. 6.1). Walling was built as two separate masonry membranes forming the exterior and interior faces of the wall, and the space between was filled with a core of mortar imbedded with loose unbonded rubble stones. This (all stone) masonry system was still used over the whole eighteenth century but in a limited number of building types. It was used extensively in church construction in urban and rural locations. It was also used in utilitarian structures such as mills, stables and outoffices. Economy dictated its use in Dublin charitable institutions such as Dr Steevens's Hospital, Mercer's Hospital and in the City Workhouse – all built in the early eighteenth century – and in the construction of terraced houses in many provincial towns and cities such as Clonmel, Kilkenny, Cashel, Cork, Limerick and Galway.

Exterior masonry could be refined by the use of cut-stone facings on the façades of one or more walls of a building. This entailed the substitution of finely worked ashlar facings and precise horizontal coursing for the random coursed rubble walling commonly used throughout the country. Although hundreds of buildings were built with local rubble, grand aristocratic houses such as Powerscourt, Baronscourt and Castlecoole were almost entirely faced with cut-stone ashlar. In Dublin, important state and institutional buildings such as the Library in Trinity College, the new

6.1 Custom House, Dublin, section of stores, by James Gandon, 1795; showing the tripartite construction of the masonry walls, NLI, AD/3219. Reproduced with permission of the National Library of Ireland.

Parliament House, the Royal Exchange and the Custom House were completely faced with cut stone.

The use of dressed ashlar as an internal wall lining is seldom encountered in Irish classical buildings, and then only in the grander works of a few neoclassical architects. Cooley introduced it into Dublin in the 1770s, in the domed interior of his Royal Exchange. Gandon, influenced by the French masonry traditions of William

6.2 Goresgrove, Co. Kilkenny, brick reveals to openings and linings to limestone walls (photograph by Arthur Gibney).

Chambers's practice, used it in the 1780s and 1790s in the north and south vestibules, and in the staircases of the Custom House, in the vestibules of the House of Lords, and in the hall of the Four Courts.

The second constructional system combined stone facings (of rubble or ashlar) with brick membranes on the interior faces of the main structural walls and, typically, brick dressings to window and door openings, brick chimneys and internal partitions (fig. 6.2). This was the most common method used to build structural walls in Irish classical buildings from the last quarter of the seventeenth century until the beginning of the nineteenth century. It was used in the construction of country houses, and in the capital in the principal buildings of Trinity College, in civic buildings such as the Parliament House, in grand urban palaces such as Leinster House and in institutions such as the Rotunda Hospital and the Blue Coat School.

Most of these buildings used structural walls of tripartite construction. The main difference between these walls and the traditional (all stone) system was the substitution of a brick internal lining for the rubble linings of the first system.

Although it is difficult to determine precisely the thickness of these brick linings, many buildings appear to have relied on slender membranes of locally made 4½-inch place bricks. This is certainly the case in country houses such as Eyrecourt and Dunsandle, Co. Galway; Summerhill and Arch Hall, Co. Meath; Kilmacurragh, Co. Wicklow; Tudenham, Co. Westmeath; Ledwithstown, Co. Longford; and Castlestrange, Co. Roscommon. Restoration work on important classical buildings in Dublin has revealed similar construction in the Royal Hospital Kilmainham, Leinster House, Charlemont House, the Blue Coat School and Newcomen's Bank.

There is evidence, however, of the use of thicker and more robust brick linings in some classical buildings. The accounts of the Trinity College Library make clear references to the use of 14-inch brick membranes, presumably as linings to the tripartite construction of the main piers above ground-floor level. This constructional pattern was probably not widely used in Irish classical buildings as it required imported stock (facing) bricks (rather than local place bricks) to ensure a proper bond. An interesting variation of this second masonry system is the use of bricks as the outer face (as well as the inner face) of one or more structural walls. This walling was used extensively in the mid-eighteenth-century ranges of Dublin Castle. It can also be seen in some early country houses such as Platten House, Co. Meath, and Mount Ievers Court, Co. Clare. However, brick exterior façades on the walls of country houses are not numerous in Ireland, and it is more convenient to discuss these houses as part of the second (combined brick and stone) system.

The third masonry system that emerged in the development of classical architecture was the use of homogeneous brick walling. Unlike the tripartite structure of the other two systems, these walls depended on bonded, or partially bonded, brick assembly to achieve strength and stability in slender masonry membranes. This slenderness made these walls particularly appropriate as interior partitions in large houses and institutions with exterior walls of composite constructions. The principal use of this third system was in the masonry of the uniform terraced houses of speculative developments such as the Gardiner and Fitzwilliam estates in Dublin, the Pery estate in Limerick and the Donegall estate in Belfast.

The development of the second and third constructional systems and their variations were the results of changes in architectural style at the end of the seventeenth century and the influence of immigrant artisans with experience of a new architectural language. Although evidence of considerable masonry skills can be found in pre-classical buildings in all parts of Ireland, the stylistic complexities of classical ornamentation, the demand for ashlar facings and the substantial use of bricks as structural masonry introduced new technical disciplines into Irish building practices before the end of the seventeenth century. This was reflected in changing organizational patterns among the building trades and the importation of new building concepts.

The increased demand for brickwork in Dublin in the late seventeenth century is reflected in the royal charter granted in 1670 to form a new and separate guild for bricklayers and plasterers who, until that date, shared the carpenters' guild with several other trades. The use of bricks, and the presence of bricklayers as a separate trade, had been established in Ireland before the mid-seventeenth century, but apart from the Dublin area, bricks were not widely used in Ireland before the beginning of the eighteenth century. At much the same time, the increased use of cut-stone ashlar and moulded entablatures on building façades introduced new skills which influenced existing masonry practices. Eighteenth-century building accounts in Ireland differentiate between the work of the common (or rough) mason who built walls in roughly dressed local rubble, and those who worked with precisely dressed ashlar and carved mouldings in stone from specially selected quarries. These specialists are commonly described in eighteenth-century Irish records as stonecutters and they were engaged contractually as a separate trade, although they were registered as masons in the guild fraternities.

The lack of defined boundaries between the work of separate trades is a common feature of seventeenth- and eighteenth-century building practice in Ireland. Like the overlapping responsibilities between carpenters and joiners, or plasterers and painters, the relationships among the three walling trades of masons, bricklayers and stonecutters are difficult to define.

* * *

The main problem in examining the responsibilities of the walling trades lies in the complexity of eighteenth-century walling construction. The first walling system we have described, the traditional rubble tripartite wall, required only common masons for its construction, though if there were to be facings of dressed stone (as was frequently the case) the common masons were joined by stonecutters, who handled their part of the masonry task.

Before examining the work of masons and stonecutters we will look at the brick trade. In Dublin, the unprecedented expansion of the city and its population from the 1670s attracted considerable numbers of English and European artisans to settle there. The development of the first speculative housing estates on the perimeter of the medieval city followed the practices adopted by speculators in post-Restoration London, following the fire of 1666. London was being largely rebuilt during this period, under the influence of new building regulations that promoted the use of brick masonry for urban houses instead of traditional English timber construction. Bricks and bricklayers were in high demand and brickwork was identified with new and fashionable house architecture. The construction of the early generations of brick town houses in Dublin on the Aungier and Meath estates were adaptations of English and Dutch models. Most building designs produced during this period were contrived by the artisans who built them. Many of them were based on vernacular patterns from abroad that were arranged to suit local conditions. Stylistic preferences ranged from versions of seventeenth-century London mansions – Molyneux House, built in 1711, with central pediment and modillion cornice is an example – to the gabled houses of the Dublin Liberties where vestigial references to classical external ornament were confined to entrance doorways and mouldings at roof level. The Dutch influence on brick housing in the Liberties and the suburbs adjoining St Stephen's Green was mostly the work of English artisans. Brick building in England had been influenced by Dutch practice and the use of Dutch housing models for a long period. There was also a considerable Dutch presence among the many foreign Protestants who came to Ireland after the Williamite wars. An early influence on Irish brickwork was provided by John Allen, a bricklayer trained in Holland who was reputedly responsible for the superbly executed brickwork of Jigginstown in Co. Kildare in 1636.

The foundation of the Dublin Bricklayers' and Plasterers' Guild must be seen in this context. It was formed at a time when new technical and interpretative skills were in short supply, and specialization in fashionable services must have been profitable. This form of market response has an immediate parallel with the formation of the Dublin Guild of Joiners, Ceylers and Wainscotters in 1700. By this time, timber entablatures, sash windows, ramped stair rails and panelling were becoming as fashionable as Flemish bonded brickwork and pedimented brick gables. The formation of the bricklayers' guild was a conscious attempt to bring together groups of expatriate specialists, to promote their skills and to identify the difference between their work and that of the common mason.

The demand for experienced craftsmen encouraged English bricklayers such as John Hearne (who became involved in the Aungier estate) and Richard Mills (who supervised the walling of the Tailors' Hall and Molyneux House) to settle in Dublin in the early 1670s.[1] During this period bricklayers enjoyed a higher profile in the city than the traditional mason. Richard Mills became assistant to the master of the city works in 1701/2 and acted as supervisor on a number of important contracts.[2] The principal walling contracts for brick and rubble stonework for the surveyor general's office and Trinity College were handled by bricklayers such as William Caldebeck or Francis Quinn, who employed journeymen masons to provide the stonework. The advantages enjoyed by this trade may still have been apparent for most of the first quarter of the eighteenth century, as the architect and master builder George Semple (whose father was a mason) started his career as a bricklayer's apprentice in 1720.[3] The bricklayer Richard Coulett, an apprentice of the stonecutter John Whinrey, received his freedom of the city in 1700.[4]

An enthusiasm for a classical brick vernacular is particularly identified with the early years of the new century, and in Dublin it is exemplified by buildings such as Robinson's and Burgh's additions to Dublin Castle, the Rubrics in Trinity College, the Tailors' Hall, Marsh's Library, Burgh's Custom House and Molyneux House. In

---

1 Rolf Loeber, *A biographical dictionary of architects in Ireland, 1600–1720* (London, 1981), pp 60, 72. 2 *CARD*, 6, p. 260.   3 DCLA, typescript, 'Roll of the freemen of Dublin'.   4 Loeber, *Architects*, p. 115.

provincial areas, most of the brick-faced buildings, apart from urban housing, were built before 1730, and the most notable of the early vernacular examples are the Uniacke House, Youghal, Co. Cork, and country houses such as Platten House, Co. Meath, Palace Anne, Co. Cork, Beaulieu, Co. Louth, and Mount Ievers Court, Co. Clare. Brickwork was considerably more expensive than rubble stonework in eighteenth-century Ireland. Even the rough brick lining used in composite walls was twice the price of equivalent rough stonework, and rubble was to remain the most commonly used walling material throughout the country.

Building accounts in Dublin and the provinces provide us with important information on the relationship between masons and bricklayers. William Caldebeck is described as a bricklayer in numerous accounts in Trinity College, but he was also paid for the construction of stone walling in 1711, and in 1712 he signed a receipt for £100 paid 'on account of mason's work [which was probably foundations] on ye College Library'.[5] His partner and successor Francis Quinn contracted for substantial quantities of brick walling on the Library from 1718 until 1723, but in 1720 he was also recorded as the walling contractor on Dr Steevens's Hospital, which was built extensively of calp-stone rubble.[6] The building accounts of Castle Durrow, Co. Laois, from 1714 to 1718 record an interesting overlap in working relationships. In 1715, the masons Denis Phelan and William Dayly agreed for walls of brick and stone in the outoffices and in the cellars of the main house; in 1717, the bricklayer Benjamin Smith was paid for 586 perch and 13ft of brick and stone walling built as part of the main dwelling house.[7] In some accounts artisans are described as both masons and bricklayers. In testimony submitted to the parliamentary enquiry into the barrack building programme of 1749–51, two artisans described themselves in this fashion. In an affidavit dealing with standards of workmanship in Carrick-on-Shannon barracks, John Byrn claimed he was a mason and a bricklayer.[8] In a similar statement dealing with workmanship at Headford barracks, Owen McGinnis stated that he traded in Galway as a mason and bricklayer.[9] However, this was uncommon in Dublin practice. Most master artisans engaged in important Dublin walling contracts (such as Francis Quinn or John Semple) saw themselves as bricklayers, although they were happy to contract for both stone and brick masonry as it was required.

The lack of clear boundaries between the contractual responsibilities of these two trades is understandable, of course, in the context of eighteenth-century tripartite walls. This constructional system required a mason and a bricklayer to work simultaneously on the erection of the same wall, the mason on the outer face and the bricklayer on the inner face of the wall. As composite wall construction (without cut-stone facings) was invariably built as one contract, both the bricklayers and masons involved in that contract worked closely together as if they were one trade.

---

5 TCD, William Caldebeck's accounts, MUN/P2/22/3; ibid., MUN/P2/23/3.   6 Ibid., MUN/P2/36/19.
7 NLI, Flower papers, MS 11455 (3), (1).   8 *Commons Journal*, 5, cxxiii.   9 Ibid., cxxviii; elsewhere (ibid., 5, lxxxix) he is described as slater.

The handling of stone and brick walling as one single contract avoided a duplication of responsibilities for the structural performance of the work and it simplified payment and measurement procedures. However, in practice it obliged either the mason or the bricklayer to physically undertake the work of both trades, or alternatively, one trade could employ members of the other trade to carry out their share of the construction. In Dublin, with its considerable tradition of brick craftsmanship, this usually resulted in journeymen masons working under the supervision of master bricklayers. In provincial areas, with strong masonry traditions and few contractual resources, it undoubtedly resulted in local masons (such as Byrn and McGinnis) undertaking both the brickwork and masonry involved in their contracts. Masons were well capable of handling the rough brick linings and dressings required in the construction of composite walls; as brick façades (other than small numbers of urban housing) were uncommon in provincial areas after the 1720s, the need for exacting craftsmanship did not arise.

* * *

The operational boundaries between the contractual activities of the common mason and the stonecutter are also confusing, as in the Dublin area both disciplines were represented by the carpenters' guild, and prominent eighteenth-century stonecutters sometimes described themselves as masons. However, surviving records of payments to building artisans reveal important distinctions between contracts undertaken by masons and by stonecutters, and the materials they used. Building records of state buildings in Dublin and of the principal buildings in Trinity College provide a clear picture of the contractual responsibilities of both masons and stonecutters. Common (or rough) masons were usually employed in the construction of structural walls of uncoursed rubble, obtained from local sources such as the calp quarries at Palmerstown, Baggotrath or Milltown. Stonecutters (or freemasons) were usually engaged with precisely coursed ashlar facings and mouldings of cut stone from selected quarries such as Ardbraccan, Co. Meath, Golden Hill, Co. Wicklow, or imported stone from the Isle of Portland in Dorset.

Stonecutters' work was measured and paid for on a different basis from the work of the common mason. Rough masonry and brickwork was paid by the volumetric perch; cut-stone facings were paid by a running foot of complicated moulding, or by surface measure of the square foot. This method of measurement reflected the complications of the stonecutter's work, as a running foot of modillion cornice was priced at a much higher rate than plain work such as architraves or plinths. Stonecutters also operated as independent contractors, although they were engaged in close association with masons and bricklayers on the erection of structural walls. Each ashlar-faced wall thus required two separate contracts, one for rough masonry and/or brickwork and the other for the work of the stonecutter.

However, the Dublin stonecutters apparently remained a part of the masons' fraternity. Thomas Burgh's accounts record several payments to the Dublin stonecutter John Whinrey between 1703 and 1723, but Whinrey is described as a mason in the Betham will abstracts.[10] Moses Darley, who undertook the limestone arcades and sandstone facings of Burgh's College Library in 1712, received the freedom of the city as a mason in 1720, as did his son Henry in 1746. Although most of the many contracts between the Darley family and the college are clearly recorded as receipts for stonecutters' work, some records make specific references to payments for masons' work. A series of payments to Moses Darley between March and December 1712 are all described as receipts for work on the new Library, variously described as mason's work, stonecutter's work and stonework.[11] In 1766 and 1767, George Darley was paid for jobbing accounts involving time charges for masons and a labourer.[12] The work described in these accounts involved routine tasks such as laying flagstones and cutting holes for fixings in stone parapets. In a letter from Dublin to William Chambers in 1769, Thomas Cooley complained of the high cost of 'mason's' work for Portland facings on his contract for the Royal Exchange.[13] This is understandable in an English context as cut-stone facings were the responsibility of the mason's trade in England.

Although a lack of building records prevents us from identifying most of the stonecutters who worked in provincial Ireland, the quality of workmanship on the façades of many country houses is evidence of a considerable market for their specialized skills. However, the style and quality of ashlar facing could vary greatly in provincial practice, especially in the first half of the eighteenth century. Some buildings such as the Bishop's Palace at Limerick (fig. 6.4) used a semi-coursed ashlar with stones of random sizes which was not unlike rubble masonry. Country houses such as Castle Durrow, Co. Laois (fig. 6.3), Doneraile Court, Co. Cork, and Summer Grove, Co. Laois, have coursed ashlar of considerable irregularity, as have the limestone façades of the townhouses of John's Square (1750s). This undoubtedly is evidence of a scarcity of sophisticated craftsmanship in the provinces during this period. The refinements to be seen in Ducart's masonry at Kilshannig, Co. Cork and the Limerick Custom House may well have required expertise brought from Dublin. The Dublin stonecutter John Whinrey made proposals to Drogheda Corporation for building a bridge over the Boyne with Thomas Burgh in 1721.[14] A stone doorcase, presumably carved by Dublin stonecutters, was shipped to Castle Forward in the 1730s.[15] George Darley was engaged on the bridge at Lismore in 1770.[16] The stonecutters working on the rebuilding of Baronscourt in 1779 under the direction of George Steuart included seventeen masons brought from London for this purpose.[17]

---

10 Genealogical Office, Betham will extracts, MS 253, pp 158–59, where his eldest son Nathaniel is described as a stonecutter. 11 TCD, Moses Darley's accounts, MUN/P2/23/18–41. 12 TCD, George Darley's accounts, MUN/ P2/145/1. 13 RIBA, William Chambers's correspondence, Cooley to Chambers, 22 Aug. 1769, CHA. 2/26. 14 Rev. T. Gogarty (ed.), *Council book of the corporation of Drogheda*, I (Drogheda, 1915), p. 350. 15 NLI, Castle Forward papers, MS 10470. 16 Jane Meredith, 'No small thing …', *Irish Arts Review Yearbook*, 14 (1998), 102–14. 17 Jacqueline O'Brien and Desmond Guinness, *Great Irish houses and castles* (London, 1992), p. 204.

6.3 Castle Durrow, Co. Laois, 1714–18, irregular coursed ashlar. Courtesy of the Irish Architectural Archive.

6.4 Entrance front of the Bishop's Palace, Limerick, © National Inventory of Architectural Heritage.

The city of Kilkenny developed a justifiable reputation as a centre of craftsmanship in stonecutting during the eighteenth century. This was due to the presence of good limestone and marble quarries near the urban centre and to the efforts of

William Colles, who became a producer of polished marble fireplaces and other marble components in the 1740s. The provision of stone cills, cornices and doorcases for the vernacular buildings of provincial towns, and of lesser country houses, was probably entrusted to local masons. These masons may have referred to themselves (on occasions) as stonecutters, but they undoubtedly (like the masons Byrn and McGinnis on the Headford and Galway barracks) were also involved in building rubble walls, brick linings and even roof slating.

Although many of the early eighteenth-century stonecutters (such as the Darleys) came from England, the organizational patterns of Irish craftsmen were not based on contemporary English practice. In England the masonry trade included freemasons (who, like Irish stonecutters, worked with cut-stone mouldings and facings but made contracts to employ masons) and rough masons who worked with structural walls of rubble masonry. In Ireland, however, as we have seen, wall construction commonly involved two separate contracts, one for rough masonry and brickwork, and the other for cut-stone facings. In England cut-stone facings and rough masonry were part of the same contract, but brickwork was built as a separate contract.

This is confirmed by records of Christopher Wren's procedure. At St Stephen, Walbrook, masons' work measured in 1674 covered both freestone ashlar and 'Rubble worke'.[18] It was the same at Hampton Court with the mason John Clarke in 1690, and in 1703 at St Paul's, where the mason William Kempster charged for the carving of a 'Festoone' and 'Corinthian Capitals' and for '34¼ rods of New Rubble'.[19] At St Paul's, separate payments are recorded to some sculptors and carvers such as Grinling Gibbons, Caius Gabriel Cibber, Jonathan Maine and others, but 'the great bulk of the carved [stone] work was carried out by the Mason contractors'.[20] Wren's bricklayers were engaged and paid on the basis of separate agreements. Wren's accounts also refer to the use of the term 'stonecutter', but in a different context from its usage in Ireland. In 1701, he purchased a marble fireplace and stone garden ornaments from stonecutters in London and Brentford, which were assembled on site by masons working at Winslow Hall in Buckinghamshire.[21] The use of the term 'stonecutter' in this context describes a craftsman who produced standard stone decorative components in a workshop which could be ordered from a catalogue. Workshops of this type, producing stone fireplaces to standard patterns, also operated in Ireland, and these workshops had the capacity to produce building components such as cills and doorcases for use on building sites by local masons. However, building records for Castlecoole, Co. Fermanagh in the 1790s clearly show the stonecutters' full involvement in both the cutting of stone components on building sites (not in workshops) and the setting of these components into the masonry fabric of buildings.[22]

Stonecutters were prominent among lists of artisans working on Irish classical buildings from the last quarter of the seventeenth century. The names of the artisans who built the Royal Hospital at Kilmainham, from 1680 until 1686, are unrecorded,

18 *Wren Soc. Vols*, 10, p. 77. 19 Ibid., 4, p. 46; 15, p. 101. 20 Ibid., 15, pp xiv, xxii–xxiv. 21 Ibid., 17, p. 62. 22 Desmond Guinness and William Ryan, *Irish houses and castles* (London, 1971), p. 164.

but £2,399 4s. 8d. was spent on stonecutters' work and materials out of a total masonry cost of £7,822 12s. 0½d.[23] John Whinrey, although he described himself as a mason, was probably the best known stonecutter operating in Dublin at the beginning of the eighteenth century.[24] He was employed on the building of St Mary's Church and he worked extensively for Thomas Burgh, the surveyor general, on contracts such as the steeple of the Royal Hospital, on Dublin Castle, on St Werburgh's Church, and on the Royal Barracks. His son Nathaniel was one of the four master stonecutters employed by Edward Lovett Pearce on the new Parliament House from 1728 until 1729.[25]

The Darley family was particularly associated with the cut-stone façades of buildings in Trinity College such as the Library from 1712 until 1722, the Printing House in 1734–6, Regent House in 1750–6, the Provost's House in 1760–5, and the Chapel and Theatre from 1777 onwards. Moses Darley's proposal for the arcaded limestone loggia in the courtyard of Dr Steevens's Hospital is dated 24 October 1720.[26] His son Henry worked under John Ensor on Richard Castle's Rotunda Hospital from 1751 until about 1756.[27] Another son, George Darley, provided the stone facings on 86 St Stephen's Green in 1766 and 1767 and Henry worked on Gandon's Custom House in the 1780s. The Darley accounts provide valuable information on stonecutters' working patterns and their part in the building process. The records of work on Burgh's Library in Trinity College and on his Dr Steevens's Hospital confirm their full involvement in the two-phase process of cutting stone components on building sites (not in workshops), and in the assembly (or setting) of cut-stone components into the masonry fabric. The accounts of Castlecoole and Baronscourt also confirm these patterns. None of the accounts differentiate between the status of artisans working as either 'cutters' or 'setters'. Both were paid on the same basis, and as part of the same contract.

Both the Trinity Library and the Dr Steevens's Hospital records specify the stonecutters' site requirements, which include the provision of equipment, site sheds, mortar and the attendance of labourers. Moses Darley's proposal for Dr Steevens's approved by Burgh in October 1720 makes this quite clear:

> Moses Darley proposeth to cutt & sett Bases, Pillars, with their Arches, & Spandrels, Quoins, & Fascias, such as are att the [Royal] Barricks for five pence per foot; Ostrigall window Stools for Seven pence per foot; The Governours furnishing stone proper for ye said work. Quarried, & laid convenient for the workmen; also shedes for the stonecutters, & to draw ye said worke where it is to be erected with Scaffolds, Centers, Labourers Morter, & all other things requisite & convenient for ye carrying on and finishing ye said worke.[28]

23 Richard Colley, *An account of the foundation of the Royal Hospital* (Dublin, 1725), p. 23.   24 On Whinrey, see Loeber, *Architects*, p. 114.   25 *Commons Journal*, 4, xxxii, xxxiii.   26 TCD, Dr Steevens's Hospital papers, building accounts, 82.   27 C.P. Curran, *The Rotunda Hospital, its architects and craftsmen* (Dublin, 1945), p. 39.   28 TCD, Dr Steevens's Hospital papers, building accounts, 82.

The Darleys, like many craftsmen who worked on early classical buildings in Ireland, were part of the great wave of foreign immigrants who came there towards the end of the seventeenth century. Henry Darley settled in Newtownards, Co. Down, where he worked as a stonecutter and became the owner of sandstone quarries in the town. His sons Moses and Hugh moved to Dublin in the early years of the eighteenth century, attracted, obviously, by the demand for new skills in the rapidly expanding capital city. This demand was for technical expertise and especially for the ability to interpret the new architectural language of classicism. Later in the century, Simon Vierpyl, another expatriate stonecutter, was to be invited to Dublin (in 1757) to introduce the stylistic sophistication of Franco-Roman masonry on the construction of the neoclassical Casino built by Lord Charlemont at Marino.

We have very little information on the identity of stonecutters who worked in Irish provincial centres, but some idea of their activities can be gleaned from the building accounts of the larger country houses. In 1717, the dimensions of his limestone facings on Castle Durrow were set out by the stonecutter Barnaby Demave.[29] In Cork city, the stonecutter John Coltsman is recorded as the builder of Christchurch and the North and South Gate bridges between 1713 and 1720. Joseph Briggs charged for stonecutter's work on Headfort House, Co. Meath, between 1769 and 1773.[30] The most prominent stonecutters in Ulster during the 1770s and 1780s were James and (his son) David McBlain. James worked for the Earl of Hillsborough on the spire of Hillsborough church and for the Earl Bishop on the spire of Derry cathedral in the 1770s.[31] From the late 1770s until 1790, the McBlains were almost continuously engaged by the Earl Bishop of Derry on the gates and façades of Downhill, on the decorative carvings on the adjoining Mussenden temple and on the façades of his second house at Ballyscullion in the 1780s.

In the 1780s, Michael Campbell is recorded as a stonecutter employed on Mount Stewart, and William Tassie worked on the stables at Blessington.[32] Robert Morton (or Martin) supplied an estimate for 'a Parapet Wall on the Casino' for the Earl Bishop in 1784, and in 1791 the stonecutter Alexander Baird was at work on the important task of cutting the Corinthian capitals of the Ballyscullion portico.[33] As we have already seen, the Earl of Abercorn brought a number of stonecutters from London and Dublin to work on the facings of Baronscourt in 1779; the Portland facings of Castlecoole required a large team of stonecutters in the 1790s and they may also have been brought there from Dublin or (in the case of some) from London.[34]

We can only speculate on the reasons for the divergence between English and Irish masonry practices, and why Irish masons involved in the specialized business of dressed facings used the term 'stonecutter' as a trade description. There was,

29 NLI, Flower papers, MSS 11455 (1).   **30** NLI, Headfort papers, MSS 26/679.   **31** On the McBlains see Peter Rankin, *Irish building ventures of the Earl Bishop of Derry* (Belfast, 1972), pp 10, 22, 29, 53. **32** PRONI, Mount Stewart account books, D654/H/1/1, p. 36; Hillsborough papers, D671/V/360, bundle 110, Nr 63.   **33** PRONI, Bristol papers, D1514/1/1/9; Rankin, *Irish building ventures*, p. 53. **34** Jacqueline O'Brien and Desmond Guinness, *Great Irish houses and castles* (London, 1992), p. 204; Guinness and Ryan, *Irish houses and castles*, p. 164.

6.5 George Miller, 'Mr Colles's Marble Mills, Millmount, Co. Kilkenny', early nineteenth-century watercolour. Reproduced with permission of the Royal Society of Antiquaries of Ireland.

undoubtedly, a connection between the choice of this description and the contractual involvement of rough masons with bricklayers in the building of composite walling. The demand for brick façades and wall linings in the Dublin area from the end of the seventeenth century promoted the bricklayer at the expense of the rough mason and, as we have seen, we find prominent bricklayers such as Richard Mills, William Caldebeck and Francis Quinn handling both stone and brick walling contracts, and describing themselves as masons and bricklayers. This never happened in England, and the skilled masons who undertook cut-stone contracts may have adopted the term 'stonecutter' as a contractual description, to distinguish the terms of their agreements from those of the common mason and bricklayer.

The masonry trade, or the stonecutting part of it, also developed specialists who, like Simon Vierpyl or Edward Smyth, extended their activities into monumental carving and figurative sculpture. Although complex tasks such as the carving of

6.6 George Darley, design for a neoclassical chimney-piece, pen and watercolour, c.1775, RIA 3/C 34/3/4. Reproduced with permission of the Royal Irish Academy.

Corinthian capitals were commonly entrusted to stonecutters, building accounts also record the specialized work of stone carvers. John Houghton carved the Ionic capitals and the royal arms on the Parliament House in the 1730s. Castle used Houghton and John Kelly to carve the arms on Carton in 1739, and Kelly's name also appears in the accounts for the Hall in Trinity College in 1746.[35] Hugh Darley used the carver James Robinson to cut the rococo garlands for the west front of Trinity College in 1756.[36] Vierpyl spent a considerable portion of his career in the execution, or the management, of stonecutting contracts in Ireland, but he had a reputation as a sculptor, and the figurative and decorative carvings on the Casino Marino (1760s) are undoubtedly his. Smyth is reputed to have started his career as a journeyman with George Darley, but he is remembered for the considerable contribution his decorative and figurative carving made on Gandon's Custom House and the Four Courts.

35 TCD, John Kelly's accounts, MUN/P2/84/6.   36 TCD, James Robinson's accounts, MUN/P2/99/4.

The manufacture of stone fireplaces also used the skills of stonecutters and carvers. John Whinrey offered to promote the sale of Lord Perceval's Irish marble, enjoying in 1715–16 an export business to England.[37] The Kilkenny entrepreneur William Colles invented a new method of cutting and polishing marble using water power in the 1740s, and his workshop produced fireplaces, cisterns, vases and other objects in marble (fig. 6.5).[38] His production method proved to be so economical that he was successful in penetrating foreign markets in Bristol, Liverpool and Glasgow. Michael Shanahan, the master builder who acted as an architect on several of the Earl Bishop of Derry's building projects, made fireplaces in Cork. His claim that he had 'a most excellent carver' in his Cork marble business was obviously convincing, as a number of his fireplaces were shipped from Cork in 1787 for use in the bishop's houses at Downhill and Ballyscullion.[39]

The advent of neoclassicism, and of professional architects such as Cooley, Ivory and Gandon in the last three decades of the century, brought increased opportunities for stonecutters and their associated trades (carvers and sculptors) in Dublin (fig. 6.6). Trade reports for the period just before the 1800s indicate the involvement of a workforce of nearly 1,000 operatives in the stonecutting trade, comprising 41 master contractors, 330 'operatives' and a large group of attendant sawyers, polishers and labourers.[40] The social and political changes introduced in the early nineteenth century following the Act of Union greatly diminished the building market and contractual activities of all the building trades. By 1832, it was claimed that the number of master stonecutters operating in the Dublin market had been reduced to fifteen contractors, while 'The number of working men now connected with our Trade, including sawyers, Polishers, &c. does not exceed 300'.[41] By this time, contractual patterns had also begun to change. The use of the contract in-gross had become commonplace, and general contractors employing journeymen had supplanted independent master artisans, such as the stonecutter, and the use of traditional single trade contracts.

---

37 BL, Add MS 46,966, ff 60, 136; Add MS 46,967, f. 18. 38 Tony Hand, '"Doing Everything of Marble" …' *IADS*, 11 (2008), 74–99. 39 Peter Rankin, *Irish building ventures of the Earl Bishop of Derry* (Belfast, 1972), p. 17. 40 NLI, 'Report of the stonecutters … 1832', MS 13,629 (8). 41 Ibid.

CHAPTER SEVEN

The introduction of brickwork

ALTHOUGH THE MEDIEVAL PATTERN of walls built entirely of stone persisted in the construction of eighteenth-century Irish churches and also in terraced houses in some provincial cities, most classical buildings were constructed with a combination of stone and clay bricks. William Robinson's extensive use of bricks in his ambitious design for the Royal Hospital Kilmainham reinforced a pattern that was consistently followed in most state and institutional building contracts and in country houses irrespective of their size. Robinson's deliberate use of stone for certain parts of his masonry structure and bricks for others is revealing. The main structural walls in the entirety of the east, west and south ranges of the hospital have exterior facing of local calp rubble (rendered) and interior linings (4½ inches) of brickwork. The partition walls, the chimneys and fireplaces are constructed with bricks. Bricks are used as dressings for window and door openings in most sections of the hospital, and as cores for the plastered impost mouldings on the piers of the cut-stone arcades.

These three ranges contain residential apartments in two storeys of masonry construction and in the attic of the tall slated roof. The north range contains the former masters' quarters and the high single-storey spaces of the hall and chapel. The masters' quarters were built (like the soldiers' apartments) of brick and stone, but the hall and chapel (like the succeeding generation of eighteenth-century churches) have stone exterior facings and stone interior linings to massive composite walls. We will examine the reasons for these unusual variations in construction later in this chapter.

The use of bricks in masonry construction was probably the most significant change introduced into Irish building practices by post-medieval building artisans. We have already described the considerable demand for brick facings generated from the end of the seventeenth century in Dublin and some provincial centres. This is exemplified by early eighteenth-century classical buildings in Dublin such as the Rubrics in Trinity College, the Tailors' Hall and Molyneux House, and in the provinces by country houses such as the Uniacke House (1703) in Youghal, Palace Anne (1714), Co. Cork, and Mount Ievers Court (1733), Co. Clare. Bricks had been used for building houses in Dublin city from the first half of the seventeenth century and they become strongly identified with the speculative terraced housing of the

---

Gibney's account of very early brickwork in Ireland, and the importation of brick, should be supplemented by recent work by Susan Roundtree, 'A history of clay brick as a building material in Ireland', MLitt, 1999, University of Dublin, Trinity College, and 'Brick in the eighteenth-century Dublin town house', in Christine Casey (ed.), *The eighteenth-century Dublin town house* (Dublin, 2010), pp 73–81.

eighteenth-century estates in Dublin, and coastal cities such as Drogheda, Derry, Limerick and Belfast.

This early eighteenth-century enthusiasm for brick façades was generated by imported architectural fashions. The streetscapes of London were substantially rebuilt with brickwork after the fire of 1666, and Christopher Wren had fully demonstrated the architectural potential of brick masonry in the design of important commissions such as the palaces at Kensington and Hampton Court. However, a second and equally important reason for the introduction of bricks into Ireland was the technical advantages it offered to architects like William Robinson in the structural design of buildings such as the Royal Hospital. In what follows we will examine the influence of both these patterns of brick usage on building practices during the century.

* * *

It is difficult to be precise about the first appearance of bricks in Ireland, but there is enough evidence to establish their use in Irish buildings from the beginning of the seventeenth century, and earlier. The brick chimneys of Ormonde Castle in Carrick-on-Suir may predate the seventeenth century and this could well be one of the first uses of bricks in the country. E.M. Jope has recorded a use of brick dressings on cannon ports in Carrickfergus Castle in the 1570s.[1] Mountjoy Fort in Co. Tyrone (1601–5) was built (unusually for its time) almost completely in brickwork and this may well be the result of the involvement of the Dutch engineer Levan de Rose, who would have been familiar with brickwork in his native land (fig. 7.1). In 1630, the Earl of Cork paid for digging earth to make bricks 'for re-edifying my decaied house in Castle Street in Dublin'.[2]

The best known example of brick masonry built in the first half of the seventeenth century is the palace at Jigginstown, Co. Kildare, built by Thomas Wentworth in 1636 (fig. 7.2). Jigginstown is unique in its construction and use of materials. Its masonry is entirely composed of carefully bonded brickwork. Several different brick sizes are used and the bricks are made with considerable skill and precision. Some of the brick types conform with the 8½ to 9-inch standard used in normal English practice, but the presence in the walls of 7 x 1½-inch and 7 x 3½-inch bricks is unexpected. The wall thicknesses (above basement level) of 27 inches and 22 inches are remarkably slender for this period, but they are justified by the quality of the materials and the precision of the bonded brick masonry.

The responsibility for the construction of Jigginstown has been attributed to John Allen, an English bricklayer who received his training in Holland. This is supported by the high quality of the masonry and by the presence of the (7-inch) brick sizes,

---

[1] E.M. Jope, 'Moyry, Charlemont, Castleraw and Richhill: fortification to architecture in the North of Ireland, 1570–1700', *Ulster Journal of Archaeology*, 23 (1960), 117. [2] Rev. Alexander B. Grosart (ed.), *The Lismore papers*, first series, III (London, 1886–8), pp 20–1.

7.1 Mountjoy Fort, Co. Tyrone, 1601–5.

7.2 Jigginstown House, Co. Kildare, 1636. Courtesy of the Irish Architectural Archive.

which are identical to bricks used in early seventeenth-century buildings in Amsterdam. It is likely that at least some of the bricks were imported from Holland. Jigginstown is impressive in terms of craftsmanship and constructional standards, but it made no apparent impact on seventeenth-century Ireland, or on the development of newer building patterns that emerged in the latter half of the century. Most surviving seventeenth-century houses built between 1630 and 1670 (if we can judge by examples such as Raphoe Palace, Burncourt, Glinsk or Leamaneagh) have massive stone walls and fortified expressions, although Raphoe Palace has fragments of brick masonry which are probably eighteenth-century alterations to its internal fabric.

The most frequently quoted authority on seventeenth-century building practices in Ireland is Gerard Boate, whose *Irelands naturall history* was published in London in 1652. Boate's first comment on bricks relates (appropriately) to their use in combination with stone masonry. He describes two forms of limestone, both grey and blue, and he outlines the problems faced by English colonists in dealing with Irish climatic conditions:

> The sort of Gray Free-stone in Ireland hath a bad qualitie, that it draweth in the moysture of the air continually to it, and so becommeth dank and wet both in and outside, especially in times of much rain. To mend this inconvenience the English [in Ireland] did wainscot these walls, with oak or other boards, or line them with a thin crust of brick.[3]

He was unimpressed with the quality of bricks made in Ireland and of the methods used to make them:

> And as for the Brick[s], they have been little used in Ireland even among the English themselves for a great while, but of late years began to be very common, as well in the countrie, as in the Cities, especially Dublin, where all new buildings (they, which not only in handsomness, but also in number doe surpass old) are all made of Brick. But that which is made in Ireland is not so good for the most part, as that of other Countries, not so much for any unfitness in the clay itself, as for want of handling and preparing it aright.[4]

Boate also describes the making of bricks in huge quantities of 200,000 to 300,000 in one firing, of which about two-thirds were discarded because of their poor quality. He is critical of the lack of uniformity in the burning process through 'the unskilfulness or neglect of those who make & fill these Kilns and of those that govern the fire'.[5] These comments have in the past supported the view that the high-quality bricks used in Jigginstown were imported from abroad.

Although no physical evidence remains of such an intensive use of brickwork in seventeenth-century Ireland, Boate's observations are supported by the Settlement

3 Gerard Boate, *Irelands naturall history* (London, 1652), p. 149.   4 Ibid., pp 159–60.   5 Ibid., p. 161.

7.3 No. 5 Henrietta Street, Dublin, *c.*1740, ground-floor window with gauged and rubbed bricks in lintel.

Commission's surveys of Irish property holdings which followed the restoration of Charles II in 1660. These records reveal a substantial use of brickwork in Dublin city and its developing suburbs. Records of a survey made in 1661 describe 'the great Brick-House in Copper-Alley'; brick houses were part of the streetscape of Patrick Street, Francis Street, St George's Lane, Cooke Street, Kevin Street, Thomas Street, Rosemary Lane and Schoolhouse Lane in the 1660s; a considerable number of houses built in the new suburb of Oxmantown in the same period used brick masonry.[6] (In the eighteenth century, when brick façades were commonplace in most of the streets in Dublin, basements, stables and boundary walls were invariably constructed of rubble stone because of the higher cost of imported facing bricks.)

Boate's description of the poor standards of brickmaking in Ireland is relevant, and it provides us with an explanation for the absence of exterior brick facings in

6 NAI, Lodge records of the rolls, vii, 13, 22, 100, 400 (microfilm MFS 42/4); xii, 48, 49, 187, 210, 226, 252, 333, 355 (microfilm MFS 42/6).

7.4 Francis Wheatley, 'Brickmakers', print after oil painting exhibited in 1786. Private collection.

many parts of provincial Ireland. An examination of bricks used as internal masonry linings in many country houses exemplifies the problems arising from poor control of the firing process, resulting in misshapen and deformed bricks. The inadequate manufacturing methods observed by Boate were obviously still in use in many areas during the eighteenth century. The better quality bricks of even rectilinear shape, used as facings on houses such as Beaulieu, Co. Louth, Mount Ievers Court, Co. Clare, or the terraces of Henrietta Street in Dublin, were mostly imported into Ireland from other countries with traditional skills in brickmaking.

Eighteenth-century customs records describe the importation of bricks from Holland and England. These bricks were usually moulded to conform with dimensions (of 9 inches x 4½ inches x 2¼ inches) laid down by English statutes, and they were possibly sometimes used as ballast in ships calling to Irish ports for cargoes of local produce.[7] Some early eighteenth-century buildings (such as Marsh's Library in Dublin) used dressings of bright red rubbed bricks which probably originated in

---

7 Richard Neve, *The city and country purchaser* (London, 1726; facsimile ed., 1969), p. 44. Gibney's views on the importation of brick have to some extent been superseded by the work of Susan Roundtree.

7.5 John Rocque, 'An Exact Survey of the City and Suburbs of Dublin', 1756, detail, Old Brick Field to the west of Sackville Mall, BL, K. Top. 53. 13. b. 11. Reproduced with permission of the British Library.

the brickfields of the Thames Valley. Wilkinson claimed that the bricks used to face many of Dublin's eighteenth-century terraced houses came from the port of Bridgewater on the Bristol Channel.[8] The surveyor general Arthur Dobbs, in a letter to his brother in 1754, recommended the importation of 'strong bricks' from Liverpool for use on his house near Carrickfergus.[9] The customs archives of the port of Zierikzee, which serviced the Dutch province of Zeeland, record many cargoes of bricks exported to Irish towns (such as Dublin and Cork) during the middle decades of the eighteenth century.[10]

8 George Wilkinson, *Practical geology and ancient architecture of Ireland* (London, 1845), p. 131. 9 PRONI, letter from Dobbs to Richard Dobbs, Mic 533/2, p. 123A. 10 Information from Erik van der Doe, Zierikzee, Holland.

These facing bricks were described as stockbricks by eighteenth-century building artisans, a name derived from a Dutch word describing the 'stock' or wooden mould that shaped the unburnt brick. Imported stockbricks were usually used only as facings; locally made bricks were used for linings to composite walls, partitions and general structural work. Bricks used for linings and for general wall construction were usually described as 'placebricks' by eighteenth-century artisans.

Brickmaking did not develop as an organized industry in Ireland perhaps until the eighteenth century. Bricks were usually made by unskilled labourers on, or near, building sites, or bought from small local producers who leased plots of land for brickmaking in the vicinity of the speculative housing estates (fig. 7.4). This involved the excavation of earth to a depth of about 4ft and its use to make bricks, which were burnt – not in enclosed kilns where temperature control could be maintained – but in continuous stacks, or clamps, as they were called by eighteenth-century brickmakers. John Rocque's map of Dublin in 1756 depicts an area between Great Britain Street and Sackville Mall called the Old Brick Field (fig. 7.5). The clay overburden on this plot of ground was undoubtedly used to make the placebricks for many of the adjoining houses in Henry Street and Bolton Street, but by 1756 it could no longer be used for brickmaking, as its soil was depleted. On Bernard Scalé's map of 1773 the area is completely developed with houses and stables.

On country estates such as Burton, Co. Cork, bricks were made in situ by labourers, for use on the building of Burton House in the 1670s.[11] In Dublin, Robert Arthur and Henry Lee (described as brick-burners) supplied bricks for Burgh's repairs to the old Parliament House from 1700 to 1708; Arthur also supplied bricks for use in building the Tailors' Hall in 1705/6.[12] Robert Ball's accounts record the purchase of 'Donoly's bricks' in 1753, for use by himself and other speculative developers of houses in Sackville Mall [now O'Connell Street].[13]

* * *

The description in Boate's *Irelands naturall history* of stone walls with brick linings confirms that this system was in use in Ireland at least thirty years before Robinson employed it in the Royal Hospital at Kilmainham. It cannot have been widely used outside of Dublin at this early period, or it would be more in evidence today, but one important example survives in the ruins of Eyrecourt, built in Co. Galway in the 1660s. Eyrecourt's importance for us lies in its relationship with aspects of an emerging constructional system and its affinity with the new architectural language. The use of 4½-inch brick linings as the interior surfaces of the peripheral walls links it with the structures described by Boate and with subsequent classical buildings of the next century. However, there are other aspects of its structural design that are

---

11 BL, Egmont papers, Add. MS 46,951B, f 107; Add. MS 46,964B, f 80.   12 Henry Berry, 'The Merchant Tailors' Gild', *JRSAI*, 48 (1918), 43.   13 NAI, Ball, MS Dublin, 43.

untypical both of existing masonry traditions in Ireland, and of the new generation of buildings identified with the growth of Irish classical architecture.

Eyrecourt, with its external plaster rendering, its uncoursed (composite) rubble walls and its brick linings, looks similar in many respects to early classical buildings such as the Royal Hospital (1680s), Kilmacurragh House (*c*.1700s), or later generations of country houses such as the King House (1730s), Ledwithstown (1740s), and Castlestrange (1750s). The main difference in the masonry at Eyrecourt is the reliance on a massive oak structural frame embedded within its walls, continuous oak lintel courses on the masonry linings and timber ties forming diagonal braces at the corner junctions of the main walls.

The system of building houses with oak structural frames – cage houses, as they were called – was not uncommon in Irish cities during the early modern period, and it was known to persist in the plantation towns of Ulster until well into the seventeenth century. Eyrecourt, however, is not a cage house. It has massive masonry walls, which were more than capable of playing their full structural role without the need of a secondary structural system of timber. Its builders were obviously unfamiliar with structural masonry and they had no confidence in either its performance or efficiency.

Eyrecourt is significant as a transitional link between different building traditions at a time when new architectural ideals were promoting change and improvization in constructional patterns. It was probably built by English artisans, carpenters rather than masons, who were attempting to relate their own working methods to local materials and practices. The limestone masonry is of a poor standard and, significantly, it is built without the use of arches, which must make this building unique in an area noted for its masonry traditions. Arches are avoided at window openings by using massive window frames that act as lintels in the support of the masonry. The window thus becomes a primary structural element that must be fixed in position before construction starts.

* * *

Before discussing exterior brickwork, we will examine the procedure, described by Boate, of lining stone walls with internal brick lining. In the 1680s, Robinson designed the Royal Hospital with masonry that contained no embedded timbers except oak lintels used as supports at window openings. This was essentially a re-use of the old traditional Irish formula of composite walls but with the addition of brick internal linings. However, we can still perceive a hesitancy and uncertainty in some aspects of the structural design. This is expressed in the massive scale of the masonry (particularly in the chimney breasts) and in the oversized floor and roof framing in relationship to modest spans. This is particularly evident in the gallery floors which use 8-inch oak beams at 20-inch centres over a span of 10ft. Robinson was obviously intent on supporting the floor, but he was also concerned with the stability of the external wall, and the closely spaced beams were ties to ensure its structural equilibrium.

7.6 Marsh's Library, Dublin, *c*.1700, ground-floor window with gauged and rubbed bricks in lintel.

Robinson employed brick linings in the rebuilding of Dublin Castle in 1685. In 1703, his design for Marsh's Library used facing bricks, placebricks and flat arches made with rubbed brick voussoirs, which may have been imported from the London area (fig. 7.6). His name has also been linked with the design of Kilmacurragh House, built in the early 1700s. Kilmacurragh (like the Royal Hospital) has massive timber framing over modest spans and, like the earlier example of Eyrecourt House, it has a timber eaves cornice and a pedimented doorcase of timber. Although Kilmacurragh's primary structure was a combination of stone and brick linings, it relied (like Eyrecourt) on timber diagonal braces to support the masonry parapet at roofplate level.

The most important building constructed in the first quarter of the eighteenth century was the Library in Trinity College, which was designed by Thomas Burgh and begun in 1712. Burgh followed Robinson's example (at Kilmainham) in his choice of masonry with stone exterior and brick interior faces. A lavish budget allowed him to clad the upper floors entirely in sandstone ashlar over an arcaded limestone base. Burgh was a more daring builder than Robinson, and the structural design of the Library shows a confidence that is missing at the Royal Hospital. One unusual aspect of the masonry construction is revealed by the Library records. Instead of the thin lining of bricks described by Boate and used in Kilmainham and Kilmacurragh, the bricklayer's (Francis Quinn's) accounts charge the cost of a 14-inch brick membrane as an internal lining.[14] An inspection of these walls shows that this membrane is carefully constructed with facing bricks.

Burgh obviously mistrusted the structural efficiency of slender unbonded brick linings and he used his ample budget to achieve higher constructional standards. In the construction of Dr Steevens's Hospital in the 1720s, his low budget forced him to build walls entirely of stone because it was half the cost of brickwork, but his rubble walls were mostly of bonded rather than of composite (tripartite) construction. While in his Library in Trinity College the window openings were crowned by brick arches rather than timber lintels, in the hospital more than half the windows are formed with rough stone arches.

These refinements provided certain advantages. The quality of the masonry construction ensured an adequate stability without the excessive use of floor ties, even in the tall double height space of the Library. The two principal façades of the Library have fenestration patterns with unusually large window to wall ratios (which suited the building's function) but which must have seemed remarkably daring in the second decade of the eighteenth century. The slender wall thicknesses in Dr Steevens's Hospital and in the Library could only have been achieved by carefully constructed masonry.

In the Library, an inspection of the two massive crosswall partitions (dividing the terminal pavilions from the main Library space) revealed the use of solid bonded brickwork formed with high quality facing bricks. The architects and builders who succeeded Burgh in Trinity College must have been impressed by his example, as Regent House and the adjoining buildings enclosing Front Square (1750s) also appear to have bonded brick membranes behind their granite facings.

Only a few years separate the final stages of the erection of Burgh's Library from the rapid construction programme of Pearce's Parliament House, which was already in use by 1732. Pearce's accounts show a considerable use of brickwork as masonry linings in his wall construction, but the thickness of the brick membrane is unknown. His country houses, such as Cashel palace, Bellamont Forest and Summerhill, all made substantial use of brick interior linings. The ruined remnants of the walls of Summerhill display typical country house constructional patterns of (tripartite) composite walls with stone facings and 4½-inch brick linings.

Bricks appear to have been in common use as linings in Dublin, behind the Palladian ashlar of urban mansions such as 85 St Stephen's Green (1730s), Leinster House (1740s), Charlemont House (1759) and the Provost's House (1760s). But (with the exception of Charlemont House) we have no indications of their precise

---

14 TCD, Francis Quinn's accounts, MUN/P2/37/65; P2/44/24.

construction. They were also used in institutions such as St Patrick's Hospital in 1749, and in state buildings in Dublin Castle in the 1750s and 1760s. In St Patrick's Hospital, George Semple placed his reliance on the skill in making cementitious lime mortar and on 4½-inch brick linings. Despite the use of sophisticated English carpentry systems in the floor framing of Charlemont House, the builders had no misgivings about the choice of composite walls and 4½-inch brick linings behind the cut-limestone façade.

The considerable boom in country house construction from the 1730s until the 1750s promoted important refinements in constructional practice, particularly in the works of Pearce, Castle and their followers. The most significant change in construction that accompanied the Palladian movement was in floor framing, in the adoption of long spanning joists in lieu of the traditional combination of beams and joists. Bricks also played a substantial role in the construction of these houses, and in the evolution of the new system of floor framing.

Locally made placebricks were used, not just as lining membranes, but as dressings, vaults and cores for plaster mouldings. Arch Hall (1730s), Kingsfort (1740s) and Ballyhaise (1740s) have extensive brick vaults over the principal rooms at ground-floor level, and the King House in Boyle has brick vaults up to roof level. In Kingsfort, Co. Meath and Ledwithstown, Co. Longford (1740s), specially shaped bricks are used as corbels at ceiling level to form cores for plaster cornices. In some houses, we can find placebricks which are just as carefully made and as well laid as facing bricks. This is so in Ledwithstown, where the use of precise relieving arches in the brick linings is in sharp contrast to the roughness of the rubble facings on the building's exterior.

* * *

In the ruins of Tudenham, Co. Westmeath (1740s), we can observe a sophisticated system for fixing timber members to the masonry walls. This consists of the recession of a brick course (by about an inch) at three different levels around the perimeter of the rooms. These recessions provided slots for continuous rough grounds to which skirtings, chair rails and cornice brackets were simply fixed without cutting into the masonry. This anticipated and controlled the work of both the carpenter and the mason and eliminated ad hoc improvization in the building process.

Bricks, as Maurice Craig has pointed out, were used early on in stone buildings because of their precision in the construction of structures of small dimensions such as chimneys.[15] Their use as dressings to window and door openings was for the same reason. Their other advantage, of course, was their modular flexibility in the interface with timber structures and fixings, particularly floor framing. It was this potential that promoted their use as wall linings.

15 Maurice Craig, *Classic Irish houses of the middle size* (London, 1976), p. 15.

7.7 Charles Fort, Kinsale, Co. Cork, joist pockets of brick within stone walls.

Boate has claimed that brick linings were introduced into seventeenth-century Irish buildings because of their capacity to absorb damp in limestone walls. There may be some factual foundation to this in terms of seventeenth-century practices, but there is enough evidence to show that their continuous use in the eighteenth century was to facilitate floor fixings. This is most evident in buildings where the use of bricks is confined to masonry areas which support timber structures. One example of the use of both stone linings and brick linings occurring in the same building can be seen in the ruins of Garretstown House, Co. Cork (1740s). The house was built with brick-lined walls on two opposite sides of the rooms and stone linings on the other two walls. The advantages of this arrangement are clear. The local stone did not need to support the floor timbers, but the more expensive brick linings supported embedded floor joists at close centres.

Another example can be seen in the ruined pavilions of the bishop's palace at Elphin, Co. Roscommon, which was built between 1747 and 1750. Here the local stone linings support intermittent cross beams at about 9ft centres, but the closely spaced rafters have their ends supported by brick linings. Other examples of the combination of stone and brick linings (supporting floor joists) can be found in the 1740s terraced houses on the North Mall in Cork city and in Stephenstown House, Co. Louth, which dates from the late eighteenth century.

All of these examples are outside the Dublin area, where brickmaking traditions were strong and where the huge demand for bricks for terraced houses ensured constant supplies at competitive prices. Even more frugal examples of the combination of local stone and bricks can be seen in Wardstown House, Co. Donegal (*c*.1740s), in the barrack buildings of Charles Fort in Kinsale (1750s) and Tyrone House, Co. Galway (1770s). In these buildings the linings of local rubble are interrupted only at floor levels, to accommodate three or four courses of brickwork in a continuous band around the building's interior. These courses of brickwork provide a housing for the floor structure (fig. 7.7). A similar arrangement can be seen in mid-eighteenth-century terraced houses in Oliver Plunkett Street in Cork.

The most conclusive evidence, however, of the relationship between brick linings and floor supports must be seen in the hundreds of classical churches built entirely with stone linings, because they required no suspended timber floors. Where floor supports were required, as in the case of the gallery in St Mark's Church in Dublin, a brick partition provided this support. There is also no indication in these stone-lined churches (or in Dr Steevens's Hospital) of the damp conditions described by Boate.

* * *

We must now look at the development of the second building pattern, the use of facing bricks on the façades of eighteenth-century buildings. Placebricks, as we have seen, were used in the interior masonry of buildings in all parts of Ireland; brick 'as a substantial building material', as Maurice Craig points out, was, with a few exceptions, confined to buildings in the vicinity of coastal towns and cities before the nineteenth century.[16] Dublin, like London, is especially identified with brick façades due to their substantial use in the streetscapes of terraced classical houses built throughout the eighteenth century

Bricks were in use in Trinity College Dublin as early as 1637, and in 1640 a contract was signed with the bricklayers James Browne and Robert Pavier to build lodgings for the Provost.[17] This contract probably involved brick façades, as (unlike an earlier contract) no mention of stone masonry is contained in the agreement. In 1672, Richard Mills, a member of the newly founded bricklayers' guild (1670), was engaged on a new building in the College designed by the carpenter John Lucas.[18] It is difficult to know if the building used any brick facings, as Mills contracted for work in both stone and bricks. In the last decade of the seventeenth century (1695–1700), an ambitious building programme was undertaken by the College to build ranges of buildings around a courtyard to provide new residential accommodation. Photographic records of this development show brick-faced buildings with high slate roofs and dormer windows. Part of these buildings survive in a much altered fashion in the College Rubrics (the bricks on the façade of which have been replaced).

We know very little about the materials and constructional methods of the urban houses built by the first leaseholders of the Aungier and Meath estates in the expansion of the city during the 1670s and 1680s. Some light has been thrown on this period by a recent discovery of a surviving four-bay house of the mid-1680s at

---

16 Ibid., p. 15.   **17** TCD, John Tallis's accounts, MUN/P2/1/16; ibid., James Brown and Robert Pavier's accounts, MUN/P2/1/24. The view in Hatfield of Trinity College, c.1592, which may be a proposal rather than a survey, shows brick façades towards the Quadrangle.   **18** TCD, Richard Mills's accounts, MUN/P2/1/27.

7.8 James Malton, 'The Tholsel, Skinners Row, Dublin', watercolour, 1792, detail showing Malton's rendering of the texture of brickwork and pointing, NGI, cat. no. 2185. Reproduced with permission of the National Gallery of Ireland.

21 Aungier Street. This house was built with brick façades (under more recently applied plaster rendering) with a combination of timber and brick structural supports. This method was commonly used in speculative house construction in London, and it may be typical of larger houses built in late seventeenth-century Dublin. A lease for a site in York Street (among the Abercorn papers) stipulated that the lessee must build a slated brick house of two storeys, with a cellar and garret, with walls one-and-a-half bricks thick, within three years of 1677.[19]

Photographic records of some of the gabled houses in the Meath estate in areas such as Poole Street and Braithwaite Street clearly indicate a construction of local limestone rubble with plaster rendering. These houses are among the earliest terraced buildings built on the estate, on foot of leases issued in 1683. Later versions, built at the turn of the century in Weavers' Square, Chamber Street and the adjoining area, have brick façades, string courses of brickwork and vestigial references to classical motifs in their doorcases. The ultimate development of these weavers' houses, built in the early decades of the eighteenth century, in streets such as Ward's Hill and Sweeney's Lane, had curvilinear gables with brick pediments. This brick house type spread rapidly from the industrial precincts of the Liberties into developing housing

---

[19] PRONI, Abercorn papers, Lease from Reading to Neive, D623/B/6/5.

7.9 Beaulieu, Co. Louth, 1720s, brick detail. Courtesy of the Irish Architectural Archive.

estates in all areas of the city, and it became a model for early uniform housing in Dublin, Cork and Limerick.

There was a conspicuous interest in bricks and classical ornamentation in the design of institutional buildings and large urban mansions from the closing decades of the seventeenth century in Dublin. William Robinson introduced a formula of brick façades built over a base of local limestone arcades into the rebuilding of Dublin Castle in the 1680s, and in 1703 he designed a brick library to house Archbishop Marsh's collection of valuable books. Marsh's Library may be the first instance of the use in Dublin of gauged arches with rubbed brick voussoirs. Richard Mills is linked with the building of the brick façades of the Tailors' Hall in 1704 and of Molyneux House in 1706. Longford House in Mary Street and the Ward mansion on Ward's Hill, both dating from the early 1700s, had brick façades and stone dressings. Burgh continued Robinson's use of bricks over stone arches in his extensions to the upper yard at Dublin Castle in 1712.

William Robinson's name is linked with the building of Platten House, Co. Meath, at the turn of the century (1698) and it used facing bricks of unknown origin. An early use of Dutch facing bricks can be seen on the Uniacke House in Youghal, built, according to local tradition, by a Dutchman called 'Leuventhen' in 1706. Palace

Anne, built at Ballineen, Co. Cork, in 1714, has the rare distinction of having brick facings on walls that are lined with local rubble, which is indicative of the expense of imported facing bricks and their scarcity in inland areas. Beaulieu, Co. Louth, which seems to have assumed its present appearance in 1722, has rendered walls, but it has a unique use of rubbed brick reveals at door and window openings, a moulded brick entablature and moulded brick cills (fig. 7.9). Rubbed bricks were uncommon in Ireland, but moulded bricks were also used on the house in the bailey at Askeaton Castle (which was rendered externally) and on Jigginstown.

Brick facings and gauged brick arches are also a feature of the Southwell Charity in Downpatrick, which carries a date stone of 1733. This building is an example of the rare use of moulded voussoirs to form undulating arches at window soffits, a feature, as Maurice Craig points out, characteristic of the Thames Valley and the east of England.[20] Another example of undulating arches can be found in the early eighteenth-century Yeomanstown House in Co. Kildare, but its arches and brick façade are now covered by a coat of plaster. Haystown House near Rush, Co. Dublin, also of this early brick building period, has been covered by applied plaster rendering. An unusual use of brick facings can be seen in the pilasters and rustications of the pavilion adjoining Clonmannon House, Co. Kildare. The modelling of the rustication recalls the use of brick in Kent's Holkham Hall in the mid-1730s. One of the last examples of this early generation of brick façades is John Rothery's use of it on the north front of Mount Ievers Court in the early 1730s. The pale pink bricks used by Rothery are reputed to have been imported as ballast from Holland, in exchange for a cargo of rapeseed.

The return of the viceregal court to Dublin in the 1660s, and the increase in population in the decades that followed, ensured a steady market for new buildings. Builders in a search of models to replace cage-houses and traditional rubble stone houses turned to the fashionable faubourgs of London (such as Covent Garden, Bloomsbury and Soho) for inspiration. The prevailing building material used in most of these areas was brickwork.

Many of the influential people involved in building early classical buildings arrived in Ireland (like Robinson and Mills) in the great wave of immigrants who settled there between 1670 and the 1700s. The use of brick façades, tuck pointing, gauged brickwork and undulating arches were, like timber structures, timber bracketed eaves, cornices, timber pedimented doorcases and internal timber cornices, part of an imported tradition that, with time, became diluted and mutated. By the 1730s many of these features had disappeared, or, like floor and roof structures, become rationalized in terms of local traditions and regional preferences.

The second generation of classical buildings with brick façades commenced just before the 1730s in the designs of Edward Lovett Pearce and the introduction of Palladian architecture to Ireland. The two most important examples of this use are

---

20 Craig, *Classic Irish houses*, p. 16.

the country mansions of Bellamont Forest at Cootehill, Co. Cavan, and Cashel Palace, Co. Tipperary. These houses owe nothing to the eclectic pattern of the earlier brick architecture. They are highly focused expressions of stylistic ideals that were also being explored during this period by the foremost architects in England.

Bellamont and Cashel are particularly interesting in the context of their geographic locations, which were inaccessible by water carriage from any of the Irish seaports. The question that arises is whether Pearce was involved in the extravagance of transporting imported bricks from the coast (as happened at Jigginstown), or whether the bricks were manufactured to unusually rigorous standards adjacent to the building sites. This is easily answered in the case of the front façade of Cashel. Building accounts of the construction record the cost of placebricks at 9s. per 1,000 and stock (facing) bricks at £1 per 1,000.[21] The presentation of these accounts suggests that both brick types were made locally, but aside from this, the figure of £1 per 1,000 could not reasonably have paid for the importation of facing bricks and their transportation from the coast.

The cost of local placebricks in Dublin was about 13s. per 1,000 over the first half of the century, but we have no comparative information on the cost of facing bricks. By the 1760s, records of brick prices in Dublin show costs of placebricks at 18s. to £1 per 1,000, and imported stock bricks at £1 16s. 0d. per 1,000.[22] The facing bricks at Cashel were obviously made locally. No accounts survive of the building of Bellamont Forest. However, examination of both the exterior facings and the linings at basement level is revealing. The basement walls are entirely lined and faced with bricks that match the quality of those on the main elevations. Bricks at basement level in Irish houses are most unusual, particularly in houses (such as Bellamont and Cashel) that have stone floors (on vaults) at ground-floor level. Country houses and urban terraced houses in Dublin were commonly built with the cheaper alternative of plastered rubble walls up to their ground-floor plinths. The use of bricks, and particularly bricks of such quality, in the basement at Bellamont was profligate by any standards in eighteenth-century Ireland. This suggests the joint ownership of the building and the brick production. The bricks were undoubtedly made by the Earl of Bellamont on his own lands, but the intervention in the process to ensure the quality required must have been organized by his kinsman and architect, Edward Lovett Pearce.

Pearce's deep interest in bricks as a locally produced building component is manifest in his introduction of a parliamentary act to regulate their manufacture in Ireland in 1729.[23] The act stressed the need for bricks of adequate strength that would reduce dependence on the purchase of bricks from Holland. It also attempted to control the dimensions of bricks by stipulating that a brick should not be less than 9½ inches long, 4½ inches wide and 2¼ inches deep. Brick facings after Pearce's death

---

21 PRONI, letter from Hearn to the Archbishop of Cashel, D562/458.   22 TCD, Richard Plummer's accounts, MUN/P2/144/10.   23 3 Geo. II, cap. 14.

in 1731 were not popular and (apart from urban houses) were mostly confined to Palladian houses. Woodlands, near Santry, Co. Dublin (of the early 1730s), a design which recalls earlier seventeenth-century English models in elevational expression, has been attributed to Pearce's own hand. Francis Bindon built brick façades at Clermont House, Co. Wicklow in 1730 and at Newhall, Co. Clare in 1751. Castle faced Dollardstown House, Co. Meath with bricks in 1735, and Ballyhaise, Co. Cavan in the 1740s. Brick façades were also used on two late Palladian houses, Davis Ducart's Kilshannig, Co. Cork, and Newberry, Co. Kildare, both in the 1760s.

CHAPTER EIGHT

Stone: its acquisition and use

Although brick dressings and brick wall linings were used in the construction of most of the important eighteenth-century country houses and institutional buildings in Ireland, the use of the traditional medieval formula of all-stone construction prevailed in some building types. The low cost and easy availability of local stone probably explains its use in provincial town houses, mills, rural cottages, stables and garden walls, but it was also used extensively in constructing churches in many parts of Ireland and in Dublin hospitals.

The use of stone interior linings in an early classical building such as the Main Guard in Clonmel (1670s) probably owed more to a scarcity of bricks and bricklayers in provincial towns during the latter part of the seventeenth century, rather than to considerations of cost. Its use in the walls of the hall and chapel of the Royal Hospital at Kilmainham is surprising, as brickwork was extensively used elsewhere in this building for both wall linings and partitions. Dr Steevens's Hospital, built in the 1720s under the direction of Thomas Burgh, is entirely constructed of Dublin calp with the exception of its chimneys and a partition supporting a subsidiary staircase. Burgh's choice of wall construction was probably dictated by economic rather than technical constraints. The hospital records make many references to its charitable status and its constant need for funds: Burgh provided his services free of charge.[1] Some walling stone was provided from a quarry owned by the surgeon general Thomas Proby, who was a member of the hospital's board of governors. Burgh's choice of rough stone interior linings and dressings (in lieu of the brickwork used on the Trinity College Library) had certain disadvantages, and these can be seen in the fabric of the hospital. One problem arising from imprecision in the formation of window reveals – due to uneven rubble dressings – had a disturbing effect on vistas down the long continuous galleries. Another was the difficulty in maintaining precise floor levels from one part of the building to another due to the inflexibility of the roughly coursed masonry.

Obviously these disadvantages were acceptable in underfunded charitable institutions of this type, as the same constructional system can be found in older parts of Mercer's Hospital, built in the 1740s, and in the surviving eighteenth- and nineteenth-century buildings on the site of the former city workhouse in James's Street.[2] They were not acceptable to Richard Castle, however, or to George Semple,

[1] T. Percy Kirkpatrick, *The history of Dr Steevens' Hospital* (Dublin, 1924), p. 29. [2] Information from James O'Beirne, B.Arch., FRIAI.

8.1 Thomas Roberts, 'Lucan House and Demesne with Figures Quarrying Stone, County Dublin', *c.*1773–5, NGI, cat. no. 4463. Reproduced with permission of the National Gallery of Ireland.

whose proposal in 1749 for St Patrick's Hospital specifies the use of bricks for dressings and wall linings.[3]

The most consistent use of the all-stone masonry system can be found in the construction of eighteenth-century Irish churches. In Dublin, early churches such as St Mary's, St Matthew's Irishtown, St Nicholas, St Luke's, St Werburgh's and St Anne's (all early eighteenth century) were substantially built of Dublin calpstone, although St Matthew's was built over a crypt with vaults of brickwork. Later churches such as St Mark's, built in the 1740s, and St Catherine's, built in 1769, were also built largely in calp, although the partition forming the entrance porch (supporting the gallery) in St Mark's was built with bricks. One early Dublin church appears to have ignored this common practice: recent rebuilding of the Presbyterian church (1720s) in Eustace Street has revealed structural walls of carefully bonded brickwork. The use of stone to form interiors and window reveals of classical churches in provincial centres also appears to be common. Christchurch and St Anne's (both 1720s) in Cork city used a combination of sandstone and limestone rubble taken from local quarries. Richard Castle's cathedral in Sligo, built in the early 1730s, used local limestone. The extensions to Raphoe cathedral in 1739 and the rebuilding of Elphin cathedral in 1758 were carried out with local rubble. John Roberts's (Church of Ireland) cathedral in Waterford and Thomas Cooley's church in Kells (both second half of the eighteenth century) were built in limestone.

If we compare the rubble masonry of eighteenth-century buildings with walls in seventeenth-century fortified houses and earlier medieval buildings, we find no significant variation in building methods. Masons working on classical buildings continued to use tripartite wall construction (see chapter 6), although walls became considerably less massive with the advent of the eighteenth century. Wall widths, as Maurice Craig has pointed out, continued to decrease in cross section as time passed. The seventeenth-century walls of the hall in the Royal Hospital, for instance, are between 56 and 58 inches thick, which made them as massive as the masonry of many earlier castles. Burgh also used massive walls of about 45 inches width in 1715 in the construction of St Werburgh's Church, but the heaviest walls he used in Dr Steevens's Hospital (in piers of the chapel) were about 36 inches wide, and most of the structural walls elsewhere in the building did not exceed widths of 26 inches.

The formation of window openings in eighteenth-century rubble walling also followed medieval practice. Masonry forming the outer face of the wall above the openings was supported by flat or low segmental arches formed with roughly cut voussoirs. These arches were usually backed by timber lintels supporting the inner lining and core of the wall. In work of higher quality, arches were also used to support the inner linings and core of the walls instead of lintels. Although we can find good examples of carefully coursed and semi-squared rubble masonry in eighteenth-century buildings such as St Mark's Church in Dublin, most masons (like their

---

3 St Patrick's Hospital, George Semple, 'A further description of the foregoing designs ...', p. 3 (xerox copy in IAA, accession no. 2008/44).

medieval predecessors) relied on random-sized stones and coursing for the construction of structural walls. Walling stones were roughly shaped with the mason's hammer, but corner stones were usually dressed with the chisel to ensure precise alignment at external wall junctions. Stone spawls, left over from the rough shaping of the walling rubble, and smaller stones were used to form the filling in the mortared core of tripartite walls.

Tripartite walls had been in common use in Europe since the construction of Imperial Rome, and there is evidence to suggest that their use in Ireland predated the Norman conquest. Richard Brash, a Victorian architect writing in 1874, records the use of 'compound walls, of masonry and concrete' in early Christian buildings such as Ardmore church, Co. Waterford, and the Gallarus Oratory, Co. Kerry:

> The facing stones were dressed, and laid both bed and joints in tolerably fine mortar; a grout was then prepared of hot lime, sand, and gravel, and the heart of the wall was filled with it; stones of various sizes were then packed into the grouting.[4]

The eighteenth-century architect and master builder George Semple was also conscious of the long traditions associated with the use of tripartite walls in Ireland. His description of their construction shows his considerable respect for sound traditional practices:

> My Father (who was a Workman about the Year 1675) often told me, and my own repeated Observations convince me, that the Methods Masons practiced in former Times, in building Churches, Abbeys, Castles or other sumptuous Edifices, in this Country, was to this effect. After they laid the out-side Courses with large Stones, laid on the flat in swimming Beds of Mortar, they hearted their Walls with their Spawls and smallest Stones, and as they laid them in, they poured in plenty of boiling Grout, or hot Lime-liquid among them, so as to incorporate them together, as if it were with melted Lead, whereby the heat of it exhausted the Moisture of the out-side Mortar, and united most firmly both it and the Stones, and filled every Pore (which as the Masons term it) set, that is, grew hard immediately, and this Method was taught to our antient masters, by the *Romish Clergy*, that came to plant *Christianity* in these countries, and I affirm that in many of such old Buildings, I have seen the Mortar, as it were, run together and harder to break than the Stones were.[5]

Semple was unique among contemporary architectural writers in England and Ireland in his descriptions of technical processes and his comments on the

---

[4] Richard Brash, 'Notes on the ancient ecclesiastical architecture of Ireland', *Irish Builder* (15 Jan. 1874), 18.
[5] George Semple, *A treatise on the art of building in water* (Dublin, 1776), p. 79.

performance of building materials. Towards the end of his career, in 1776, he published *A treatise on building in water*, which described the innovative methods he used in the reconstruction of Essex Bridge in 1753–5. Like many master builders of his generation, he had closely studied the works of Vitruvius, Alberti and Palladio, and curiosity about Palladio's references to coffer-dams encouraged him to procure a copy of Bernard De Belidor's *Architecture hydraulique*. Belidor's descriptions of the technologies used by the École des Ponts et Chaussées in Paris enabled Semple to design and construct coffer-dams as foundations for Essex Bridge. The treatise also allowed him opportunities to expand on his experiences in the handling of timber and masonry materials. His comments provide us with valuable insight into the theoretic and practical problems that confronted eighteenth-century builders.

In his treatise, and in a written proposal addressed to the governors of St Patrick's Hospital (which he built in 1749/50), Semple places considerable emphasis on preferred methods of making mortar.[6] Mortar, as he suggests, played a considerable part in the structural characteristics of masonry walls. Composed of sand, lime and water, its strength and efficiency depended mostly on the quality of the lime used, and how it was mixed with the other ingredients before its use in wall construction. Lime was produced by burning limestone at high temperatures (of over 850°F) in limekilns. This process produced roachlime which was mixed with water to form a cementitious putty called slack (or slacked) lime. Sand, obtained from sandpits, rivers or the seashore, was added to make mortar. In some countries ground seashells or brick dust were mixed with the sand. Imported tarras, a volcanic stone from the banks of the Rhine, in Germany, was sometimes used by English and Irish builders (such as Wren in England and Coltsman in Cork) to make hydraulic mortar for use in water works such as cisterns and bridges.[7] Pozzolan, a volcanic ash used extensively in Italy, had similar properties.

Limestone was obtainable in every county in Ireland except Wicklow, but the quality of lime depended largely on the chemical properties of different limestones. In Italy, classical tradition exemplified in the writings of Vitruvius and Palladio prescribed the use of the whitest and hardest stones (such as marble) for making strong lime. Isaac Ware, however, preferred to use 'bluish or reddish' limestones for mortar mixing.[8] Semple claimed that the best lime was obtained from the hardest, the heaviest and closest-grained stones. His contemporary, the naturalist Dr John Rutty, preferred lime made from Dublin calp to that made from London chalk, but he particularly recommended limestone from Sutton, which makes a strong cement 'like Terras', and Carlow limestone, 'one of the best … in the Kingdom: and I am Informed that the *Dutch* are so well acquainted with the excellency of our *Irish* lime, as to have imported it hence'.[9] Semple expressed a view that the quality of lime

---

6 Semple, 'A further description of the foregoing designs …'.   **7** *Wren Soc. Vols*, 14, p. 112; 15, pp 101, 128; 19, p. 106; Richard Caulfield (ed.), *The council book of the corporation of the city of Cork* (Guildford, 1876), p. 364.   **8** Isaac Ware, *A complete body of architecture* (London, 1756), p. 79.   **9** John Rutty, *An essay towards a natural history of the county of Dublin*, II (Dublin, 1772), pp 92, 98–9.

mortar as a cement was directly influenced by the mixing methods employed by contemporary artisans. In his proposals for the building of St Patrick's Hospital in 1749 and for new public record offices in 1758 he provides a precise description of his preferred mixing process. For St Patrick's he writes:

> It is not intended that the morter, which is to be made use of in this Building, Should be made in the usual way; particularly for the out side walls. But the principal methods, which I intend to be taken, are Chiefly, To bring the lime in roach from the Kiln to the Work: To Slack but a small quantitie of it at a time, and to cover & mix that with sand directly, ready for the riddle (Whilst the spirit of the lime is hot & quick). But not to be in a hurry to riddle it, But to give it time to cool & infuse its strength among the sand. That the proportion of sand to lime (I mean for instance such sand as is generaly got at Island Bridge) Be not richer than four of Sand to one of roach lime (That is about 2 to 1 of slack) That after it is riddled & turn'd up, That it be allow'd as much time to soak as conveniently the Work will admit of. That when the Workmen are making use of it that the Labourers shall only cut down a small bed of it at a time. And that Two of them – the one opposite to the other [–] must Labour each of them small beds, three or four times over with the beaters & then turn it by for the Hodd men etc And above all, that there be as little Water made use of in tempering it as possible. But to apply very hard Labour to supply the usual place of water.[10]

Semple's formula for mortar lays emphasis on the laborious process of turning and beating the matrix in a semi-dry condition to ensure the compaction of the materials. The addition of water would have made this process less laborious, but Semple had obviously learned from experiment and experience that water (in excess of an amount needed to hydrate the lime) weakened the mortar. His insistence on river sand rather than sand from a sandpit was to ensure the absence of clay and organic matter that would have interfered with the chemistry of the matrix. Sea sand was also used in mortar mixes in Semple's time, but its saline content – as Dr Rutty pointed out – was a serious disadvantage.[11] This well-defined formula for mixing mortar, and the careful choice of local limestones with proven performance records, were designed to produce the strong cements seen by Semple as good building practice. However, his commission to replace Essex Bridge in 1752 and his work on Ormond Bridge promoted his interest in hydraulic mortars and encouraged him to investigate their special properties. He became fascinated with what he described as the 'the petrifying Qualities of Lime-stone, Lime or Lime-water' and the inherent capacity of some limes to make mortars as hard as stone, even under water.[12] His

---

[10] Semple, 'A further description of the foregoing designs …', pp 5–6. [11] Rutty, *Towards a natural history of the county of Dublin*, p. 22. [12] Semple, *A treatise on the art of building in water*, pp 75, 81.

findings anticipated the considerable development of strong, fast-setting mortars (such as Roman cement), which influenced building practices towards the end of the eighteenth century.

The hardening (or carbonation) of mortars made from many limestone strata was conditioned by the exposure of the mortar to the air for a considerable period and the evaporation of its water content to the atmosphere. An initial hardening happened rapidly, through the absorption of water into the adjoining stonework, but the carbonation process continued for many years before the mortar could develop its full strength. Pockets of mortar, isolated from the air in the middle of the wall, might remain soft indefinitely. The carbonation of lime mortar could result in a contraction of its volume, shrinkage and unequal settlement of the masonry around window opes. Thomas Humphreys, a Dublin measurer writing about Belfast in 1813, records another consequence of slow-setting mortars:

> I will therefore beg to arrest the attention of the gentlemen and merchant [sic] of Belfast, while I observe to them, that their taste in architecture needs a little refinement, particularly, they ought to endeavour to remove that odious appearance which almost all their new buildings, of whatever denomination, have, by being for years after they are built, propped by large beams at every angle, until the lime and brick gets sufficient time to cement.[13]

Because of the massive dimensions of seventeenth- and early eighteenth-century masonry walls, the limitations of lime mortar as cements may not have unduly influenced building patterns, but as wall thicknesses become progressively thinner, problems of structural stability must have been noticeable. One consequence of these problems was the extensive use of bond timbers as load spreaders and wall ties, especially in the slender masonry of urban terraced houses.

Semple, of course, had already faced more difficult problems as a bridge builder in 1753.[14] The foundations of the piers in his design for the new Essex Bridge were to be built 4½ft under low-water level and the carbonation of common mortar at this level was questionable. However, his early preparations for the task had given him considerable confidence. He had already (in 1752) visited England and discussed his bridge design with Charles Labelye, who had constructed the recently built Westminster Bridge. He had examined the construction works at Ramsgate Harbour and sought the advice of its engineers. He had purchased chain-pumps, several kinds of tarras (with similar properties to pozzolan) and (probably on the advice given him) lime from Leigh near Warrington, which he was told could set under water just as well as tarras. Semple's treatise has left us with a remarkable description of the construction of the bridge and its coffer-dams, but he provides no information on his

---

13 Thomas Humphreys, *The Irish builder's guide* (Dublin, 1813), p. 69.   14 Much of the information in this paragraph and the next comes from Semple, *A treatise on the art of building in water*, pp 28–9, 55, 81.

use of local lime mortar or the performance of the imported English lime and tarras. However, his comments on his discovery of old (petrified) mortar at the base of the previous Essex Bridge, and in the foundations of the nearby Ormond Bridge, leaves us with an optimistic view of the hydraulic properties of local limes. He confirms this view with unequivocal statements such as 'I believe, no Lime-stone whatever can have more excellent Qualities than such as we have in, perhaps, every county in this Kingdom' and 'our Lime-stone will make exceedingly good Tarrass for Water-works'.

Semple was fairly safe in his assertions about Dublin calp, but he was wrong about many other Irish limestones. By the time he published his treatise in 1776, new discoveries about the production of hydraulic limes were beginning to influence English building practices. John Smeaton's investigations into English limestones, before his construction of the Eddystone Lighthouse in the 1760s, had established the chemical properties of fast-setting mortars that developed hardness and cohesive strength without exposure to the atmosphere. Smeaton's experiments proved that pure high-calcium limestones (such as white marble or Portland stone) were no better than London chalk for the production of mortar. He found the qualities he required in impure limestones such as the Dolomite and Blue Lias strata and particularly in the Aberthaw limestones, which he found near Glamorgan, in Wales. These stones contained impurities such as clay, magnesium and alumina, which, when calcined at high temperatures with calcium, produced a cement with similar properties to tarrras or pozzolan.

There are no Blue Lias strata in Ireland, and Dolomite formations are limited to a few areas in Munster and Leinster, but the impure argillaceous Dublin limestone (known locally as calp) had the necessary requirements for making hydraulic lime. Wilkinson uses the word calp to describe beds of impure limestone in Dublin, Meath, Longford, Donegal and Sligo, and these limestones had hydraulic qualities.[15] But while hydraulic limes could be found in Ireland, they were not widespread. The pure crystalline limestone of Cork and the chalk used in Antrim probably made very weak mortars. This is confirmed by Thomas Humphreys's criticism of the performance of mortars in Belfast and the use of imported tarras by the stonecutter John Coltsman in 1714 for the construction of both the North Main Street and South Main Street bridges in the city of Cork.[16]

* * *

However, the main uses of limestone were as rubble walling by masons, and as facings and entablatures by stonecutters. Facing stone was chosen mostly from selected Irish limestone, sandstone and granite quarries, and in some cases it was imported from quarries in England and Scotland. Walling stone (for loadbearing structure) was usually taken from the nearest and most economical source. We will now examine the

---

[15] George Wilkinson, *Practical geology and ancient architecture of Ireland* (London, 1845), pp 37, 43.
[16] Richard Caulfield (ed.), *The council book of the corporation of the city of Cork* (Guildford, 1876), p. 364.

distribution and use of masonry materials in walls made entirely of stone and of combined stone and brickwork.

Walling stone was obtained for urban buildings from established quarries in cities such as Cork, Limerick and Dublin, but stone used in the walls of country houses was usually excavated by building workers on the building owner's estate or on adjacent land. Sedimentary stones such as shales, sandstones and limestones were commonly used for rubble walls in most parts of Ireland, but walls of harder igneous stones, such as granite, can be encountered in counties Wicklow, Down and Carlow. Basalt was extensively used for rubble walls in Co. Antrim.

Limestone in Ireland is widely distributed: it underlies most of the central plain in a broad band extending westwards from Dublin Bay to Galway, northwards as far as Bundoran and Armagh, and southwards to Kilkenny and the borders of Cork and Tipperary. It also occurs in west Clare, in the eastern and northern part of Kerry and in a narrow seam running westwards from Midleton to Cork city and southwards to the sea coast at Little Island.

Sandstone formations occur principally along the coastal zones in the eastern and southern parts of Ireland, in many parts of Ulster (such as Donegal, Londonderry, Fermanagh, Monaghan, Antrim and Down) and interspersed with limestone strata in Leitrim, Roscommon, Offaly, east Clare, south Kilkenny and Tipperary. Granite and basalt are not as widely distributed as sedimentary stones. Granite can be found in south county Dublin, on the elevated heights of the Mourne and Wicklow mountains, in Co. Carlow, on the south coast of Co. Galway and the western coast of Donegal. Basalt underlies most of Co. Antrim and parts of Co. Londonderry.

Walling stone was usually procured from the nearest available source, but preferences were for stones that could be quarried and formed into masonry courses without the need for expensive tooling. Calp, the muddy limestone underlying the Dublin area, was an ideal walling stone in this respect. Formed in shallow beds of about 3 to 12 inches in thickness, it could be easily removed from quarries in orthogonal blocks which could be broken into walling stones with the mason's hammer (fig. 8.1). Sandstones also offered advantages as walling materials. They were softer than limestones, easily split into tabular building blocks and their cleavage joints – perpendicular to their beds – allowed them to be removed easily and economically from the quarry face. Fissile rocks such as shales, which were interspersed among sandstones and the Dublin calp formations, were sometimes used as walling stones, although they were less durable than sandstone or limestone.

Granite was used extensively as a facing stone and entablatures in Leinster and parts of Co. Down, but its use as a structural material was limited because of its hardness and unyielding nature. Basalt, an even harder and more cohesive stone than granite, was popular with masons in counties Antrim and Londonderry because (like sandstone) it had cleavage joints that allowed it to be easily removed in convenient sizes from the quarry and used immediately as a masonry material. The choice of stone for facings, dressings and moulded ornaments was influenced by practical

8.2 George Wilkinson, 'Black marble quarry, Co. Galway …', G. Wilkinson, *Practical geology and ancient architecture of Ireland* (London, 1845), p. 41.

considerations such as cost, workability and performance, and, in many cases, by the stylistic preferences of prevailing architectural fashions. Facing stone was usually obtained from selected quarries, and it was frequently transported over considerable distances from quarry to building site. Most Irish sandstones were softer than local limestones and easier to use as stone facings, but their use on moulded entablatures was limited because of their poor weathering qualities and lack of durability. Their use as dressings and carved mouldings was probably more extensive in the north of Ireland than elsewhere, although local sandstones were commonly used as plain ashlar facings in southern counties such as Wexford, Tipperary, Cork and parts of Kilkenny.

Florence Court, Co. Fermanagh, has cornices, quoins, window cases, doorcases and string courses of a brown sandstone quarried near Glenfarne, Co. Leitrim.[17] Michael Priestley's courthouse at Lifford and houses such as Portsalon and Wardstown, Co. Donegal, are all dressed with a cream coloured sandstone of the type found at Mountcharles. On the façades of the Earl Bishop of Derry's Downhill in the 1780s, Michael Shanahan used sandstone from both the Dungiven quarries in Co.

[17] Information from Kenneth James, Geology Dept., Ulster Museum.

8.3 St Anne's Church, Shandon, Cork, 1726. Photograph by Brendan O'Connell.

Londonderry and the Ballyvoy quarries in Ballycastle.[18] Henry Aaron Baker may have used Ballyvoy stone to build the Bishop's Gate in Derry city in 1790. The pale brown sandstone used by Shanahan for the ashlar and colonnaded portico of the Earl Bishop's later house at Ballyscullion, Co. Londonderry, was quarried locally in the mountains nearby.[19]

Although local sandstones were used as facings and entablatures on buildings such as Damer House (1730s) at Roscrea and Marlfield (1770s) near Clonmel, there is a persistent pattern of the use of limestone dressings with sandstone ashlar or rubble walling in certain parts of Ireland. The Main Guard in Clonmel has yellow sandstone (plain ashlar) wall facings combined with limestone engaged columns, cornice and window cases. St Anne's Church in Cork city (fig. 8.3) and the clock tower in Youghal (1771) are good examples of the use of white Cork limestone used as dressings on buildings faced with the local purple-red sandstone. Woodstock (1740s) and Mount Juliet, Co. Kilkenny (1760s), are both built with local sandstone

18 Peter Rankin, *Irish building ventures of the Earl Bishop of Derry* (Belfast, 1972), p. 22.   19 Ibid., p. 55.

8.4 Kilshannig, Co. Cork, 1760s, detail of entrance front. Photograph courtesy of the Irish Georgian Society.

rubble and dressed with Kilkenny limestone. Roundwood House, Co. Laois (1750s), has a similar combination of sandstone walls with limestone quoins, cornices and dressings.

These examples express the most rational and appropriate use for both materials. Sandstone, which could be split and easily worked into orthogonal forms, made an ideal ashlar and walling material. The more durable limestone, which could be carved into precise mouldings, was appropriate for dressings and decorative entablatures. Of course, most of the buildings we have noted are either situated in areas where deposits of both stones were located (such as Co. Cork) or built near the banks of a navigable river (such as the Nore in Co. Kilkenny), which made transportation of limestone into sandstone areas economical. The absence of an easily transportable limestone in most of Ulster forced a reliance on local sandstone dressings or the importation of stone from Scotland and England. Another good example of the rational use of different masonry materials can be seen in the city of Armagh. The dense light-grey local limestone, quarried (according to Wilkinson) near the city boundary, made a superb and durable facing stone, but its hardness made it difficult to work and limited its use as a structural material.[20] The walling stone used locally was a pink (mostly sandstone)

20 Wilkinson, *Practical geology*, p. 315.

conglomerate quarried in the adjacent townland of Dromargh.[21] Combinations of both stones can be seen in George Ensor's infirmary (1760s), in the Gaol (built by Cooley, Johnston and Murray between the 1780s and the 1850s), and in eighteenth-century houses in English Street and Castle Street.

Some eighteenth-century buildings have eccentric and unusual combinations of sandstone and limestone. Davis Ducart's Kilshannig, Co. Cork (1760s), is mostly built of (local) purple-red sandstone with Cork limestone cornices, quoins and windowcases other than the brick front façade. However, the three-bay frontispiece framing the main entrance is constructed with a harder and more durable brown sandstone, which was not of local origin (fig. 8.4). Its Doric entablature, piers, modillion cornice, triglyphs and guttae are precisely carved in this stone, but for some reason, and possibly because of their complexity, the metopes are carved in limestone. Richard Morrison's courthouse in Clonmel (1799) has an ashlar facing and a Corinthian entablature with engaged columns constructed of local yellow sandstone. The capitals, however, strike a discordant note, as they are carved in a grey carboniferous limestone. Is it possible that Morrison or his masons opted for this practical but incongruous choice, or were these capitals a later replacement, after the originals (like Morrison's sandstone capitals at Ballyfin) had weathered badly over a period?

Although granite was not commonly used as a walling material in the Dublin area, its potential as a cut-stone facing was clearly recognized by eighteenth-century builders, and by the 1740s it had replaced Dublin calp as the principal local stone used for ashlar and decorative facings. Known to masons and stonecutters as mountain stone, it was obtained mostly from quarries in the Dublin and Wicklow foothills, and it was used extensively for public buildings in the city and for country houses in the counties of Wicklow and Carlow.

Early eighteenth-century uses of granite in Dublin can be seen in the doorcase of St Matthew's Church (1703) at Irishtown (fig. 8.5) and in the gates of St Sepulchre's, which must have been built about the same period. Its employment on public and institutional buildings became fashionable a few decades later after Pearce picked it for plain and rusticated ashlar on the new Parliament House in 1728. Its successful use as ashlar there, in combination with dressings and entablatures of Portland limestone, established an important pattern that was repeated in many of the city's most ambitious building contracts such as the Rotunda Hospital, the mid-eighteenth-century buildings of Trinity College, the Blue Coat School, the Custom House and the Four Courts. Even the softest granites were coarser in grain and more difficult to cut than sandstone and most limestones, and their rational use was in dressings with plain surfaces and simple mouldings. This is exemplified on Dublin's private houses too, such as Castle's design for the eastern (and more economic) façade of Leinster House (1740s), which is simpler and more austere than the handling of the

---

21 Philip Doughty, 'The stones of Armagh' in *The buildings of Armagh*, prepared by Robert McKinstry, Richard Oram, Roger Weatherup and Primrose Wilson (Belfast, 1992), p. 28.

8.5 St Matthew's Church, Ringsend, Dublin, 1704, detail of front.

Ardbraccan limestone on the western façade. Castle probably used granite more adventurously than most eighteenth-century designers in buildings such as Powerscourt (1730s) and Russborough (1740s), both in Co. Wicklow. These grand palazzi are completely faced in local granites, Powerscourt in a silvery grey stone quarried at Glencree, and Russborough in the brown-bed granite from Golden Hill at Blessington. Powerscourt's linked composition of different building units and dramatic massing provided the architect with an opportunity to use the inherent qualities of this robust material that is missing in the flat and static elevations of Leinster House.

Limestone was the predominant stone used for cut-stone facings and dressings in most midland counties and in many of the larger urban centres such as Dublin, Cork, Limerick, Waterford, Galway, Kilkenny and Drogheda. Most midland and coastal limestones were mid-grey in colour, but darker (almost black) stones and blue-grey stones were not uncommon. A pale brownish-grey stone was available from Ardbraccan, Co. Meath. The quarries at Armagh produced a beautiful hard light-grey limestone, but it was seldom used elsewhere because of the costs of transportation. In county Cork, an almost white crystalline limestone was quarried in the city itself, and light-grey variations of this stone could be found in Midleton and elsewhere in the county.

The grey native limestones were not so easily worked, nor as fashionable as the imported limestones from the south of England, but they were used successfully as facings and entablatures on a great number of country houses such as Castletown, Co. Kildare (1720s), Tudenham, Co. Westmeath (1740s) and Tyrone House, Co. Galway (1770s); they were also used on important urban buildings in provincial centres such as Cashel Palace in the 1720s, the garden front of Limerick Custom House in the 1760s and the cathedral at Waterford in the 1780s. They were used in Dublin for doorcases (such as those on 86 St Stephen's Green and on Ely House) but apart from Leinster House and the Provost's House they were less common than Portland as ashlar facings or as entablatures on public buildings.

Although a high quality grey limestone from the Sheephouse quarry near Drogheda could be economically brought by sea to Dublin, there appears to have been a preference in the capital for the pale grey-brown limestone from Ardbraccan, Co. Meath, which was more expensive to transport and harder to work than the stone from Drogheda. The first important use of this stone was on country houses such as Summerhill, Co. Meath in the 1720s and Carton, Co. Kildare in the 1730s; Castle's choice of it for the main façade of Leinster House introduced it to Dublin in the 1740s. It was obviously seen as a more attractive substitute for imported limestone than granite or grey common limestone, as it was chosen by Simon Vierpyl to face Chambers's Charlemont House in the 1760s. It was also used for the front of the Provost's House, one of the few mid-eighteenth-century buildings in Trinity College built without Portland stone dressings. Of course, Dublin's own local limestone, the dark grey calp (known among the trades as blackstone), was used extensively up to the 1730s on the façades of important city buildings. Robinson used it on the Royal Hospital and on St Mary's Church, and Burgh used it on the arcades of the College Library and on Dr Steevens's Hospital. However, apart from its colour, which was undoubtedly unfashionable after the advent of Palladian classicism, its hard unyielding density made it difficult to carve, and stone of a quality suitable for facings was only available from a few sources such as the quarries at Palmerstown and Leixlip. Cost was another disadvantage. Although walling stone could be produced inexpensively from the city quarries, the labour involved in cutting and dressing the local calp for facings was expensive. The costs of plain blackstone ashlar used on building the Parliament House from 1728 to 1731 was 12 pence per superficial foot. This was poor value in comparison with the price of the granite ashlar at 10 pence per superficial foot.[22] The attractive combination of granite masonry with Portland stone dressings, and its lower cost, inhibited the use of calp on the important façades of Dublin buildings for the remainder of the eighteenth century.

22 *Commons Journal*, 4, app. xxxiv.

The most significant influences on the choice of stone for the façades of the principal buildings in Dublin were the stylistic preferences of architects and those citizens who had been exposed to new cultural patterns coming through England from France and Italy. The white limestone quarried in the Isle of Portland was already established, by the end of the seventeenth century, as the most widely used facing and decorative masonry in the London area. Its use by Wren and Hawksmoor on the city churches and palace buildings identified it firmly with the classical imagery originating in Europe. Its affinity with the white Istrian limestone used to build the temple fronts of the Veneto may have secured its continued popularity with Burlington and the new English Palladian movement in the 1720s. Its choice by Pearce in 1728 for the pediments and the colonnades of the ambitious new Irish Parliament House was almost an inevitability. This was not the first use of English stone on Irish classical buildings. Robinson's accounts of Royal Hospital at Kilmainham (1680–6) include costs expended on Portland stone used to build the pedimented openings at its four entrances.[23] The frontispiece of Kilkenny Castle, which probably also dates from Robinson's time, has giant Corinthian pilasters of local grey limestone with Portland stone capitals and decorative swags. Trinity College imported 38 tons of Whitehaven stone in 1713, probably for Burgh's Library.[24] Burgh also used it (or something resembling it) on St Werburgh's in 1715 (fig. 8.6).

Although the choice of white Portland stone by Pearce for the Parliament House was undoubtedly governed by stylistic preferences, there were other practical reasons for the use of imported stone. Moses Darley's stonecutting accounts on Burgh's College Library record several payments for work with 'the freestone'. Freestone was a term loosely used to describe stones which (like many sandstones) were soft and easily worked by stonecutters and sculptors. However, the term properly refers to stones that were granular rather than stratified in structure, and could thus be carved freely in any direction, because of an absence of directional grain. Most sedimentary rocks such as limestones and sandstones have a distinctive grain related to their bedding planes.

The true freestones were the oolitic limestones such as Bathstone and Portland stone, which occur in thick beds without minor bedding planes, and these stones have granular structures. Portland stone is particularly soft when it is newly quarried, due to the presence of mineralized ground water, or 'quarry sap', which slowly migrates to the surface layers and forms a hard crystalline skin that develops a high resistance to weather. The oolites had important advantages for ambitious architects. The thickly bedded Portland stone promoted the use of large masonry modules that were needed for column construction. Pearce, Cooley and Gandon designed free-standing porticoes with colonnades of a scale that required stones of considerable size. Columnar masonry drums over 5ft in height helped to articulate the scale and

---

23 Richard Colley, *An account of the foundation of the Royal Hospital of King Charles II* (Dublin, 1725), p. 23.   24 TCD, Thomas Edmund's accounts, MUN/P2/25/39a.

8.6 St Werburgh's Church, Dublin, 1715–19. Photograph by David Davison.

grandeur of giant columns. Corinthian capitals on these columns required stones of at least this magnitude to accommodate their complex profiles, and it is doubtful if a suitable Irish stone could have been easily found for this purpose. Robinson's decision to use painted timber capitals on his Portland stone piers at the entrance of the Royal Hospital may have been due to a shortage of the correct stone for the purpose, or the lack of suitable craftsmen to undertake the carving. There were few attempts made to build porticoes with free-standing colonnades outside the Dublin area until the last decade of the eighteenth century. The portico on Pearce's Bellamont Forest, Co. Cavan (1730s), is relatively modest in scale, and its local grey limestone columns are probably made with their longitudinal axes parallel with their bedding planes.

The fine grain of the Portland limestones, combined with their initial softness, was another advantage in carved and moulded work such as cornices and capitals. A comparison between the ornate precision of Cooley's Portland modillion cornice on the Royal Exchange (1770s) and the much coarser granite to the Doric entablature of Smyth's St Catherine's Church (1760s) illustrates the characteristics of both materials. Hugh Darley's comment in 1756, on James Robinson's carving on the West Front of Trinity College that 'such Works have not before been done in this Kingdom', reveals the impact this sophisticated workmanship had in Dublin at this time.[25] It is doubtful if these highly ornamental capitals, or Gandon's capitals on his House of Lords colonnade, could have been executed with such confidence in the Irish stones that were available.

A reference to the curious eighteenth-century practice of oiling Portland stone to preserve and harden it is found in Wren's records of the building of St Paul's Cathedral: 'The interior … where softer Stones were found … was laid in Oil several times over'.[26] There is no mention of the oil used but presumably it was linseed oil, which was used extensively in paint and putty fabrication. It was also mentioned by Charles Robert Cockerell, who discussed this practice in Dublin with Francis Johnston.[27]

Pearce's decision to use an imported freestone on such a grand scale in 1728 must be seen not only in the context of stylistic preferences, but also in terms of the practical feasibility of building his ambitious design. The preferences of William Conolly (the Speaker of the Commons) for the use of native materials were well known to Pearce, and the architect's memorandum to the building committee of the Parliament House included assurances on the use of Irish stone (such as Kilkenny marble) on the building's interior.[28] His decision to use a local granite around the inside walls of the piazza as a foil to the Portland peristyle may have been a gesture to patriotic pride, but this combination was highly successful and it provided a formula for subsequent buildings built during Dublin's classical era. The use of Dublin blackstone as an ashlar on the east and west elevations was less successful. This may also have been a concession to local prejudice. Of course, Pearce's original ambitions might well have conceived the Parliament House as a building entirely clad with white freestone, like so many classical buildings constructed in London by this period. The

---

25 TCD, James Robinson's accounts, MUN/P2/99/5.   **26** *Wren Soc. Vols*, 16, p. 169.   **27** Lynda Mulvin, 'Charles Robert Cockerell, Francis Johnston and the dissemination of neo-classical principles' in Lynda Mulvin (ed.), *The fusion of neo-classical principles* (Dublin, 2011), pp 165, 168, n. 12, who adds that 'the buildings of Front Square, Trinity College … were also sampled and proved positive for an oil-like substance; oiling of the stone later became part of the building maintenance'.   **28** Edward McParland, 'Edward Lovett Pearce and the Parliament House in Dublin', *Burlington Magazine*, 121 (Feb. 1989), 93.

8.7 Thomas Cooley, the Royal Exchange, 1770s and Thomas Ivory, Newcomen's Bank, 1780s, Dublin. Photograph by Graham Hickey.

image of an entirely white classical temple was to await realization in the Dublin area until the 1760s, when Chambers's neoclassical Casino at Marino was almost entirely faced with Portland stone by Vierpyl. The refinements of Thomas Cooley's Royal Exchange (1770s) and of Thomas Ivory's Newcomen's Bank (1780s) owe a lot to the inherent qualities of their Portland masonry claddings (fig. 8.7).

Outside Dublin, the use of imported facing stones was relatively uncommon. This was due no doubt to the expense of transportation costs and also to a lack of demand for civic buildings of a monumental character, such as we find in Dublin. Nevertheless, although country houses and buildings in provincial towns relied mostly on local stones for facing materials, distantly sourced stone was sometimes used for special features on their façades.

8.8 John Nixon, 'Quarries at Portland', 1789. Courtesy of the Earl Belmore.

A stone doorcase for Castle Forward, Co. Donegal, produced presumably by stonecutters in Dublin in the 1730s, was shipped to Derry in timber cases for delivery to the building site.[29] Accounts for Carton, Co. Kildare, record the purchase of small amounts of Portland stone in the late 1730s, used in conjunction with the Ardbraccan limestone and other Irish stones in its reconstruction.[30] Windele records the presence of 'a handsome pediment of Portland stone supported by fluted Doric columns' on

29 NLI, Castle Forward papers, MS 10470.   30 Desmond Guinness and William Ryan, *Irish houses and castles* (London, 1971), pp 184–5.

8.9 James Malton, 'The West Front of St Patrick's Cathedral, Dublin', watercolour, 1793, detail showing a man with a hod used for carrying brick, stone or mortar, NGI, cat. no. 2620. Reproduced with permission of the National Gallery of Ireland.

the street-front of the King's Old Castle (the eighteenth-century courthouse) in his historical descriptions of Cork city.[31] The most ambitious use of imported facing stones, of course, was on some of the larger country houses in Ulster.

The use of the famous Bath freestone as plain and rustic ashlars, and for the pedimented frontispiece with engaged Ionic columns on Castleward, Co. Down (1765), may not have been as extravagant as it appears. The Ward family owned their own ships, and Bristol (adjacent to Bath) was one of the ports most frequently used by Irish mercantile traders. The transportation of the stone as ballast might have been as inexpensive as taking stone overland from quarries in Ireland. George Steuart's accounts for the building of Baronscourt, Co. Tyrone, in 1779–80, record the use of eight different stones used as structural walling material and for facings.[32] One of the largest accounts (£603 15s. 6d.) is for Dungiven sandstone from Co. Londonderry, and this must have been used extensively on the façades of the house

31 J. Windele, *Historical and descriptive notices of Cork* (Cork, 1839), p. 26.   32 PRONI, Abercorn papers, D623/C/3/1, f. 8.

during this period. However, Steuart also records substantial sums of £735 17s. 2½d. for stone from Scone, of £179 1s. 6½d. for stone shipped from Liverpool and of £130 18s. 3½d. for stone from Greenock.

One late-eighteenth-century use of imported stone in rural Ireland, which attempted to match its ambitious use in Dublin by such architects as Gandon and Cooley, can be seen in the realization of James Wyatt's refined elevations of Castlecoole, Co. Fermanagh, in the 1790s. Here, Portland stone was used without restraint on all façades of the house, on its side pavilions, in the freestanding giant columns of its Ionic entrance portico, in the colonnades articulating the façades of the pavilions and those linking them with the central block of the main house. This was an extravagant use of materials by any standards in Ireland, and its owner, Lord Belmore, was embarrassed by its subsequent cost. By comparison, a house of similar architectural qualities, built during the same period at Emo Court, Co. Laois, appears almost frugal. Emo was based on a plan provided by James Gandon in the early 1790s, and it was he who was undoubtedly responsible for the introduction of Portland stone into its elevational treatment, although he was not involved in the subsequent execution of the design.

Emo is just as ambitious as Castlecoole in its use of double height freestone porticoes and its formal articulation of linked pavilions. The monumentality of its concept has a civic quality lacking in other Irish country houses. However, the realization of this concept suffers from a bland handling of masonry surfaces. How much grander and more monumental would it appear if the Portland stone had been combined with Leinster granite (instead of plaster) in the manner of Gandon's Custom House, or his other Dublin buildings. By the 1790s, Ireland had entered the canal age and granite ashlar could have been inexpensively transported to the site from Carlow, but, sadly, this opportunity to promote the abstract qualities of the design was overlooked and lost.

CHAPTER NINE

The roofing trades: the work of the slater and the plumber

SLATERS FIXED TILES AND slates to timber roof structures and (occasionally) to masonry surfaces such as walls and chimneys (fig. 9.1). Plumbers worked mostly with lead in the provision of a number of building components. Both trades worked as separate contractors, but it is convenient to discuss them in tandem because of the overlap of their work on the construction and repair of eighteenth-century roofs.

Slate, always common, was the principal material used on the roofs of eighteenth-century classical buildings. Clay tiles and timber shingles were used extensively on seventeenth-century roofs, but their use was limited during the next century. Roof-gutters, rainwater pipes (trunks) and flashings (dressings to chimneys and along the party wall/parapet of adjoining buildings) were usually made from lead. Lead was also used as a cladding to cupolas, domes, platform (flat) roofs and the low-pitched roofs of pediments.

Plumbers were responsible for the formation of gutters, trunks and flashings and the cladding of domes, dormers and cupolas. The main materials used by the plumber were solder (a fusible alloy of lead and tin) and cast lead sheeting. In the formation of components such as rainwater pipes and gutters, individual sections of sheeting were fused together with hot solder, and solder was used to repair damaged leadwork. Plumbers also made sash-weights, they provided lead pipework, storage cisterns and pumps for the supply of water. On buildings with ashlar facings, they poured the lead bedding for iron cramps in the cut-stone masonry, and they covered the projecting upper surfaces of stone cornices and doorcases with lead dressings. Plumbing involved specialized skills in the casting and fusion of hot metals and the design of patterns for lead cladding on complex geometric surfaces. These skills may have been difficult to acquire without the dedicated training of the guild system that operated in the main towns and cities of the kingdom. Slating was a more accessible undertaking, and it should not surprise us to find it widely practised by local masons in the Irish provinces. We know nothing about the origins of the plumbers' and slaters' trades, but helliers (slaters and tilers) are recorded with millers and masons as members of the Dublin carpenters' guild in 1508.[1] By the beginning of the eighteenth century the slating trade seems to have been well established in Dublin,

1 Mary Clark & Raymond Refaussé, *Directory of historic Dublin guilds* (Dublin, 1993), p. 17.

9.1 Slate-hung bow-fronts on the Grand Parade, Cork, © Anthony Barry Archive.

and the term slater was widely used to describe specialists who worked with tiles and slates. Plumbers were also members of the carpenters' guild in Dublin by the eighteenth century, but the plumbers in Cork were represented by the guild of goldsmiths.[2]

2 John Windele, *Historical and descriptive notices of Cork* (Cork, 1839), p. 104.

9.2 *The book of trades; or, Library of useful arts* (London, 1815), part 1, 'Plumber'.

Wars and weather have combined to destroy almost all the physical evidence of roofing construction in many Irish seventeenth-century buildings and in most medieval buildings. The survival rate for eighteenth-century buildings is much better. Many roofs of prominent classical buildings still retain their original timber roof structures, but the weathering membranes (of slate and lead) have been replaced many times in continuous attempts to resist the weather. With the exception of Neve's *City and country purchaser* (first published in 1703) none of the well-known eighteenth-century building manuals make a serious attempt to discuss the theoretic background to contemporary slating or plumbing practices.[3] Our examination of these practices will mostly rely on building records of the main eighteenth-century institutions in Dublin and a few country houses. One familiar aspect of these records, through the century, is the recurring employment of several generations of the same

---

3 Richard Neve, *The city and country purchaser* (London, 1726; facsimile ed., 1969), p. 182 onwards, and p. 240 onwards.

family in plumbing and slating contracts. The most prominent slaters involved on contracts in the Royal Hospital Kilmainham and Trinity College from the 1670s until the 1740s were the Heatleys. Three other families were also engaged in the college slating contracts: the Elliots from the 1750s until the 1820s, the Cape family from 1718 until the 1740s, and the Pikes from the 1750s until about 1815.

Another persistent pattern in these records is a remarkably high incidence of roofing failures resulting in repair contracts, replacement of slates and lead, and in some institutions (such as Trinity College and the Royal Hospital) a series of almost continuous maintenance contracts. Leaking roofs can only have been caused by bad workmanship, poor materials, or by an inability to understand the technical characteristics of the materials in use. The disastrous performance of lead pipes supplying water to Dublin institutions in the early years of the century (and their subsequent replacement by wooden pipes) further illustrates the state of contemporary plumbing practices, and some institutional records also complain about bad slating practices. In 1705/6, for instance, criticism of slating repairs carried out by Robert Wharton at the Royal Hospital caused his dismissal and the appointment of Abraham Heatley to maintain the roofs. Heatley also failed to satisfy the governors.[4] He was asked to explain his poor performance of the maintenance contract in 1715; he was accused of negligence in 1717, and he was dismissed in 1720.[5] In 1743, there was renewed concern at the bad state of the roof.[6] The problems of slating maintenance were not confined to the early decades of the century. Despite extensive re-slating in the late 1790s at Dr Steevens's Hospital, the board agreed in 1801 to petition parliament for aid with re-roofing.[7]

The failure of leaden roof membranes to keep out the weather is also recorded frequently. The roof of the Tholsel (1680s) was a subject of considerable anxiety to Dublin Corporation. In 1696, a proposal to replace the existing leadwork was placed before the assembly; in 1702, the cupola needed extensive repairs, and six years later it was decided to face it with slates to protect it from the weather.[8] The roof needed further renovation in 1712, and in that year Sir John Rogerson was paid £68 19s. 4d. for the lead used in its repair.[9] Similar problems affected the platform roofs erected by William Robinson on the northern range of the Royal Hospital in the 1680s. By 1719, cracks had appeared in the lead covering over the hall and chapel which were repaired by the use of lead solder; in 1725, a decision was taken to replace the lead on these roofs at the considerable cost of £269.[10] The lead used by Jonathan Cape on Burgh's Library in the early 1720s must have deteriorated badly by the 1740s, as, in 1746, Ruth Cape (his daughter-in-law) was paid for the supply of over 13 tons of lead

---

4 NAI, Royal Hospital Kilmainham minute books, 1, RHK 1/1/1, f. 321 v, 331 r. **5** Ibid., 3, RHK 1/1/3, 16 Aug. 1717; 4, RHK 1/1/4, 29 Jan. 1722. **6** Ibid., 5, RHK 1/1/5, f. 16 v. **7** TCD, minutes of governors and guardians of Dr Steevens's Hospital, 1782–1806, 3 May 1779, 26 July 1799, 7 Nov. 1801, 7 Dec. 1801. **8** CARD, 6, pp 145, 269, 383. **9** Ibid., p. 458. **10** NAI, Royal Hospital Kilmainham minute books, 3, RHK 1/1/3, 8 Aug. 1719; 4, RHK 1/1/4, 21 Apr. 1725; the estimate for new lead was £527; old lead to the value of £258 could be reused.

used to repair the roof.[11] The platform roofs of the Royal Hospital were still causing problems at the end of the century. Vincent Waldré's report to the hospital governors in 1804 urged the total replacement of the lead with copper, because 'the Lead … is so bad that it is Irreparable and if these places [Hall and Chapel] are Covered with lead again the expense would be Considerable and in a few years become full of holes as at present, by the Attraction of the Sun'.[12]

Waldré's comment about the influence of the sun on the hospital roofs referred to the ductility of soft metals, such as lead, and the problems caused by expansion of the metal due to increases in temperature. Expansion (or creep) in lead is an inherent characteristic of the metal, and an imperfect knowledge of its implications could easily result in cracks and fractures. Defects arising from fixing methods that limited movement probably account for many of the problems experienced with lead used on eighteenth-century roofs. It is more difficult to speculate on the defects found in slated roofs and why they were so prevalent in eighteenth-century buildings. In what follows we will examine the origins and supply of roofing materials, how they were applied to roofs, and how roofing contracts were organized. We will start with the work of the plumber and his materials.

* * *

Lead was mined in several areas in Ireland during the seventeenth and eighteenth centuries. Boate, in his survey of 1657, remarked on lead deposits in Antrim, at Sligo Harbour and at the mine near Kilmore, Co. Tipperary, which supplied the lead for the roof of the O'Brien castle at Bunratty, Co. Clare.[13] The growth of the building market in the middle of the eighteenth century may have promoted an increase in lead production. Pococke noted lead mines at Ardmore, Co. Waterford, and at Loughlinstown (near Dublin) on his travels in Ireland in 1752; in 1757, the *Belfast Newsletter* advertised a vacancy for a paymaster for a lead mine in Co. Armagh; Willes recorded the presence of lead mines at Silvermines in Co. Tipperary in 1760.[14] In 1780, Robert Stewart, the Marquis of Londonderry, started to develop lead deposits on his Co. Down estates at Bangor and Newtownards.

The cost of refining local lead deposits, or the cost of transporting such a heavy material overland, may have limited the use of Irish lead and considerable quantities of lead were imported. Customs records from the 1760s until the 1790s show a steady importation of lead sheet or pigs and lead ingots (over 500 tons in 1773 and 1787).[15] In the mid-eighteenth century the Dublin plumber William Murphy was sent to Wales to organize the supply of lead for the roofs of buildings in Trinity College.[16]

---

11 TCD, Jonathan Cape's accounts, MUN/P2/48/2; Ruth Cape's accounts, MUN/P2/90/2.   12 NAI, Royal Hospital Kilmainham minute books, 7, RHK 1/1/7, 31 Oct. 1804.   13 Gerard Boate, *Irelands naturall history* (London, 1657), pp 141–2.   14 John McVeagh (ed.), *Richard Pococke's Irish tours* (Dublin, 1995), pp 112, 126; *The Belfast Newsletter*, 6 Sept. 1757; James Kelly (ed.), *The letters of Lord Chief Baron Edward Willes* (Aberystwyth, 1990), p. 69.   15 NLI, Customs import and export ledgers, MSS 353 (2), 358 (1).   16 TCD, William Murphy's accounts, MUN/P2/99/3.

Most of the cargoes of lead imported into Irish ports were in the form of lead pigs (roughly cast ingots of metal), which were small enough to be manhandled over short distances. Pig-lead was cast into sheet form for use in the manufacture of pipes and other building components. The difficulties of transporting heavy rolls of lead sheet obviously encouraged the practice of casting lead on building sites. An account of 1755 in Trinity College records a payment of £3 per ton for casting lead pigs into sheeting.[17]

The eighteenth-century process of casting sheet lead was described in detail by Neve in his *City and country purchaser*.[18] The sheets were cast by pouring molten metal onto a timber table covered by a layer of damp sand. The thickness of the cast sheet was controlled by two adjustable timber battens fixed to two opposite sides of the table; thicknesses of $\frac{1}{10}$, $\frac{1}{8}$ and $\frac{3}{16}$ inches were obtained by battens of corresponding depths. The thickness of the sheet was determined by the simple method of pulling a skimming board along the two peripheral battens, thus removing lead that was in excess of the required thickness. Sheets were cast in lengths of up to 18ft. Sheet lead weighed from approximately 6lb per square foot to approximately 12lb per square foot. This means that an approximate hundredweight of 12lb sheet was capable of covering a square yard of roofing.

This simple production method had advantages, in that it could be set up on building sites or workshops without elaborate equipment or controls. Lead was melted in steel crucibles over furnaces and charcoal braziers and manually poured over the bed of sand. The siting of casting beds adjacent to the building under construction allowed the production of large and heavy lead sheets ready for use. This had one important disadvantage. Although two peripheral battens controlled the lead's maximum thickness, they could not control the minimum thickness of the sheet. As this was affected by such variables as the surface of the sand bed, and the flow pattern of the molten metal, it must have been difficult to maintain a uniform thickness in all parts of the leaden sheet. The reduction in cross section of an $\frac{1}{8}$-inch lead gutter to a lesser thickness in certain areas could introduce potential weak spots that were liable to fracture when the gutter contracted or expanded. The problems of producing a uniform thickness in lead sheeting was ultimately solved by the use of rolling mills, that extruded the metal in precise thicknesses, under controlled workshop conditions. Lead, thus milled, was not unknown in the eighteenth century, although there are no records of its use in Ireland. However, its use on early classical buildings in England proved to be unsuccessful. Neve warned builders against the dangers of milled lead, and quoted a parliamentary inquiry into the disastrous failure of the roofs of Greenwich Hospital, which brought the verdict that 'milled lead was not fit to be used'.[19]

Lead and solder were sold by weight, lead usually by the ton or the hundredweight and solder by the pound. Occasionally, on jobbing work, plumbers priced lead

---

17 Ibid.   **18** Neve, *The city and country purchaser*, p. 183, onwards.   **19** Ibid., p. 188.

piping by length (in yards and feet) but on larger contracts pipes, rainwater trunks and fabricated components were usually priced by weight, and at unit costs that were higher than the cost of sheet lead. Thus an account of Jonathan Cape's for work on Burgh's Library in 1721 charged lead sheet at 16s. per hundredweight and lead pipes at £1 8s. 0d. per hundredweight.[20] The difference in cost (12s. per hundredweight) paid Cape for his time involved in fabricating the pipe from lead sheeting.

Plumbing contracts were unusual in that all contractual agreements (for repairs, maintenance and new roofing works) were organized on a time and material basis. Slating contracts in the college also had a high percentage of time and material agreements, but this may been caused by the need for extensive maintenance; slating works on all new buildings were invariably carried out as measured contracts. The reasons for not using measured agreements on major plumbing contracts are not clear, but it may have been difficult to establish a unit of measurement (such as the mason's perch or the slater's square) to define the combined costs of work and materials. Another explanation may lie in the unusual ratio between the cost of workmanship and the cost of materials in large plumbing contracts. For instance, in 1745, Matt Cape was paid a total of £319 0s. 11½d. for work and materials used on Richard Castle's bell tower, involving over 13 tons of sheet lead; the cost of workmanship alone came to £12 3s. 6d.[21] Out of an account of £1,316 9s. 0d. paid to Alexander Thompson for work and materials on the West Front in 1755, the total cost of workmanship amounted to a mere £52 6s. 0d.[22]

These high material costs obliged architects and building supervisors to make precise inventories both of the amount of lead used on roofing contracts and also of the residual amount of waste material (cuttings) left unused after fabricated lead sections were fixed to roof structures. On early contracts such as the College Library, the lead was weighed by Nathan Hall the head porter, and payments were made on the basis of certificates signed by him and Thomas Burgh. By the 1740s, Castle was using the services of measurers to check plumbers' time and materials accounts. A certificate of Castle for replacement of lead on the Library in 1745 includes William Keating's endorsement: 'I have Compared this Acct wth John Kanes Book and find it to answer'.[23] This practice of checking plumbers' materials (by weight) as they were furnished on site continued through the century under the direction of architects such as Hugh Darley and Graham Myers. Although plumbers' accounts for major roofing contracts were presented as bills for time and materials, they were effectively handled as measured accounts by architects, measurers and clerks of work because of the necessity of checking the weight of the lead used in the contract.

The high purchase cost of lead, combined with the ease with which it could be melted down and recycled (as lead sheet), ensured a high second-hand value for waste cuttings and old leaden roofing components. Many accounts in the College show the

20 TCD, Jonathan Cape's accounts, MUN/P2/48/2. 21 TCD, Matt Cape's accounts, MUN/P2/94/10. 22 TCD, William Murphy's and Alexander Thompson's accounts, MUN/P2/125/95, ff 95d–f. 23 TCD, Ruth Cape's accounts, MUN/P2/90/1.

value of old lead (removed from defective roofs during repair contracts) as a credit on plumbers' accounts. In the 1760s, John Reed the plumber was paid from 15s. to 18s. 6d. per hundredweight for old lead, and from 18s. 6d. to £1 2s. 6d. per hundredweight for new lead (4d. per hundredweight was deducted from his bill for old lead because it had to be cleaned).[24]

The softness and malleability of sheet lead made it an ideal material to cover curved roof surfaces such as domes and cupolas. The capacity to make sheets of the dimensions described by Neve also allowed it to be used on platform roofs that were too low in pitch for slates or tiles. He recommended the use of thinner lead (weighing between 6 to 9 lbs per square foot) for gutters, and heavier (8 to 12 lbs) for platform roofs.[25] Some idea of the weight of the lead sheeting in use on the buildings of Trinity College can be gleaned from the 1746 account of over 13 tons supplied by Ruth Cape for use in the repair of the Library roof.[26] There is no indication in her account of the relative weight (per square foot) of the sheets supplied, or whether the lead was of the thinner variety (used for gutters) or the thicker sheeting used for roof cladding. Her account also shows considerable variation in the weight of the sheets. This is surprising, as they were all undoubtedly cast on the Cape family's sandbed, and they should have been all (roughly) of the same dimensions. Some variations can probably be explained by the need to provide two thicknesses of lead, but the considerable differences in sheet weights suggest random sheet thicknesses arising from poor control of the casting process. Variations in the quality of lead produced by contemporary casting methods is clearly indicated in some eighteenth-century roofing accounts. Fluctuations in the price of lead sheeting in the first half of the century, during the long period of cost stability, can only be attributed to differences in quality of production. A hundredweight of lead cost 16s. in 1721 on the contract for Burgh's Library; Burgh sanctioned costs of 22s. per hundredweight for lead used on Dr Steevens's Hospital in 1729; in 1753 new lead used on the Royal Hospital cost 22s. per hundredweight (with old lead at 18s.) and c.1750 the lead used on the Parliament House cost 19s. per hundredweight.[27] Significant variations in prices could occur within short periods and even on the same job. At Trinity, between 1755 and 1758, William Murray charged £1 5s. 6d. per hundredweight for sheet lead while Alexander Thompson charged £1 and £1 1s. 0d.; Murray charged £1 12s. 6d. per hundredweight for lead pipes while Thompson charged £1 8s. 0d.[28]

None of the records of roofing contracts in the Dublin institutions provide us with a clear picture of how eighteenth-century plumbers fabricated gutters from sheet lead, or how they fixed lead panels as claddings on domes, or platform roofs. Plumbers' accounts invariably include materials other than lead sheets, such as solder, nails, pipes and component parts of water pumps. Solder was used extensively to join

24 TCD, John Reed's accounts, MUN/P2/138/10–12.   25 Neve, *The city and country purchaser*, p. 186.
26 TCD, Ruth Cape's accounts, MUN/P2/90/2.   27 TCD, Jonathan Cape's accounts, MUN/P2/48/2; ibid., Dr Steevens's Hospital building accounts, 1540; NAI, Royal Hospital Kilmainham Minute Books, 5, RHK 1/1/5, 7 June 1753; *Commons Journal*, 5, xlvii.   28 TCD, William Murphy's and Alexander Thompson's accounts, MUN/P2/125.

9.3 Hand-forged nails, all (except that on top left) from Palace Street, Dublin, 1760s. Peter Pearson Collection, photograph by David Davison.

pipe sections together and to repair fractures in lead gutters and roofs. Jobbing contracts involving roof repairs with solder are clearly recorded, but payments for solder also occur in accounts dealing with new roofing contracts. Cape's 1746 account for the supply of the large quantity of sheeting to replace the lead on Burgh's College Library also included the cost of 24lbs of solder and 2000 clout nails.[29] Clout nails had short shanks and large circular heads that were suitable for securing soft materials (such as lead and leather) to timber supports.

We can only speculate on how platform roofs were fixed in Ireland and how panels of sheet lead were joined together, but the considerable roof failures we have noted in the Royal Hospital and in Trinity College must have been caused either by fixings that inhibited thermal movement, or by lead panels that were too large to accommodate expansion without undue stress. The use of solder to join sections of lead into a continuous gutter could inhibit expansion and cause stress fractures; the

29 TCD, Ruth Cape's accounts, MUN/P2/90/2.

overuse of clout nails to fix lead panels to timber supports would cause similar problems.

English plumbers were aware of the elastic limits of lead and the problems of 'creep' in lead panels. Neve provides a description of English plumbers making a standing seam between two lead panels on a platform roof and the dressing of this seam around a circular timber batten. This method of providing a weatherproof joint that allows two panels of lead to expand (around the batten) without constraint, is still in use today. He also describes the views of a London plumber on the need to break long gutters with a stepped joint to accommodate expansion 'for by this Means … the Lead (being cut into two pieces which are shorter) is not so subject to crack (by being dilated and contracted with Heat and Cold) as otherwise it is'.[30]

On the other hand, Neve's description of a plumber forming a gutter on the roof of a London church is not reassuring:

> When he sodder'd the sheets of lead that are fixed into the wall on one edge, and with the other edge lap over the ends of those which are seam'd in the platform, at every other sheet, in the middle betwixt the seams, he sodded the Lapping-sheet down to the other.

While it is difficult to understand fully the process described, it is evident that solder was used extensively to form fixed joints; and this, we know, could inhibit expansion.

The indiscriminate use of solder, lack of control over the casting process leading to variations in thickness (and weak spots) in sheet lead, oversized lead panels and excessive use of nailed fixings may have all contributed to roofing failures in the first half of the eighteenth century. To overcome the problems of stress caused by expansion, plumbers tended to use thicker sheeting (such as the heavy 12lb sheets recommended by Neve) in the mistaken belief that it could resist movement fractures. This may have been successful in some cases, as the considerable difficulty in handling heavy panels on high roofs would have forced a reduction in panel sizes with a consequent reduction in expansion.

Unfortunately, the lack of records of roofing contracts after the 1750s limits our discussion on the durability of leaden roof membranes. We have no information on how the cladding on the dome of Pearce's Parliament House performed between 1730 and 1792, the year it was destroyed by fire; we cannot say if stress fractures influenced decisions to remove the bell-tower Castle built in Trinity College in 1745. Although Chambers relied on leaden roofs in his design for Charlemont's Casino at Marino in the 1760s, Cooley opted for the use of copper sheeting on the dome of the Royal Exchange in the 1770s. There are no other references to the use of copper on Dublin buildings before the nineteenth century, but Whitmore Davis described his episcopal house at Ferns as being 'covered with Copper' in an advertisement for his *Architectura Hibernica* in 1789.[31] In a report to the governors of the Royal Hospital in 1804, Francis

---

30 Neve, *The city and country purchaser*, pp 186–7.   **31** *Dublin Evening Post*, 5 Mar. 1789.

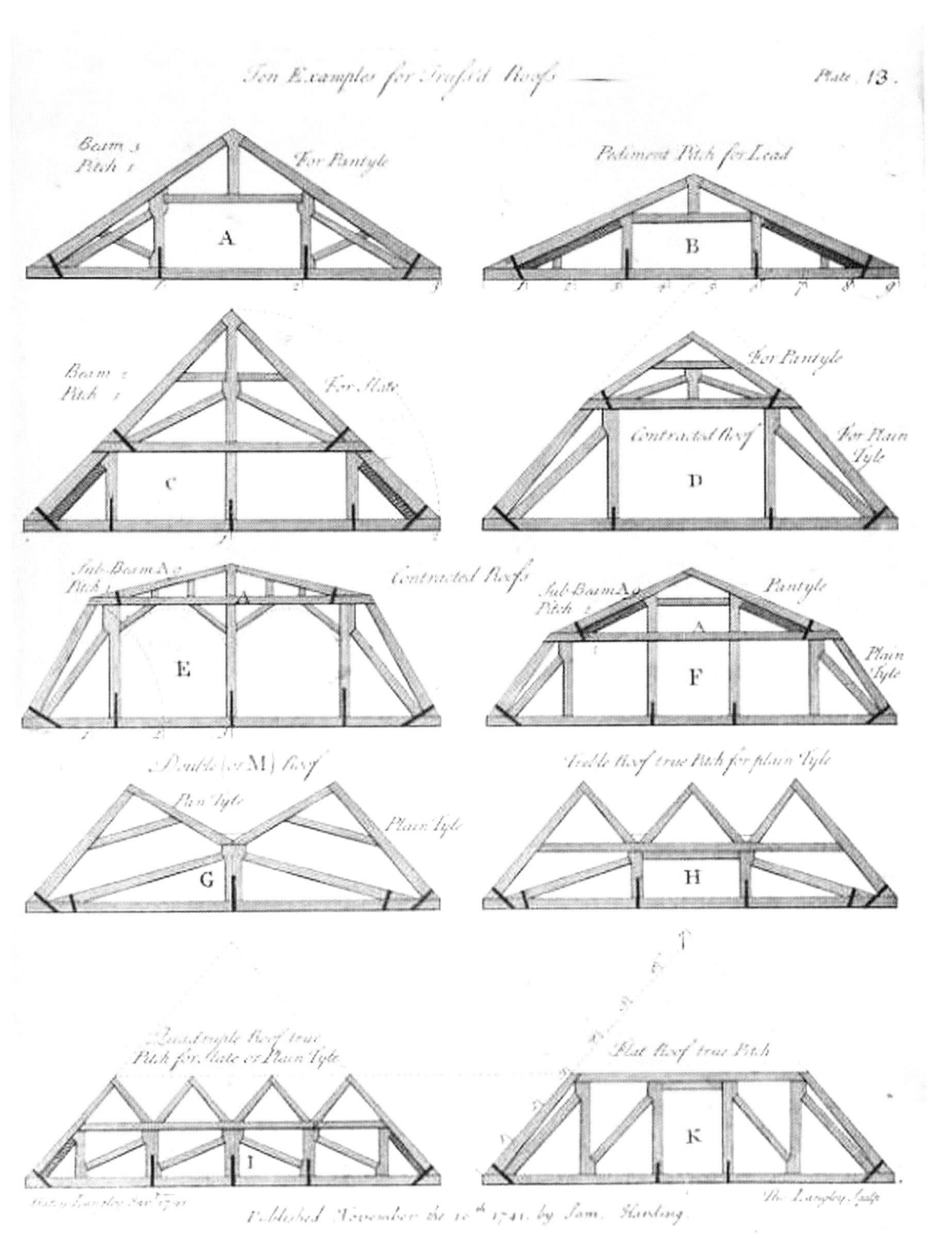

9.4 Trusses providing different pitches of roof to accommodate a variety of roofing materials, slate, pantile, plain tile, lead etc., B[atty] L[angley], *The city and country builder's and workman's treasury of designs* (London, 1770), appendix, plate 13.

Johnston recommended copper for the flat roof and pediments, but he pointed out the difficulty of finding 'good Copper layers Even from England' with the necessary experience of laying copper roofs.[32]

The decision to use flat platform roof construction at the ridge level of the hospital was influenced by William Robinson's concern for the profile of his roof. Most of the hospital's residential accommodation was organized in three ranges around a central courtyard, and Robinson planned the larger public spaces (such as the Hall and Chapel) in the fourth (northern) range. The apartments required a building depth of 29ft, which allowed the residential ranges to be roofed with a simple framed truss and coupled rafters supporting slates at a pitch of 45 degrees. The northern range that contained the large high spaces of the hall and chapel required trusses with clear spans of 50ft. The design of these trusses incorporated the same 45-degree rafter system as the other ranges to allow the continuity of slated roof surfaces around the four ranges of the building, but the top of the truss (spanning over the central part of the range) was constructed as a flat platform covered with lead. The need to keep the roofs of the four ranges of the hospital at the same height was a central aspect of Robinson's design. The use of a flat platform on the central part of the roof allowed the ridge levels of all the roofs to remain at the same height. A 45-degree rafter system would yield a higher roof ridge on a 50ft span without that platform.

The relationship between roof pitch and the choice of roofing materials was an important consideration in the design of early classical buildings, particularly in countries with heavy rainfall such as England and Ireland. The new generation of building manuals that followed the emergence of the Palladian movement in the 1720s provided comprehensive details on the design of roof trusses for different building configurations. The information given was mostly concerned with carpentry practice, but some authors produced relevant data on the suitability of roof pitches for different roofing materials. Francis Price, writing in 1735, defined a pediment pitch (suitable only for lead) as having a vertical height equal to a quarter of the roof span.[33] This produced pediment roofs with a pitch of about 27 degrees. His roof designs indicate pitches of 38 degrees for pantiles and 45 degrees for plain tiles. By the 1740s the architectural problems of combining high roof profiles with classical façades were probably influencing building practice, as in 1741 Batty Langley published a series of truss designs with lower pitches (fig. 9.4).[34] Langley promoted a common pitch for plain tiles and slates of 45 degrees and a pitch of 35 degrees for pantiles.

These empirical formulae were merely rough guides for contemporary practice, but they emphasize the problems that early eighteenth-century builders experienced with roofing materials. Lead, if properly applied and jointed, could be used on any

---

32 NAI, Royal Hospital Kilmainham Minute Books, 7, RHK 1/1/7, 7 Nov. 1804.   **33** Francis Price, *The British carpenter; or, A treatise on carpentry* (London, 1735), p. 15 and plate G.   **34** Batty Langley, *The city and country builder's and workman's treasury of designs* (London, 1745), appendix plates 13, 14.

low pitch down to a few degrees, because it was available in large panels. Pantiles had more advantages than plain tiles because they were larger in size, and because they could be interlocked horizontally on the roof surface to provide a better barrier to rainwater. Plain tiles were usually about 6 inches broad, 10 inches long and ½ inch in thickness. They had the same disadvantage as the smaller varieties of slates (such as singles), as the difficulty in providing a sufficient overlap between courses (due to their small dimensions) prevented their use on roof pitches under 45 degrees.

* * *

In 1657, Boate noted the use of slates, clay tiles and also timber shingles on Irish roofs:

> In sundry parts of Ireland Slate is in great abundance, and that nothing deep within the ground, just in the same manner as the Freestone, so as it may be raised with little charge and labour; wherefore at all times it hath been much used by the English inhabitants for the covering of their houses and other buildings. Nevertheless some years since in places near the sea, especially at Dublin, that kind of Holland Tiles, which by them are called *Pannen* began to be used generally, the Merchants causing them to be brought in from thence in great abundance, because in Ireland they had neither convenient stuff to make them of, nor work-men skilfull in that business: although the common Tiles usual in many parts of England and other Countries, were made and used in several places within the land ... Besides these there was another kind of covering in use, both for Churches and houses, to wit, a certain sort of wooden Tiles, vulgarly called Shingles; the which are thight enough at the first, but do not many yeares continue so, it being necessary to change them often.[35]

Boate's description of the availability and use of slate in many parts of Ireland meets our expectations of building practices during this period. His references to the use of clay tiles (in coastal areas) and timber shingles as roofing materials are more surprising but they are supported by some evidence.

Roof tiles were in use in Ireland before the seventeenth century. The Kilkenny city records show the presence of two tilers operating there between 1491 and 1519, even though the civil survey records only the presence of slate and thatch (and occasional shingles) on the city roofs in the 1650s.[36] An excavation of the medieval castle at Trim revealed fragments of curvilinear roof tiles in the earth surrounding the keep. Tiled roofs are recorded in Oxmantown and Thomas Street in Dublin in the late 1660s.[37] A Walter Vincent is described as a 'tyler' in the vestry accounts of Christ

---

35 Boate, *Irelands naturall history*, p. 151.   **36** W.G. Neely, *Kilkenny, an urban history, 1391–1843* (Belfast, 1989), pp 67–8; Robert Simington (ed.), *The civil survey A.D. 1654–1656, County of Waterford* ... (Dublin, 1942), appendix F.   **37** NAI, Lodge records of the Rolls, xii, 48, 355 (microfilm MFS 42/6).

Church, Cork, in the late 1660s, when 2,700 tiles were imported for the use of the church. The purchase around the same time as 'tile pins' suggests the tiles were used for the roof rather than paving.[38] Tiles were used extensively on the roofs of the early building in Trinity College, as maintenance accounts of Abraham Heatley's from 1704 until 1720 include several payments for pantiles.[39] Pantiles were also used later in the century on the Printing House in the mid-1730s and the new Dining Hall (not current building) in the 1740s. Boate's description refers to the use of two different roof tiles in Ireland: 'pannen' from Holland and 'common tiles', which were used extensively in England. The Holland tiles were probably pantiles, large double curved tiles used extensively in Europe and known in some parts of England as Flemish tiles. The common tiles referred to must have been the tiles known in England as plain tiles. Boate seems certain that plain tiles were manufactured locally in Ireland, but it is likely that many of these tiles used on Irish roofs came (like the tiles in Cork) from the south of England.

The manufacture and use of plain tiles in England was well established from medieval times, and their dimensions were controlled under a statute of Edward IV. Neve quotes the dimensions as measuring $6\frac{1}{4} \times 10\frac{1}{2}$ inches with a thickness of $\frac{5}{8}$ an inch at least (though he notes tiles of different dimensions too).[40] His dimensions for pantiles were $14\frac{1}{2} \times 10\frac{1}{2}$ inches. He describes their shape as 'bent (breadthwise) forward and backward in the Form of an S, only one of the Arches is at least three times as big as the other', and 'the lesser Arch, or Hollow of another Tile … lies over the edge of the great Hollow of the former Tile'. This method of connecting pantiles horizontally on the slope of the roof provided better weather protection than the simple horizontal overlap used in slating and plain tiling, particularly if the tiles were bedded, or pointed with mortar. According to Neve, pantiles had 'no Holes for Pins, but hang (on the Laths) by a knot of their own Earth'.

Clay tiles were more in demand than slates as roof coverings in London and its hinterland during the early decades of the eighteenth century. Neve provides a comprehensive review of tiling practices in his *City and country purchaser*, but his brief reference to blue slates describes them as being 'commonly us'd in Covering of Summer, and Banquetting-houses in Gardens'.[41] Langley refers to tiles but not to slates in his 1729 edition of the *Builder's vade-mecum*, in the chapter 'Of the several Materials relating to Buildings'.[42] This preference for tiles may have been due to the availability of suitable clays in the Thames Valley area and also to traditional manufacturing skills that were present there from Tudor times. These same conditions produced the high quality stock bricks that formed the eighteenth-century London streetscapes. His commentary clearly indicates that the fixing of tiles on roofs was commonly the responsibility of the bricklaying trade.[43] Imported pantiles may

38 Representative Church Body Library, 'Liber Parochialis Eccles, S.S. Trinit Cork …', ff 32, 37 (P527, 7.1). 39 TCD, Abraham and Thomas Heatley's accounts, MUN/ P2/13/7, P2/16/10, P2/19/15, P2/20/35, P2/38/26, 27. 40 Neve, *The city and country purchaser*, p. 265. 41 Ibid., p. 240. 42 Batty Langley, *The builder's vade-mecum* (London, 1729), pp 64–6. 43 Neve, *The city and country*

have been preferred to plain tiles (despite their cost), because of the additional protection they provided against rainwater. Because of their corrugated profile, pantiles could be manufactured to larger dimensions than plain tiles, and they required a minimal (horizontal) overlap on account of their shape. For plain tiles, Neve quotes a cost of 15 to 17s. per 1,000 in Sussex (where they were fabricated) and costs of up to 25s. in the London market.[44] For pantiles, the cost quoted of 70 to 80s. per thousand appears excessive, but this must be measured against their economy in use: a given area could be roofed with fewer pantiles.

The other advantage offered by pantiles was their suitability for use on low-pitched roofs. This was exploited in 1631 by Inigo Jones, who successfully used them at pediment pitch on his St Paul's Church in Covent Garden. Wren's ample budgets allowed him to use leaden roofs on many of his major buildings, but he was content to use high slated roofs on several London churches and on his Royal Hospital at Chelsea. To some members of the architectural generation that followed Wren in the 1720s and 1730s, the necessity of maintaining low roof profiles was just as essential a design feature as Venetian windows, rusticated ashlar or other Palladian motifs. This is exemplified in drawings of Burlington's house at Chiswick in 1726, in his house for General Wade in 1724, in his Assembly Rooms at York in 1730, and in Kent's work on Holkham Hall and the Horse Guards building in the 1750s.

This concern for the diminution of the roof profile can also be glimpsed in Ireland during this period, but only in the work of a few dedicated Palladians. Pearce introduced the use of low-pitched Italian roof trusses into Ireland in 1725 in the roofs of Castletown, Co. Kildare, which had 35-degree pitches to parapet gutters at the façades, and 45-degree pitches to internal valley gutters. His pediment pitched roofs on the new Parliament House in 1730 were even lower (at 20 degrees) but this was achieved by the expensive expedient of using lead instead of slates. The roof of the 1730s Printing House in Trinity College is particularly interesting, as it has a pediment pitched roof of 27.5 degrees and is currently covered with large slates which would have been unobtainable in the first half of the eighteenth century. Castle's building estimate (c.1733) reveals that it was originally covered with imported pantiles.[45]

Castle's use of pantiles on the Printing House should not surprise us. The only alternative choice for low-pitched roofs during this period was lead, and because of its cost, lead was used only on roofs of important civic buildings. There were good precedents in Palladio's own work for tiled roofs, and Inigo Jones, faced with the identical problem of a tight budget, had used the same formula to produce a Palladian temple in Covent Garden a century earlier. Pearce's slated roofs on Castletown and Castle's pantiles on the Printing House were particularly daring uses of these materials for this period. Francis Price (as we have seen) advocated a minimum pitch of 38 degrees for pantiles and a 55-degree pitch for slates in 1733. The typical pitch of slated roofs in Ireland in the first half of the century was about 45 degrees. A series

purchaser, pp 268–70. 44 Ibid., pp 266, 267, 270, 271. 45 TCD, Richard Castle's accounts, MUN/P2/65/5.

of college accounts dealing with contracts under Castle's direction during the early 1740s are more surprising. In 1743, a bursar's payment of £69 0s. 3d. is recorded to Thomas Gibson for '9860 best glased Holland Pantiles at seven pounds per thousand'.[46] The use of these pantiles is suggested by a subsequent payment to the slater Thomas Heatley in 1744 for 'Tileing & Slateing' the old Hall.[47] The present Dining Hall was built under the supervision of Hugh Darley in the 1760s, and it is likely that he redesigned the roof framing at a higher pitch (40 degrees) to facilitate the use of slates, which were much easier to obtain in Dublin than pantiles. An interesting aspect of the existing hall complex is that the roof pitch of the old kitchen building is only 35 degrees. Was this also covered with glazed Holland pantiles by Castle, or was it rebuilt by Darley and roofed with tiles recovered from the wreckages the former Dining Hall?

* * *

Another roofing practice noted by Boate in seventeenth-century Ireland was the use of timber shingles. Neve is critical of their high cost, which limited their use to roofs of churches, to pyramidal steeples and to buildings in areas where tiles were unavailable.[48] The economics of using any roofing material were related to its production price, the cost of its transportation to building sites and its efficiency in covering the surface of the roof. He quoted the cost of (supplying and laying) shingles at between 30 to 60s. per 1,000, depending on their quality; he described the typical shingle as measuring 4 to 5 inches broad and 8 to 12 inches long, and he calculated that it required 1,000 shingles to cover a square of roofing surface.[49] This explains the high cost of English shingles: plain tiles (as we have seen) cost between 15 to 25 shillings per 1,000, and 600 to 800 tiles covered a square of roofing surface. Coupled with that, shingles required the additional expense of a layer of boarded sheeting, nailed to the roof structure (under the shingles) as further protection against the weather.

Shingles were made exclusively from oak, from 'quarter'd Oaken-boards'.[50] Neve described the best shingles as 'wedge' shaped, about an inch at the thicker end, following the radius of the circular tree trunk. Quarter sawn, or radially cut oak, was more expensive than flat sawn timber, but it had better weathering qualities and resisted shrinkage and warping in damp conditions. Despite their uneconomic value in England, we can well understand the economical use of shingles in seventeenth-century Ireland. Oak was cheap and plentiful in many parts of the country in the first half of the century, and shingles could be cut from smaller boughs that were unusable as framing timbers because of their size and curvature. They must have been more easily procured and a cheaper alternative to slates in the new plantation towns of

[46] TCD, Thomas Gibson's accounts, MUN/P2/85/10. [47] TCD, Thomas Heatley's accounts, MUN/P2/84/5. [48] Neve, *The city and country purchaser*, pp 238, 239. [49] Ibid., pp 238, 239, 240. [50] Ibid., p. 238.

Ulster such as Draperstown, Moneymore and Magherafelt. The indigenous woodlands of the Bann Valley had to be cleared, because they harboured rebellious natives, and the first generation of buildings in these frontier towns (following English traditions) were of oak cage construction. However, references to the use of oak shingles on specific buildings are more elusive than the evidence for the use of tiles. The records of the Dublin Philosophical Society in 1707 depict a house in Co. Down with shingled roof.[51] A description of the town of Lisburn, Co. Antrim, records the use of shingled roofs on many houses before the town was nearly entirely destroyed by fire in 1707.[52] The medieval spire of St Canice's Cathedral in Kilkenny had a covering of shingles in the early eighteenth century. Bishop Edward Synge's correspondence in relation to his palace at Elphin in 1747 also records the use of a shingled roof in his 'Landry-Room'.[53]

One of the most interesting records of early roofing contracts, involving both slates and shingles, is contained in the building accounts of Castle Durrow, Co. Laois, erected by William Flower between 1714 and 1718. Flower obviously regarded shingles as superior to slates obtained locally, as he used shingles to roof his dwelling house and slates to roof his stables and barns.[54] His preference is reflected in the cost he paid for both materials. In 1715 he purchased 21,000 slates at 10s. per 1,000 and in 1717 11,000 shingles (costing £16 10s. 0d.) at 30s. per 1,000. Another account from 1716 records the purchase of oak boards including 255ft of ½-inch board for use as shingles.[55]

Flower's slates soon proved unsatisfactory. A memorandum of 1720 in his accounts reads:

> Whereas the Slating work of the stables in Durrow done about four years past by Andrew Moore of Ballyragget is very much out of Repair ... it is this Day agreed ... that the said [John] Fannin [a slater from Kilkenny city] shall forthwith begin to new slate ... so as to make the said Roof perfectly staunch.[56]

All the roofs of Castle Durrow today are covered with slates, but there is no indication in Flower's accounts that his shingled roof was unsatisfactory. The slates used by Moore in the first contract were obtained at Ballyring quarry. Flower's accounts above clearly indicate that the shingled roofing of the castle was part of the carpenter's contract, undertaken by John Owens and John Coltsman. An item in their roofing agreement for 'Shrouding Boards ... Close Joynted' confirms the use of boarded undersheeting specified as a necessity by Neve. However, the Durrow account for ½-inch oak boards indicates that the shingles used by Flower were sawn rather than cleft, and they were obviously of even thickness (like tiles) unlike the wedge-shaped shingles described by Neve.

51 K. Theodore Hoppen (ed.), *Papers of the Dublin Philosophical Society, 1683–1709* (Dublin, 2008), 2, pp 785–8.   **52** TNA, SP/63/363, f. 85.   **53** Marie-Louise Legg (ed.), *The Synge letters* (Dublin, 1996), p. 77.   **54** NLI, Flower papers, MSS 11455 (1–3).   **55** Ibid., 11455 (2).   **56** Ibid., 11455 (3).

The difficulties in obtaining supplies of oak in Ireland from the early decades of the eighteenth century must have seriously inhibited the use of shingled roofs. William Flower had to transport oak for his buildings overland from the west bank of the Shannon to Durrow in 1715, and the continuous demand for oak for iron smelting contributed to increasing prices. The cost of 30s. per 1,000 for the shingles at Durrow resulted in a very expensive roofing contract. Slates in Dublin in 1710 cost 15s. per 1,000, and slate prices showed a marked decrease between that date and the mid-century.[57] In 1746, slates for Waterford Barrack cost 6s. per 1,000; in 1750, slates for the fortifications in Cork Harbour cost 4s. 6d. per 1,000.[58]

* * *

Slate was the predominant material used to cover Irish roofs from the medieval period until the beginning of the present century. The records of the construction of a new meeting hall (built with timber cagework) for the Dublin tailors' guild in 1583 describe payments for 10,000 slates.[59] Slate is a hard, fine-grained argillaceous stone, formed by immense pressure and heat. Owing to its fissile formation it contains cleavage planes enabling it to be split with a cleaving chisel into thin laminae, or slates.

Slate deposits, as Wilkinson noted in 1845, can be found in many coastal and inland counties in Ireland, but the number of Irish quarries producing marketable slates during his time was relatively small.[60] Wilkinson listed quarries at Killaloe in Co. Clare, Valentia Island in Co. Kerry, Bantry and Kinsale in Co. Cork, Ashford in Co. Wicklow, Corbally in Co. Tipperary and Moate in Co. Westmeath (fig. 9.5). In 1752, the eighteenth-century traveller Richard Pococke noted slate quarries on the Ards Peninsula, at Castlebar in Co. Mayo, and in 1758 at Kilmeadon, Co. Waterford and at Dunmanway, Co. Cork.[61] By Wilkinson's day many small local quarries had closed down because their markets had been taken over by the importation of slates from quarries in north and south Wales. In the eighteenth century the Welsh quarries had begun to dominate the markets on the east coast, and particularly in Dublin.

It is difficult to trace the origins of slates used in eighteenth-century building contracts, as sources of supply were recorded in only a few instances. Thomas Burgh's account of 18s. per square for 'Slating with best Carnarvon Slates' for the Dublin barracks in 1709 is evidence that the use of Welsh slates was established from the early years of the century.[62] William Flower, as we have seen, used a local quarry at Ballyring to roof the stables and barns of Castle Durrow in 1715. In the 1730s, slates were procured from a local quarry at Downhill for the roofing contract at Castle Forward, Co. Donegal.[63] In George Semple's proposal for building St Patrick's Hospital in 1749, his prescription for slating 'with Gray abby or with Ballywalter

---

57 TCD, Abraham Heatley's accounts, MUN/ P2/19/15.   58 *Commons Journal*, 5, ccii, ccxliii.   59 Henry F. Berry, 'The Merchant Tailors' Gild', *JRSAI*, 48 (1918), p. 41.   60 George Wilkinson, *Practical geology and ancient architecture of Ireland* (London, 1845), Tables 349.   61 McVeagh, *Richard Pococke's Irish tours*, pp 36, 79, 110, 189.   62 *Commons Journal*, 2, cxcix.   63 NLI, Castle Forward papers, MSS 10470.

9.5 George Wilkinson, 'Roofing slate quarry at Valentia, Co. Kerry', G. Wilkinson, *Practical geology and ancient architecture of Ireland* (London, 1845), p. 30.

slates, or with the Doubles of Carnarvon' established that the Ards Peninsula quarries were a viable alternative to Welsh slate in the Dublin market during the mid-century.[64] George Ensor's contract for building the Sessions House in Roscommon in 1762 specified the use of slates from the quarries at Killaloe with 'Dutch Tiles for the Ridge'.[65] Thomas Cooley's estimate for building the church at Kells in 1778 includes the provision of slates from Ballyjamesduff in Co. Cavan, but he also suggests the expensive alternative (doubling the cost) of ton slates from Caernarvon.[66] It is clear from the patterns emerging from these records that transportation cost had a considerable influence on market choice. The quarries at Caernarvon, the Ards Peninsula and Killaloe had the advantage of a location beside seaports or the banks of a navigable river. The cost of transporting slates from Killaloe to Roscommon by the Shannon was probably cheaper than that of bringing them along the much shorter distance overland from the quarries at Moate.

[64] St Patrick's Hospital, George Semple, 'A further description of the foregoing designs …' p. 19 (xerox copy in IAA, accession no. 2008/44).   [65] NLI, Pakenham Mahon papers, MS 10770 (2)   [66] NLI, Kells church accounts, MS 25304.

Daniel Mussenden's decision to transport 52 tons of Welsh slates to Belfast instead of purchasing them locally at the Ards quarries is easily explained. Mussenden was a merchant engaged in shipping timber and other commodities from the Baltic ports to Belfast, Dublin and ports on the west coast of Britain. His ships returning to Belfast from these ports would pick up cargoes of local produce as part of their normal trading operations. Mussenden was competing with the local quarries in the sale of slates in Belfast and its hinterland. The use of imported slates on roofs at Mount Stewart is more difficult to explain, especially as its owners, the Stewarts, also owned slate quarries in Co. Down at Ballyhiney and Craiganu.[67]

It is an indication of the demand for better quality and (possibly) larger slates that allowed architects to design lower pitched and more protective roofs. Cooley's suggestion for the use of extra-large ton slates on the roof of Kells church is another indication of this tendency. However, apart from the great mansions of the nobility such as Mount Stewart, many country houses, and houses in country towns, must have relied on slate supplies from small local quarries. There appears to have been a considerable number of these local quarries operating in the north-eastern part of Ireland. The Ballyhiney quarry yielded good results: in the two weeks starting 20 June 1808, a team of 11 men, some working part-time, produced 11,500 slates.[68] Thomas Smith, the quarry foreman, was a carpenter, his pay was 2s. per day and presumably the other 5 men were labourers. The slates were sold locally in 1807 for 30s. per 1,000.

In some areas in the west of Ireland the use of thin stone slabs (in lieu of slate) may have been common. In an affidavit sworn in 1749 presented to a parliamentary inquiry into barrack building, Owen McGinnis, a slater from Galway, promoted the use of 'Bophin and Molbay Slates [as being] preferable for Strength and Lasting to either Welsh or Killaloe Slates'.[69] He was defending the slating on the roof of the recently completed barrack at Gort, and presumably the slates praised in his evidence were the shallow bedded limestone slabs quarried on the coast of Co. Clare at Malbay and Liscannor. This practice of using stone flags for roofing is confirmed by a report of a visit to Galway by Daniel Augustus Beaufort in 1787, which observed that 'The houses are roofed with large heavy flags near an inch thick'.[70]

None of the records of slating contracts describe the process followed by eighteenth-century slaters in fixing slates to roofs, but lists of materials in daywork accounts provide enough information to make reasonable assumptions on the methods employed. Accounts include costs of slates (sold by the 1,000), pins (sold by the 1,000), nails (sold by the 1,000), lime (sold by the hogshead) and sand (sold by the cartload). Amounts for ridge tiles (sold by the dozen) often occur in accounts. Some larger contracts, particularly in the latter part of the century, record purchases of slates by the ton.

The slates were obviously fixed to the slating laths that were nailed transversely across the sloping rafters. Lime and sand were used to make a mortar bedding for the

---

[67] PRONI, D654/H/1/1,2; D654/H/7/B/1. [68] PRONI, D654/H/7/B/1. [69] *Commons Journal*, 5, app. cxxx. [70] TCD, 'Journal of a tour ... 1787', MS 4026, f. 56.

slates and some jobbing accounts simply refer to charges for mortar instead of its component ingredients. The slates were fixed to the laths with the pins, but to fully understand the difference between nails and pins we must look further than the slater's accounts. Neve says very little about slating, as it was uncommon in the London area during his period, but he refers to 'Slates hang'd on Tacks, and laid with finer mortar than tiles'.[71] Elsewhere, he is very specific about pins, which he describes as made of heart-oak and used to fix tiles to roofing laths. An account of 1750 for the purchase of 18,000 slates to roof buildings in Cork Harbour includes an amount for slaters' pegs which, of course, is another way of describing timber fixing pins.[72]

A clear description of a fixing system is contained in George Semple's proposals for St Patrick's Hospital in 1749 and for his Public Offices in 1758.[73] His Public Offices specification is more elaborate and expensive than his demands for the hospital, but his slate fixing is similar, except for the provision of continuous timber sheeting (nailed to the rafters) instead of slating battens. Neve refers to this arrangement as a necessity with slates but there are no records of its use in Trinity College, and Semple did not consider it necessary on the roofs of St Patrick's Hospital. His description of the roofing process is revealing:

> Those four Buildings, are to be cover'd, either with Stout, London Laddys, Double doubles, or Some other sort, of exceeding sound, and large Slates, Each of which, must have two holes, in them. The holes in the heads, must be about three eights of one Inch wide, in the Largest Stu'f and in the smaller Stuff, they may be some what less in proportion ... Through each, & every of s'd holes, there must be another hole, Board [i.e., bored] down through the Slit dale sheeting, with a spike Gimble, of the exact same size of the respective holes, through which there must be, a Sound dry neat Oak pin, drove to the head, and so as it may not only fill, the hole in the Slate, but also ti[gh]tly fill, the hole in the sheeting. And besides each Slate, being so pin'd down, to the Sheeting, Each of them must also have, a very Stout fourpen'y nail, made in A sixpenny mould, drove through each of the Shoulder holes, into the sheeting.

Oak pins were used as slate fixings because of the vulnerability to rust of eighteenth-century iron nails, which could easily detach the nailhead from its shank on roofs exposed to bad weather conditions. Oak pins would tend to swell in wet conditions, and this provided an advantage in securing the slates to the laths. Semple's device in driving a nail into the centre of the pin further tightened the pin in its hole. Rust would not have the same effect on these nails, as their heads and shanks were

---

71 Neve, *The city and country purchaser*, p. 240.   72 *Commons Journal*, 5, ccxliii.   73 King's Inns Library, [George Semple], 'Publick-Offices, &c. (January 25: 1758) ...', MS HI/1-1, pp 17, 18; St Patrick's Hospital, George Semple, 'A further description of the foregoing designs ...' p. 19 (xerox copies of both in IAA, accession no. 2008/44).

countersunk into the oak pin. His specification introduces some other important aspects of contemporary slating practice. His reference to largest stuff and smallest stuff must relate to the use of differently sized slates and inevitably to the use of diminishing courses graded from a maximum at the eaves to a minimum at ridge level. His insistence on 'laddys', double doubles and large slates focuses on the most important requirement of size, the procurement of slates large enough to provide a weathertight overlap, vertically and horizontally.

The first indication in the Trinity College building accounts of a new demand for larger slates came in the 1750s with the introduction of two different slate sizes, described respectively as singles and doubles.[74] The singles at 18s. per square (slates and workmanship) cost the same as in measured contracts in the Dublin area over the previous thirty years. The doubles, at £1 2s. 6d. per square, obviously involved a better quality and larger slate which had not previously been used in the college. Their use also introduced additional charges in the 1760s for heavier slating laths, which rose in price from 2s. to 4s. per 100, but in time these charges were reduced again.[75] Doubles were in common use in the college from the 1760s until the end of the century, and their use may have contributed to the evident reduction of roofing failures in the college buildings during this period.

Semple was anxious to promote the most advanced constructional systems in his design for the Dublin Public Offices, and his proposal refers to even larger slates, such as London laddys (ladies) and double doubles. Slate had begun to replace tiling in the London market by the second half of the eighteenth century, and it was undoubtedly the production of larger slates from the Welsh quarries that promoted this change. Semple's description referred to a slate size identified with London practice but not quarried locally. By the end of the century, the industrialized production systems developed in the Bangor quarries could produce slates with dimensions up to 3ft. The largest slates produced, the ton slates, were (as their name suggests) sold by weight. These slates were commonly used for eaves courses on Irish buildings such as the Royal Hospital Kilmainham and Dr Steevens's Hospital.

To get a clear picture of the sizes and classification of slates we must turn to the early nineteenth-century building manuals. In 1830 John Nicholson provided the following table for Welsh slate used in the London area:[76]

Doubles	average size	13 inches x 6 inches
Ladies	average size	15 inches x 8 inches
Countess	average size	20 inches x 10 inches
Duchess	average size	24 inches x 12 inches
Queens	average size	36 inches x 24 inches
Imperials	average size	30 inches x 24 inches

74 TCD, Thomas Kelly's accounts, MUN/P2/87/8, P2/97/7.   75 TCD, Obadiah Bolton's accounts, MUN/P2/144/1.   76 John Nicholson, *The builder's practical guide* (London, 1830), p. 621.

The manuals produced by Irish measurers, such as Thomas Humphreys in 1813 and William Stitt in 1819, relate this classification to Irish practice.[77] Humphreys recommended Irish slates from Killaloe, Ballywalter and Kinsale, but he confirmed the substantial use of slates from both north and south Wales. Bangor (Caernarvon) slates were popular in Dublin, but slates from Cardigan in south Wales were sold in Cork, Waterford and Belfast. The most commonly used slates in Dublin were doubles, countesses and queens. Stitt's tables of slate sizes and their relative roof coverage puts the classification into a measurable context:

1,000 singles	covers	1 square of roofing
1,000 doubles	covers	2–2¼ square of roofing
1,000 ladies	covers	3 square of roofing
1,000 countess	covers	6 square of roofing
1,000 duchess	covers	10 square of roofing

Humphreys relates this coverage factor to the products of the principal Irish slate quarries. The slates commonly supplied from Kinsale (by the 1,000) covered 1½ squares of roofing, from Ballywalter 'a little better than two' squares, and from Killaloe from 1½ to 3 squares, depending on size and quality. This meant that slates such as doubles could be obtained from Ballywalter and doubles and ladies could be supplied from Killaloe. The omission of the small slate called singles from Nicholson's classification table indicates its unreliability as a practical roof covering. This slate was used extensively in Dublin during the first half of the eighteenth century, and the almost continuous need for roofing repairs in Trinity College may have been a result of its use there. Nicholson also expressed reservations about the use of the smaller slates such as doubles and ladies without the provision of boarded sheeting under the slates. The use of sheeting on rafters was typical of high quality roof construction in the nineteenth century, but there are few indications of its use in eighteenth-century Ireland.

Nicholson indicated average slate sizes of 15 x 8 inches for ladies and 13 x 6 inches for doubles. We have no information on the size of the singles slate, but it is unlikely to have been more than 12 x 5 inches. The width of a slate was its most crucial dimension as the horizontal lap between joints was relatively small. The use of closely spaced slating laths could ensure considerable vertical overlap even with small slates, but the normal horizontal lap with singles slating was only 2½ inches. The English common tile with dimensions of 10½ x 6¼ inches was probably more efficient in use than the singles slate.

The availability of larger slates from Wales and the principal Irish quarries in the second half of the eighteenth century must have ensured more waterproof roof coverings and less maintenance. This is clear from the reduction in the amount of

---

[77] Thomas Humphreys, *The Irish builder's guide* (Dublin, 1813), pp 169–70; William Stitt, *The practical architect's ready assistant* (Dublin, 1819), p. 337.

9.6 General Wade's house, London, garden front, 1723, Colen Campbell, *Vitruvius Britannicus*, 3 (London, 1725), plate 10.

jobbing contracts in Trinity College and particularly from the absence of salaried maintenance agreements. Abraham Heatley was working on an annual salary of £20 in 1686, an arrangement renewed in 1730 for £45; a Thomas Heatley, slater, was on an annual salary of £45 in 1746.[78] There are no indications of maintenance payments to Heatley's successors such as Obadiah Bolton or James Elliot.

Semple's demand for slates such as ladies or double doubles in 1758 indicates that a variety of slate sizes were available in the Dublin market at this period. However, building supervisors in Trinity College must have been happy with the performance

---

78 TCD, Abraham Heatley's accounts, MUN/P2/2/20, P2/3, 4, P2/60; TCD, Thomas Heatley's accounts, MUN/P2/90/7.

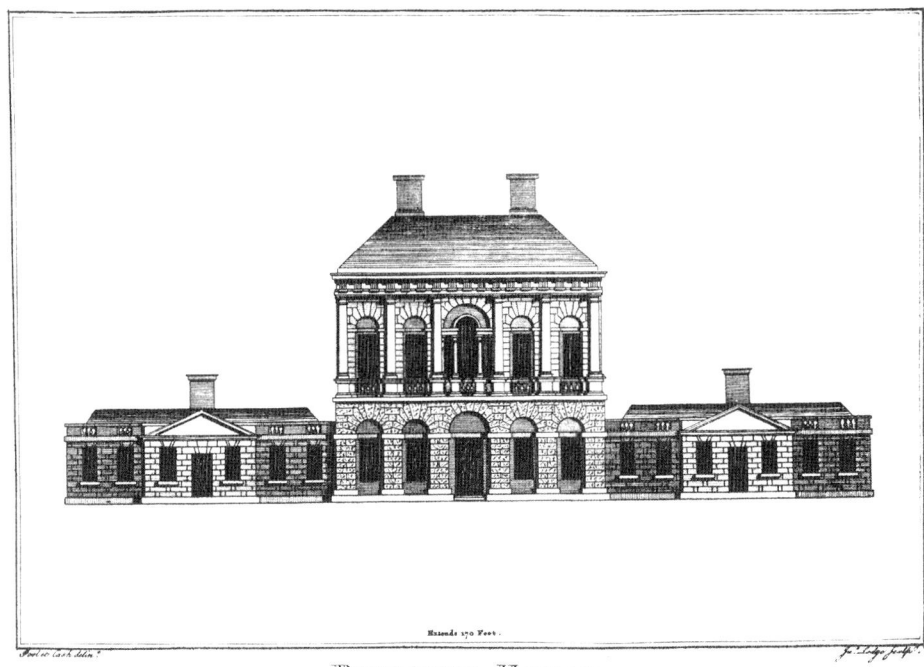

9.7 The Provost's House, Trinity College Dublin, 1760s, Robert Pool and John Cash, *Views of the most remarkable public buildings … in Dublin* (Dublin, 1780).

9.8 'Front to the Inns Quay of Design for the Publick Offices', Thomas Cooley, 1776, King's Inns Library. Reproduced with permission of the King's Inns.

of the 13 by 6 inch doubles, as most of the contracts from the 1750s until the early 1800s were carried out with this small slate. The use of larger slates in the lower courses (at the gutters) may have been introduced before the end of the century, as in 1801 James Elliot was paid for slating on the New Chapel using a combination of Bangor doubles and ton slates. This provided considerable protection at one of the roof's most vulnerable weak spots.

The later slating accounts (from the 1770s onwards) in Trinity College contain some variations in their material content, which require comment. None of the accounts contain references to wooden slating pins, and the possibility that the use of iron nail fixings may have been introduced (with larger slate sizes) cannot be ignored. Both the early eighteenth-century accounts and later accounts contain payments for lime and sand, but the later accounts refer to the process of rendering (plastering rather than bedding) with mortar. In the earlier period, the use of small slates (such as singles) and four fixings in each slate (four pin bond) required closely spaced slating laths. This allowed slaters to apply a mortar bed underneath the slates in the same way that plaster was applied to ceiling laths. With the later use of larger slates and widely spaced laths, it was impossible to provide support for mortar bedding, and the slates were rendered by an application of mortar on their under-surfaces from inside the roof structure.

It is interesting to look at the effects larger slate sizes had on eighteenth-century roof design. The introduction of bigger slates brought two important advantages: they improved the weathering qualities of pitched roofs and they allowed the use of lower roof profiles. Predictably, most mid-eighteenth-century Irish builders accepted the advantage of a better technical performance, but ignored the visual potential of lower roof pitches. Semple, for instance, specified a larger slate (ladies or double doubles) on his Public Offices in 1758, rather than the doubles he used on St Patrick's Hospital in 1749, but both buildings were designed to have 45-degree roof pitches. A comparison between Burlington's house for General Wade in London (in 1723) and the Provost's House in Trinity College (in 1758) shows that the Dublin building copied all the essential aspects of the London façade except the low roof profile (figs. 9.6 & 9.7).

The continuous use of small slates in Trinity College may have been responsible for the conservative policy on roof profiles there, even in the 1770s. Christopher Myers's adaption of Chambers's designs for the Chapel and Theatre used roof profiles which would have been considered obtrusive in London during this period. By this time, Chambers, like his contemporaries Wyatt and Adam, was using the full capacity of the Caernarvon slates to minimize the bulk of his roofs.

The first design in Dublin to exhibit the potential of larger slate sizes was Thomas Cooley's proposal for Public Offices in 1776. Cooley's elevational treatment showed low roofs at 30 degrees which did not obtrude on the primacy of the central pediment (fig. 9.8). This illustrates the daring of Pearce's slated roofs in Castletown with a pitch of 35 degrees. Cooley's building was incorporated into Gandon's Four Courts in the late 1780s, but by that time Gandon had already executed his design for the Custom House with its low roofs brilliantly concealed behind stone balustrades. In the work that followed in the 1790s, and especially in cases where his slated roofs were visible (such as the houses at Emsworth, Abbeville and the Royal Military Infirmary), the roof pitches were low enough to be unobtrusive. The succeeding generation of Irish neoclassical architects followed his example and there are few nineteenth-century classical buildings with roof pitches higher than 35 degrees.

CHAPTER TEN

The glazier and the development of eighteenth-century window patterns

GLAZING APPEARS TO HAVE BEEN established as a separate trade in Dublin from the end of the sixteenth century. There is no mention of glaziers in the city freedom rolls before 1576, but between that date and 1596 we find the names of eight artisans enfranchised as glaziers by the city corporation.[1] Earlier glazing contracts may have been undertaken by other established trades such as plumbers and blacksmiths. The medieval use of casement windows made with iron frames and glazing bedded in soldered leadwork involved materials and techniques familiar to both these trades. The emergence of the glazing trade in England and Ireland was encouraged by the development of the Tudor window type with its transoms, mullions, casements and elaborate fenestration. The introduction of manufacturing facilities in seventeenth-century glasshouses in both England and Ireland made window glass more available, and promoted its use in domestic buildings in the cities and towns of both kingdoms. Changing building patterns (following architectural fashions) and the widespread use of classical designs at the beginning of the eighteenth century offered new opportunities for trades such as bricklayers, painters and glaziers. One of the most significant changes, the use of the sliding sash window (which made its appearance in Dublin during this period), was rapidly introduced into many building types in all parts of Ireland.

Glaziers were members of the smiths' guild (of St Loy), which received a royal charter in 1474. This guild represented several other trades that dealt with the fusion of hot metals such as braziers, founders, tinplate workers and trunk makers, but it also represented ironmongers, girdlers and embroiderers. Although eighteenth-century accounts provide no records of trades other than glaziers undertaking glazing work, there is evidence of seventeenth-century glazing contracts being handled by a blacksmith. William Vizer (enfranchised as a smith in 1662) sought payment in 1683 for glazing the city Tholsel, and he was employed by Trinity College on several glazing contracts from 1684 until 1686.[2]

Vizer may have been apprenticed as a glazier and loosely described as a smith in the freedom rolls because of the glaziers' affiliation with the smiths' guild. On the

---

This chapter should be read in conjunction with a more recent study by Nessa Roche, *The legacy of light: a history of Irish windows* (Bray, 1999). 　1 DCLA, typescript, roll of freemen of the city of Dublin. 2 *CARD*, 5, p. 310; TCD, William Vizer's accounts, MUN/P2/1/36, P2/2/45 onwards.

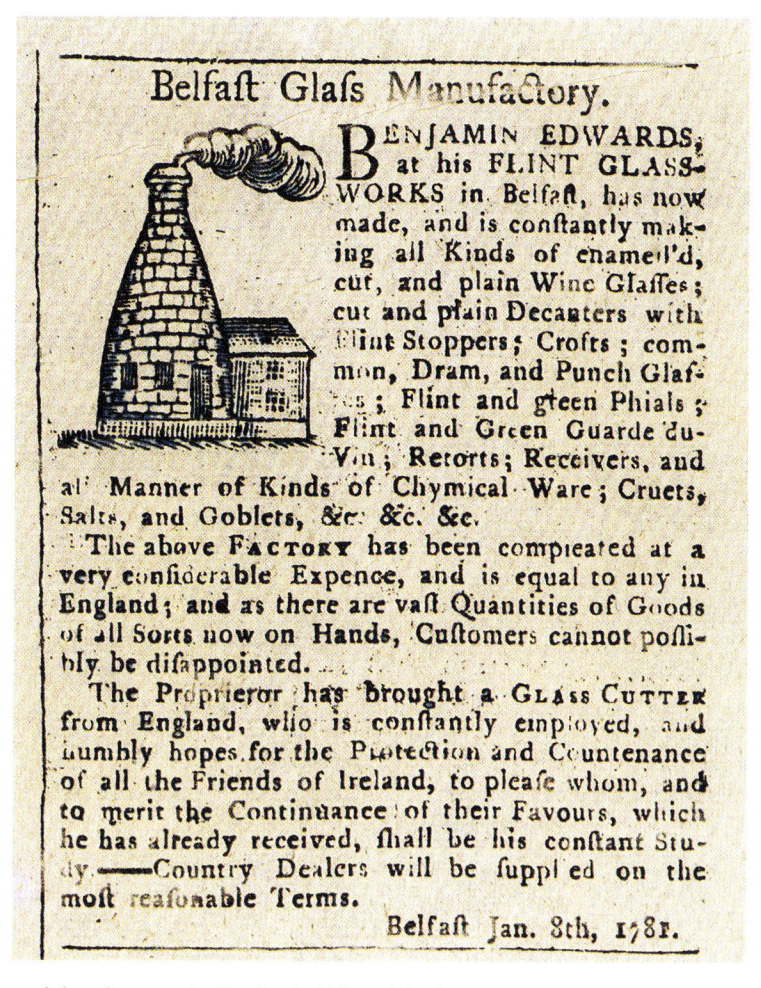

> **Belfast Glass Manufactory.**
>
> BENJAMIN EDWARDS, at his FLINT GLASS-WORKS in Belfast, has now made, and is constantly making all Kinds of enamell'd, cut, and plain Wine Glasses; cut and plain Decanters with Flint Stoppers; Crofts; common, Dram, and Punch Glasses; Flint and green Phials; Flint and Green Guarde du-Vin; Retorts; Receivers, and all Manner of Kinds of Chymical Ware; Cruets, Salts, and Goblets, &c. &c. &c.
>
> The above FACTORY has been compleated at a very considerable Expence, and is equal to any in England; and as there are vast Quantities of Goods of all Sorts now on Hands, Customers cannot possibly be disappointed.
>
> The Proprietor has brought a GLASS CUTTER from England, who is constantly employed, and humbly hopes for the Protection and Countenance of all the Friends of Ireland, to please whom, and to merit the Continuance of their Favours, which he has already received, shall be his constant Study.——Country Dealers will be supplied on the most reasonable Terms.
>
> Belfast Jan. 8th, 1781.

10.1 Advertisement for Benjamin Edwards's glasshouse, Belfast, 8 January 1781.

other hand, he may have enjoyed the reciprocal benefits of dual training within the guild system. There are several examples of painters (such as Isaac Chalke and William Wall) who were trained (and operated) also as plasterers. Smiths were responsible for the fabrication of iron casement frames in the seventeenth century, and the additional skills in soldering leadwork were not difficult to acquire for artisans used to handling hot metals. However, prominent glazing contractors working in Dublin during this period (1680–1720) appear to have been apprenticed within the glazing trade in the usual manner. Andrew Rock (enfranchised in 1660) worked under Burgh on the old Parliament House, and he was engaged on a maintenance contract at the Royal Hospital Kilmainham in 1692; George Delane replaced William Vizer in Trinity College in the 1690s, and is the only glazier recorded there until 1720;

Erasmus Taylor (enfranchised in 1697) glazed the first construction phase of the new Parliament House from 1728.[3]

Some prominent eighteenth-century glazing contractors such as James Hull (who succeeded Rock in the Royal Hospital in 1712), John Rowlett (who glazed in Trinity College and *c*.1750 at the Parliament House) and Thomas Silcock (who gave evidence on glass prices to a parliamentary inquiry in 1752) are not recorded in existing copies of the freedom rolls, and we cannot be certain of their trade or guild affiliations.[4] However, by the 1730s, most of the windows used in Irish contracts were being fabricated by joiners and carpenters, and these Dublin glaziers were never involved with timber fabrication. On the other hand, the building records of barrack construction (1750–60) provide evidence of carpenters being paid for glazing sashes in provincial areas of Ireland.[5]

* * *

The principal materials used by eighteenth-century glaziers were window glass and glazing putty. Putty, a mastic made from whiting and linseed oil, was used to fix and seal glass panes into the rebates of timber sashes. Casement windows of timber and iron were still in use in the early decades of the century. The earlier method of glazing with soldered lead that persisted throughout the seventeenth century in Ireland and England was also in use in the first half of the succeeding century. Glass was made in furnaces by the fusion of silica (sand), soda (soda ash) and lime (limestone or chalk). Materials (such as manganese) were often added to counteract the green discoloration caused by the presence of iron in sand. Kelp is recorded as an additive used by eighteenth-century glassmakers in Ireland, but not for flint glass.[6] All of these materials could be produced in Ireland, but many glassmakers found it more economical or convenient to import materials such as sand or soda ash (in the form of potash) from abroad. In his description of the glasshouse at Birr, Co. Offaly, Boate states that sand was imported from England.[7] The accounts of an Irish glasshouse in 1622 record the use of ashes obtained from burning ferns in the manufacture of glass; Neve also refers to the use of salts obtained from the ashes of ferns in glassmaking in England.[8]

Many producers of window glass also made flint glass or crystal tableware, which required siliceous sand of considerable purity. This was mostly imported from Lynn in Norfolk and from the Isle of Wight. Potash was imported from Baltic ports by the Belfast merchant Daniel Mussenden in the 1750s.[9] In 1784, the crown glass and bottle

3 *Commons Journal*, 2, ccviii; NAI, RHK minutes, RHK 1/1/1, f. 45 *v*; TCD, George Delane's accounts between MUN/P2/8/11 and P2/41/11; *Commons Journal*, 4, xxxiii.   **4** NAI, RHK minutes, RHK 1/1/2, f. 179; *Commons Journal*, 5, lxii; TCD, John Rowlett's accounts, MUN/P2/61/18, 19; *Commons Journal*, 5, lxxvii.   **5** *Commons Journal*, 6, ccxcix, cccxxii.   **6** M.S. Dudley Westropp, *Irish glass*, ed. Mary Boydell (Dublin, 1978), pp 27, 30, 173–4.   **7** Gerard Boate, *Irelands naturall history* (London, 1657), p. 162.   **8** Marsh's Library, MS Z3.1.3 (12); Richard Neve, *The city and country purchaser* (London, 1726; facsimile ed., 1969, 'Glass').   **9** PRONI, Mussenden papers, D354/771.

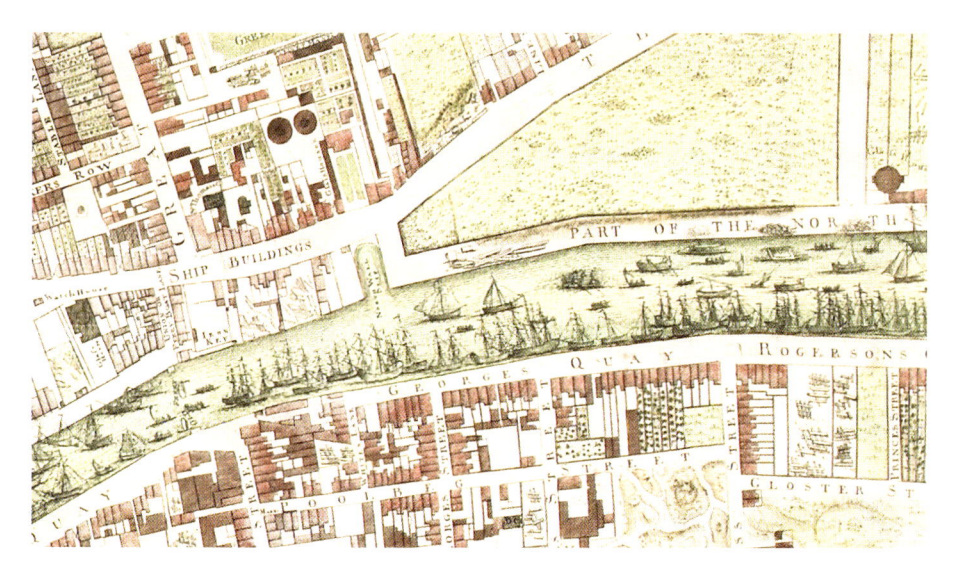

10.2 John Rocque, 'An Exact Survey of the City and Suburbs of Dublin', 1756, detail, glasshouses on the North Wall and Marlborough Green, BL, K. Top. 53. 13. b. 11. Reproduced with permission of the British Library.

manufacturers of Dublin petitioned parliament against a newly imposed duty on imported sand for glassmaking.[10] Up to this time sand had not attracted customs duties, as it was commonly shipped as ballast. Some Irish glasshouses used local sand in their process. Dublin bottle manufacturers procured suitable sand from beaches at the Bull Island.[11] The *Dublin Journal* of 19 June 1773 carried an advertisement for a glasshouse near Dungannon, described as having sand and other materials available in its vicinity. A siliceous sand obtained from Muckish mountain in Donegal was successfully used in Belfast for the production of crystal tableware in 1802.[12]

Fuel for glass furnaces was another important requirement of the manufacturing process. The abundance of oak woodlands in Ireland in the early part of the seventeenth century promoted the establishment of glasshouses in the vicinity of country estates. Boate mentions a number of glasshouses set up by English colonists, such as the one at Parsonstown (Birr), which supplied window and drinking glasses to the Dublin market.[13] Boate also refers to the absence of glass manufacturing in Dublin and other cities during the first half of the seventeenth century; this may have been because of their distance from fuel supplies. This was to change due to the scarcity of timber in the eighteenth century when most of the principal glasshouses operated in coastal cities to avail of imported supplies of coal.

Westropp tentatively dates the start of glass making in Ireland to *c*.1585: George Longe, 'who first brought to pass making of glass in Ireland', kept a glasshouse near

10 *Commons Journal*, 11, p. 222.   11 Much of the information in this and the following three paragraphs comes from Westropp, *Irish glass*.   12 Ibid., pp 169–70.   13 Boate, *Irelands naturall history*, p. 162.

10.3 Lord Mark Kerr, 'View of Ballycastle', Co. Antrim, with glasshouse, early nineteenth century. Courtesy of the Hector McDonnell Collection.

Curryglass in Co. Cork.[14] A glasshouse operating in the 1620s supplied window glass to glaziers in Youghal, Limerick, Cork and Dublin.[15] In 1623, Sir Lawrence Parsons of Birr Castle signed a lease with the glassmaker Abraham Bigo that deterred him from making glass or procuring timber on any land outside of the Parsons estate; about 1670 Ananias Henzy set up a glasshouse near the new town of Portarlington.[16] Henzy and Bigo were both French craftsmen whose families originally came from glassmaking centres in Lorraine. The names of workmen recorded in the accounts of the glasshouse at Ballynagerah, Co. Kerry, also suggest French origins. The earliest glasshouse recorded in the neighbourhood of Waterford was at Gurteen, and dates from the 1720s; in 1731 we read of 'The Glass-house near Waterford' preparing to make 'best London crown and other glass for windows'.[17]

The transportation cost of coal for glass furnaces and the proximity of expanding markets were key factors in the development of glass production in the eighteenth century. Rocque's map of 1756 shows the presence of five glass cones in Dublin city, all of them sited on the northern side of the Liffey within a short distance of the quays (fig. 10.2). One was built on the quays at the North Wall, two were adjacent to it at Marlborough Green, a fourth was sited with frontages to Bachelors Walk and Abbey Street and the fifth at the junction of Bradogue Lane and St Mary's Lane. The presence of a colliery at Ballycastle, Co. Antrim, may have promoted the building

14 Westropp, *Irish glass*, pp 20–4.   15 Ibid., p. 29.   16 Ibid., p. 33.   17 Ibid., p. 68.

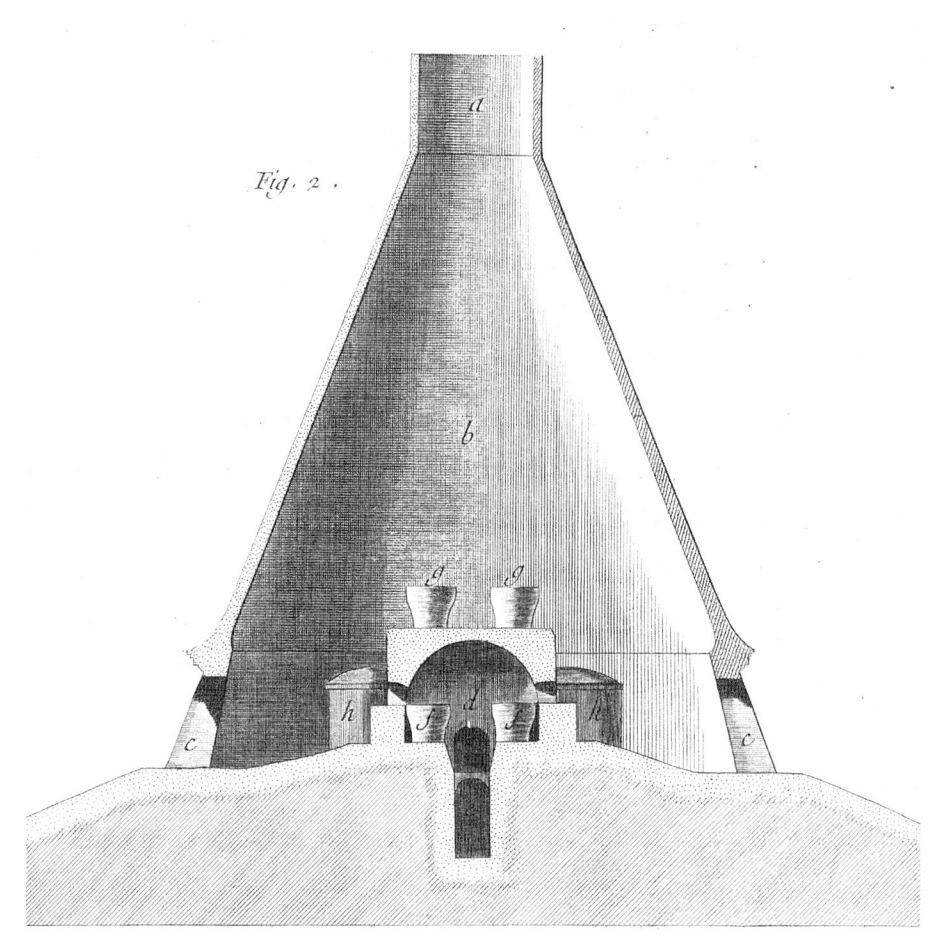

10.4 Denis Diderot, 'Verrerie Angloise' [English glasshouse] *Encyclopédie* (1751–72), plate III of Verrerie Angloise.

there of a glassworks making bottles and window glass in the 1750s. Hugh Boyd, who owned the colliery, was also an owner of the glass factory (fig. 10.3). An advertisement for the Drumrea Glasshouse (near Dungannon) in the *Dublin Journal* of 12 July 1772 described it as being part of the Tyrone Collieries. Bottle, window, plate and flint glass were produced in Cork city by 1783.[18] The *Belfast Newsletter* of 19 August 1785 announced the erection of a glasshouse at the Long Bridge for the supply of bottles and window glass.

* * *

18 *Commons Journal*, 11, p. 75.

The main technical influences on glassmaking in seventeenth-century Ireland and England came from well-established *verreries* in France (fig. 10.4). Two methods of producing window glass were used in Europe during this period. The most common method, used in Holland, Germany, Lorraine and Burgundy, produced a glass known as cylinder glass, or broad glass. The other method, commonly used in Normandy, produced glass known as crown glass. The accounts of the products sold by the glasshouse noted earlier included reference in 1622 to 'broad wyndow-Glasse'.[19] The influence of expatriate glassmakers from Lorraine developed the production of broad glass in England and Ireland during the seventeenth century. Crown glass production was introduced into London in the last decades of the century and it became the most commonly used window glass there by the middle of the nineteenth century. Broad glass was produced by blowing a ball of molten glass into an elongated cylinder that was cut down its length with shears and flattened gradually (in a furnace) into sheet form. The flattening process also interfered with the diaphanous transparency of the material and left streaks and other imperfections.

Crown glass was initially blown into a globular shape that was spun (on an iron rod) with sufficient velocity to flatten the globe into a perfectly circular disc. These discs (known as tables in the trade) were slightly curved (dished) in surface with a characteristic thickening (or bullion) at their centres where the rod had been attached to the glass. Because the surface of the glass was untouched in the flattening process, it retained the brilliance and diaphanous transparency imparted by the fire. The cutting of a circular table of crown glass into rectangular sash squares obviously involved more wastage than the division of broad glass. McGrath and Frost describe how 'Tables' of glass varied from 40 inches to 5ft in diameter, the last size 'calling for great skill and strength' on the part of the glassblower.[20] This latter size would have produced six sash squares of the 18 x 13 inch proportion used in many Palladian buildings, but possibly only four of the larger (22 x 16 inch) panes used in later buildings. The demand for crown glass was based on its surface qualities of colour, iridescence and transparency; wastage was part of its price. These qualities can still be perceived in surviving examples of this glass in sashes in Dublin streets (such as Molesworth Street) and in several buildings in Trinity College, but we cannot be certain of its age (fig. 10.5). The only examples of crown glass that are undeniably eighteenth-century in origin are those in the bookcases of the Worth Library (in Dr Steevens's Hospital), which date from the 1740s. Wastage, of course, was not such a serious problem in areas where surplus glass could be recycled in local glasshouses. Another important use for glass selvedge at the edges of crown tables was in the tapering panes used in the production of fanlights. This was also part of the glazier's responsibilities.

The credit for the introduction of the crown glass process into England has been attributed to John Bowles, who managed the Bear Garden glasshouse at Bankside

---

[19] Marsh's Library, MS Z3.1.3 (12).   [20] Raymond McGrath and A.C. Frost, *Glass in architecture and decoration* (London, 1937), p. 21.

10.5 Trinity College Dublin, Parliament Square, 1750s, example of crown glass.

(London) from 1678 to 1691. According to McGrath and Frost, the descriptive term 'crown' developed from the custom of embossing the central bullion of each table of glass produced by Bowles with a crown.[21] Neve records the early development of the crown process $c.$1691 at the Bankside factory, but the management transferred the production of window glass to another London premises at Ratcliff.[22]

Broad glass was undoubtedly still used for cheaper work and for situations such as basement or dormer windows. McGrath and Frost were of the view that crown glass became the predominant choice for eighteenth-century windows because of its inherent qualities. D.B. Harden, on the other hand, maintained that broad glass was in constant use, recommended, no doubt, for its cheapness and low wastage ratio.[23]

---

21 Ibid., p. 22.   22 Neve, *The city and country purchaser*, p. 145.   23 D.B. Harden, 'Domestic window glass' in E.M. Jope (ed.) *Studies in building history* (London, 1961), p. 55.

Broad glass was made from a flattened cylinder into tables that had two parallel sides. There are many examples (possibly of nineteenth-century) crown glass still to be seen in Ireland but surviving examples of broad glass are difficult to find. There are some panes of white glass in the early sashes in Marsh's Library that have all the appearance of the inherent defects of the broad glass fabrication process. The making of plate glass in Cork by 1783 provided glaziers with an alternative to crown or broad glass.[24] Plate glass was produced by pouring molten glass onto a steel casting table, rolling it into a thin sheet and subsequently grinding and polishing. This glass could be made in sheets of unprecedented size and its polished surface provided less distortion than crown, or broad glass. However, high manufacturing costs inhibited its use for windows in the eighteenth century and most of the plate glass produced was used to make mirrors.

Neve provides a valuable description of different window glasses available in the London market in the early years of the eighteenth century. He lists the products of the local glasshouses making crown glass (at Ratcliff and Lambeth) and glass brought from both Newcastle ('most in use here in *England*') and Bristol ('very rare … in *London*').[25] London, like Dublin during this period, also used imported glass from France, Holland and Germany. Neve promoted the qualities of London crown glass, which he clearly preferred to the broad glass produced in Newcastle or in European glasshouses. He described the dimension of the crown glass tables produced in London as being 42 to 44 inches in diameter, which produced 9 to 10 sq ft of window glass. Ratcliff crown was described as being 'a light Sky-blew Colour'; Lambeth crown he described as 'inclining something to a Green'.[26] He referred to the ash-coloured Newcastle glass as the cheapest and most commonly used glass in England, but he was critical of its quality and its lack of transparency. Newcastle glass was produced in sizes which contained 5 to 7 sq ft per table. Its economy was based on cheap fuel supplies and cheap transportation of cases of glass (embedded in coal) in the holds of colliers. He was aware of the quality of Bristol glass but he found it difficult to obtain in London because of transportation problems.

Window glass was made in Dublin in the 1730s and there were plans in 1731 to make it near Waterford; however, no reference has been found in contemporary building accounts of the use of this glass.[27] French glass was used extensively in early classical buildings in Dublin. It was used in the Tholsel in *c*.1680 and in the Royal Hospital in 1711.[28] Accounts from the second decade of the eighteenth century in Trinity College record the use of French, Dutch and English glass.[29] A dealer named Thomas Seagrave supplied eleven cribbs of French glass (costing £2 8s. 0d. each) there in 1723, and French glass was used on several college buildings by the Dublin glazier John Rowlett between 1730 and 1735.[30]

24 *Commons Journal*, 11, p. 75.   25 Neve, *The city and country purchaser*, pp 146–8.   26 Ibid.   27 Westropp, *Irish glass*, pp 45, 68.   28 *CARD*, 5, p. 310; NAI, RHK Minute Books, 2, RHK 1/1/2, f. 162 r.   29 TCD, George Delane's accounts, MUN/P2/24/10-13, P/32/9–13.   30 TCD, Joan Delane's accounts, MUN/P2/51/15; John Rowlett's accounts, MUN/P2/61/19; P2/62/12, 13; P2/70/18.

After the 1730s, building records are less specific about the origins of window glass, but imports of crown glass from both Bristol and London are recorded. London glass was used in the building of Castle Forward in Co. Donegal in the 1730s.[31] References to the costs of Bristol glass are recorded in accounts for glazing the Parliament House in 1749 and in an enquiry into provincial barrack building in 1752.[32] In 1749, the Bishop of Elphin specified the use of panes of Bristol crown glass for the 'Lanterns' of his new palace.[33] The purchase of eleven cases of Bristol crown glass from the merchant Isaac Mee, reported in 1752 for such a utilitarian contract as the barracks at Carlow, is a good indication that cheaper local alternatives were not available.[34] The earliest records of the use of Dublin glass in building accounts were in contracts for the reconstruction of provincial barracks in 1760. In that year, John Magill, the Comptroller of Works, issued a directive on construction standards on barrack contracts in Athlone, Castlebar and other towns in the north-west circuit. His prescriptions may have been particularly pertinent, as his comments were not intended primarily for glaziers, but for carpenters, who handled glazing in remote areas as part of their window contracts. He recommended:

> Dublin Glass, to be well bedded in Putty, when first put in, then well pegged, and afterwards to be well puttied on both Sides, and the Panes to be cut the full Size of the Square, and not to have any wants in the Corners.[35]

George Ensor agreed in 1762 to build the Sessions House in Roscommon glazed 'with best Dublin Crown Glass'.[36] 'Window Glass and Flint Glass' were produced in Abbey Street in Dublin by Thomas Smith Jeudwin and John Landon, who came from London in 1759 'having learned that the Art of manufacturing Window Glass was not known in *Ireland*'; they claimed in 1761 that having 'brought Artists from abroad' and having invested £12,000 in the window glass business, their glass could 'equal in Goodness any Window Glass imported here from *Newcastle* or *Bristol*'; further petitions followed in 1763 and 1765.[37] Smith Jeudwin and Lunn were also involved for a period in the glasshouse in Ballycastle.

In the 1770s, crown glass was also fabricated in the Marlborough Green glasshouse in Dublin and was available from the Long Bridge glasshouse in Belfast by 1789, while a local glasshouse in Ringsend advertised Dublin 'window glass of a large size and good colour' in 1798.[38] This availability of crown glass from local sources from 1760 onwards should have reduced costs and encouraged the use of larger pane sizes. The claim of the Abbey Street glasshouse for a reduction of 25 per cent on imported glass prices in 1761 was significant, but local glass may have been inferior in quality. The continuous importation of crown tables from Bristol, and

---

31 NLI, Castle Forward papers, MS 10,470. **32** *Commons Journal*, 5, lxii, lxxxvii. **33** Marie-Louise Legg (ed.), *The Synge letters* (Dublin, 1996), pp 123–4. **34** *Commons Journal*, 5, lxxvii. **35** *Commons Journal*, 6, cccxxii. **36** NLI, Pakenham Mahon papers, MS 10,770 (2). **37** *Commons Journal*, 7, pp 38, 208–9; 8, pp 34–5. **38** Westropp, *Irish glass*, pp 62, 107.

especially London, indicates some variant in either size or quality. Of course, the production of crown glass in Dublin glasshouses may not have been a continuous process throughout the second half of the century. In 1789, the Dublin glass merchant John Raper offered a wide choice of window glass from Belfast, Bristol, Dumbarton and London; by 1798, he was advertising window glass from his 'infant manufactory' at Ringsend which, he says, is 'at least equal' to most of the glass imported to Dublin.[39] In 1778 the estimate for glass of different quality was presented to the board of the Royal Hospital in Kilmainham:[40]

	s.	d.
London Crown	2	8 per foot
Best Bristol Crown		8 per foot
2nd Best [Bristol ditto]		7 per foot
3rd Best [Bristol ditto]		6 per foot
Newcastle crown glass (same price as Bristol)		
Irish Crown Glass		6 per foot
White English glass		5 per foot

These prices indicate considerable variations in quality, particularly in the three different glasses from Bristol. In the estimates for works at the Parliament House in 1749, 120ft 'of new Glass' (of unspecified origin) was charged at 10*d*. per foot; in the same estimates 'new Bristol Crown Glass' came in at 7*d*. per foot; the glazier later demanded 9*d*. per foot, although 'it appeared that 7d per Foot was the usual Price'.[41] The high cost of London crown confirms its superior quality and possibly its availability in large sizes and, of course, its additional shipping cost. The English white glass was obviously a broad glass. Cooley was replacing the existing casements in the attic dormers in Kilmainham with sashes at this time and the cheaper broad glass was probably under consideration for use in these windows.

* * *

Although the disposition of fenestration openings in early classical buildings in England and Ireland shows a clear break with previous traditions, the casement windows used were identical to those in use in the sixteenth century. They were outward opening windows hung on iron hinges (or springs). Window openings were usually formed with identical widths, except where requirements at ground-floor level or the punctuation of long façades required a particular emphasis. Windows varied in height to suit internal room dimensions and the importance of certain apartments. The emphasis, particularly in the lower levels, was on tall proportions, usually in a

---

39 Ibid., pp 62–3.   **40** NAI, RHK Minute Books, 6, RHK 1/1/6, f. 132 r.   **41** *Commons Journal*, 5, lxii, liii, lxii, xlvi.

ratio of at least 5:3. This ratio frequently diminished in upper storeys and particularly at attic level.

This formula produced designs such as Inigo Jones's Italianate façades at Covent Garden in the 1630s and Lincoln's Inn Fields in the 1640s. Attics, mostly lit by dormers, were glazed with side-hung (coupled) casements closing against a central mullion. The windows of important apartments at first-floor level were designed with a transom and central mullion, forming four separate lights. Two large casements were hung below transom level, with two fixed or top-hung casements above the transom. William Robinson's fenestration in the Royal Hospital and the state apartments in Dublin Castle followed this pattern in the 1680s.

The transom windows were similar in most respects to the croisé (or cross) window used almost universally in classical buildings in France and other European countries in the seventeenth century. It had advantages in that the transom (fixed above eye level) did not interrupt views, and that the lower casements could act as doors with access to balconies. These advantages were not perceived in Britain and Ireland because of climatic conditions and the relative opacity of seventeenth-century glass and lead glazing.

Much has been made in the writings of both Harry J. Powell, and McGrath and Frost, of the superior qualities of crown glass that allowed it to dominate the glazing market in eighteenth-century England. The demand for this glass and its popularity must be linked with the introduction and development of the sash window. Sashes were first used in London in the 1660s, and they were popularized by use on a massive scale by Wren in his programme of palace contracts at Whitehall, Hampton Court and Kensington in the years between 1685 and 1696. The first indication we can find of sashes used in Ireland was in the Duke of Ormonde's apartments in Kilkenny Castle in 1680; early uses in Dublin were in the Rubrics ranges in Trinity College in 1700 and in Marsh's Library in 1703; sashes by 'an English Joyner' were proposed for Burton, Co. Cork in 1703, perhaps with crown glass in the main windows, as 'Ordinary Glass' was proposed for the garrets.[42]

Apart from their lower material costs, sash windows provided important advantages over the traditional transom (or cross) windows used in most seventeenth-century buildings. On a practical level they allowed building occupants considerable control over the amount of ventilation admitted into buildings and a choice of ventilation at different room heights. This was an important consideration in the cold and wet conditions experienced in northern countries like Britain and Ireland. Their most attractive advantage, however, was in the capacity of sashes to accommodate much larger panes of glass than leaded glazed casements. There was no advantage in using crown glass in leaded glazing because the close spacing of the lead cames (holding the glass pieces in place) obscured exterior vistas. Sash glazing exploited the

---

42 HMC, Ormonde, new series, 5, p. 292; TCD, building accounts for the Rubrics refer to 'ye joyner for sashes, Casements &c', MUN/P2/5, while George Delane's accounts of 1699 refer to 32 'new sash squares' in the Provost's House, MUN/P2/8/11; BL, Egmont papers, Add. MS 46964A, ff 34–6.

10.6 James Malton, 'The Tholsel, Skinners Row, Dublin', watercolour, 1792, detail showing two mullioned windows with casement opening in the Tholsel, NGI, cat. no. 2185. Reproduced with permission of the National Gallery of Ireland.

full potential of the brilliance and transparency of crown glass; the combination of larger pane sizes provided clear exterior vistas within an open and graceful fenestration.

Although sashes rapidly became the predominant fenestration pattern in eighteenth-century England and Ireland, casements were still in use in the early part of the century. They were used in small houses and often in curious proximity to sash windows in the attics and more unobtrusive parts of larger buildings. James Malton depicted the survival of large leaded casements alongside sashes in his view of the Dublin Tholsel in 1791 (fig. 10.6). Maintenance and repairs to existing leaded glazing were an extensive part of glaziers' contracts up to the 1740s. This is particularly evident in the accounts of the Royal Hospital, where leaded windows were gradually replaced by sashes at intervals during the century. Some uses of lead glazing revealed in early eighteenth-century records are quite surprising. An estimate of Thomas Burgh's for glazing the Dublin barracks in 1709 contains no references to sash windows, but it stipulates a cost of 3s. 6d. each for 'Casements with four Iron Springs' and 6d. per foot for glazing, 'the Lead being very strong'.[43] An account of George Delane's for work in Trinity College on the 'New building on the North side of the Library Square' (Rotten Row) in 1723 included twenty-eight sash windows on the first and second floors, and twenty-seven leaded windows at ground-floor and garret levels.[44]

We can understand Robinson's use of transom windows in the Royal Hospital and in Dublin Castle in the 1680s, although the Duke of Ormonde (who promoted both these building contracts) had used sashes in Kilkenny Castle a few years previously. The use of such outmoded windows in the Green Coat School in Cork city in 1715 is more difficult to understand. Barracks reports indicate the removal of old transom windows in Tullamore barracks in 1760.[45] An account of John Rowlett's for glazing in Trinity College in 1730 provides an interesting picture of the diverse glazing patterns in use in Dublin at this time of the century: 'To 17 large sash squares at 8d each ... To 50 new Ledd squares ... [at 2d each]', all for the Provost's House; 'To 25 new Quarries at 1d each ... To 1 Light new banded 6d', in the Library; and 'To 7 foot of new Glass at 6d per foot' in the Engine House.[46]

Sash squares was a term used in eighteenth-century accounts to describe the rectangular panes of glass fitted into the rebates of sash windows and sealed with a putty pointing. The term 'square' was possibly derived from early uses of the sash in England (such as Somerset House), where the pane proportions were marginally higher than a square in an approximate ratio of about 6:5. Eighteenth-century sash panes were always higher than their widths, in ratios such as 3:2 or 4:3. Pane sizes varied in size in relation to window openings, and they tended to increase in size as the century advanced.

---

43 *Commons Journal*, 2, cxcix. **44** TCD, Joan Delane's accounts, MUN/P2/52/11. **45** *Commons Journal*, 6, ccclxvii. **46** TCD, John Rowlett's accounts, MUN/P2/61/18.

Lead squares were smaller rectangular panes fitted into lead glazing sections (cames) which were extruded with a channel on each side in an 'H' form. Rowlett's cost for banding a light in the library refers to the support of iron bars, fixed horizontally to the window at regular intervals to brace the glazing against buckling stresses. One of the disadvantages of lead glazing was its inherent inability to withstand wind pressure and storms without regular supports. The smallest pane of glass described in Rowlett's accounts was the quarrey. The cost of quarreys at 1*d*. each indicates dimensions that were much smaller than lead squares. However, Neve's description of quarreys clearly describes a non-rectangular shape of diamond pattern. Quarreys, according to Neve, 'for the most part are 6 Inches in length from one Acute Angle to the other, and in breadth from Obtuse Angle to Obtuse Angle 4 Inches'; quarreys were glazed with soldered lead cames and were usually cut (in London) from Newcastle glass.[47]

The unit prices for glass in Rowlett's account can tell us quite a lot about the glass used. The 'new' glass priced at 6*d*. per square foot was undoubtedly crown glass. Delane was using 'new Glass', 'new sash squares', and 'English sash squares', at 6*d*. per foot, in the College by 1712–13 at the latest.[48] The large sash squares at 8*d*. each (e.g., 'French sash squares') were also cut from crown glass. Assuming that they also cost 6*d*. per square foot, the 8*d*. panes must have measured 192 square inches in area which would indicate pane sizes of possibly 12 x 16 inches in height. Both the lead squares and the quarreys (at 2*d*. and 1*d*. each) were considerably less than a square foot in area and they were cut from a poor quality broad glass. Burgh's estimate for (heavy) leading and glazing in 1709 was 6*d*. per foot.[49] As we have already seen, the usual price of Bristol crown glass in Dublin in 1749 was 7*d*. per foot. Rowlett's reference to the replacement of a leaded window in the new College Library is surprising, as its building records for the new Library show substantial payments to the joiner John Sisson for the installation of sash windows from 1716 until 1719.[50] The twenty-five quarreys referred to in his account must relate to repairs to the earlier Library, which was still in use at the time; Burgh's Library was not fully completed and in use until 1732.

Casements were made in both iron and timber, but surviving records of lead glazing in Ireland refer only to iron casements. A good example of leaded timber casements in a seventeenth-century London house (in Clifford's Inn) was illustrated by McGrath and Frost in 1937. Iron, of course, may have been preferred by builders, as the substantial weight of lead glazing needed strong support, and heavy timber framing could be unsightly, particularly if casements were hung in large transom and mullion windows. Each big leaded window depicted by Malton in the Dublin Tholsel in 1793 had a mullion and a transom and six casements hung in pairs. The casements appear to have been made of iron.

47 Neve, *The city and country purchaser*, pp 153, 154. 48 TCD, George Delane's accounts, MUN/P2/22/11, 13; P2/24/11. 49 *Commons Journal*, 2, cxcix. 50 TCD, John Sisson's accounts, MUN/P2/31/15–17; P2/37/69–71; P2/39/71.

The proportions of early sash windows were directly related to the limitations of the glass available at the end of the seventeenth century and to prevailing practices of the period. The earliest models were single-hung with weights attached only to the bottom sashes, and pane sizes were not significantly larger than the traditional lead squares.[51] These small sash squares resulted in multiple pane divisions. Sashes fabricated in horizontal modules four and five panes in width were quite common in the late seventeenth century.

The most advanced use of the sash in the seventeenth century can be seen in Wren's extension to the palace at Hampton Court (1695–8). Here, the scale and proportion of sashes (and pane sizes) were closely related to the importance of different storeys and the different uses of rooms in these storeys. The largest windows, lighting the royal apartments and reception rooms at first-floor level, were 13 x 6ft, a common classical ratio slightly larger than a double square. Most of these windows were four panes wide, in a pane arrangement of sixteen over sixteen, but the windows of the Queen's Drawing Room were three panes wide in a formation of nine over six. The ground-floor windows were five panes in width, in a formation of fifteen over fifteen, while the attic windows were six panes wide, in a formation of twenty-four over eighteen. Wren's control over the diversity of scale in the front façade depended upon the use of sash panes of different sizes and an unprecedented use of exceptionally large panes in the first-floor windows. His attic windows used conventional glazing of the period with panes of $10\frac{1}{2}$ x 8 inches in size, but the windows of the main reception rooms (at first-floor level) had panes with dimensions of 18 x $13\frac{1}{2}$ inches. His three windows lighting the Queen's Drawing Room (in the central pavilion) received special emphasis with ultra large sheets of glass measuring 29 x 21 inches. The large sash divisions of the drawing room relied on sheets of plate glass that were undoubtedly imported from Europe. McGrath and Frost held the view that this glass came from a source such as the French St Gobain glasshouse, which commenced plate glass production in 1693.[52] The dramatic scale and clear luminosity of Wren's glazing must have made a considerable impact on building development at this time. It particularly promoted the use of larger windows with sliding sashes and larger window panes of crown glass. London quickly developed as a centre for the manufacture and supply of crown glass.

This influence was felt in Ireland from the beginning of the eighteenth century, although there is no evidence of the use of larger pane sizes and crown glass until 1715. The rare survival of five early sashes in Marsh's Library (1703) gives a good indication of a predictable pattern during this period. The windows are four panes in width, designed in a twelve over twelve formation to accommodate 12 x 9 inch panes of glass. They were probably glazed originally with broad glass, but today they have panes of modern sheet glass, crown glass and what could be either broad glass, or inferior crown glass. These windows are similar in scale and construction to the attic

---

51 H.J. Louw, 'The origin of the sash-window', *Architectural History*, 26 (1983), 49–72, 144–50.
52 McGrath and Frost, *Glass*, pp 98, 99.

10.7 Trinity College Dublin, Old Library, ground-floor window in the west pavilion.

windows in Hampton Court, but they are not as competently designed as Wren's sashes. They use the same early form of glazing bar made up of two separate moulded sections with a simple mitred joint at pane intersections, on the inner face of the window. The jointing of the inner section (an astragal moulding) is poorly controlled, suggesting a hesitancy and lack of familiarity with sash construction.

Although there is not a great deal of evidence left to confirm it, it is likely that the common use of four-pane (wide) sashes prevailed in Ireland until the Palladian era. The presence of a surviving four-pane window of obvious antiquity in the west pavilion of the Trinity College Library permits the reasonable assumption that this was one of Burgh's original windows, installed before 1720 (fig. 10.7). A four-pane sash with small pane divisions survives as a casement in the basement of Buncrana Castle, which dates from 1718. Durrow Castle has replicas of four-pane sashes at basement level, which suggests that the windows installed in 1716 were of similar design. The early eighteenth-century casements in the Brazen Head tavern in Dublin are four panes wide, with panes of similar scale to those used in Marsh's Library. All the façades of Mount Ievers Court in Co. Clare (1736) have retained their four-pane sashes and small sash panes. The large windows at ground- and first-floor level are arranged in a sixteen over sixteen pane formation. With the exception of Burgh's Library window, all these windows have small panes. The Library window has panes measuring 12 x 18 inches, in sashes with a pane formation of twelve over twelve. These sashes were probably glazed with London crown glass, which was in use in the college during this period.

* * *

By the 1720s, with the emergence of the Palladian movement, larger sash panes were easier to obtain, sash divisions were reduced in number and the three-pane (wide) sash became widely used. Greater emphasis was placed on proportional relationships and the modulation of window openings within the composition of the façade. Palladian theory favoured a proportional system starting with the window dimensions of the principal rooms and a series of diminishing ratios for rooms at higher or lower levels. Palladio's preferred dimensions for the largest windows were 'two squares and a sixth part of their breadth more in height' or a ratio of 13:6, and a progressive reduction of ⅙ in the heights of the windows in upper storeys. A great advantage of this proportional system was the inclusion of two important primary ratios in its series, a ratio of 6:6, which produced square window openings, and a ratio of 12:6, which produced windows with the proportions of the double square.

In Ireland, judicious interpretations of this proportional system can be seen in early Palladian buildings. The work of Edward Lovett Pearce, in particular, relied on the powerful combination of these primary proportions. In 1730, his new Parliament House presented an ashlar front to College Green that was unbroken save for a central doorcase and a line of first-floor windows, all designed as double squares. The front façade of Cashel Palace (1730) has a composition of double squares, flanked by Venetian windows and a row of roof dormers that optically appear as squares, while the main elevation of Bellamont Forest in Co. Cavan, designed during this period, had four window bays of double squares, surmounted by four square windows at attic level. Summerhill in Co. Meath, attributed to his hand, owed much of its monumentality to its incisive punctuation with square and double square window openings.

Richard Castle's façades also made good use of Palladian proportional principles. Pool and Cash's engraving (in 1780) of the original front of Tyrone House (1740) depicts bays of double square openings at ground and first floor, surmounted by six square attic windows above cornice level (fig. 10.8). His Clanwilliam House façade (1740s) on St Stephen's Green was designed with two long 13:6 ratio windows flanking its entrance door. Leinster House (1745) had a similar fenestration pattern

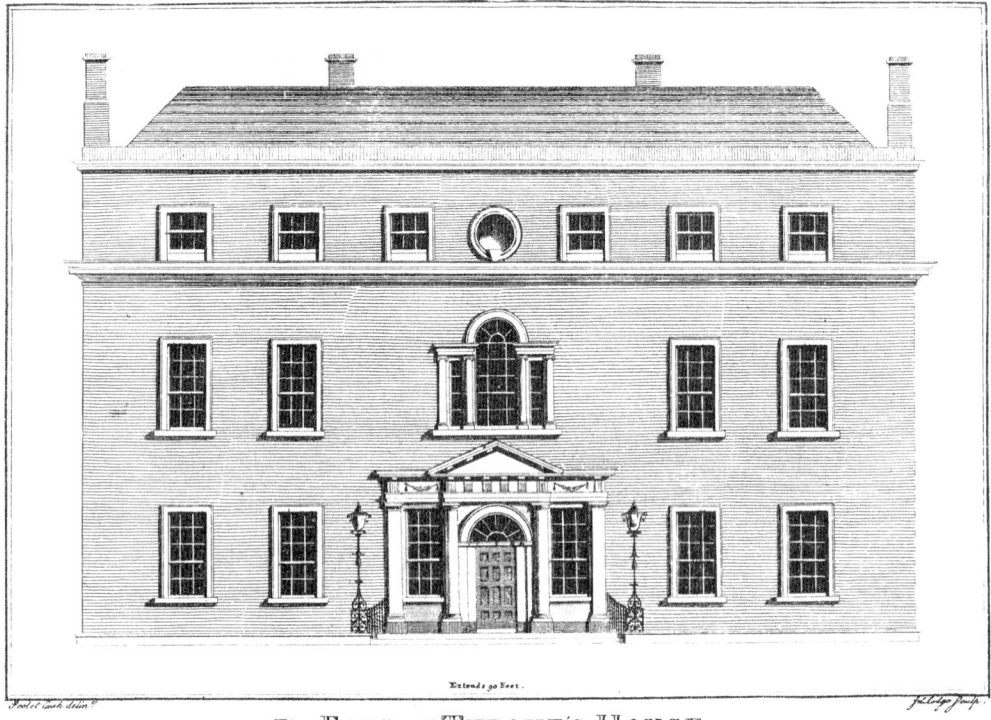

10.8 Tyrone House, Dublin, 1740, Robert Pool and John Cash, *Views of the most remarkable public buildings ... in Dublin* (Dublin, 1780).

to Tyrone House, with square attic windows over two storeys of double square openings. The Rotunda Hospital's (1750) fenestration design had double square windows on both lower levels and 9:6 ratio windows lighting the top floor.

Pearce's use of primary proportions had advantages. They combined the use of preferred classical ratios with an easy integration of the sash and its subdivisions. Because of their modular affinity, they could be aligned without difficulty with masonry courses. The square and double square windows could be simply subdivided to permit the use of two sashes of identical dimensions, glazed with sash panes of identical size. If an intermediate ratio was required, the most suitable was the relationship of 9:6. This was a useful proportion, as it integrated easily with subdivisions of the double square, but it usually required the use of unequal sashes with a subdivision of six panes over three.

O'Dwyer has adverted to the peculiarly Irish custom of lighting the important rooms of eighteenth-century buildings with unequal sashes, subdivided in a nine over

10.9 James Malton, 'Leinster House, Dublin', aquatint, 1792, detail of fenestration.

six pane formation.[53] This is rarely encountered in English fenestration patterns. The use of this window formation was particularly common in grander houses and institutional buildings of the Palladian era. Its introduction might reasonably be attributed to Richard Castle, as it was used extensively in his designs from the 1740s onwards, and it was not apparently used by Pearce. Engravings of Pool and Cash in 1779 and Malton in 1791 depict its use in Tyrone House, Leinster House, the Rotunda Hospital, Trinity College, Dublin Castle and the Provost's House (fig. 10.9). This fenestration pattern provided an extended range of window heights using panes of identical dimensions. In four-storey elevations such as the front of Trinity College, or the façade of 86 St Stephen's Green, this could be a big advantage. It worked perfectly as a method of controlling sash pane subdivision, but it was difficult to integrate some of its modules with Palladian proportions.

[53] Frederick O'Dwyer, 'Proportion and the Georgian window' in T.J. Fenlon (ed.), *The town: conservation in the urban area*, proceedings of the IGS Conference (1995), p. 30.

It is interesting to look at how Palladian architects handled the integration of different sash sizes and pane divisions in relation to classical proportional principles. Pearce's designs presented no problems because of his careful choice of window modules and relationships. Castle was more adventurous in his choice of relationships and in his ability to compromise. In his design for Clanwilliam House we find him engaged in the typical Palladian transitions between long 13:6 ratio windows at entrance level and double square arched windows flanking his Venetian window in the first-floor saloon. He solved his sash design problem by using identical nine over nine pane sashes at both levels, with minutely adjusted dimensions to absorb the 8 inches difference in heights. The additional ½ inch in height in the ground-floor sash panes and the lower height of the timber sub-cills at first-floor level are not noticeable from the street. We find him playing the same visual tricks in Tyrone House and Leinster House. Pool and Cash record the use of double square windows at ground- and first-floor levels in both buildings, although the measured dimensions in Leinster House reveal a slightly taller window designed, no doubt, to conform with the masonry coursing. Both façades have the strong terminal punctuation of square attic windows. Castle, of course, was well aware that the three over three pane sash relationships (established by the proportions of the lower windows) were not high enough to use as a square. This difference in dimensions was absorbed by an exceptionally high timber sub-cill, which is clearly delineated in the 1780 engraving of Tyrone House. He was also confident that these cills would never be visible from ground level. In both houses, they are obscured by the masonry, and in the case of Tyrone House by a massive salient cornice positioned just under attic level. Theodore Jacobsen's front façade of Trinity College (1752) has a design which successfully controls the diminution of scale in a complex four-storey composition, but his upper windows (at second-floor and attic level) do not conform with Palladian proportional ratios. The difficulties in keeping identical pane sizes in windows of different proportions aligned with precisely coursed masonry façades were considerable. The more accommodating scale of brickwork, or the stucco used extensively by Palladio in the Venetian provinces, allowed more freedom in the determination of window ratios.

After the 1760s, two important changes in glazing patterns are evident. The use of Palladian nine over six pane sashes in windows became less fashionable and six over six pane divisions were increasingly used in the main windows of large houses and institutions. This was due, to some extent, to the influence of English architects and their Irish commissions during this period. Designs such as Charlemont House, the Royal Exchange and the Hibernian Marine School (all six over six) were under construction, or already built, in Dublin in the 1770s. In the provinces, houses such as Castleward, Co. Down, and Abbeyleix, Co. Laois (both six over six sashes), were also built during this period. Malton's views of Dublin streetscapes show terraced houses with both nine over six pane divisions and six over six panes divisions in the 1790s.

By the 1780s, the popular demand for thinner glazing sections and larger glazed areas is noticeable, particularly in urban terraced houses. This is evident in the taller proportions of windows in later neoclassical houses in Merrion Square, and in the adjoining streetscapes. Also noticeable are attempts to alter windows in older 1760s houses in Merrion Street and the north side of Merrion Square, which were fashionably enlarged by lowering their cill heights. Castle's largest windows in his urban houses of the 1740s were 4ft in width and 8ft 8 inches in height. The enlarged windows of Merrion Square maintained the 4-ft window bay but increased window heights to 10ft and higher. Sash divisions were changed to conform with stylistic preferences during the century but changes in pane sizes may have been more influenced by limitations of manufacture and supply than fashions. The crown glass used by Rowlett in Trinity College in 1730 was described as 'large sash squares'.[54] The glass dimensions in the four-pane sashes in the College Library (presumably an original 1715–19 window) are 18 x 12 inches. Castle's windows in the 1740s, to judge by measurements of his main Dublin buildings, mostly had panes sizes about 18 x 13 inches. The 1750s windows in the front of Trinity College had panes no larger than 15 x 12½ inches.

In the 1760s, however, the modules of the large windows in 86 St Stephen's Green (attributed to Robert West) indicate pane sizes 22 x 16 inches. This sudden increase in pane size in a traditional Palladian fenestration pattern was possibly a result of newly established manufacturing facilities for crown glass in Dublin. The arrival of expatriate London glassmakers in Dublin in 1759, and the availability of crown glass tables from the Abbey Street glasshouse in the 1760s, must have been an advantage to local architects and builders. The market for better quality glass was assured by the continuous progress of the Gardiner estate to the north of the Liffey, and by the ambitious inauguration of the Fitzwilliam estate to the south. For their part, the London experts (Landon and Smith Jeudwin) must have been anxious to impress Dublin master builders (such as Darley, West and Ensor) with the claimed superiority of their product and its availability in large pane sizes.

The demand for large pane sizes increased as the century advanced and particularly with the use of 6 over 6 pane sashes in tall neoclassical window openings. McGrath and Frost referred to the common use of panes with dimensions of 24 x 15 inches in London before the end of the eighteenth century, and panes measuring 27 x 17 inches can be found in late eighteenth-century houses in Dublin's Harcourt Street.[55] On the other hand, Gandon used relatively modest (22 x 15½ inch) panes in the Custom House in the 1780s, and his introduction of nine over nine sashes in the terrace of houses in Beresford Place in the 1790s was an obvious attempt to use tall neoclassic proportions without increasing pane sizes.

Glazed fanlights over entrance doors made an important decorative contribution to eighteenth-century façades. Early fanlights were fabricated in timber, using sections that were identical to the glazing bars used in sash construction. Unlike sash construction, however, fanlights were made with the moulded surface of the bar

---

54 TCD, John Rowlett's accounts, MUN/P2/61/18.   55 McGrath and Frost, *Glass*, p. 98.

10.10 James Malton, 'The West Front of St Patrick's Cathedral, Dublin', watercolour, 1793, detail showing open butchers' stalls, NGI, cat. no. 2620. Reproduced with permission of the National Gallery of Ireland.

10.11 'A Prospect of the Parliament House in College Green, Dublin …', c.1753, print after J. Tudor, detail. Courtesy of the Irish Architectural Archive.

facing the exterior, and glass was fixed into the rebates of the bar from inside the building. Timber fanlights were usually semi-circular in form, and designed mostly in a fan shape with glazing bars radiating from a central hub. An alternative design was based on the use of curvilinear glazing bars in the form of intersecting pointed arches. Good examples of the former type can be encountered in early Dublin houses in South William Street and Eustace Street, and in the provinces in Cashel Palace and Belvedere in Co. Westmeath. Examples of the latter type can be seen in Newberry Hall in Co. Kildare and over the entrance door of the Rotunda Hospital in Dublin. The post-Palladian demand for lighter and more elegant glazing design promoted the use of thinner timber sections in sash construction and the use of metal glazing sections in fanlights. Timber sash bars were gradually reduced from the 1½- to 2-inch sections down to the ½-inch glazing bars used in neoclassical sashes. The difficulty in using slender timber sections in curvilinear patterns inevitably introduced metal bars that were sufficiently malleable to bend and strong enough to use in thin sections.

Iron fanlights were sometimes used in England and Scotland, but metallic Irish fanlights were mostly made of a combination of zinc and lead. This was an ideal combination: the zinc glazing section, in the shape of a T, provided the structural stiffness required while the lead was used as a facing. The zinc was cut and soldered into the required design pattern and an extruded lead U-section was applied as an exterior cover flashing around the cross arm of the T-section. The glass was inserted

10.12 James Malton, 'Royal Exchange, Dublin', watercolour, 1795, detail showing curved shop windows on Cork Hill. Courtesy of the Henry E. Huntington Library and Art Gallery.

from the inside into the zinc section and fixed with a putty painting. Decorative lead enrichments were frequently applied to the lead cover sections with solder.

Glazed shop windows were another important aspect of the glazier's work. The medieval shopfront persisted into the seventeenth century; it was usually unglazed and consisted of removable timber shutters attached to trading counters that were opened in the daytime to expose the merchandise on offer. Something of the sort survived as butchers' stalls visible in Malton's view of St Patrick's Cathedral (fig. 10.10). The advent of glass shopfronts is identified with eighteenth-century enterprise and its development was promoted by the introduction of crown glass and larger window panes. The earliest glazed shopfronts were the lean-to outshots such as are visible in Joseph Tudor's engraving of College Green in 1752 (fig. 10.11). These appear to be built of timber framework, infilled with windows and roofed with low single pitched leaded roofs. Malton's views of Dublin show a variety of shopfronts in the latter part of the eighteenth century (fig. 10.12). His print of Essex Bridge depicts two adjoining but dissimilar fronts in Capel Street, each with two large shop windows

10.13 'Front to Astons Quay', watercolour, 1800, showing shop fronts proposed by the Wide Streets Commissioners, DCLA, WSC map 383/1. Reproduced with permission of the Dublin City Library and Archives.

flanking an entrance door. One shopfront is flush with the brick superstructure overhead. The other (a lottery office) projects onto the pavement in shallow curved bow windows. The flush-fronted premises had tall (four-pane wide) windows with elegant fanlights, of similar design to the (three-pane) sashes used in the upper storeys, but of fixed (not opening) construction. The projecting front had a timber cornice and fascia following the curved window bows. The Wide Street Commissioners in Dublin erected (and made proposals for) several glazed shop fronts at the end of the eighteenth century: some of these contained up to thirty-five panes of glass to promote the maximum display of merchandise (fig. 10.13). The glass panes (to judge from surviving eighteenth-century bow-front shops in London) were flat and not curved to align with the shapes of the glazing bars, their economic use awaited the nineteenth century and the age of the plate-glass shopfront.

CHAPTER ELEVEN

Plastering and stuccowork

Plastering was clearly established as a separate trade in medieval Ireland. The Dublin freedom rolls contain frequent references to admissions of 'plaisterers', and the survival of fine Elizabethan stuccowork from the Ormonde manor house at Carrick-on-Suir Castle, from the chapel at Bunratty Castle and from Quin Abbey in Co. Clare points to the presence of a body of skilled artisans working in the country before the advent of the classical builders. During the classical period, and particularly in the middle decades of the eighteenth century, the artistic quality of decorative plasterwork in Ireland was rivalled in only a few areas of Europe. This was due to the influence and intervention of foreign master craftsmen earlier in the century. The ability of local artisans to respond to new stylistic and technical challenges was centred on their inherited skills and traditions. Up to the latter part of the seventeenth century, plasterers in Dublin operated with other building trades (such as masons and slaters) as members of the carpenters' guild. The expansion of the city and the building boom that followed the restoration of the monarchy in 1661 promoted rapid changes in building practice. One consequence of change was the combination of bricklayers and plasterers in the new Guild of St Bartholomew, which received a royal charter in 1670.

Plasterers operated quite independently from their fraternal guild brothers the bricklayers, but they shared a dependence on some common materials. Most of the plaster used in Irish building contracts was made with identical materials to walling mortar, a mixture of lime (calcium oxide), sand and water. As roach lime (fresh from the kiln) was too caustic for immediate use, it was slaked in water for several months. Sand for plaster was chosen for its sharpness and freedom from organic matter. River sand was commonly used, but pit sand was suitable if its residual soil content was removed by washing. Sea sand was seldom used, as it caused saline efflorescence in plaster membranes.

This mixture of lime and sand was used on both exterior masonry walls and on interior wall surfaces and ceilings. However, the formation of decorative plaster surfaces (or stucco) often required different materials added to, or substituted for, common lime plaster. The stucco used in ancient Rome was described by Vitruvius as a mixture of pulverized marble dust mixed with lime and water.[1] This was applied in a series of thin coats over common (lime and sand) plaster. Vasari, in his life of

---

Important recent research on Irish plasterwork has been carried out by Christine Casey, Conor Lucey and Joseph McDonnell; see Select Bibliography.   1 Vitruvius, 7, iii, 6.

Giovanni da Udine, described the development of an identical stucco used in Renaissance Italy based on the use of lime mixed with marble dust instead of sand. This was promoted in its use by Raphael and Giulio Romano in the loggias of the Villa Madama in Rome and in the interior of the Palazzo del Te in Mantua. The Italian stucco tradition was carried across northern Italy and over the Alps into parts of Switzerland, the Tyrol and southern Germany by itinerant sculptors and stuccodores. It was strongly developed in the late baroque period in the border lands between Como and Lugano and in the Italian-Swiss canton of the Ticino. Its high point in the first decade of the eighteenth century came in its fusion with French-inspired rococo forms in the hands of local artisans from the Vorarlberg and southern Bavaria. The influence of this tradition was also felt in England and Ireland. It came to England in the first decade of the eighteenth century with Giovanni Bagutti and Giuseppe Artari, who hailed from the Ticino and worked with Vanbrugh on Castle Howard in 1710 (Bagutti), and with Gibbs on St Martin-in-the-Fields in 1724. In 1735, two expatriate Ticinesi craftsmen, Paolo and Filippo Lafranchini, moved from England to Ireland and worked in Dublin and the provinces with Richard Castle and Davis Ducart. Bartholomew Cramillion, a stuccodore with remarkable sculptural skills, came to Ireland from Europe in 1755 at the invitation of Bartholomew Mosse to work on stucco interiors in the Rotunda Hospital. An undated estimate, possibly from the hand of Richard Castle, calculating the cost of finishing the staircase in the Library of Trinity College provided for 116 yards 'of stucco Ceiling Done in the Italien Manner'.[2]

The Italian word 'stucco' was loosely used in eighteenth-century England and Ireland to describe decorative plasterwork on either interior or exterior building surfaces. Its name was derived from the texts of Vitruvius and Vasari and from the introduction (into sixteenth-century England) of Italian experts in stucco plaster called 'stuccatori', a term that became mutated by use to the word 'stuccodores' as a description for specialists in modelled or cast plaster ornamentation. From the mid-eighteenth century onwards the work of native-born Irish stuccodores such as Robert West and Michael Stapleton is particularly noticeable. Although the quality of their work indicates the acquisition of highly specialized skills, these craftsmen operated as both general plastering contractors as well as specialists in decorative stucco. West's accounts for his contract on the Rotunda Hospital in 1755 indicate payments for both '[plain] Plaistering and Stucco Work'.[3] Stapleton's extensive accounts for work in Trinity College between 1780 and the 1790s include items for plastering, stucco work and painting; West, as Curran has pointed out, described himself at various times as a plasterer, stuccodore and master builder.[4] Stapleton's name appears in the *Dublin directory* of 1777 as a 'Plasterer and Stucco-worker', and in 1797 as a 'Stucco-plaisterer and Painter'.

2 TCD, estimate for finishing the Library, MUN/P2/28.   3 *The case of the Bartholomew Mosse ... 1755* [Dublin, 1755].   4 TCD, Michael Stapleton's accounts, e.g., MUN/P2/174/16; C.P. Curran, *Dublin decorative plasterwork of the seventeenth and eighteenth centuries* (London, 1967), p. 3.

Wall and ceiling plaster was usually applied in three separate coats, a pricking-up coat, floating coat and a final setting coat. The undercoats were scratched with incisions to provide better adhesion between coats. The setting coat was mixed with finer particles of sand than the two base coats and it was trowelled to a smooth finish. The coarser undercoats were usually reinforced with some fibrous materials such as animal hair, obtained from goats and cattle. A typical account of the plastering contractor Isaac Chalke, for work on the Royal Hospital Kilmainham in 1706, included payments for three barrels of hair and quantities of sand, lime, laths and nails.[5] The thickness of plaster membranes varied depending on the alignment of wall or ceiling surfaces. The minimum depth of internal wall plaster was about ¾ of an inch in thickness, but in buildings with rubble stone wall linings (such as Dr Steevens's Hospital) thicknesses over an inch could occur. In some cases where walls were particularly uneven, or where the spatial geometry of the room demanded it, plaster was applied on timber laths, fixed to battens nailed to the structural walls. Laths were also used to produce a key for plaster applied to stud partitions.

Ceiling plaster was also applied on timber laths nailed to the soffits of floor joists or (in more expensive work) to a separate system of ceiling joists suspended from the timber floor structure. The combined depth of plaster coats on ceilings usually exceeded ¾ of an inch in thickness, and the considerable weight of the plaster membrane needed continuous support. This was simply achieved by trowelling wet ceiling plaster into the narrow gaps between ceiling laths to form an upper continuous seam (or key) wider than the gap between the laths. Ceiling laths were split (or riven) from narrow timber scantlings, as surface irregularities were preferred (to a sawn surface) because they provided a better key. A purchase of 10,000 'good heart oak laths not less than foure feet long nor less than Inch broad' at £1 3s. 0d. per thousand from Thomas Annsley of Mountmellick was recorded in the accounts of Castle Durrow in 1715.[6]

The use of an expensive material such as oak for ceiling laths was unusual, even in the early years of the eighteenth century. White deal (spruce) was commonly used for laths in most Irish buildings and lath thicknesses could vary depending on the quality of the work. Pat and John Wall's accounts for plastering the buildings forming Parliament Square in Trinity College between 1756 and 1761 refer to both 'stucco laths' and 'slating laths'; the latter were used for ceiling the Regent House, which carried heavy enrichment.[7] No information on lath sizes was provided in the account but the unusual reference to the use of slating laths, normally an inch thick, obviously related to some especially heavy ornamentation. Laths used in speculative house development could be remarkably economical. Lath dimensions in a recently renovated 1720s house at 25 Eustace Street were an inch broad and a mere ⅛ inch in thickness.

5 NAI, Royal Hospital Kilmainham minute books, 1, RHK 1/1/1, f. 333 v.   6 NLI, Flower papers, MS 11455 (3).   7 TCD, Pat and John Wall's accounts, MUN/P2/139, pp 5, 11.

It is difficult to determine, either from observation or the examination of building records, what specific ingredients were used in the production of stucco plasterwork in Ireland in the seventeenth, or even the eighteenth century. Bankart maintained that the *stucco duro* introduced by Italian stuccodores on mid sixteenth-century English buildings (such as Nonsuch Palace at Epsom in *c.*1538, or Longleat in Wiltshire in the 1540s) was superseded on Elizabethan buildings by traditional English plaster mixes of sand and lime.[8] Italian stucco was not to appear again until the arrival of a new wave of expatriate artisans in England during the long period of peace which started with the last decade of the seventeenth century. However, English stuccodores may have mixed additional ingredients with lime plasters to give them additional plasticity. Fast-setting gypsum plaster was also used in England in combination with lime plaster in the latter part of the seventeenth century. There are similarities between Elizabethan plasterwork in England and the aforementioned examples of contemporaneous plasterwork in Ireland at Bunratty Castle, and at the manor house at Carrick-on-Suir Castle. It is not unreasonable to presume that the technical execution and materials used in these Irish examples were based on English practice.

What little we know of the uses of decorative plaster in the succeeding decades of the seventeenth century (the 'fretting' of the gallery in Sir Richard Boyle's house at Youghal in 1614; the stucco coat of arms decorated by Richard Morland in the Dublin Tholsel in *c.*1620; the plaster decorations on the vault of the early Chapel in Trinity College; and the elaborate stucco in Blessington Manor in the 1670s) suggests that these correspond with contemporary English practice.[9]

The highly decorated ceiling of the Royal Hospital at Kilmainham, executed about 1685, shows this English influence in its design and formal organization. Although the present ceiling is a papier mâché replica of the original stucco ornamentation it shows an obvious debt to seventeenth-century English ceilings at Coleshill in Berkshire of 1660 and Edward Goudge's work in the chapel at Belton in Lincolnshire in 1688. Barbara FitzGerald, in unpublished research, has also pointed out similarities in style between the Royal Hospital and Edward Martin's stucco ceilings at Arbury Hall, Warwickshire, in 1678 and Burghley, Northamptonshire, in 1682.[10] On the other hand, although the hospital stucco work is similar in configuration and pattern to these examples, it has a wild exuberance in its modelling that is missing in the more ordered English ornamentation. It is difficult to imagine that the richly modelled ornamentation of the chapel ceiling was produced by a mixture of lime and sand, the same humble materials used to make mortar for its walling construction. Lime plasters were commonly mixed with glutinous substances such as gelatine or size to improve their plasticity and tensile strength. It is unlikely that the high modelling of the ceiling could be easily produced in lime without some such

---

8 George Bankart, *The art of the plasterer* (London, 1908), (reprint ed. 2002), pp 45, 48, 56, 87.   9 C.P. Curran, 'Dublin plaster work', *JRSAI*, 70 (1940), p. 3; *CARD*, 3, p. 111; Edward McParland, 'Trinity College, Dublin – I', *Country Life* (6 May 1976), 1167; Edward McParland, *Public architecture in Ireland, 1680–1760* (New Haven & London, 2001), p. 66.   10 Barbara FitzGerald, 'Problems with a ceiling [in

additive. Beard refers to the probable use of gelatine (obtained from horses' hoofs) in lime plaster to improve its plasticity and workability.[11]

There is also the reasonable doubt that ceilings of the complexity of Kilmainham or Coleshill would have been executed during this period without the use of gypsum, particularly in the making of cast ornamentation. Gypsum, a sulphate of lime, was known widely by its trade name of 'plaster of Paris' because of the presence of substantial deposits at Pantin, near the Parisian suburb of Montmartre. Gypsum plaster had remarkable potential as a decorative medium. It could be modelled, cast, carved, incised, coloured and gilded. It had advantages over lime plaster in the production of decorative ornament. Its fast setting time (a matter of minutes) and its cohesive strength made it particularly suitable for work in high relief such as we find in the Royal Hospital. It also expanded during the setting process, which was useful in filling gaps or joints between different applications of plaster. Plaster of Paris was undoubtedly obtainable for use as an ingredient in stucco mixes in the seventeenth century in England. Large deposits of gypsum were available in Derbyshire and Nottinghamshire. A use of plaster of Paris in England is recorded as early as 1519 in William Hormann's *Vulgaria*.[12] Balthazar Gerbier, the architect of Hampstead Marshall (a 1670s house in Berkshire with stucco ceilings), advanced the opinion in 1663 that a 'Tun of Playster of Paris' covered 29 square yards to a thickness of ¾ of an inch.[13] This reference to ¾ inch thickness of plaster is relevant, as this was the nominal thickness of plaster ceilings.

On the other hand, gypsum plaster may have presented problems to certain Irish stuccodores (such as Robert West or the Lafranchini brothers) whose work depended to a great degree on the in-situ modelling of wet plaster into ornamental forms. The fast setting time of gypsum was a disadvantage in the refinement of modelled surfaces, as the rapidly hardening stucco lost its moisture and its plasticity. Vitruvius was unequivocal in his comment that gypsum should never be used in stucco mixes because its rapid setting could keep the work from drying uniformly.[14] This could cause cracks in the plaster membrane. There is evidence that fast-setting stucco mixes required the addition of retarding agents to delay the setting time sufficiently to enable stuccodores to refine their surface modelling. P.N. Sprengel, writing in 1772 on German practice, prescribes the use of retarders such as beer, milk and wine.[15] Irish stuccodores must have made full use of such retarders to produce their highly modelled ornamentation.

The arrival in Ireland in 1735 of Paolo and Filippo Lafranchini initiated in Irish stuccowork a new sculptural quality, which had its roots in the Italian baroque tradition. They were born, like Artari and Bagutti, in the Italian-Swiss province of the Ticino and they (like their fellow countrymen) had associations with Gibbs in

the Royal Hospital Kilmainham]', (BA, TCD, 1987). **11** Geoffrey Beard, *Decorative plasterwork in Great Britain* (London, 1975), p. 9. **12** Quoted in ibid., p. 23. **13** Ibid., p. 12. **14** Vitruvius, 7, iii, 3. **15** Andreas F.A. Morel, *Andreas und Peter Anton Moosbrugger: zur Stuckdekoration des Rokoko in der Schweiz* (Bern, 1973), p. 23.

11.1 Florence Court, Co. Fermanagh, 1760s, lantern and plasterwork (no longer surviving). Courtesy of the Irish Architectural Archive.

London before coming to Ireland. Their early work between 1735 and 1745, in Riverstown, Co. Cork, in Carton, Co. Kildare, in Russborough, Co. Wicklow, and Clanwilliam House in Dublin, introduced large-scale figurative compositions into Irish interiors and overlaid local Palladian tastes with flavours of international classicism. Their work also introduced a new element of plasticity into Irish stucco decoration that was to become a characteristic of the native school of Irish rococo stuccodores that emerged in the mid-1750s. This plastic development of surfaces into figurative and floral forms, in rapid gradation from low to high relief, anticipated the free-flowing arabesques associated with the work of Robert West, Patrick Osborne and James McCullagh. The spontaneity and plastic quality of rococo plasterwork depended largely on the stuccodore's skill in modelling wet plaster in situ before it became dry and unresponsive. This was influenced by the characteristics of the plaster used and how long it took to reach an initial set.

This reintroduces the difficult subject of plaster mixes and the ingredients used to make in-situ stucco ornamentation that remained soft enough for control over its form and cohesive enough to encourage forms in high relief. The Lafranchini brothers had the advantages of growing up in an area that had inherited the Italian stucco tradition and of international experience gained in Germany and in England.

Can we assume that the stucco mixes used by them were (like those introduced into Tudor England by Italian stuccodores in the 1540s) based on the formula quoted by Vasari that is, essentially, a mixture of lime and marble dust? Other additives such as volcanic ash (pozzolan) were commonly added to mortar mixes in Italy and, as we know from our examination of masonry mortars, such mixtures produced hydraulic mortars which were fast setting and cohesive. The advent of Bartholomew Cramillion and the introduction of rococo ornament into Ireland in the mid-1750s is another factor that may have influenced stucco techniques. His ability as a figurative sculptor suggests an Italian apprenticeship, but his stylistic affinity with rocaille decorative motifs at this time has strong links with the emerging mid-European stucco tradition influenced by Cuvilliés, the Feichtmayrs and Domenicus Zimmermann. Joseph McDonnell's attribution to Cramillion of the superb figurative modelling in ceilings of the former Mespil House and the La Touche bank implies that his influence on his Irish contemporaries must have been considerable.[16]

It is fascinating to dwell on the effects of this influence on such stuccodores as Robert West and the emerging masters of the Irish rococo tradition. West had already completed a substantial contract for 'Plaistering and Stucco Work' at the Rotunda Hospital before Cramillion's arrival and he had been paid a total of £895 12s. 10d. by 1755.[17] Cramillion's appointment in the same year for the ambitious job of decorating the Rotunda chapel can hardly be seen as an encroachment on West's position at the time. Bartholomew Mosse's ambitions for the completion of the chapel clearly called for a figurative sculptor of known experience. West had only finished his apprenticeship three years previously in 1752 and the intervening years must have been entirely taken up with his Rotunda contract.[18] West, of course, may have been responsible for the stucco ceiling and wall enrichment of the stair hall in the hospital, but the only evidence for this is his payment for stucco (as well as plastering) in 1755. If this attribution is correct, it would confirm West's involvement with the motifs of French rococo ornament before the arrival of Cramillion. There has always been a hesitancy about combining West's name with this competent but rather static stucco design. The Rotunda staircase has none of the artistic animus and individuality of later work attributed to West in his own house at 20 Dominick Street (1755–9), in 9 Cavendish Row (1757), in Mornington House (1760) or in 86 St Stephen's Green (1760–6) (fig. 11.2). We can only guess at the formative influences that produced this high point of creative artistry and the formidable technical skills that accompanied it. Cramillion's stucco modelling appears to be the most likely influence for West's almost seamless fusion of surfaces and his subtle gradation of curving planes. This is given additional credence by McDonnell's claim for his involvement in the ceilings in Mespil House and the La Touche bank.

16 Joseph McDonnell, *Irish eighteenth-century stuccowork and its European sources* (Dublin, 1991), pp 21, 25–6; Joseph McDonnell, 'The art of the sculptor-stuccatore Bartholomew Cramillion in Dublin and Brussels, 1755–1772', *Apollo* (September 2002), 41–49, where McDonnell establishes Cramillion's Flemish origins.   **17** *The case of the Bartholomew Mosse … 1755* [Dublin, 1755].   **18** DCLA, Gilbert Library, typescript, roll of freemen of the city of Dublin.

11.2 No. 20 Lower Dominick Street, Dublin, built by Robert West, 1758–60, detail of plasterwork in staircase hall.

Links sometimes suggested between Irish rococo plasterwork and that of the Wessobrunn school in Bavaria might have important connotations, as there can be no doubt about the composition of stucco used in that area.[19] Andreas Morel, in his study of the work of Andreas and Peter Moosbrugger in Switzerland, is unequivocal about the part played by gypsum in the making of stucco: he specifies gypsum, sand and chalk as the chosen ingredients of stuccodores working north of the Alps in the seventeenth and eighteenth centuries.[20] We can be in no doubt also of the French dependence on gypsum. The steady export trade of plaster of Paris from the medieval period onwards must have been based on a buoyant home market. It was also used extensively in English plasterwork. Apart from Hormann's and Gerbier's references, there are several records of Wren's use of plaster of Paris in the 1680s and 1690s, including a reference to the purchase of 9¾ tons for use in St Paul's in February 1686/7.[21] A laboratory analysis of stucco samples taken from rococo ceilings of the 1750s in Uppark in Sussex (in 1989) revealed a mix of 52% sand, 28% lime or chalk, 10% gypsum and 10% assorted materials such as glue and hair.[22] This supports Beard's contention that gypsum was sometimes used by stuccodores as the finishing coat.[23] We can also be sure that gypsum played an important role in the work of the Irish stuccodore. An eighteenth-century description of the (seventeenth-century) chapel at Newtownards Manor in county Down describes 'the compass ceiling divided into nine Panels and curiously adorned with stuccowork in Plaister of Paris, well crafted in various Wreaths, Foliages and Figures of Angels'; in 1747 Edward Synge's letters to Dublin requested 'more Plaister of Paris' for use in his new episcopal palace at Elphin.[24]

* * *

We must now address the sequence of operations involved in plastering practice and the relationship between in-situ work and cast ornamentation. As we have seen, plain (undecorated) plastering involved the application of three coats of common (lime and sand) plaster to ceiling laths and wall surfaces, with gypsum used sometimes in the final coat. The plaster was mostly applied with steel trowels but the final (setting) coat was brought to a smooth surface with a timber trowel (or float). Before the application of the (second) floating coat to the wall, narrow (2–3 inch) vertical bands of plaster called screeds were applied to establish a true alignment of wall surfaces. The floating coat, which established the level alignment of the wall, was then applied between these vertical screeds. The final setting coat was usually less than 3/16 of an inch in thickness to enable the lime to combine with carbon dioxide from the air and to set hard.

19 McDonnell, *Irish eighteenth-century stuccowork*, p. 13; Wijnand Freling, 'Rococo stuccowork in the Netherlands' in Christine Casey and Conor Lucey (eds), *Decorative plasterwork in Ireland and Europe* (Dublin, 2012), p. 159. **20** Morel, *Andreas und Peter Anton Moosbrugger*, p. 23. **21** *Wren Soc. Vols*, 14, p. 21. **22** Information from Séamus Ó hEocha. **23** Geoffrey Beard, *Decorative plasterwork in Great Britain* (London, 1975), p. 9. **24** Rolf Loeber, 'Irish country houses and castles of the late Caroline period', *BIGS*, 16 (Jan.–June 1973), 20; Marie-Louise Legg (ed.), *The Synge letters* (Dublin, 1996), p. 30.

Large plaster cornices required some form of structural support. This was usually provided by timber brackets (nailed to the wall and ceiling structure) supporting continuous horizontal laths. Buildings with vaulted floor structures (as in Kingsfort House, Co. Meath) sometimes used corbelled brick courses at impost level (in lieu of timber) as support cores for plaster cornices. This system of brick supports for plaster ornament was widely used in classical buildings in northern Italy and it may have been imported into Ireland during the Palladian era. Designs for decorative stucco ornamentation were drawn as full-scale cartoons and transferred onto wall and ceiling surfaces through perforations made at close intervals in the delineated design. In-situ modelling in stucco could be built up in applied coats or modelled directly (like cornices) with profiled modelling tools. Some of the decorative foliage in the rococo ceiling on the second floor of Mornington House (*c.*1760) was formed by incised depressions in the setting coat in lieu of relief modelling. This could mean that the initial stages of modelling may have been executed before the flat plaster background was set. A recent restoration of this ceiling revealed that some of the linear foliage consisted of real twigs taken from bushes and coated with a thin coat of stucco.

The casting of stucco ornament was common in early classical work in Ireland and in Palladian buildings up to the 1730s. Its use also developed progressively from the 1770s onwards with the development of neoclassical ornament. Ceilings in the chapel of the Royal Hospital Kilmainham (1685), in Castle Durrow (1715) and in Beaulieu, Co. Louth (1728), with their dependence on natural forms in high relief, made use of plaster moulds. These castings could be bonded to the in-situ setting coat of the ceiling with an adhesive of lime putty and size if they were small and light, but heavier ornaments required a direct connection to the timber ceiling structure with nails, wire or other suitable materials (fig. 11.3). An architectural report made by William Murray in 1842, on the dangerous condition of the chapel ceiling of the Royal Hospital, records some fixing methods employed:

> The recent occurrence of one of the heavy plaster ornaments being thrown down by the storm which took place in the 25th ultimo shows the imperative necessity there is for securing the innumerable pendant ornaments which are at present suspended by rotten twigs of heath and decayed wire, very many of the melons and pomegranates are of very ponderous weight and although they have the appearance of being imbedded into the plaster there is reason to suspect that the oak dovetailed dowells by which they were secured are completely decayed as in the instance of the pomegranate which recently fell.[25]

The use of plaster moulds for applied stucco ornamentation involved an initial modelling of the ornament in modelling clay, covering this clay model with plaster to make a mould and casting the ornament, by pouring a liquid plaster slip into the

25 NAI, Royal Hospital Kilmainham minute books, XVI, RHK 1/1/16, 11 Feb. 1842.

mould. An armature of metal or wood was usually inserted into the mould before the casting process was complete. This protruded from the cast ornament and provided a fixing when it was planted onto the ceiling surface. Gypsum plaster was an ideal material for mould making and casting, and samples of cast ornaments taken from ceilings in Charlemont House (1750s) and Mornington House (1760) indicate its use during the mid-eighteenth century in Dublin.

The considerable use of coffered ceilings by the Palladians in Ireland also encouraged an extensive use of repetitive stucco ornament made on casting benches and applied to soffits. The 1730s ceilings of Bellamont Forest in Co. Cavan, and of 9 Henrietta Street in Dublin are good examples of this application, but later applications can be seen in William Chambers's ceilings in Charlemont House and the Marino Casino (1750s). Even the most elaborate architectural features such as Corinthian capitals and entablatures could be cast as a series of individual mouldings and assembled as a composite whole. The modillion cornice that frames the in-situ rococo ceiling and the Corinthian capitals of the columnar screen in the hall at Castletown Cox, Co. Kilkenny, were assembled from casts by the provincial stuccodore Patrick Osborne in about 1770. The renowned English neoclassical stuccodore Joseph Rose had eight packing cases containing moulds and casts for the capitals and frieze of the saloon at Castlecoole ready for dispatch from his London workshop in 1795.[26] The execution of an elaborate stucco entablature started with in-situ modelling of the plain cornice and the receding planes of the frieze and architraves. Mouldings such as egg-and-dart were commonly produced from plaster moulds in sections which were joined together (on assembly) to the bed mould. Variations in size of different sections of egg-and-dart mouldings in the same cornice can be seen in the 1750s rococo ceiling – taken from Johnstown-Kennedy, Co. Dublin – installed in the hall of Dr Steevens's Hospital and in ceilings in Mornington House (1760). This may have been due to the deterioration of plaster moulds through use, or to the use of different moulds for increased production.

Where ornament required timber moulds, these were usually made from boxwood. Timber moulds were a logical choice for dentil courses and plain modillions. Scrolled modillions with decorative enrichment on three faces and undercut curving surfaces could require complex piece moulds of carved timber. The Dublin stuccodores working in the 1760s on Mornington House bonded a considerable amount of cast decorative ornament onto entablatures with a plaster adhesive, presumably made with lime putty, gypsum and size. The heavier ornate modillions were fixed with long iron nails. Plain modillions taken from the King House in Boyle (1730s) and scrolled modillions from Charlemont House in Dublin (1750s) had recessed sockets cast into their upper (bedding) surfaces to receive metal or timber fixings.

Ornamental friezes such as those in the saloon at Carton, Co. Kildare (1739), Grove House, Milltown (1750s), and Newbridge, Co. Dublin (1760), were modelled

---

26 Beard, *Decorative plasterwork*, p. 20.

11.3 Plaster ornaments in the shape of urns with metal armatures, from South Frederick Street, Dublin, mid-18th century. Peter Pearson Collection, photograph by David Davison.

in-situ in wet stucco. This practice prevailed into the 1770s in Osborne's stuccowork at Castletown Cox. By this time, Robert Adam's decorative work had begun to influence the design of wall and ceiling ornamentation in Britain. A recent survey of friezes in the ruins of Adam's Dalquharran Castle in Ayrshire (1785) revealed incised scoring of the in-situ plaster (following the lines of the design) to provide a key for the cast stucco decoration. Presumably details such as the elegant neoclassical garlands applied by Michael Stapleton on walls and ceilings in Trinity College (1770s–90s), in Belvedere House (1780s) and Mount Kennedy, Co. Wicklow (1780s), were applied in a similar manner. The vast amount of repetitive ornaments employed by Robert Adam in early works, such as the long gallery and drawing-room at Syon House in Middlesex in the 1760s, promoted the economics of the casting table as part of the development of neoclassical decorative practice. Neoclassical stuccodores such as Michael Stapleton and Charles Thorpe used in-situ modelling for the geometric framework of their designs, but they relied on the repetition of cast ornament in low relief for much of their decoration. This encouraged the use of shallow timber press moulds, which enabled craftsmen to produce ornament economically.

* * *

11.4 Castletown Cox, Co. Kilkenny, entrance hall, *c*.1767, plasterwork by Patrick Osborne.
Courtesy of the Irish Architectural Archive.

11.5 Castletown Cox, Co. Kilkenny, staircase hall, *c.*1767, detail of plasterwork by Patrick Osborne. Courtesy of the Irish Architectural Archive.

It is interesting to look at comparative costs of plain plaster and stuccowork and how costs varied with the complexity of ornamentation. Patrick Osborne's final account for his contract at Castletown Cox (dated 1774) provides comprehensive information on a considerable variety of plain and decorative applications.[27] Plain plastering on walls, for instance, cost 5*d.* per square yard. The preparation of plaster wall coats for wallpaper (probably lacking the final coat) cost 3*d.* per square yard. The higher cost of 6*d.* per square yard for ceilings obviously reflects the additional provision of ceiling laths. Plain cornices (run in situ) cost a mere 5*d.* per foot, but ornamented cornices (in the hall corridors) cost 2*s.* 6*d.* per foot. The great Corinthian entablature (in the hall and drawing room), with a decorated cyma (obviously cast) and applied cast mouldings such as egg-and-dart, scrolled modillions, roses, dentils, beaded astragals and frieze, cost 5*s.* per foot. The Doric entablature (in the stair hall), with cast cyma, mutules, triglyphs and metopes, also cost 5*s.* per foot. Surprisingly, the four large (cast) Corinthian capitals on the columns in the hall cost only £11 7*s.* 6*d.* or less than

[27] Brian de Breffny, 'Stucco work by Patrick Osborne at Castletown Cox,' *The Irish Ancestor*, 13:1 (1981), 15–17.

£3 a piece. The modelled in-situ ceilings in the drawing room and saloon, with their swirling rococo ornament, cost £45 10s. 0d. and £45 0s. 0d. respectively (figs. 11.4 & 11.5).

A comparison with some Dublin accounts for similar work executed in the 1760s reveals the considerable difference between city and provincial rates. Patrick and John Wall's payments for plastering and stuccowork on the Parliament Square buildings of Trinity College c.1760 show prices for plain ceiling plastering of 12d. per square yard, which is double the provincial rate, but their plain wall plastering at 3½d. per square yard is considerably less than the 5d. paid at Castletown Cox.[28] The rate of 10d. per foot for plain cornices is also double Osborne's rate. The rates for decorative stucco entablatures, however, are not dissimilar. Wall's Ionic entablature, with five enrichments, including modillions and roses, cost 4s. 6d. per foot, which is identical to Osborne's price. In Dublin, a large cornice with three enrichments cost 3s. per foot, and a cornice with two enrichments cost 1s. 8d. These compare with Osborne's ornamented cornice in the Castletown hall corridors at 2s. 6d. per foot and his enriched cornice under the gallery at 2s.

The parity with Dublin rates for the more complex cast stucco entablatures probably arose because of Osborne's special expertise as a stuccodore. He obviously executed the highly skilled tasks himself and left routine plastering to assistants. His ability to model complex architectural features, such as Corinthian capitals, would have commanded top rates of pay anywhere in Ireland. Although his creative skills and individuality could not be compared with those of Robert West, his mastery of his medium and the stylistic motifs of the period is evident. Osborne's proficiency, of course, raises the question of how a provincial plasterer from Waterford developed such skills. Competence in plain plastering, walling and structural carpentry might be expected in eighteenth-century provincial Ireland, but specialists in decorative crafts such as stonecutting, joinery and stucco were not easily found. This is evident in Bishop Edward Synge's mid-eighteenth-century correspondence on the construction of Elphin Palace, Co. Roscommon.[29] His letters reveal a reliance on Dublin sources for materials and for competent artisans such as house (interior) carpenters and plasterers. The accounts of contracts at Baronscourt, Co. Tyrone, c.1780, record six carpenters, two plasterers and one plumber from London; at Castlecoole, Co. Fermanagh, in the 1790s, they show a reliance on English specialists such as carvers, stuccodores and painters to handle decorative work.[30]

Brian de Breffny's association of Osborne's skills with experience gained working under the Lafranchinis is not an unreasonable assumption. Ducart, the Italian architect of Castletown Cox, probably employed the Lafranchinis at Kilshannig, Co. Cork in the 1760s (fig. 11.6). They obviously used Irish assistants on such contracts

28 TCD, Patrick and John Wall's accounts, MUN/P2/139. 29 Legg, *The Synge letters*, pp 16, 29, 30, 43, 119, 123, 131. 30 PRONI, Abercorn papers, MS D623/c/1, f. 4; Desmond Guinness & William Ryan, *Irish country houses and castles* (London, 1971), p. 164; Castle Coole (National Trust [guidebook], 2008), pp 8, 12.

11.6 Kilshannig, Co. Cork, detail of plasterwork in library ceiling attributed to Filippo Lafranchini, 1760s. Courtesy of the Irish Architectural Archive.

for routine tasks, and an ambitious assistant with a natural aptitude for decorative modelling could learn a lot from such an experience. Something similar happened in Dublin between the 1750s and the 1770s. The serial impact of the Lafranchinis modelled work in the 1740s, followed by Cramillion's influence from 1755 onwards, promoted a new dynamic among local craftsmen in an enthusiastic pursuit of stylistic ideas and techniques. Their lack of training as figurative sculptors was a disadvantage, but it did not inhibit their adoption of the in-situ modelling process and their control over its plastic potential. The published designs of French decorators such as Oppenord and Meissonier provided a framework that allowed scope for this potential. The Jarratt album in the Irish Architectural Archive is one example of how the development from rocaille curves into looser, individual compositions, which characterized the work of West and his followers, utilized the plastic potential of the stucco medium to its fullest extent. The combination of floral wreaths, fruit clusters, trophies and birds in high and low relief, and often in asymmetrical sequence, became identified with the stuccodores of the Dublin rococo school.

11.7 Staircase hall and landing, Powerscourt House, Dublin, plasterwork by James McCullagh with Michael Reynolds, 1774. Courtesy of the Irish Architectural Archive.

Variations in the handling of important decorative elements within the same ceiling, in buildings such as 85 St Stephen's Green (1760s) and Mornington House (1760s), show the hands of more than one craftsman working simultaneously on decorative detail. West's payment in 1755 for his Rotunda contract indicates the employment of a considerable workforce and, apart from his brother John, he must have employed other skilled assistants.[31] The considerable amount of work executed in Dublin in the same style, but not always to the same standards, points to a group of artisans working under one influence.

The plastering trade expanded considerably in Dublin during the middle decades of the century from the 1740s until the 1760s. The city freedom rolls show the admission of fourteen plasterers between 1720 and 1740. Between 1741 and 1761, thirty-eight admissions are recorded, among them the West brothers, William Lee who also worked on the Rotunda Hospital and James McCullagh, who was to handle the stuccowork on the stair hall of Powerscourt House (fig. 11.7). Acknowledged ability as a stuccodore in eighteenth-century Ireland brought large rewards and even public recognition. West, both master builder and plasterer, became a man of considerable substance. McCullagh was master of his guild in 1778 and a member of the common council of the city corporation. Stapleton's name is absent from the freedom rolls, but this never seemed to interfere with his career, and he owned houses in the Mountjoy Square area by the 1790s.[32] Charles Thorpe also owned several houses in Mountjoy Square; he became an alderman in 1792, and subsequently lord mayor of Dublin in 1800.

---

31 *The case of the Bartholomew Mosse ... 1755* [Dublin, 1755].   **32** On Stapleton's speculative building career see Conor Lucey, *The Stapleton collection* (Tralee, 2007), chapter 4.

CHAPTER TWELVE

Painting

U NLIKE CRAFTS SUCH AS CARPENTRY, masonry, slating and plastering, painting does not appear to have been a well-established building trade in medieval Ireland. There are only two admissions of painters as freemen in the Dublin freedom rolls before 1671, and the first significant mention of a trade presence in the city was in 1670 with the formation of the Guild of St Luke to represent the three separate trades of cutlers, painter-stainers and stationers.[1] Combinations of separate trades to form a city guild was a normal procedure. The reliance by less established trades on other trade associations with strong market control and powerful patronage was also common. The cutlers were undoubtedly the most influential trade in the 1670 combination and their involvement may have been an essential factor in the grant of a royal charter. The charter of October 1670 records the names of thirteen founder members, eight cutlers including the first guild master Samuel Cotton, three painter-stainers and two stationers.[2] The painter-stainers were Richard Carney, Isaac Chalke and Thomas Wiseman. Carney was one of two elected wardens, which secured him a seat on the common council of the city. He became master of the guild in 1686. Thomas Wiseman was recorded as guild master in 1678 and Chalke in 1679.[3]

The choice of the descriptive term 'painter-stainers' was based on an older use of the same title by the London company of painter-stainers, established in 1502. This title was derived from the application of paint on solid surfaces such as timber, stone and iron and of 'stains' on fabrics such as cotton, canvas, leather and silk. The London and Dublin fraternities encompassed all levels of the art and craft, from heraldic painters to portrait painters and house painters. The organization of painters in the Dublin guild closely followed London practice and its membership was drawn from the same assortment of craftsmen.[4] The lack of clear demarcation between painters engaged in pictorial representation, heraldic designs and decorative building finishes was part of an earlier pattern that prevailed up to the middle of the eighteenth century, until the development of the academies of drawing and the structured pursuit of training in the fine arts. Seventeenth-century workshop practice involved

---

1 DCLA, typescript, roll of freemen of the city of Dublin, Rudolfus Cotton 1600, Thomas Cotton 1650. 2 Oliver Snoddy, 'Charter of the Guild of St Luke, 1670', *JRSAI*, 98 (1968), 80–1. 3 Walter G. Strickland, *A dictionary of Irish artists* (Dublin, 1913), I, p. 158; *CARD*, 5, p. 155; NLI, records of the Guild of St Luke, MS 12,122, f. 14 *v*. 4 Jane Fenlon, 'The painter stainers companies of Dublin and London' in Jane Fenlon, Nicola Figgis & Catherine Marshall (eds), *New perspectives: studies in art history in honour of Anne Crookshank* (Dublin, 1987), pp 102–4.

apprentices in identical tasks irrespective of their vocational ambitions and ultimate specializations. Paints used on pictorial altarpieces, on carved escutcheons, or on panelled wainscotting were made from the same pigments, obtained from the same sources, and laboriously mixed with binders such as oils or glue-sizes by apprentices or assistants before application. However, the Dublin directories make a clear distinction after the 1750s between 'house-painters' as a description for artisans engaged in building contracts and 'herald painters' engaged in commissions for signs, escutcheons, banners and illuminated parchments.

The late emergence of the painting fraternity as an organized trading association in Dublin can be variously explained. While commissions for armorial insignia, banners and pictorial panels might have been common enough in the medieval city, the work involved could be handled by a small number of workshops. The building market provided limited opportunities for skilled decorative craftsmen. Urban houses were built either of rubble stone with cut-stone dressings, or of oak cage construction with wattle infill covered by lime plaster. There was little necessity for paint on domestic exteriors, windows were usually of lead, and doorcases of oak or carved limestone. Internal wall and ceiling surfaces were simply and economically decorated with water-based paints or distempers that did not require the skills necessary in the making and application of oil-based paints. Distempers were paint pigments mixed with glue-size, binder and water. The most commonly used distemper was whiting, made with powdered chalk (or sometimes lime) and often used as a ceiling finish. Powdered pigment colours such as ochre, umber, sienna and vermilion were frequently used in mixtures with whiting and lampblack to make distemper.

Seventeenth-century building records in Ireland reveal attempts by members of the plastering trade to contract for painting work. This is understandable in the context of the limited decorative potential of pre-classical interiors. Whiting and glue-size were materials in everyday use in plastering contracts and the use of distemper could be seen by plasterers as normal operational practice. Changing patterns in building practices with the advent of classical ornament provided new opportunities for painting skills. The competition between plasterers and painters to control this developing market resulted in a public enquiry in 1677 to define the responsibilities of both trades in the application of paint. Something similar had happened in London more than half a century earlier, which helped establish the dominance of the painting fraternity in the control of their craft.

The end of the great age of timber building in England and the advance of European architectural ideals in the early years of the seventeenth century opened up new markets for decorative skills. Inigo Jones's design for the Queen's Apartments in Somerset House in 1628 included a carved doorcase decorated by the painter Matthew Goodrich in imitation of white marble enriched with gold; the interior was described as 'walls ornamented with 218 panels of grotesque work … on a white ground with gilded mouldings'; the faces of the stone window were in gold arabesque on white with an edge of gold next to the glass; the chimney-piece was white, blue bice (obtained from azurite) and gold. The decoration extended to the balcony 'where the railing was painted cobalt blue, the stanchions and iron balls gilded, the soffit of the balcony stone colour, and the four cartouches supporting it, blue and gold'.[5]

Over ten years previously, in 1616, Jones initiated the first use in England of compartment ceilings in his design for the Queen's house at Greenwich. This promoted a new decorative formula in English interior design that was fully exploited by successive architects such as Webb at Wilton (Wilts), in 1650, Pratt at Coleshill (Berks), in 1660, Burlington at Chiswick in 1725 and even by Chambers in his 1760s interiors. The organization of structural coffers to form circular or oval bays as central features – as in the Whitehall Banqueting House – encouraged commissions for decorative ceiling paintings in important civic buildings and grand country houses. The use of distinguished foreign artists (such as Rubens, Sabatini, Laguerre and Verrio) to execute many of these ceiling decorations exposed English painter-stainers to techniques employed in the great European decorative workshops. This influence would have been eagerly absorbed by local craftsmen engaged in decorating the architectural background to these artworks.

By the 1660s, changing constructional patterns in urban domestic architecture began to alter and increase the scope of English painting contracts. The substitution of Norwegian and Baltic softwoods (spruce and fir) for English oak in domestic interiors greatly increased the use of painted timber surfaces. Softwood panelling, cornices, entablatures, doors and staircases – unlike plaster surfaces – needed oil paints or varnishes for durability. This process required a careful preparation of the surface itself, and the application of priming and undercoatings as a base for the final paint-coat. The availability of highly skilled carpenters, carvers and joiners in the London area promoted the extensive use of timber ornamentation on the exteriors of early classical houses. Modillion eaves, cornices of timber, hooded doorcases with elaborately carved consoles, and dormers with timber pediments were in common use. These enrichments, like the timber sashes which became common in the 1680s, required painting as protection against the weather.

The foundation of the Dublin fraternity of painter-stainers must be seen in the context of the growth and development of the painter's craft in England and in the expectation of new opportunities created by changing building practices. The expansion of the Dublin suburbs had already begun in 1670 and patterns that were already evident in London urban developments were beginning to emerge. The subsequent progression of the Meath and Aungier estates south of the river, and the Jervis, Ellis and Drogheda estates to the north, justified these market expectations. However, these expectations were shared by members of the Dublin plastering trade who were strongly established in the city and who also decided to consolidate their position in the market. This resulted in the formation of another new association in 1670 called the Guild of St Bartholomew, which represented the trades of plastering

---

5 John Harris & Gordon Higgott, *Inigo Jones, complete architectural drawings* (London, 1989), p. 194.

and bricklaying. Fortunately, some early records of the Guild of St Luke have survived, and they provide a rare opportunity to study the activities and operation of a city guild in full exercise of its powers. The group of painter-stainers associated with the guild, in the decades between its foundation in 1670 and the early 1700s, is particularly interesting. The variety of skills and background experience among this group can only be explained by the considerable overlap of responsibilities inherent within the building crafts, particularly in this period of transition and change.

Richard Carney, a founder member and one of the first wardens of the guild, typifies this pattern. Strickland outlines his career: described as a herald, a limner and a portrait painter, he was appointed Athlone Pursuivant in 1661 and Ulster King of Arms in 1683, after which he was knighted.[6] He is recorded as a contractor for decorative work in St John's Church in Dublin in 1681, involving the gilding of seven dials and the statue of St John and he was master of the guild in 1686. Isaac Chalke, another founder member, also had an unusual career. He trained as a plasterer and received his franchise through this trade in 1654.[7] He undoubtedly operated as both a plasterer and painter and his involvement in St Luke's guild in 1670 was designed to secure his position as a painting contractor. However, he was equally intent on furthering his interests as a plasterer, as we find his name among the founder members of the new Guild of St Bartholomew, which also received its charter in 1670.[8]

Chalke's confidence in the promotional advantages of the guild system was not misplaced. His name, and that of his son (Isaac Chalke junior), were linked with contracts for plastering, painting and gilding for the city corporation (in the Tholsel).[9] Chalke's name appears, as painter and plasterer, in the surveyor general's accounts for 1706/7 and at the Royal Hospital Kilmainham in 1715.[10] Records of these accounts clearly show payments for plastering and painting as one single contract. Chalke and his son (enfranchised in 1683) were undoubtedly the most likely choice as contractor for this lucrative commission although the stucco enrichments in the chapel ceiling may have justified the involvement of a specialist. By 1679, when Chalke became guild master, the membership had increased to sixty-five sworn brethren including fifteen painter-stainers.[11] The list included names such as Thomas Spencer, who was enfranchised as a plasterer in 1669, Aaron Crossley, who operated as a heraldic painter, and Thomas Carleton, who was a portrait painter.[12] The name of William Robinson, who was better known as the surveyor general and architect, is also recorded; he became master of the guild in 1696.[13] Robinson's participation is not

---

6 Strickland, *Dictionary*, I, pp 157, 158.   7 DCLA, typescript, roll of freemen of the city of Dublin.   8 DCLA, charter of the Dublin guild of bricklayers and plasterers, MS 81.   9 *CARD*, 5, pp 399, 400, 409.   10 TNA, T. Burgh's accounts, 5/6 Sept. 1707, WO/55/1984; NAI, Royal Hospital Kilmainham minutes, III, RHK 1/1/3, 18 Aug. 1715; Richard Colley, *An account of the foundation the Royal Hospital of King Charles II* (Dublin, 1725), p. 23.   11 NLI, records of the Guild of St Luke, MS 12,122, ff 14v–15v.   12 DCLA, typescript, roll of freemen of the city of Dublin; Charles T. Keatinge, 'The Guild of Cutlers, Painter-Stainers and Stationers', *JRSAI*, 30 (1900), 139; Strickland, *Dictionary*, I, pp 156–7.   13 NLI, records of the Guild of St Luke, MS 12,122, f. 60 v.

surprising: he also became a founder member of the plasterers' and bricklayers' guild in 1670 and the guild of joiners, ceylers and wainscotters in 1700.[14] We can be reasonably sure that his membership of these new building fraternities was on foot of invitations from prominent artisans who sought access to state contracts. Tradesmen such as Chalke and Spencer were ideally positioned to take advantage of close contacts of this nature. Robinson might also have benefited from association with the building fraternities. He was known as a trader in foreign merchandise and an importer of materials such as building timber. His liaison with prominent contractors in the network had advantages.

The increase in membership in the last two decades of the seventeenth century reflects the growth of the city and its population. By 1719, the roll books of the Guild of St Luke recorded the names of 193 members of whom 86 were painters.[15] The membership of the painter-stainers continued to represent an assortment of skills and different backgrounds. It included limners, heraldic painters, portrait painters, landscape painters and plasterers. Prominent pictorial artists among these members included Thomas Pooley (admitted 1683), Gaspar Smitz (admitted 1681) and Martin Skinner (admitted 1698).[16] Prominent plasterers recorded as members included Nathaniel Spencer (admitted 1701), Edward Burne (admitted 1706), George Spike (admitted 1699) and William Wall (admitted 1715); Wall was appointed guild master for 1726/7.[17]

The strong presence of plasterers in the painters' guild is curious in view of the rivalry between these trades, and the public dispute about their operational responsibilities which occurred in 1677. On June 24 in that year, a petition from the Guild of St Luke requesting new regulations to control the encroachment of plasterers in painting contracts was placed before the Dublin City Assembly. The petition claimed that:

> Whereas alsoe the painterstainers of the guild of Saint Luke, the Evangelist, Dublin, formerly petitioned to the assembly of this city, shewing that divers of the corporation of plaisterers, of the citty of Dublin, did exercise the art of painting worke, the which, as the petitioners humbly conceived, properly belonged to the petitioners trade, the petitioners therefore humbly prayed the said assembly to take the premisses into their serious considerations and to ordeine and appoint to which of the said trades painting worke did properly belonge, it being for the distinction of trade.[18]

The painter-stainers also asked the assembly to introduce regulations for plasterers based on established London practice. They cited an act of parliament which, they

---

[14] DCLA, Gilbert Collection, charter of the Dublin guild of bricklayers and plasterers, MS 81; Henry Guinness, 'Dublin trade guilds', *JRSAI*, 52 (1922), 162.   [15] Keatinge, 'The Guild of Cutlers', 137.   [16] Strickland, *Dictionary*, II, p. 251; DCLA, Gilbert Library, typescript, roll of freemen of the city of Dublin.   [17] NLI, records of the Guild of St Luke, MS 12,122, ff 75 r, 76 v, 91 r, 69 v, 117 v, 121 r; MS 12,123, pp 214–19.   [18] *CARD*, 5, pp 145–6.

claimed, prohibited London plasterers 'from laying any manner of colours whatsoever, and [which] directed [them] onely to use whitening, blacking, red lead, red oker, yellow oker, and russet, mingled with size onely, and not with oyle, on pain of five pounds for every offence'. The city assembly accepted the case presented by the painter-stainers. They restricted members of the plasterers' guild to contractual conditions similar to those operating in London, but the new regulations contained the following provision which protected existing plasterers:

> It is therefore ordered and agreed upon, by the authority aforesaid, that such of the brethren of the corporation of plaisterers as have used to lay colours and paintings in oyle, paying for each person the summe of twenty shillings a peece to the corporation of painter-stainers, shall have libertie, dureing their residence here, to use and lay such colours and paintings, and for the future noe other person or persons whatsoever shall use or exercise or laying colours in oyle, ... but ... members of the said corporation of painterstainers, their servants and apprentices.[19]

The records of the Guild of St Luke for 19 January 1703 show that two apprentices, John Tomson and John Sisson, were refused admission because they were articled as plasterers, and their master Richard Sisson (also a plasterer) held his guild membership on condition that he 'work in oyle with his Own hands' and was 'not to bring up any apprentice to work in oyle'. The intention behind the Dublin painters' demand for the introduction of the London regulations was clearly to confine plasterers to colouring internal plaster surfaces with water-soluble paints (distempers) from a limited and unexciting range of colours. The dependence on size as a binding medium produced paints that were unsuitable for use on timber surfaces or for external use. The six pigments allowed by the regulations were among the cheapest and most utilitarian colours in everyday use. The omission of rich colours such as verditer or bright yellow (both used in the eighteenth century at Ledwithstown in Co. Longford) was a serious disadvantage.[20] Equally serious was the lack of a green and of a blue pigment that could be used for its own qualities or mixed with yellow to make a range of greens.

Whiting made a very dependable distemper that was commonly used to produce white ceilings and wall surfaces. It was also used as a cheap extender (or adulterant) with the more expensive white lead as an oil paint. It was made from crushed chalk, which was mostly obtained from the south-east of England or from northern France. Its lack of opacity and covering power limited its use in an oil paint. However, its low cost encouraged its use on contracts with low budgets. Thomas Burgh's accounts for

---

[19] Ibid., p. 146.　[20] Mary McGrath, 'Report on Ledwithstown House', 1993, unpaginated, copy in the Irish Architectural Archive. It was difficult to date precisely the use of paints in Ledwithstown (early eighteenth-century), but bright yellow was 'one of the earliest colours found', and the verditer is probably eighteenth-century.

painting woodwork in the Hall and Chapel in the Royal Hospital Kilmainham in 1705 refer to a paint called 'Spanish white', which was essentially a mixture of whiting and linseed oil.[21] In Ireland, the term whiting must have also described a distemper (or whitewash) made with lime instead of chalk, as there are no references to chalk in building accounts. Lime was available locally and was in common use on building sites, especially by plasterers. Burgh's 1705 account (referred to above) in the Royal Hospital approved payments 'for the White washing ye cieling of ye Hall & Galery', and 'For Cleaning & Brushing ye cieling in ye Chappell & white washing ye same twice over & stopping all ye Cracks'. Stitt refers to the use of 'Lime white' used on walls and ceilings by plasterers in 1819; Bristow quotes another early nineteenth-century reference to the superiority of lime white over chalk white for ceilings and its infrequent use in London due to the prevalence of chalk and the scarcity of limestone.[22]

Whiting also played an important role in adjusting the tonality of colours in mixtures with other pigments. The limited scope of pigments in the plasterer's range could be adjusted with judicious mixtures of yellow, or red, with whiting and black. Tints such as stone colour, olive green, buff and French grey could be achieved using yellow ochre as a base. Dull reds, terra cotta and browns could be produced with a base of red ochre, russet or red lead. The opportunities available to painter-stainers with an extended palette of colours such as smalt blue, verditer, Indian (crimson) lake, verdigris, umber, orpiment yellow and vermilion (all available in the seventeenth century) were much more exciting. Smalt blue was discovered among early paint samples taken from the gates of the Royal Hospital; verditer was probably used in the eighteenth century to pick out the frames of panels on the walls of Ledwithstown House; in 1774, Lady Louisa Conolly coloured the ceiling of the gallery at Castletown, Co. Kildare in colours of scarlet, white and gold.[23]

Blacking was probably a pigment known as lamp black, which was the cheapest and most common black in use in the late seventeenth century. It was essentially a soot, obtained, according to Dossie, by 'burning oil in a number of large lamps in a confined place'.[24] A pigment made from soot was used in varnish on internal doors in Ledwithstown House, but this may have been a brown pigment called bistre, made from calcined beechwood; the black pigments used in both distempers and oil mixes in Ledwithstown were found to be carbon-based and probably made from charcoal.[25]

The most useful pigments in the plasterer's range were the ochres, red and yellow. Yellow ochre could be found in several European countries as a naturally coloured earth. Red ochre was made from calcined yellow ochre. Dossie refers to supplies of ochre from Oxfordshire, which appears to have been one of the main sources of supply in England during the eighteenth century.[26] We have no information on Irish

---

21 NAI, Royal Hospital Kilmainham minutes, I, RHK 1/1/1, f. 295.   **22** William Stitt, *The practical architect's ready assistant* (Dublin, 1819), p. 346; Ian Bristow, *Interior house-painting colours and technology, 1615–1840* (London, 1996), p. 8.   **23** Bristow, *Interior house-painting colours*, pp 16, 171–2; McGrath, 'Ledwithstown House'.   **24** Robert Dossie, *The handmaid to the arts* (London, 1764), i, p. 139.   **25** McGrath, 'Ledwithstown House'.   **26** Dossie, *The handmaid to the arts*, p. 69.

sources of supply other than at Avoca, Co. Wicklow, but Bristow records the common use of ochre from Bristol, which was probably available on the Irish market before the nineteenth century.[27] Yellow ochre is an opaque pigment with considerable covering power. It was one of the main ingredients used in paints mixed to simulate oak, and it also played an important role in paints simulating Portland stone. Its use has been identified in Ledwithstown in distempers mixed with black, to make a grey green.[28] It was also used ground in oil, as an undercoat on grained timberwork (doors and skirtings) in the entrance hall at Ledwithstown. According to Dossie, Venetian red is a native red ochre, 'generally used by house-painters in imitation of mahogany'; red ochre, he adds, 'is chiefly brought from Oxfordshire'; Spanish brown, which is 'nearly of the same colour with Venetian red', is another native earth.[29] Venetian red may well have been the base for the (iron oxide) terracotta distemper, observed in the dado of the sitting room at Ledwithstown. Its low cost and quick drying capacity as an oil paint made it an ideal primer and undercoat on joinery.

The six basic pigments selected for use by plastering contractors also included two other reddish colours, russet and red lead. There are no references to a pigment described as russet in seventeenth- or eighteenth-century painting records and it seems reasonable to accept russet as a colour combination of red ochre and yellow ochre. Red lead may have been useful to plasterers as a water-based distemper, but its use as a colour finish in oils was inhibited by its reputation for turning black with time. Its most consistent use was as a primer and undercoat, where its covering power and quick drying properties were advantages. It was frequently used as a primer on exterior ironwork and as an undercoat for the more expensive red vermilion.

The range of pigments permitted for use in plastering contracts was capable of providing adequate but unexciting wall and ceiling decorations in distemper. Its limitations lay in the narrow basis for choice, the absence of bright yellows, bright reds and an almost total lack of blues and greens. The combinations revealed in the examination of eighteenth-century distemper used in Ledwithstown provide an indication of proper requirements for good decorative practice at this time. The plasterer's lack of specialized training in the subtle blending of tints and tonalities was also a disadvantage. Expertise in the application of paint could be acquired without great difficulty, but the real skill of the trained painter was in mixing and compounding different pigments to achieve the precise decorative values demanded by contemporary taste and fashion.

The oil most commonly used in paint mixes was linseed oil obtained from the seed of the flax plant. Nut oil, obtained from walnuts, was occasionally used, especially with white lead pigment, which tended to become yellow in time when mixed with linseed oil. John Wall's accounts in Trinity College record 684 square yards of white paintwork in the Provost's House using 'London Lead and Nut Oyle', measured in 1753.[30] The proper application of oil paint required considerably more

---

27 Bristow, *Interior house-painting colours*, p. 30.   **28** McGrath, 'Ledwithstown House'.   **29** Dossie, *The handmaid to the arts*, pp 54, 55, 69.   **30** TCD, John Wall's accounts, MUN/P2/96 (1).

labour and preparation than the use of distemper. The painting of timber surfaces involved preliminary treatment such as knotting, stopping, priming and several undercoats that were pumiced and sanded before the application of a final finish. Pigments such as red lead and Spanish brown were commonly used as primers and undercoats because of their covering power and fast drying properties. Knotting was an essential measure in the painting of softwood to prevent the resinous emission from knots staining the finished work.

Joseph Emerson recommended red lead mixed with size as a knotting preparation for wainscotting in 1744.[31] Red lead mixed with oil was a more common application and oil-based mixes were essential in all exterior situations. Stopping was the process of filling, with a plastic filler, cracks, gaps and joints (in joinery) in the surface to be painted. This filler was usually a putty made from linseed oil and whiting. White lead and red lead were often added to putty mixes. The bye-laws of the Guild of St Luke stressed the importance of proper preparation for painting surfaces, especially in a bye-law of 1676:

> If any person of this Guild being a painter-stainer shall at any time hereafter paint or Coulor any oyle work whatsoever that is to stand & be without doores in the weather, and shall insteade of an Oyle primeing use Size milk [?] etc., or that shall not stopp the Crackes or slyffts in timber with Oyle putty, or shall Lacker any worke whatsoever that is to abide the weather instead of Gold … the party soe offending shall for the first offence pay to the Master of the said Guild for the use of the said Corporation Six shillings, Eight pence sterling, and for the second offence and all other more offences of this nature the full vallue of his or theire worke.[32]

These regulations were taken seriously. In April 1700, William Sherrif was fined for external oil painting in York Street that was 'insufficient and defective'.[33] And in 1704, the heraldic painter Aaron Crossley was censored on foot of a complaint by Elizabeth Gunn concerning the painting of a 'signe of a ship' and he was told that he 'ought to finish it, and soon'.[34]

The mixing of pigments and binders to make specific colours was commonly carried out by tradesmen and their apprentices, but in eighteenth-century London the demand for oil paint encouraged the establishment of commercial paint workshops or 'colourmen'. The making of distemper was a simple matter, involving the suspension and mixing of powdered pigments in buckets of hot size. Oil paint was a more complicated process, involving the grinding of dry pigment with oil on a marble slab to achieve an even absorption of the colour particles. This was a laborious and time-consuming task, particularly when large quantities of colour were required.

---

[31] Ian Bristow, 'Ready mixed paint in the eighteenth century', *Architectural Review*, 161: 962 (April 1977), 246–8.   [32] NLI, records of the Guild of St Luke, MS 12,121, p. 21.   [33] Keatinge, 'The Guild of Cutlers', 139.   [34] NLI, records of the Guild of St Luke, MS 12,123, p. 90.

Some London colourmen industrialized the process by the use of horse-driven mixing mills. There is insufficient information on Irish painting practice to enable us to determine how painters procured their materials. The accounts of the new Parliament House in 1731 refer to the purchase of colours from a William Walker, but there is no information on whether the colours were already mixed into a paste for immediate use, or supplied as pigments to be processed by the painter George Spike before application on the building.[35]

On contracts where speed or economy were important, distemper could be used on wall and ceiling surfaces and oil paints reserved for timber joinery. The alkaline content of newly applied lime plaster precluded the use of oil paint in new buildings for a period of a year or more. This did not deter ambitious builders from exploiting the decorative potential of oil-bound colours. Bristow records the expensive practice of decorating new buildings initially with distemper followed by a final application of oil paint a year or two later.[36]

Eighteenth-century fashions promoted a colour range based on certain fixed conventions. Many of the most commonly used colours simulated natural produce and materials. The London colourman Alexander Emerson advertised colours in the 1730s such as stone, lead, oak, cedar, mahogany, chocolate, straw, pea green and walnut tree colour.[37] Some of these paint colours have been recorded in Irish building accounts. George Spike's account for painting in the Provost's House, Trinity College, in 1717 refers to 'Dantzick oak Collour on the great staircase' and to 'Cedar collour painting in the Provost's Closet'.[38] Oak and mahogany colours were used in the Provost's House in the 1750s; doors and windows in the north range of Parliament Square were painted 'white and mahogany colour' in 1756; mahogany was used again in the Provost's House for doors in 1790 and in rooms in Lord Caledon's house in Cavendish Row in 1799.[39] William Stitt recorded contractual rates for oil paints described as 'Chocolate or lead colour', mahogany and 'Grey or Portland stone colour' in 1819.[40]

The colour range advertised by Emerson was sold to the general public as well as house painters, and some of these colours were commonly used by eminent decorative designers, although the pigment mixtures employed may have been more sophisticated than those sold by commercial coulourmen. Pea green was a highly fashionable colour in the mid-eighteenth century. Robert Adam estimated for its use in the Assembly Room of the Shire Hall in Hertfordshire, and William Chambers used it for Lord Charlemont.[41] Chambers also liked stone colour, which he described in a letter to a merchant in Leith as a paint which 'will last best & is Cheapest' in parlours for common use.[42] He used it in Somerset House, and Adam used it in both

---

35 *Commons Journal*, 4, pp. xxxii.   36 Bristow, *Interior house-painting colours*, p. 111.   37 Bristow, 'Ready mixed paint in the eighteenth century', 246–8.   38 TCD, George Spike's accounts, MUN/P2/34. 39 TCD, Patrick and John Wall's accounts, MUN/P2/96/1,11; MUN/P2/102; Michael Stapleton's accounts, MUN/P2/152/14; PRONI, Caledon papers, D2433/B/1/3/27.   40 Stitt, *The practical architect's ready assistant*, pp 347–8.   41 Bristow, *Interior house-painting colours*, pp 163–4; RIA, Charlemont correspondence, Chambers to Charlemont, 7 Sept. 1775, MS/12/R/13.   42 Geoffrey Beard, *Decorative*

Osterly Park and the Register House in Edinburgh; straw colour was also used in Osterly Park.[43]

Dossie was critical of the quality of the paints mixed in London by commercial colourmen. He was an admirer of the decorative ideals practised in France, which he described (in 1764) 'at this time the source of nearly all invention of fashions'.[44] Chambers's prescriptions for the decoration of the saloon of the Marino Casino (described in a letter to Lord Charlemont in 1769) might have consoled him. He recommended that

> the Entablature doors &c. of the room should be dead white touched with blew and that the cove part of the Ceiling be done with Izing glass & flake white to be of a more brilliant white than the Entablature ... the coffers of the Cove a light blew as also the ground of the Galoss running round the flat part of the Ceiling in oyle and that the Apollos head and rays be flake white & the flat ground round it of as faint a blew flat in oyle as it is possible to make. if your Lordship should not approve of this method the Walls may be blew to the top of the Entablature but it should be a light blew and rich with gold upon the ornaments and with regard to all the Ceiling parts the White must predominate but the Coffers & Ground of the Galloss may be blew the mouldings gilt and the Appollos head & Rays white & only heightened or streak'd with gold for if it be solid Gold it will look clumsy.[45]

Charlemont accepted most of the suggestions in the first alternative proposed by Chambers. This was essentially a composition of two different whites against a light blue background, presumably designed as a foil for the blue wallpaper described elsewhere in Chambers's letter. The more brilliant white was bound with isinglass, a particularly expensive size obtained from the carcase of the sturgeon fish. Dossie recommended isinglass in 1764 as a binder for high quality distemper.[46] Flake white was a superior and expensive form of white lead pigment much used by pictorial artists. Dead white describes the use of a flat or matt oil finish which was fashionable in interior designs in the mid-eighteenth century.[47] Matt finishes were usually obtained by the use of turpentine mixed with oil-bound paints.

The blue on the walls in the Casino and in the hexagonal coffers of the ceiling was complimented by the deeper blue of a lapis lazuli plaque forming a centrepiece of the white marble fireplace, and by an elaborate table with a lapis lazuli top made by the London sculptor Joseph Wilton. This combination of blues and whites surmounting a richly patterned parquet floor must have made a stunning impact on local sensibilities. The architecture of Chambers's Casino had already encouraged leaders

---

plasterwork in Great Britain (London, 1975), p. 20.   **43** Bristow, *Interior house-painting colours*, pp 172–3.   **44** Dossie, *The handmaid to the arts*, 1, p. vi.   **45** RIA, Charlemont correspondence, Chambers to Charlemont, 22 Mar. 1769, MS/12/R/12.   **46** Dossie, *The handmaid to the arts*, 1, p. 188.   **47** Bristow, *Interior house-painting colours*, p. 102.

of public taste in Dublin to look abroad for architectural ideas in 1768, in the design competition for a new Royal Exchange.

* * *

By this time, the trade lists in the Dublin directories used the term 'house painter' to describe artisans specializing in painting buildings, and 'herald painter' to describe those involved in graphic work. Although an increase in specialization may have developed since the end of the seventeenth century, some overlap of responsibilities was still discernible at this time. Strickland refers to a former house painter called Peter Shee who became well known as a landscape painter in the 1760s.[48] He also records the activities of a limner and heraldic painter called George Rencher, an expatriate Londoner who promoted himself in *Faulkner's Journal* in 1751 as a painter of ceilings and staircases 'after the new French mode'.[49] It is also evident, from descriptions of James McCullagh (as stuccodore and painter) and Michael Stapleton (as stucco plasterer and painter) in the Dublin trade directories, that these well established plastering contractors were engaged in painting contracts in the last quarter of the eighteenth century. Stapleton's accounts for work in Trinity College clearly indicate an involvement in both distemper and oil colours in his contracts.

We cannot be certain if the agreements regulating the plastering and painting trades at the end of the seventeenth century were still in force in the latter half of the next century. However, we can be confident that McCullagh and Stapleton were engaged in a well-established tradition initiated nearly a hundred years earlier by contractors such as Isaac Chalke, Nathaniel Spencer and William Wall, who were members of both the plasterers' and painters' guilds and who dominated the contracting market for both these services.

It is unlikely that plasterers such as Chalke and his son (Isaac Chalke junior) or William Wall would have been considered for appointment as masters of St Luke's without an established competence in the craft of oil painting. Their appointments on important contracts (for painting and plastering) by the surveyor general and Trinity College is clear evidence of their training and skill in both disciplines. Chalke (as we have observed) and George Spike, who also worked for the surveyor general and Trinity College, were both described in Burgh's accounts as 'painter and plasterer'.

It is apparent from contractual records that Chalke, Spike and Wall and the generations of eighteenth-century painter-plasterers that followed (such as Patrick and John Wall, James McCullagh and Michael Stapleton) were in a special category of craftsmen as members of two trades. There were, of course, many other plasterers, among them Edward Semple and Robert West, who did not appear to work as painters or, at least, who did not work with oil paints. There were also members of St Luke's (such as Maurice Tyrrell and William Meighan, who worked with Pearce on

---

48 Strickland, *Dictionary*, 2, pp 347–8.   49 Ibid., pp 274–5.

the new Parliament House in 1730, and James Adam, who worked on the Royal Hospital Kilmainham in the 1750s) that contracted only for painting work and who obviously were not trained as plasterers.[50] The Dublin market for painting was apparently shared by three different categories of tradesmen – plasterers, who painted walls and ceilings in a limited range of distemper colours, painters, who contracted for oil and distemper work, and painter-plasterers, who also worked in oil and distemper. Here again we are confronted with an example of how imported trade practices became mutated by existing Irish traditions. While the Dublin Guild of St Luke was based on well-established patterns developed in London, its absorption of a strongly established group of plasterers who practised as painters developed new patterns in Ireland. As in the case of the Irish stonecutter who emerged as a separate trade category, this was a clear break with English practice.

In London, the early seventeenth-century trade regulations were still in force in the eighteenth century, but they were rationalized to make a clearer division between the work of the painter and the plasterer. Bristow describes trading patterns in the mid-century which placed the responsibility for all work in distemper (in an unlimited range of colours) on the plastering trade and all work in oil colours on the painting trade. This contractual agreement was still in use in the early decades of the nineteenth century.[51]

---

50 *Commons Journal*, 4, xxxii; NAI, Royal Hospital Kilmainham minutes, RHK 1/1/5, 17 Jan. 1759.
51 Bristow, *Interior house-painting colours*, p. 111.

Epilogue

THE INTRODUCTION OF CLASSICAL architecture into Ireland in the latter part of the seventeenth century brought with it significant changes in building patterns and uses of new materials. These changes were anticipated as early as the 1670s by Dublin artisans in the reorganization of trade affiliations. In 1670, the bricklayers and the plasterers left the long-established carpenters' guild and formed the new Guild of St Bartholomew. In that year also, the painters, who shared a growing but competitive market with the plasterers, formed the new Guild of St Luke in combination with the stationers and the cutlers.

The implications of these changing organizational patterns are clear. They reflect an expanding market for imported architectural fashions and a demand for new decorative and structural materials. Traditional urban houses built with local limestone rubble (or occasionally with timber framing and plastered infill) were being replaced with houses of brickwork, similar in most respects to the designs developed in London during this period. The foundation of the Guild of St Bartholomew promoted the ascendancy of the bricklayer's trade at the expense of the traditional walling mason; Dublin bricklayers such as William Caldebeck and Francis Quinn contracted for both brick and stone walling but they employed local journeymen masons in the construction of rubble wall linings.

The scarcity of oak precluded its use in all but the most expensive early classical buildings and, even in these buildings, its use was mostly limited to roof members and wainscotting. It was replaced by imported fir for floor and roof framing but the extensive use of fir in entablatures, panelling, wainscotting, doors, windows and cornices introduced the need for protective finishes of oil-paint. This developed a new and lucrative market, which promoted the foundation of the Dublin Guild of St Luke and the advancement of the house painter, a relatively new trade. The plasterers, who had traditionally handled painting contracts (as well as plastering work) in pre-classical buildings, formed the Guild of St Bartholomew to protect their interests and obtain a more direct representation in the city assembly.

The formation of the guilds in the same year (1670), within months of each other, was hardly a coincidence. By 1679, the painters had persuaded the city fathers to introduce regulations limiting the plasterers' encroachment of the market. This may have affected some plasterers, but several well-established artisans (such as Isaac Chalke, George Spike and William Wall) continued to contract for painting and plastering work in important Dublin buildings because of their membership of both guilds.

The enthusiasm for brick façades continued into the 1700s, with their use on important civic and institutional buildings in Trinity College (such as the Rubrics), in Dublin Castle, in Marsh's Library and in the Tailors' Hall, all in the opening years of the century. The use of cut-stone facings was limited in the early years of the century to local calp dressings in rubble walling and semi-coursed ashlar, such as we see in the Church of St Nicholas Within in Dublin, built in 1707. The first use of ashlar on a grand scale occurred in Burgh's granite façades of the Royal Barracks in 1701. This was followed in 1712 by a more ambitious choice of sandstone (above ground-floor arcades of local calp) in the Library of Trinity College. This huge commission enticed the stonecutter Henry Darley and his son Moses to move from Newtownards to Dublin to undertake the stone cladding contract. The peculiarly Irish use of the term 'stonecutter' was applied throughout the eighteenth century to describe masons such as the Darleys and their contemporaries, the Whinreys, who carved freestone dressings, moulded entablatures and ashlar facings. The adoption of the term was obviously intended to distance them from the rough masons who commonly worked on walling contracts with bricklayers.

Burgh's somewhat clumsy handling of the rusticated ashlar on the east and west façades of the Library may have been due to inexperience, or to difficulties inherent in the material. Calp was a difficult stone to work and in 1715 we find him again using imported sandstone on the façade of St Werburgh's Church. Pearce's introduction of the combination of pale Wicklow granite with Portland stone in the sophisticated design of the Parliament House in 1728 established a masonry tradition that was used on most of Dublin's civic buildings over the next century.

The new demand for decorative timber mouldings on both the exterior and in the interior of early classical buildings introduced the joinery trade to new markets in building components. Panelled interiors with moulded skirtings and cornices, carved exterior door surrounds and external modillion cornices (such as that used in the Royal Hospital Kilmainham) required a precise control of workmanship not usually demanded of the carpentry trade. The complex construction of the sash window, introduced into Dublin buildings such as Marsh's Library in about 1700, was another important requirement of this developing market.

The ascendancy of the joinery trade in the first three decades of the eighteenth century was marked by the formation of the new Guild of Joiners, Ceylers and Wainscotters in 1700. John Sisson, the first guild master, was a favoured contractor of Thomas Burgh. He worked on state contracts such as the Old Parliament House, the Royal Barracks and on buildings in Trinity College such as the Library. The foundation of the joiners' guild was an attempt to control a market that the joiners shared with (their former guild brothers) the carpenters. They did succeed in dominating this market for a few decades, but by the 1720s carpenters had learned to make complex components such as sash windows, and by the 1740s the supply of doors, windows, staircases and other fitted timber components was mostly under the control of carpentry contractors.

The sash window is particularly identified with classical architecture in Ireland and England. Its stylistic and operational superiority over the earlier leaded casements was apparent from its first appearance in Ireland, and it came into common use in many parts of the country by the 1720s. In the Royal Hospital Kilmainham the gradual replacement of the 1680s lead casements by sliding sashes was started by Thomas Burgh in 1711. As the century advanced, practical and stylistic considerations introduced modifications in window design, such as concealed sash boxes behind masonry reveals, lighter and more elegantly moulded sash bars, and from the 1780s onwards, a tendency to use taller windows, from floor to cornice level, and larger panes of glass.

The introduction of timber sliding sashes had implications for trades other than carpenters and joiners. The limitation on pane sizes in leaded casements usually resulted in the use of broad glass, which was cheaply produced but not completely transparent, because of surface defects arising from its production process. The relative stiffness of timber glazing bars accommodated larger pane sizes and promoted the use of crown glass, which combined a high level of transparency with an iridescent surface that was particularly attractive. The earliest records we find of the use of crown glass in Ireland was in Trinity College in 1712/13. By 1720, the long sandstone façade of Burgh's Library with its continuous punctuation by large sashes and glazed with the new crown glass, must have presented an unusual and impressive sight to Dubliners. The best crown glass came from London, from either the Ratcliff or the Lambeth glassworks. Bristol crown glass was used extensively in many parts of Ireland from the 1740s onwards. Irish crown glass, made in Dublin glasshouses, was available at certain periods from the 1760s until the 1790s.

The most far-reaching influence on Irish architectural concepts, as well as building practices, came in the late 1720s with the introduction of Palladian architecture. Pearce's ambitious design for the new Parliament House in 1728, with its giant Ionic colonnade, well-articulated masonry design, low Italianate roofs, parapet gutters and high stepped dome, must have made a surprising impact on contemporary sensibilities, and presented the large team of artisans contracting for its construction with unprecedented challenges. The records of the first phase of its construction reveal levels of management skills that were uncommon in this period. The completion of a building of this quality and complexity (costing over £19,000) in a period of 3½ years was in itself unusual. The detailed estimates of projected costs (totalling almost £6,000) for the completion phase was based on a most precise and professional analysis of the materials and work required. The contrast with Thomas Burgh's casual handling of contracts and lack of control of building programmes and budgets is very evident.

The Parliament House was the first use of the masonry combination of Portland limestone (columns and entablature) with plain and rustic granite ashlar obtained from local sources. Such a combination used the best qualities of both materials in an economic balance. This was to prove such a successful formula for Dublin façades that it was used repeatedly in buildings in Trinity College, the Blue Coat School, the Custom House, the Four Courts, the King's Inns and a number of important nineteenth-century classical buildings. This was also the first experience in Ireland of the construction of giant freestanding colonnades, and John Houghton's carved Ionic capitals exhibit a remarkable control and confidence. William Robinson's use of painted timber capitals on his stone pilasters at the entrance of the Royal Hospital Kilmainham in the 1680s is indicative of the lack of suitable skills in stone carving in an earlier period.

One of the most interesting aspects of the Palladian movement in Ireland was its influence on roof design, in terms of both its structural efficiency and its formal configuration. The difference between the roof framing systems used before and after the 1730s can be seen in contrasts between the structural clarity of the king-post trusses used in the Parliament House, and the confusing arrangement of earlier truss designs in buildings such as the Drogheda Schoolhouse, Dr Steevens's Hospital and the Royal Hospital at Kilmainham.

The derivation of Pearce's trusses is easily found. They follow closely the design of the simplest (single post) trusses illustrated by Palladio, spanning the cloisters of his Carità convent or the upper storeys of his Egyptian Halls. Another likely source was the illustration of the king-post published in Daniele Barbaro's *Vitruvius*. The design of these trusses could also be seen in the work of several of Pearce's contemporaries practising in London. These designs were subsequently popularized in the 1730s and 1740s in the carpenters' manuals published by Francis Price and Batty Langley.

Pearce's first use of Italianate trusses was as early as 1725 in the roofs of Castletown, Co. Kildare. Here the trusses are quite unusual in that they are asymmetrical, with lower pitched (35 degree) principals on the side of the truss spanning on to the façade walls and a higher (45 degree) pitch spanning onto an internal spine wall and a valley gutter. The lower pitched framing on the elevational sides of the trusses in Castletown raises another important aspect of Palladian orthodoxy. Classical principles called for the reduction of the mass of the roof and the primacy of the parapet and eaves cornice. Italian roofs were normally pitched at angles of around 30 degrees; Irish roof slopes (in this period) were seldom less than 45 degrees. Pearce succeeded in using remarkably low roofs at pediment pitch on the Parliament House by using expensive lead roof coverings. Nevertheless, his determination to fully conceal the Parliament House roofs led to the use of high masonry parapets, more a Roman than a Vicentine invention.

The problem faced by Irish Palladian builders in adopting classical roof profiles was the difficulty in finding suitable roofing materials other than lead, which was expensive. The slates available in the first half of the eighteenth century were too small for use on roof slopes under the 'common pitch' of 45 degrees. The high frequency of roof failures (and resulting repairs) in Trinity College and the Royal Hospital Kilmainham (even with high pitched roofs) is indicative of this problem. Even as late as the 1760s, we find in the Provost's House and Davis Ducart's Limerick Custom House, high roofs, which appear awkward and provincial when compared with classical models.

The persistent ambitions of the early Palladians to conform with classical canons can be perceived in Castle's choice of Dutch pantiles on roofs of the 1730s Printing

House and the 1740s Dining Hall (not the present building) in Trinity College. Pantiles were efficient at low pitches and they also reflected Italian practice. The Printing House still retains its low roof profile with a modern slate roof. The roof framing of the Dining Hall was replaced in 1759 with a conventional (high) slate roof of the period, whereas the pantiles previously used must have been specially selected to cover a lower roof profile. Castle also appears to have followed Pearce's example at Castletown in using asymmetrical roof trusses on Leinster House in the 1740s, with 35 degree slopes to the external parapets and a 45 degree slope to an internal valley gutter. How these roofs were made watertight, with the small slates available at this time, cannot be explained.

The industrialization of the Welsh quarries after the mid-century introduced larger slates into Irish and English markets. However, with exceptions, Irish builders remained cautious about the use of low roof profiles until the neoclassical era. The works of Cooley, Ivory, Wyatt and Gandon fully exploited the availability of larger slates imported from Wales and roofs became a less dominant feature of Irish buildings.

It is from the Palladian era, and from the work of Richard Castle in particular, that we begin to notice an important divergence between English and Irish building practice. The difference is most noticeable in the design of floor framing but it is also apparent in other aspects of carpentry practice such as roofs and timber partitions. Eighteenth-century English floor framing involved the use of up to three structural members to support the floors. Floor joists rested on binders, which they crossed at right angles. The binders were in turn stiffened by traverse girders. Plaster ceilings were then hung from a separate system of ceiling joists attached to the underside of the binders. The maximum span of floor joists was regulated by the London building acts which, for some strange reason, stipulated that joists should not carry loads over distances of more than 10 feet. Early eighteenth-century floor framing in Ireland was similar to English practice but somewhat simpler in design, in that only two structural members were used. Binders were eliminated in Irish floors and joists spanned directly into a primary structure of timber girders. This was the system used by Robinson in the Royal Hospital Kilmainham and Marsh's Library, by Burgh in Trinity College and Dr Steevens's Hospital, by Pearce in Castletown, Co. Kildare, in the Parliament House and in the early houses in Henrietta Street.

By the 1740s in Ireland, we can find examples of even more radical floor construction in which the use of girders is eliminated and floors are solely supported on what George Semple described as 'through joists' spanning from wall to wall. This is so in Leinster House, in Tudenham and Belvedere in Westmeath, and in the later houses in Henrietta Street. In the second half of the century almost all Irish buildings with the exception of those designed by English architects (such as Chambers and Gandon) used long spanning joists as sole floor supports.

An obvious advantage of the Irish joisted floor system was its economy in use and its simplicity of construction. Another important characteristic was the elimination of complex timber joint connections such as mortises, tenons and cog-joints, which were extensively used in English floors and in early eighteenth-century Irish floor framing. This must have appealed to Irish builders, who inherently relied on masonry rather than carpentry traditions. The tendency to replace timber structures with masonry supports is evident in the development of Irish construction. It can be seen in the early gabled Dublin houses that avoided the use of roof trusses by using masonry supported purlins. A similar use is visible in provincial town houses (such as the 1740s house at Pope's Quay in Cork) where, instead of roof trusses, purlins are supported by crosswalls. It is also visible in the absence (except in the Irish work of Chambers and Gandon) of the trussed partition.

The price paid by Irish builders for their preferences can sometimes be seen in a lack of flexibility in room planning due to the persistence of masonry supports. Irish plans on upper floors usually follow the plan configuration of lower floors except for the occasional and uninspiring use of stud partitions; James Gandon and Francis Johnston were occasional exceptions. English planning was more imaginative. Ironically enough, in the nineteenth century, English builders discarded their traditional system of floor framing (girders and bearers) and adopted the use of the Irish system of long spanning through joists.

The eighteenth century was a unique period in Ireland in terms of cultural, political and social development. Historians have tended to see building artisans in Ireland from a nineteenth-century viewpoint. Eighteenth-century craftsmen in Irish cities like Dublin were essentially part of a middle-class milieu with access to the same opportunities as members of the merchant community. Many artisans working in Irish cities were English or of recent English origin. Their status as freemen of the city and their adherence to the Protestant faith provided important privileges and considerable social mobility. It should not surprise us to find the architect William Robinson's name recorded as a member of both the painters' and joiners' guild during his tenure as surveyor general, or the Ball family founding their merchant bank on the proceeds of their (previous) carpentry practice, or the former carpenter 'Buttermilk Jack' Magill ending his career as commissioner of the Barrack Board with a seat in parliament.

Unlike their nineteenth-century counterparts, eighteenth-century artisans such as carpenters, stonecutters and bricklayers had full control over their standards of workmanship and productivity. They could enter into single-trade contracts on their own behalf, on terms which were totally uncompetitive and which guaranteed comfortable profits. Many artisans working in Dublin became affluent and, like the Wills, the Darleys, the Rudds and the Sproules, they also became the owners of large property holdings.

However, the unique aspect of their operational practice was their engagement as architectural designers. Many artisans were involved in the interpretation, as well as the execution of classical ornamentation: others, like John and Isaac Rothery, Michael Wills and the Ensor brothers, were fully engaged in architectural practice. Their career as architects, however, was not on what would now be regarded as a professional level, as it was rarely divorced from the building process. It was part of their responsibilities as master builders in contracts for the design and construction of entire buildings. This, of course, involved them in the employment of artisans from other trades as subcontractors.

The construction of urban housing estates in cities such as Dublin provided lucrative opportunities for developers from the early decades of the eighteenth century. These ventures were particularly attractive to building artisans, because their skills and experience could minimize building costs and maximize profits. Many of the carpenters, bricklayers, plasterers and stonecutters who were engaged in single-trade contracts on important public buildings acted as sole developers for houses in urban estates. The construction of the Aungier, Dawson, Molesworth, Gardiner and Fitzwilliam estates provided a continuous supply of housing sites in Dublin city over the whole century. Some housing ventures realized a quick sale and profit for developers, but many artisans retained leases on houses they had built. Such was the basis of some building dynasties, e.g. those of the Darleys and the Semples, which lasted well into the nineteenth century.

The process of controlling the architectural design, as well as the construction of urban houses, provided artisans with invaluable experience in architectural practice and in the management of craft skills other than those of their own trade. This, coupled with the influence of building literature and tuition from the schools of the Dublin Society, developed a corpus of craftsmen with confidence in the interpretation as well as the execution of architectural motifs. This confidence can be seen in the entrepreneurial master builders of the mid-century who began to handle a wider range of building types than houses. Builder architects such as George Semple and the brothers John and George Ensor are typical of this process. The combination of practical knowledge with highly developed theoretic views enabled Semple to tackle the problem of designing and building Essex Bridge in the 1750s, and more general structures such as St Patrick's Hospital and the spire of St Patrick's Cathedral. During the 1760s, George Ensor designed and built buildings as varied as Roscommon Courthouse, charity schools in Roscommon and Athlone, Armagh Hospital and the Church of St John the Evangelist in Dublin.

Eighteenth-century architects came from a variety of backgrounds. Some were ex-soldiers, such as Burgh and Pearce, whose position as surveyors general allowed them full scope to exercise their talents. Some were gentlemen and important office holders, such as Nathaniel Clements and the Earl Bishop, whose wealth and position allowed them to indulge in architecture as an absorbing hobby. Many, like George Ensor or Samuel Sproule, were apprenticed as craftsmen in the guild system and combined architectural ability with expertise in building practice. This operational mobility reflects the persistent overlap we have found among the trades, where bricklayers contracted for masonry, carpenters provided joinery, plasterers engaged as painters, and officials such as Sir William Robinson held membership of both the Dublin joiners' guild and the painters' guild during his period as surveyor general.

Most artisan designers saw the pursuit of architecture as an extension of their existing skills, which could provide opportunities to increase their incomes. Few fitted easily into the professional category expressed in Loeber's criterion of a 'supervisory rather than executive' involvement in building practice. They had supervisory roles as architects but they also had contractual responsibilities and they received direct financial rewards from the building process. There are instances, of course, where artisans did become completely involved as architects and supervisors. John Ensor acted in this capacity after Castle's death on Bartholomew Mosse's hospital and Rotunda in the 1750s. Hugh Darley also took over Castle's position as architect to Trinity College (on the basis of a salary). Darley's new career may have kept him away from stonecutting contracts but it did not prevent him building houses in the Gardiner estate. John Ensor also became deeply involved in building speculative houses in Cavendish Row in the 1750s and he subsequently contracted as a master builder with his brother George.

To Semple, the Ensor brothers and their like, the chief advantage of architectural skills was the freedom to build to their own designs without the interference of supervisory authorities. This enabled them to make their own bargains and to control the building process. This control ensured the provision of building information to their employees, the avoidance of delays that were usually at the builder's expense and the realization of prices with high margins of profit. Such design-and-build contracts were particularly suitable to provincial districts where skilled craftsmen were unobtainable. George Ensor's contracts in Roscommon, Athlone and Armagh in the 1760s are indicative of this market. After the 1770s, however, the uses of master builders and design-and-build contracts became less common.

The last quarter of the eighteenth century in Ireland was a period of rapid change in building patterns. The advent of neoclassicism promoted new architectural fashions and introduced formally trained English architects such as Cooley and Gandon to Irish commissions. Another aspect of change was the continuous increase in wages and material prices from the end of the 1760s. This made the prior estimation of building costs difficult to predict and as a consequence, limited the contractor's ability to make fixed-cost agreements. As fixed-cost agreements were an important objective of design–and-build contracts this inhibited the use of such contracts.

By the end of the century the problem of continuous cost increases led to demands for competitive prices from builders. Accurate prices could only be obtained through the provision of higher standards of building information, such as detailed working drawings. This promoted the career of independent professional architects such as Gandon and Johnston at the expense of artisan architects contracting as master builders. The early nineteenth century saw the introduction of the general contractor engaged on the basis of competitive tenders. This was the end of the artisan architect and the operational mobility between craftsmen that so characterized the building activities of the eighteenth century.

Select bibliography

[*amplified by the editors*]

MANUSCRIPTS

Belfast
Public Record Office of Northern Ireland
    Abercorn papers
    Blessington papers
    Bristol papers
    Londonderry papers
    Mussenden papers

Dublin
Dublin City Library and Archive
    Roll of freemen
Irish Architectural Archive
    Blessington House building accounts (copies)
    Drogheda Schoolmaster's House (Grammar School) folio
    George Semple specifications for Public Offices and for St Patrick's Hospital (xerox copies)
    Michael Wills's cash book
    Thomas Eyre papers
National Archives
    Ball accounts
    Bryan Bolger papers
    Royal Hospital Kilmainham board minutes
National Library
    Castle Forward building accounts
    Clements papers
    Flower of Castle Durrow papers
    Kells church accounts
    Kilmainham papers
    Limerick (Sexton Pery) papers
    Pakenham Mahon papers
    Records of the Guild of St Luke
Registry of Deeds
    Indexed abstracts of deeds
Representative Church Body Library
    Parish vestry records

Royal Irish Academy
   Charlemont papers
Trinity College
   Archive of the Incorporated Society in Dublin for Promoting (English) Protestant Schools in Ireland
   College muniments (MUN/P2 series)
   Diaries and travel journals of Daniel Augustus Beaufort
   Dr Steevens's Hospital records

Limerick
Jim Kemmy Municipal Museum
   Minutes of the Guild Company of Masons, Bricklayers, Slaters et al., 1747–57

London
British Library
   Egmont papers
The National Archives
   Ledgers of imports and exports Ireland (CUST 15)

CONTEMPORARY NEWSPAPERS

Belfast Newsletter　　　　　　　　*Dublin Journal*
Dublin Evening Post　　　　　　　*Freeman's Journal*

THESES

Byrne, Helen, 'Simon Vierpyl (c.1725–1810). new light on his work in Ireland', MA, 1995, School of Art History, UCD.
Casey, Christine, 'Books and builders: a bibliographical approach to Irish eighteenth-century architecture', PhD, 1991, University of Dublin, Trinity College.
Cloonan, Nicki, 'Nineteenth-century floor tiles in Ireland', MUBC, 2005, UCD.
Cole, Alexander, 'The restoration of Newman House (1989–1994)', BA, 2013, School of Art History, University of Dublin, Trinity College.
Collins, Bridget, 'The history of the attitudes towards preservation and conservation of Dublin's eighteenth-century buildings', BA, 1994, Department of the History of Art and Architecture, TCD.
Coughlan, John, 'The merchant house in eighteenth-century Cork', MUBC, 1997, UCD.
Crimmins, Cathal, 'Henrietta Street: a conservation study', MArch, 1987, UCD.
Cuffe, Ann, 'Dr Steevens's Hospital: a study in the construction, nature and future of an eighteenth-century hospital in Dublin', MUBC, 1988, UCD.
Doyle, Aine, 'Chimneypiece design in Ireland c.1728–1751: the work of Richard Castle and the Pearce-Castle School', MA, 1995, School of Art History, UCD.
Duggan, Anthony, 'The development of Parnell Square: its houses, decoration and fittings', MUBC, 1990, UCD.
Ferran, Emer, 'The Grand Opera House, Belfast: a theatre restored', BA, 1986, Department of the History of Art and Architecture, TCD.

Fitzgerald, Barbara, 'Problems with a ceiling [in the Royal Hospital Kilmainham]', BA, 1987, Department of the History of Art and Architecture, TCD.
Geoghegan, Anne, 'The carved tablet of the chimneypiece in Dublin in the second half of the eighteenth century', MA, 1997, School of Art History, UCD.
Hand, Tony, 'The Kilkenny marble works: a family enterprise', PhD, 2011, University of Dublin, Trinity College.
Hanley, Roisin, 'The history of decorative plasterwork: with reference to the development of the composition and techniques of plasterwork and the role of the stuccodore', MUBC, 1999, UCD.
Harris, Gillian Ann, 'Medieval timber roof structures in Ireland', BA, 1996, Department of the History of Art and Architecture, TCD.
Hayes, Melanie, 'Anglo-Irish architectural exchange in the early eighteenth century: patrons, practitioners and *pieds-à-terre*', PhD, 2015, University of Dublin, Trinity College.
Lindsay, Alistair, 'An investigation into the historic use of lime in some buildings in Ireland', MArch, 1998, UCD.
Lucey, Conor, 'Made in the new taste: domestic neoclassicism and the Dublin building industry, 1765–1801', PhD, 2008, UCD.
Lyons, Charles, 'Irish roof timbers 1550–1640 and 1680–1708', MUBC, 2004, UCD.
MacRory, Rachel, 'A study of No. 12 Fumbally Lane, Dublin 8', BA, 1990, Department of the History of Art and Architecture, University of Dublin, Trinity College.
Malone, Sheena, 'Robert West, plasterer and masterbuilder', MA, 2002, School of Art History, UCD.
O'Connell, Katherine, 'Restoration in context: the Dining Hall, Trinity College Dublin', BA, 2010, Department of the History of Art and Architecture, TCD.
O'Connor, Elizabeth, 'Wyatt's Irish interiors: the interior design of James Wyatt for houses in Ireland', MA, 1994, School of Art History, UCD.
O'Connor, Justin, 'The Georgian doorcase: design, construction and conservation', MUBC, 2012, UCD.
O'Neill, Garrett, 'The source and use of roofing slates in nineteenth-century Ireland', MUBC, 2007, UCD.
O'Reilly, Barry, 'Corrugated iron in Ireland', MUBC, 1999, UCD.
O'Rourke, Mona, 'The protection of historic interiors in Ireland', MUBC, 1993, UCD.
O'Shea, Aoibhe, 'The origins of the statutory protection of ancient Irish monuments in the nineteenth century', BA, 1993, Department of the History of Art and Architecture, TCD.
Popplewell, Sean David, 'Eighteenth-century domestic decorative painting in Ireland', MA, 1976, School of Art History, UCD.
Roundtree, Susan, 'A history of clay brick as a building material in Ireland', MLitt, 1999, University of Dublin, Trinity College.
Scannell, John, 'Conservation of Gandon's terrace, 1–5 Beresford Place [Dublin]', MUBC, 1993, UCD.

PRINTED SOURCES

Aalen, F.H.A., Kevin Whelan & Matthew Stout, *Atlas of the Irish rural landscape* (Cork, 1997; 2nd ed., 2011).

Anon., *Hydrographia Hibernica; or, a view of the considerable rivers of Ireland* ([Dublin], 1710).
Ayres, J., *Building the Georgian city* (New Haven & London, 1998).
Baggs, A.P., 'The earliest sash window in Britain?', *Georgian Group Journal*, 7 (1997), 168–71.
Bankart, George, *The art of the plasterer* (London, 1908).
Beard, Geoffrey, *Decorative plasterwork in Great Britain* (London, 1975).
— *Stucco and decorative plasterwork in Europe* (London, 1983).
Boate, Gerard, *Irelands naturall history* (London, 1652).
Boutcher, William, *A treatise on forest trees* (Dublin, 3rd ed., 1784).
Boyers, D., *The builder's companion* (London, 1807).
Brash, Richard, 'Notes on the ancient ecclesiastical architecture of Ireland', *Irish Builder*, 15 Jan. 1874.
Bristow, Ian, *Interior house-painting colours and technology, 1615–1840* (New Haven & London, 1996).
Burrows, Malcolm, 'Measurers of architecture 1750–1850', *Chartered Quantity Surveyor*, Dec. 1980.
Campbell, Robert, *The London tradesman* (London, 1747).
Casey, Christine, *Making magnificence: architects, stuccatori and the eighteenth-century interior* (New Haven & London, 2017).
— (ed.), *The eighteenth-century Dublin town house: form, function and finance* (Dublin, 2010).
Caulfield, Richard (ed.), *The council book of the corporation of Kinsale from 1652 to 1800* (Guildford, 1879).
Clark, Mary & Raymond Refaussé, *Directory of historic Dublin guilds* (Dublin, 1993).
Clarke, Linda, *Building capitalism* (London, 1992).
Clune, Revd George, *The medieval gild system* (Dublin, [1943]).
Colley, Richard, *An account of the foundation of the Royal Hospital of King Charles II …, near Dublin* (Dublin, 1725).
Craig, Maurice, *Dublin, 1660–1860* (London, 1952; Dublin, 2nd ed., 2006).
— *Classic Irish houses of the middle size* (London, 1976; Dublin, 2nd ed., 2006).
— *The architecture of Ireland from the earliest times to 1880* (London and Dublin, 1982).
Curran, C.P., *Dublin decorative plasterwork of the seventeenth and eighteenth centuries* (London, 1967).
Curran, Joanne et al., *Stone by stone: a guide to building stone in the Northern Ireland environment* (Belfast, 2010).
D'Arcy, Fergus, 'Wages of Dublin labourers in the Dublin building industry, 1667–1918', *Saothar*, 14 (1989), 17–32.
D'Arcy, Fergus, 'Wages of skilled workers in the Dublin building industry, 1667–1918', *Saothar*, 15 (1990), 21–37.
Darling, John, *The carpenters rule made easie* (London, 8th ed., 1727).
De Breffny, Brian, 'Stucco work by Patrick Osborne at Castletown Cox', *The Irish Ancestor*, 13:1 (1981), 15–18.
Department of the Environment, *Conservation guidelines*, a series of pamphlets with text by various conservation architects including *Windows* (by Frederick O'Dwyer & Nessa Roche); *Mortars, pointing & renders* (by Maura Shaffrey); *Decorative plasterwork* (by Andrew Smith); *Brickwork & stonework* (by David Slattery); *Ironwork* (by Ciaran O'Connor); sources of information (by David Griffin) etc.

Department of Arts, Heritage and the Gaeltacht, *Architectural heritage protection: guidelines for planning authorities* (Dublin, 2011).
Dixon, Hugh, *An introduction to Ulster architecture* (Belfast, 2nd ed., 2008).
Dobbs, Arthur, *Observations of the trade and improvement of Ireland* (Dublin, 1729–31).
Dossie, Robert, *The handmaid to the arts* (London, 1764).
Farrelly, J., 'Decorative render in the late sixteenth/early seventeenth century' in C. Manning (ed.), *From ringforts to fortified houses* (Dublin, 2007), pp 237–48.
Fenlon, Jane, 'The painter stainers companies of Dublin and London' in Jane Fenlon, Nicola Figgis & Catherine Marshall (eds), *New perspectives: studies in art history in honour of Anne Crookshank* (Dublin, 1987), pp 102–4.
Gailey, Alan, *Rural houses of the north of Ireland* (Edinburgh, 1984) (concerns mainly vernacular houses).
Georgian Society records of domestic architecture and decoration in Dublin, 5 vols (Dublin, 1909–13; reprint Shannon, 1969).
Gilbert, J.T. & R.M. (eds), *Calendar of ancient records of the city of Dublin*, 19 vols (Dublin, 1889–1944).
Gogarty, Revd T. (ed.), *Council book of the corporation of Drogheda* (Drogheda, 1915).
Grosart, Revd A.B. (ed.), *The Lismore papers* (London, 1886–8).
Guinness, Henry, 'Dublin trade gilds', *JRSAI*, 52 (1922), 143–63.
Hand, Tony, '"Doing Everything of Marble …": some descriptive accounts of the Kilkenny Marble Works', *Irish Architectural and Decorative Studies*, 11 (2008), 74–99.
— 'The White Quarry, Ardbraccan', *Irish Architectural and Decorative Studies*, 8 (2005), 138–59.
Harden, D.B., 'Domestic window glass' in E.M. Jope (ed.), *Studies in building history* (London, 1961), pp 39-63.
Hawney, William, *The compleat measurer* (London, 1717).
Herbert, Robert, 'The trade guilds of Limerick', *North Munster Antiquarian Journal*, 2:3 (Spring, 1941), 121–34.
Hodgson, P. Levi, *The modern measurer* (Dublin, 1793).
Hoppus, Edward, *Practical measuring now made easy* (London, 1736).
Humphreys, Thomas, *The Irish builder's guide* (Dublin, 1813).
Jones, Huw, 'Wren tests restorers', *New Civil Engineer*, 27 Oct. 1988, 28–31.
Jope, E.M., 'Moyry, Charlemont, Castleraw and Richhill: fortification to architecture in the North of Ireland, 1570–1700', *Ulster Journal of Archaeology*, 23 (1960), 97–123.
Journals of the House of Commons of the kingdom of Ireland, 19 vols (Dublin, 1796–1800); index, 2 vols (Dublin, 1802).
Keatinge, Charles T., 'The Guild of Cutlers, Painter-Stainers and Stationers', *JRSAI*, 30 (1900), 136–47.
Kelly, James (ed.), *The letters of Lord Chief Baron Edward Willes* (Aberystwyth, 1990).
Keohane, Frank (ed. Graham Hickey), *Irish period houses, a conservation guidance manual* (Dublin, 2015) (with useful guidance for further reading).
Kirkpatrick, T. Percy, *The history of Dr Steevens' Hospital* (Dublin, 1924).
Langley, Batty, *The builder's vade-mecum* (Dublin, 1729).
— *The city and country builder's and workman's treasury of designs* (London, 1745).
Legg, Marie-Louise (ed.), *The Synge letters* (Dublin, 1996).

Loeber, Rolf, *A biographical dictionary of architects in Ireland, 1600–1720* (London, 1981).
— et al. (eds), *Architecture 1600–2000*, vol. 4, *Art and architecture of Ireland* (New Haven & London, 2014).
Longfield, Ada, 'The manufacture of "raised stucco" or "papier mâché" papers in Ireland, c.1750–70', *JRSAI*, 78 (1948), 55–62.
Louw, H.J., 'The origin of the sash-window', *Architectural History*, 26 (1983), 49–72, 144–50.
Lucey, Conor, 'The scale of plasterwork production in the metropolitan centres of Britain and Ireland' in Christine Casey and Conor Lucey (eds), *Decorative plasterwork in Ireland and Europe* (Dublin, 2012), pp 194–218.
— *The Stapleton collection* (Tralee, 2007) (with an important chapter on Michael Stapleton's house-building practice).
— '"Rooms neatly coloured": painting and decorating the Dublin town house, 1789–1810', *Georgian Group Journal*, 18 (2010), 137–51.
McAfee, Pat, *Irish stone walls* (Dublin, 1997).
— *Stone buildings* (Dublin, 1998).
— *Lime works* (Dublin, 2009).
McCracken, Eileen, *The Irish woods since Tudor times* (Newton Abbot, 1971).
McDonnell, Joseph, 'Continental stuccowork and English rococo carving at Russborough', *Irish Architectural and Decorative Studies*, 14 (2011), 110–27.
McGrath, Raymond & A.C. Frost, *Glass in architecture and decoration* (London, 1937).
McKinstry, Robert et al. (eds), *The buildings of Armagh* (UAHS, Belfast, 1992).
McParland, Edward, 'The papers of Bryan Bolger, measurer', *Dublin Historical Record*, 25:4 (1972), 120–31.
— 'Trinity College Dublin–I', *Country Life*, 6 May 1976.
— *James Gandon, Vitruvius Hibernicus* (London, 1985).
— 'The office of the surveyor general in Ireland in the eighteenth century', *Architectural History*, 38 (1995), 91–101
McVeagh, John (ed.), *Richard Pococke's Irish tours* (Dublin, 1995).
Morel, Andreas F.A., *Andreas und Peter Anton Moosbrugger: Zur Stuckdekoration des Rokoko in der Schweiz* (Bern, 1973).
Moxon, Joseph, *Mechanick exercises* (London, 3rd ed., 1703).
Neely, W.G., *Kilkenny, an urban history, 1391–1843* (Belfast, 1989).
Neve, Richard, *The city and country purchaser* (London, 2nd ed., 1726).
Nicholson, John, *The builder's practical guide* (London, 1830).
O'Boyle, Aidan, 'Aldborough House, Dublin: a construction history', *Irish Architectural and Decorative Studies*, 4 (2001), 102–41.
O'Dwyer, Frederick, 'Proportion and the Georgian Window', in T.J. Fenlon (ed.), *The town: conservation in the urban area*, proceedings of the IGS Conference, 1995, p. 30.
O'Neill, Conor, 'In search of Bossi', *Irish Architectural and Decorative Studies*, 1 (1998), 146–75.
Pain, William, *The builder's companion* (London, 1758).
—, *The practical house carpenter* (London, 1788).
Patton, Marcus, *The bedside book of dormers and other delights: a guide to traditional architectural details in Ulster* (Belfast, 2011).
Price, Francis, *The British carpenter; or, A treatise on carpentry* (London, 5th ed., 1765).

Rankin, Peter, *Irish building ventures of the Earl Bishop of Derry, 1730–1803* (Belfast, 1972).
Roche, Nessa, *The legacy of light: a history of Irish windows* (Bray, 1999).
Rudd, Mary Amelia, *Records of the Rudd family* (Bristol, 1920).
Rutty, John, *An essay towards a natural history of the county of Dublin* (Dublin, 1772).
Rynne, Colin, *Industrial Ireland, 1750–1930* (Cork, 2006) (with chapters on iron and steel, non-ferrous metals and minerals, building materials, etc.).
Semple, George, *A treatise on the art of building in water* (Dublin, 1776).
Severens, Kenneth, 'A new perspective on Georgian building practice: the rebuilding of St Werburgh's Church', *Bulletin of the Irish Georgian Society*, 35 (1992–3), 3–16.
Shaffrey, Patrick & Maura, *Irish countryside buildings* (Dublin, 1985) (with an appendix on building materials).
Skinner, David, *Wallpaper in Ireland, 1700–1900* (Tralee, 2014).
Smith, James, *The carpenters companion* (London, 1733).
Stitt, William, *The practical architect's ready assistant* (Dublin, 1819).
The Buildings of Ireland series (Penguin Books and – from 2005 – Yale University Press): Alistair Rowan, *North-West Ulster* (1979); Christine Casey and Alistair Rowan, *North Leinster* (1993); Christine Casey, *Dublin* (2005); Kevin Mulligan, *South Ulster* (2013); all contain in their Introductions an account of local building materials.
Thompson, F.M.L., *Chartered surveyors: the growth of a profession* (London, 1968).
Truxes, Thomas, *Irish-American trade, 1660–1783* (Cambridge, 1988).
UAHS in association with the Environment Service (NI) Historic Monuments and Buildings, *Directory of traditional building skills* (Belfast, 1994) (with useful guidance for further reading).
Ware, Isaac, *A complete body of architecture* (London, 1756).
Westropp, M.S. Dudley (ed. Mary Boydell), *Irish glass* (Dublin, 1978).
Wilkinson, George, *Practical geology and ancient architecture of Ireland* (London, 1845).
Windele, John, *Historical and descriptive notices of the city of Cork* (Cork, 1839).
The Wren Society, 20 vols (Oxford, 1923–43).
Wyse Jackson, P.N., *The building stones of Dublin* (Dublin, 1993).
Yeomans, David T., 'Early carpenters' manuals, 1592–1820', *Construction History*, 2 (1986), 13–33.
— 'Managing eighteenth-century buildings', *Construction History*, 4 (1988), 3–19.
— *The architect and the carpenter* (London, 1992).
— *The development of timber as a structural material* (Aldershot, 1999).
— *The repair of historic timber structures* (London, 2003).
Young, Arthur, *A tour in Ireland* (London, 1780).

Index

compiled by Julitta Clancy
Page references in italic refer to illustrations.

Abbeville, Dublin, 207
Abbeyleix, Co. Laois, 228
Abercorn, 8th Earl of, 136
Adam, James, 264
Adam, Robert, 206, 245, 261–2
Aheron, John, 46
Alberti, Leon Battista, 25, 163
Alexander, Nathaniel, 105, 122
Alexander, Robert, 105, 122
Allen, John, 129, 141
Amsterdam, 143
Annsley, Thomas, 236
Arbury Hall, Warwickshire, 237
Arch Hall, Co. Meath, 127, 151
Archbold, Pierce, 24, 50–6, 100, 123
Architectura Hibernica (Davis), 190, 192
architectural publications, manuals, etc., 16, 25–6, 58–61, 66, 70, 74, 78, 81–3, 85, 87, 88–92, 90, 91, 101, 103, 105, 108, 115, 162–4, 192, 203, 219; *see also under* individual authors
Ardmore, Co. Waterford
  church, 162
Ardress House, Co. Armagh, 55
Armagh, 42, 55, 83, 170–1, 272
  gaol, 171
  hospital, 48, 55, 271
Armstead, Francis, 95
Armstead, John, 99
Armstead, Thomas, 95
Artari, Giuseppe, 235, 238
Arthur, Robert, 147
Asherton, William, 95
Ashford, Co. Wicklow, 198
Askeaton Castle, 156
Athenry barracks, Co. Galway, 51, 53
Athlone, Co. Westmeath, 42, 83, 272
  barracks, 217
  charity school, 48, 55, 271

Avoca, Co. Wicklow, 259
Avondale, Co. Wicklow, 16

Bagutti, Giovanni, 235, 238
Baird, Alexander, 136
Baker, Henry Aaron, 58, 169
Ball, Benjamin, 34, 36, 44, 80, 99, 100, 101, 116
Ball family, 24, 270
Ball, Robert, 26, 29, 56, 84, 99, 100, 101, 110, 111, 118, 147
Ballineen, Co. Cork, 156
Ballycastle, Co. Antrim, 169
  glasshouse, *212*, 212–13, 217
Ballyfin, Co. Laois, 171
Ballyhaise, Co. Cavan, 151, 158
Ballynagall, Co. Westmeath, 122
Ballynagerah glasshouse, Co. Kerry, 212
Ballyscullion, Co. Londonderry, 136, 139, 169
Bangor (Wales): slates, 31, 202, 203, 206
Bankart, George, 237
Barbaro, Daniele, 66, 268
Baronscourt, Co. Tyrone, 38, 39, 48, 103, 105, 122, 124, 132, 135, 136, 179–80, 248
barrack building programme, 26, 33, 37, 42, 43, 49, 84, 95, 123, 134, 135, 152, 198, 221, 270
  contracts and contractors, 24, 50, 51–5
  parliamentary inquiry (1752), 24, 28, 48–55, 130, 134, 200, 210, 217
Barrow valley, 114
Beard, Geoffrey, 238, 242
Beaufort, Daniel Augustus, 200
Beaulieu, Co. Louth, 26, 98, 100, 130, 145, *155*, 156, 243
Bective, 1st earl of, 84
Belfast, 42, 84, 85, 105, 109, 122, 141, 165, 166, 200, 203, 210, 211, 218
  Donegall estate, 127

281

Belfast (*contd*)
 glasshouses, 213, 217; Edward's glassworks, 209 (advertisement)
 Linenhall Library, 85
 Rosemary Street Presbyterian church, 48, 84
Bellamont Forest, Co. Cavan, 150, 157, 176, 225, 244
Belmore, 1st Earl, 180
Belton chapel, Lincolnshire, 237
Belturbet barracks, Co. Cavan, 42
Belvedere House, Co. Westmeath, 116, 231, 245, 269
Bennis, Mitchell, 22
Bigo, Abraham, 212
Bindon, Francis, 158
Birr, Co. Offaly
 castle, 212
  glasshouse, 210, 211
  Parsons estate, 212
Blessington House, Co. Wicklow, 42, 47, 237
Board of Works, 33, 40
Boate, Gerard, *Irelands naturall history*, 113, 143–5, 147–8, 150, 152–3, 185, 193, 194, 196, 210, 211
Bolger, Bryan, 40
Bolton, Obadiah, 204
Bonvillete, Maximilien, 121
Borrowdale (stonecutter), 81
Bowles, John, 214–15
Boyd, Hugh, 213
Boyers, D., *The builder's companion*, 105, 106
Boyle, Co. Roscommon, 114; *see also* King House
Boyle, Michael, Archbishop of Armagh, 42, 47; *see also* Blessington House
Boyle, Richard, 1st Earl of Cork, 237
Boyle, Richard, 2nd Earl of Cork, 86
Boyle, Richard, 3rd Earl of Burlington, *see* Burlington, Lord
Boyne River, bridge over, 132
Brash, Richard, 162
braziers, 11, 22, 208
bricks
 facing bricks (stockbricks), 20, 127, 145–7, 149, 150, 153, 155, 156, 157
 manufacture of, 143, 144–5, *145*, 147, 151, 152, 157–8
 placebricks, 147, 151, 153, 157
Briggs, Joseph, 136

Bristol, 139, 179, 218, 259
 crown glass, *see* crown glass
Bristow, Ian, 258, 259, 261, 264
Broderick, Allen [Alan Brodrick], 95
Brooking, Charles (carpenter), 42, 98
Brookings, Charles, *A map... of Dublin*, *19*
Brown, Thomas, 47
Browne, James, 153
Buncrana Castle, Co. Donegal, 224
Bundoran, Co. Donegal, 167
Bunratty Castle, Co. Clare, 185, 234, 237
Burgh, Thomas, 28, 33–5, 40, 81, 83, 94–6, 112, 115, 129, 131–2, 135, 147, 174, 222, 266–7, 271
 Custom House, Dublin, 44, 129
 Dr Steevens's Hospital, 48, 135, 150, 159, 173
 Dublin Castle, 155
 Old Parliament House, 209
 Royal Barracks, 53–4, 198, 221, 263
 Royal Hospital Kilmainham, 257–8
 St Werburgh's church, 99, 161, 263
 Trinity College Library, 20, 34, 39, 96, 98, 112, 117, 132, 149–50, 173, 184, 187, 188, 189, 222, 224, 225, 263, 267, 269
Burghley, Northamptonshire, 237
Burke (barrack master), 52
Burlington, Lord (Richard Boyle, 3rd Earl of Burlington), 174, 195, 206, 254
Burncourt, Co. Tipperary, 143
Burne, Edward, 256
Burton, Decimus, 56
Burton House, Co. Cork, 42, 47, 113, 147, 219
Bush, John, 113
Butler, James, *see* Ormonde, Duke of
Byrn, John, 130, 131, 134
Byrne, Edward, 51, 52, 54

cage houses, 18, 57, 148, 156, 197, 198, 253
Caldebeck, William, 28, 39, 42, 129, 130, 137, 265
Caledon, Viscount, 261
calp, 11, 28, 159, 161, 163, 166, 167, 171, 173, 176
 quarries, 131, 166
 rubble, 130, 131, 140
Campbell, Colen, *Vitruvius Britannicus*, 58, 85, 204
Campbell, Michael, 136
Campbell, Robert, 57

Cape family, 184–5, 187, 188
Cape, Jonathan, 184, 187
Cape, Matt, 187
Cape, Ruth, 184–5, 188, 189
Cappoquin barracks, Co. Waterford, 37, 51, 53
Cardy, Samuel, 24, 52, 53, 54
Caritá convent (Venice), 268
Carleton, Thomas, 255
Carlow barracks, 50, 51, 53, 120, 217
Carney, Richard, 252, 255
carpenters, 21, 28–30, 36, 57, 82, 88, 90–2
    designers, as, 83–5, 91–2
    guilds, 20–3, 26, 57, 95
    tools, *89*, 90
    training and education, 57–8, 85
carpenters' manuals, *see* architectural publications, manuals, etc.
Carrickfergus Castle, Co. Antrim, 141
Carrick-on-Shannon barracks, Co. Leitrim, 51, 54, 130
Carrick-on-Suir, Co. Tipperary
    barracks, 51
    Ormonde Castle, 141, 234, 237
Carrigglas, Co. Longford, 73
Carton House, Co. Kildare, 30, 47–8, 138, 173, 178, 239, 244
casement windows, 31, 93, 94, 208–10, 218–19, *220*, 221–2, 225, 266, 267
Casey, Christine, 26, 61, 85
Cash, John, 58; *see also* Pool, Robert and Cash, John
Cashel, Co. Tipperary
    barracks, 51
    Bishop's Palace, 39–40, 150, 157, 173, 225, 231
Castle Dobbs, Co. Antrim, 146
Castle Durrow, Co. Laois, 34, 39, 40, 98, 114, 130, 132, *133*, 136, 197, 198, 224–5, 236, 243
Castle Forward, Co. Donegal, 100, 178, 198, 217
Castle Howard, Yorkshire, 235
Castle, Richard, 17, 23, 34–5, 45–6, 50, 68–71, 80–1, 83, 95, 116, 138, 151, 158, 159, 172–3, 195, 225–9, 235, 268–9, 272
    Clanwilliam House, 228
    Leinster House, 171–2, 173, 225–6
    Rotunda Hospital, 135
    Sligo cathedral, 161

Trinity College, 40, 195–6; bell tower, 187, 190; Dining Hall, 30, 45; Printing House, 38, *41*, 98, 112, 116, 195
Castlebar, Co. Mayo, 198, 217
Castlecoole, Co. Fermanagh, 48, 124, 134–6, 180, 244, 248
Castlestrange, Co. Roscommon, 127, 148
Castletown, Co. Kildare, 15, 38, 47–8, 110, 173, 195, 206, 258, 268–9
Castletown Cox, Co. Kilkenny, 15, 244, 245, *246*, *247*, 247–8
Castleward, Co. Down, 179, 228
Chalke, Isaac, 32, 209, 236, 252, 255, 256, 263, 265
Chalke, Isaac, junior, 255, 263
Chambers, John, 50–6, 84, 100, 123
Chambers, William, 73, 76, 122, 125–6, 132, 173, 177, 190, 206, 244, 254, 261–3, 269, 270
charcoal, 114, 186, 258
Charlemont, 1st Earl of, 48, 136, 190, 261, 262
Charles Fort, Kinsale, Co. Cork, 33, 37, 45, 152, *152*
Charles II, 144
Christiania (Norway), 103, 106, 109
churches, 23, 82, 84, 124, 136, 140, 153, 159, 161–2, 193, 196; *see also* Belfast; Cork; Dublin; Kells; London
Cibber, Caius Gabriel, 134
Clanrickard, 9th Earl of, 101, 114
Clarecastle, Co. Clare, 51
Clarke, John, 134
Clements, Nathaniel, 271
Clermont House, Co. Wicklow, 158
Clonmannon House, Co. Wicklow, 156
Clonmel, Co. Tipperary, 124
    barracks, 51
    courthouse, 171
    Main Guard, 159, 169
Cobh, Co. Cork, 37
Cockerell, Charles Robert, 176
Coleshill, Berkshire, 237, 238, 254
Colles, William, 134, 139
Coltsman, John, 42, 98, 136, 163, 166, 197
Como (Italy), 235
Company of Bricklayers and Tilers (London), 23
Company of Goldsmiths (Cork), 22
Connell, John, 123
Connor, Bartholomew, 86

Conolly, Lady Louisa, 258
Conolly, William, 176
Cooke, Edward, 54
Cooley, Thomas, 33, 44, 46–7, 83–4, 125, 132, 139, 171, 174, 180, 218, 269, 272
    Kells church, 42, 161, 199, 200
    Public Offices, *205*, 206
    Royal Exchange, 176, *177*, 190
copper roofs, 30, 190, 192
Corbally, Co. Tipperary, 198
cordwainers, 11, 22
Cork, 20, 28, 30–1, 37, 38, 42, 59, 72, 120, 124, 136, 139, 146, 155, 163, 167, 179, 203
    barracks, 84
    Christ Church, 136, 161, 193–4
    glassmaking, 213, 216
    Grand Parade, *182*
    Green Coat School, 94, 221
    guilds, 22, 182
    harbour, 201; fortifications, 37, 198
    King's Old Castle, 179
    North and South Gate Bridges, 136, 166
    North Mall, 152
    Oliver Plunkett Street, 153
    Pope's Quay, 270
    St Anne's Church, Shandon, 161, 169, *169*
Cork, Earl of, *see* Boyle, Richard
Cotton, Samuel, 252
Coulett, Richard, 129
Craig, Maurice, *Classic Irish houses of the middle size*, 15, 151, 153, 156, 161
Craiganu, Co. Down, 200
Cramillion, Bartholomew, 235, 240, 249
Cranfield, Richard, 30
Cranfield, Thomas, 30, 58
Crawley, Benjamin, 34, 40
Cromwell, Oliver, 113
Crossley, Aaron, 23, 255, 260
crown glass, 32, 210, 212, *215*, 216–19, 223, 267
    Bristol, from, 32, 216–18, 222, 267
    Dublin, from, 217–18, 229, 267
    London, from, 32, 217–18, 225, 267
    manufacture of, 214–18, 223, 229
    shopfronts, 232
Cubitt, Thomas, 56
Curran, C.P., 235
Curryglass, Co. Cork, 212
Cuvilliés, Francois, 240

Dalquharran Castle, Ayrshire, 245
Damer House, Roscrea, 169
Danzig (Gdansk), 104, 106, 110, 122
Darley family, 24, 132, 134, 135–6, 229, 270, 271
Darley, George, 101, 132, 135, *138*, 138
Darley, Henry, 30, 100, 132, 135, 136, 266
Darley, Hugh, 23, 40, 45, 136, 138, 176, 187, 196, 272
Darley, Moses, 27, 97, 132, 135, 136, 174, 266
Davis, Whitmore, 190
Dawson's Grove, Co. Monaghan, *25*
Dayly, William, 130
De Belidor, Bernard, *Architecture hydraulique*, 163
de Breffny, Brian, 248
De Keyser, Willem, 30
de Rose, Levan, 141
Delane, George, 209, 221
Demave, Barnaby, 136
Derry, 20, 122, 141, 178
    Bishop's Gate, 169
    cathedral, 136
Derry, Earl Bishop of, *see* Hervey, Frederick Augustus
Diderot, Denis, 'Verrerie Angloise,' *213*
Dobbs, Arthur (surveyor general), 33, 42, 122, 146
Dollardstown House, Co. Meath, 158
Doneraile Court, Co. Cork, 132
Dorchester, Dorset, 24
Dossie, Robert, 258, 259, 262
Downhill, Co. Londonderry, 30, 109, 136, 139, 168, 198
Downpatrick, Co. Down
    Southwell Charity, 156
Drammen (Norwegian port), 102, 104, 105
Draperstown, Co. Londonderry, 197
Drogheda, Co. Louth, 141, 172, 173
    barracks, 24
    Boyne River, bridge over, 98
    Schoolmaster's House/Grammar School, 48, *63* (section), 66, 106 (table), 107, 110, 116, 268
Drogheda Corporation, 132
Dromargh, Co. Armagh, 171
Dromoland, Co. Limerick, 46
Drumrea Glasshouse, Co. Tyrone, 213
Drumshambo, Co. Leitrim, 114

Dublin, 30, 38–40, 46, 47, 53, 60, 71, 81, 84, 85, 88, 93, 94, 100, 113, 121, 124–5, 127, 131, 135, 136, 140, 143, 152, 155, 157, 171–2, 174, 180, 190, 196, 200, 202, 203, 211, 214, 244, 249, 264, 266
  Abbeville, 207
  Aston Quay shopfront, *233*
  Aungier estate, 71, 128, 129, 153, 254, 271
  Aungier Street (No. 21), 153–4
  Ballast Board, 114
  banks: Bank of Ireland, 47; La Touche, 240; Newcomen's, 127, 177, *177*
  Blue Coat School, *21*, 86, 126, 127, 171, 267
  Brazen Head tavern, 225
  brickmaking, 147
  Bride Street (No. 96), 93
  Bull Island, 211
  Casino at Marino, 48, 122, 136, 138, 177, 190, 244, 262–3
  Castle, 15, 34, 39, 44, 49, 50, 84, 95, 127, 129, 135, 149, 151, 155, 219, 221, 227, 265
  Cavendish Row, 261, 272; (No. 9), 240
  Charlemont House, 73, *75*, 127, 150, 151, 173, 228, 244
  Chichester House, 34, 95
  churches, 44, 70, 135, 153, 161–2, 176, 255; Eustace Street Presbyterian church, 161; St Anne's, 161; St Catherine's, 161, 176; St John's, 83, 255, 271; St Mark's, 70, 153, 161; St Mary's, 135, 161, 173; St Matthew's, Ringsend, 161, 171, *172*; St Nicholas Within, 161, 266; St Patrick's Cathedral, *179*, *230*, 232, 271; St Sepulchre's, 171; St Werburgh's, 82, 99, 135, 161, 174, *175*, 266
  Clanwilliam House, 225, 228, 239
  College Green, 225, 232; *see also* Parliament House (below)
  Custom House: Burgh's, 44, 129; Gandon's, 15, 30, *125*, 125–6, 135, 138, 171, 180, 207, 229, 267
  Dawson estate, 271
  Dr Steevens's Hospital, 16, 24, 34, 40, 44, 48, *63* (section), 66, 76, 84, 106, 110, 115, *116*, 124, 130, 135, 150, 153, 159, 161, 173, 184, 188, 202, 236, 244, 268, 269; Worth Library, 79, 214

Dominick Street: Lady Hume's house, 34, 44, 116; (No. 20), 240, *241*; (No. 40), 79
Doneraile House, 71
Drogheda estate, 254
Earl of Cork's house, Castle Street, 141
Ellis estate, 254
Ely House, 173
Essex Bridge, 83, 108, 163, 164, 166, 232, 271
Eustace Street, 231; (No. 25), 16, 107, 236
Fitzwilliam estate, 83, 127, 229, 271
Four Courts, 15, *119*, 126, 138, 171, 206, 267
freemen, 22, 23, 24, 208, 210, 234, 251, 252
Gardiner estate, 127, 229, 271, 272
glasshouses, *211*, 212, 216, 217, 218, 229, 267
Grove House, Milltown, 244
guilds, *19*, 20–4; *see also* guilds
Harcourt Street, 229
Henrietta Street, 71, 80, 108, 145, 244, 269; (No. 5), *144*; (No. 13), 15, *80*, 107; (No. 14), *80*
Island Bridge, 164
Jervis estate, 254
King's Inns, 267
La Touche Bank, 240
Leinster House, 15, 71, 80–1, 106, 108, 116, 126, 127, 150, 172, 173, 225–7, *227*, 228, 269
Liberties, 129, 154–5
Longford House, Mary Street, 155
Marine School, *119*, 228
Marsh's Library, 32, 76, 88, 115, 117, 129, 145–6, 149, *149*, 155, 216, 219, 223, 225, 265, 266, 269
Meath estate, 71, 128, 153, 154, 254
Mercer's Hospital, 124, 159
Merrion Square, 55, 56, 107, 229
Merrion Street, 229; (Nos. 20-25), 107
Mespil House, 240
Molesworth estate, 71, 271
Molyneux House, 66, 128–9, 140, 155
Mornington House, 15, 240, 243, 244, 251
Mountjoy Square, 55, 251
North Great George's Street (No. 35), 15
O'Connell Street Upper (No. 42), 79
Ormond Bridge, 164, 166
Oxmantown, 144, 193

Dublin (*contd*)
   Parliament House (Chichester House), 34, 95
   Parliament House (College Green), 20, 26, 27, 34, 35, 40, 44, 46, 68, 81–2, 98–9, 101, 106, 110, 117, 123, 125, 126, 135, 138, 147, 150, 171, 173–6, 188, 190, 195, 209, 210, 217, 218, 225, *231*, 261, 264, 266, 267, 268, 269; roof trusses, *68–9* (sections), 69–70
   Powerscourt House, *250*, 251
   Public Offices, *61* (section), 201, 202, *205*, 206
   Ringsend, 44, 217, 218
   Roslyn Park, 73
   Rotunda (Lying-in) Hospital, 99, 126, 135, 171, 226, 227, 231, 235, 240, 251, 272
   royal arms, 29, 30, 138
   Royal Barracks, 53–4, 135, 198, 221, 266
   royal charter, 1670, 127–8
   Royal Exchange, 44, 83, 125, 132, 176, 177, *177*, 190, 228, *232*; architectural competition, 42, 263
   Royal Hospital Kilmainham, 15, 20, 30, 31, 33, 34, 39, 46, *62* (section), 66, 86, 97–8, 115, 127, 134–5, 140, 141, 147–50, 161, 173, 174, 175, 188, 202, 209, 210, 216, 218, 219, 221, 236, 237, 238, 243, 255, 264, 266–7, 269; chapel, 159, 243, 258; hall, 159, 161, 258; roof, 30, 66, 184, 185, 189, 192, 268
   Royal Military Infirmary, 207
   Rutland Square (Parnell Square), 26, 83, 100, 101
   Sackville Mall (O'Connell Street), 26, 101, 147
   St Patrick's Hospital, 48, 70, 83, 104, 106, 107, 151, 161, 163, 164, 198, 201, 206, 271
   St Stephen's Green, 71, 129, 135, 225; (Nos. 14–17), 82; (Nos. 42–3), *93*; (No. 85), 150, 251; (No. 86), 135, 173, 227, 229, 240
   shopfronts, *232*, 232–3, *233*
   Sir John Rogerson's Quay, *119*
   Smithfield, 123
   Smock Alley Theatre, 83
   South Frederick Street (No. 10), *70–1* (drawings)
   South Wall, 108, 114
   South William Street, 231
   Tailors' Hall, 129, 140, 147, 155, 265
   Tholsel, 32, 86, *154*, 184, 208, 216, *220*, 221, 222, 237, 255
   timber merchants, 101, 122–3
   Trinity College, 23, 29, 32, 33–6, 40, 42, 44, 45, 86, 96, *97*, 101, 112, 118, 123, 126, 129–31, 138, 150, 171, 186, 189, 190, 201–10, 214, 216, 227, 228, 235, 245, 263, 266, 269; bricklayers, 28, 153; building contracts, 45, 46, 49, 204; carpentry and joinery, 95–6, 98, 99, 104, 105, 107, 117; Chapel, 96, 122, 135, 206, 237; Dining Hall, 30, 45, 117, 194, 196, 269; New Chapel, 206; Parliament Square, 236, 248, 261; Printing House, 38, *41*, 98, 107, 112, 116, 135, 194, 195, 268–9; Provost's House, 96, 98, 135, 150, 153, 173, *205*, 206, 221, 227, 259, 261, 268; Regent House, 98, 135, 150, 236; roofs, 184, 185, 187–8, 194, 206; Rotten Row, 221; Rubrics, 129, 140, 153, 219, 265; Theatre, 98, 135, 206; west front, 138, 176, 187; windows, 31, 32, *215*, 221
   Trinity College Library, 16, 24, 34, 39, 44, 76, *97*, 112, 135, *224*, 235, *see also* Burgh, Thomas; glazing, 221–2, 224–5, 229, 267; joinery, 96–9, 266; *see also* Sisson, John; lead and plumbing, 184–5, 187–9; masonry and masons, 24, 27, 124, 127, 130, 132, 135, 149–50, 159, 173–4, 266; *see also* members of Darley family; timber, 20, 115, 117, 122; seventeenth-century library, 86
   Tyrone House, 225–8, *226*
   University College Dublin: James Joyce Library, 85; School of Architecture, 15
   Usher's Quay, 123
   viceregal court, 156
   Ward mansion, Ward's Hill, 155
   weavers' houses, 153–4
   Wide Streets Commissioners, 233, *233*
   York Street, 23, 154, 260
Dublin Bay, 167
Dublin City Assembly, 32, 114, 256–7
Dublin Corporation, 184
Dublin Philosophical Society, 197
Dublin Society, 82, 271
   schools, 58, 83, 85

Ducart, Davis, 132, 158, 171, 235, 248, 268
Dumbarton, 218
Duncannon, Co. Waterford, 37
Dundalk, Co. Louth, 122
Dungannon, Co. Tyrone, 211, 213
Dungarvan, aqueduct, Co. Waterford, 36
Dunmanway, Co. Cork, 198
Dunmurry, Co. Antrim
    Presbyterian church, 84
Dunsandle, Co. Galway, 127
Dunsoghly Castle, Co. Dublin, 66
Durrow, Co. Laois, 114; *see also* Castle Durrow
Dutch Billies, 71–2

Ecole des Ponts et Chaussées (Paris), 26, 163
Eddystone Lighthouse, Devon, 166
Edinburgh, 262
Edwards, Benjamin, *209*
Edward IV, 194
Elliot family, 184
Elliot, James, 204, 206
Elphin, Co. Roscommon
    Bishop's Palace, 110, 121, 152, 197, 217, 242, 248
    cathedral, 161
Emerson, Alexander, 261
Emerson, Joseph, 260
Emo Court, Co. Laois, 180
Emsworth, Co. Dublin, 207
England, 20, 40, 66, 72, 93, 94, 99, 108, 113, 115, 121, 132, 134, 145, 156, 163, 165, 166, 170, 173, 174, 186, 192, 193, 200, 210, 219, 221, 231, 235, 239, 253, 257, 258
English building practices, 18, 20, 42, 43–4, 50, 60, 70–4, 76, 79, 81, 87, 115, 128, 151, 208, 210, *213*, 214–16, 237, 270; *see also* architectural publications, manuals, etc.
Enniscorthy, Co. Wexford, 117
Ensor brothers, 24, 40, 51, 52, 81, 92, 229, 270
Ensor, George, 26, 33, 37, 42, 43, 48, 58, 80, 82, 83, 171, 199, 217, 271, 272
    barracks building inquiry, 49, 50–3, 54–5
Ensor, Job, 24, 81, 99
Ensor, John, 26, 43, 50, 51, 54, 55, 83, 101, 135, 271, 272
Esdall, George, 83, 123
Eyre, Thomas (surveyor general), 33, 35, 36–7, 45, 55
Eyrecourt House, Co. Galway, 127, 147–8, 149

fanlights, 214, 229, 231–2, 233
Fannin, John, 197
Feichtmayr family, 240
Ferns, Co. Wexford
    Bishop's Palace, 190
Ferrard, 1st Baron, 26
fir, *see* timber
FitzGerald, Barbara, 237
Flanders, 99
Flemming, Anthony, 86
floor construction, 16, *73*, 76, *76*, 77, *78*, 78–9, *79*, 80, *80*, 151, 269
    framing, 72–81, 117, 269
    joists. *see* joists
    trussed girders, 72–3, *74*
Florence Court, Co. Fermanagh, 168, *239*
Flower, Colonel, 98
Flower, William, 197, 198
Foxford, Co. Mayo, 114
France, 26, 113, 174, 214, 216, 219, 223, 257, 262
Friedlieb, Andreas, 108, 117, 118

Gallarus Oratory, Co. Kerry, 162
Galway, 124, 172
    barracks, 50, 51, 52, 53, 54, 134
Gandon, James, 46, 58, 73, 76, *78*, 83, *102*, 125, 135, 138–9, 174, 176, 180, 206–7, 229, 269, 270, 272
Garretstown House, Co. Cork, 152
George I, statue of, 117
George II, statue of, 46
Gerbier, Balthazar, 238, 242
Germany, 101, 163, 214, 216, 235, 238, 239
Gernon, Patrick, 51, 52, 53, 54, 122
Gibbons, Grinling, 134
Gibbs, James, 60, 66, 235, 238–9
Gibson, George, 95
Gibson, Thomas, 196
Gilbert (stonecutter), 81
Glamorgan (Wales), 166
Glasgow, 139
glass; *see also* crown glass
    broad glass, 214, 215–16, 267
    French glass, 32, 216, 223
    plate glass, 216
    prices, 32, 216, 217, 218, 222
glassmaking, 210–18
    glasshouses, 208, *209*, 210–13, *212*, *213*, 214–15, 217–18, 223, 229

Glencree, Co. Wicklow, 172
Glenfarne, Co. Leitrim, 168
Glens of Antrim, 114
Glinsk, Co. Galway, 143
goldsmiths, 22
Goodrich, Matthew, 253
Goodwin, William, 82, 99, 100
Goresgrove, Co. Kilkenny, *126*
Gort barracks, Co. Galway, 51, 53, 200
Goudge, Edward, 237
Granard barracks, Co. Longford, 54
granite, 24, 28, 167, 171–3, 176, 180, 266–7
   Carlow, from, 167, 180
   facings, 150, 166, 167, 171, 266
   quarries, 171–3
Guild of Joiners, Ceylers and Wainscotters, 20, 21, 86, 94–5, 129, 256, 266
Guild of Masons, Bricklayers, etc. (Limerick), 22, 23–4
Guild of St Bartholomew, 234, 254–5, 265
Guild of St Loy, 208
Guild of St Luke, 15, 21, 23, 32, 161, 252, 255–7, 260, 263, 264, 265
guilds, 15, 18, *19*, 20–4, 26, 32, 56, 83, 84, 198, 208, 265; see also journeymen
   bricklayers and plasterers, 20, 22, 23–4, 26, 28, 127–8, 129, 153, 234; see also Guild of St Bartholomew
   carpenters, 20–1, 24, 26, 86, 181, 182
   glaziers, 208–9
   joiners, 86, 266; see also Guild of Joiners, Ceylers and Wainscotters
   membership, 21, 22
   painters, 21, 22, 32, 252–5; see also Guild of St Luke
   plumbers, 21, 22, 24, 182
   slaters, 22, 181
   smiths, 208–9
   stuccodores, 32
Gunn, Elizabeth, 260
Gurteen glasshouse, Co. Waterford, 212
gutters, 45, 195, 206
   lead, 30, 181, 188, 189, 190
   oak, 108, 114
gypsum plaster, *see* plaster of Paris

Halfpenny, William, 81, 85
Hall, Nathaniel, 112, 187
Hampstead Marshall, Berkshire, 238
Hampton Court Palace, Richmond, 44, 93, 94, 115, 134, 141, 219, 223–4
Hand, Thomas, 33–4
Harden, D. B., 215
Hart, John, 95
Hawksmoor, Nicholas, 18, 34, 60, 66, *67*, 68, 174
Hawksworth, Abraham, 34
Hawney, William, *The complete measurer*, 59
Haystown House, Rush, Co. Dublin, 156
Headford barracks, Co. Galway, 51, 53, 130, 134
Headfort House, Co. Meath, 136
Hearne, John, 129
Heatley, Abraham, 184, 194, 204
Heatley family, 184
Heatley, Thomas, 196, 204
Henzy, Ananias, 212
Herne, John, 24
Hervey, Frederick Augustus, Earl Bishop of Derry, 109, 136, 139, 168, 169, 271
Hillsborough church, Co. Down, 136
Hillsborough, 1st Earl of, 136
Hoban, James, 58
Hodgson, Philip Levi, *The modern measurer*, 32, 59, 60, 78, 104, 105, 106, 109n, 112, 113
Holkham Hall, Norfolk, 156, 195
Holland, 20, 72, 99, 122, 129, 141, 143, 145, 156, 157, 214, 216
Holmes, John, 122
Hoppus, Edward, *Practical measuring now made easy*, 59–60
Hopson, Charles, 94
Hormann, William, *Vulgaria*, 238, 242
Hothard, George, 95
Houghton, John, *29*, 30, 58, 138, 267–8
Howell, Thomas, 86, 95
Hull, James, 210
Hume, Lady, 34, 44, 116
Humphreys, Thomas, 28, 165, 166, 203
hydraulic lime, 11, 163, 164, 166, 240
Hydrographia Hibernica, 121

Iredall, Peter, 95
Irish oak, 20, 101, 108, 113–14, 116–17, 196, 198, 211
Isle of Wight, 210
Italian stuccodores, 237, 238–40, 248–9
Italy, 163, 174, 235, 243
Ivory, Thomas, 58, 83, 139, 177, 269

Jacobsen, Theodore, 228
Jamaica, 121
James, John, 60
Jarratt, Joseph, 33, 46, 82
Jarratt, Thomas, 33, 37
Jigginstown House, Co. Kildare, 28, 129, 141, *142*, 143, 156, 157
Johnston, Francis, 47, 55, 122, 171, 176, 192, 270, 272
Johnstown Kennedy, Co. Dublin, 244
joists, 30, 57, 103, 106–7, 115, 269
    ceilings, 74, 76, 79, 96, 236, 269
    floors, 57, 73, 74, *76, 77*, 80, 81, 107, 108, 114, 115, 116, 152; Irish system, 76, 78–9, *79*, 108, 151, 269–70
Jones, Inigo, 195, 219, 253–4
Jope, E.M., 15, 141
journeymen, 11, 21, 23, 26, 36–7, 42, 57, 84, 129, 131, 139, 265

Kanes, John, 187
Keating, William, 187
Keatten, Edward, 22
Kells, Co. Meath
    Church of Ireland, 42, 84, 161, 199, 200
Kelly, John, 30, 138
Kempster, William, 134
Kenn, Benjamin, 47
Kenn, Captain William, 47
Kent, William, 156, 195
Kessel, Matthew, 86
Kilkenny, 124, 133–4, 139, 167, 168, 170, 172, 176, 193
    barracks, 51, 53, 54
    Castle, 31–2, 86, 174, 219, 221
    St Canice's Cathedral, 197
Kilkenny Corporation, 86
Kilmacurragh House, Co. Wicklow, *62* (section), 66, *76, 77*, 88, 115, 127, 148, 149, 150
Kilmeadon, Co. Waterford, 198
Kilshannig House, Co. Cork, 132, 158, *170*, 171, 248, *249*
King House, Boyle, 148, 151, 244
King, Richard, 40
king-post trusses, *see* roof trusses
Kingsfort House, Co. Meath, 151, 243
Kinsale, Co. Cork, 42, 86
    fortifications, 38; *see also* Charles Fort
    slate quarries, *see* quarries
Kinward, Thomas, 93

La Touche, James Digges, 22
Labelye, Charles, 165
Lafranchini brothers, 235, 238–40, 248–9, *249*
Lambeth glassworks, 216, 267
Landon, John, 217, 229
Langley, Batty, 59, 70, 76, 85, 87, 92, 192, 268
    The builder's vade-mecum, 78, 81, 90, 194
laths, 12, 30, 194, 236
    ceiling, 12, 32, 79, 206, 236, 242, 243, 247
    slating, 12, 20, 194, 200–1, 202, 203, 236
latten-workers, 12, 22
Lawe, Robert, 51, 52, 53, 54
lead, 30, 181, 185–90
    glazing, 31, 209, 210, 222
    roofs, 181, 185–90, 192–3, 195; *see also* gutters
Leamaneagh House, Co. Clare, 143
Ledwithstown House, Co. Longford, 71, 127, 148, 151, 257, 258, 259
Lee, Henry, 147
Lee, William, 251
Leigh, Warrington, 165
Leon, Michael, 109
Letgeredge, James, 86
'Leuventhen' (Dutch builder), 155
Leyden, Thomas, 16
Lifford courthouse, Co. Donegal, 168
Limerick, 28, 72, 124, 141, 155, 172, 212
    barracks, 24, 51, 53
    Bishop's Palace, 132, *133*
    Custom House, 132, 173, 268
    guilds, 22, 23–4
    Pery estate, 127
limestone, 20, 22, 24, 28, 135, 149, 155, 163, 167, 171, 176, 200; *see also* hydraulic lime; marble; Portland stone
    Ardbraccan stone, 24, 28, 131, 172, 173, 178
    Armagh, from, 172–3
    Cork, from, 169, 170–3
    Dublin, from, 28, 131, 166, 173; *see also* calp
    quarries, 28, 93, 133–4, 170, 172–3, 174
Lisburn, Co. Antrim, 20, 197
Lismore, Co. Waterford, 132
    castle, 86
Little Island, Co. Cork, 167
Littledall, John, 95
Liverpool, 139, 146, 180
Loeber, Rolf, 272

London, 18, 56, 73, 88, 128, 132, 136, 141, 149, 154, 156, 190, 201, 202, 218, 219, 233, 239, 248, 253, 254, 260, 264, 268
- Bloomsbury, 18, 156
- building regulations, 18, 74, 76, 115, 128, 256–7, 264
- Chiswick Villa (Burlington), 195, 254
- churches, 20, 23, 93, 103, 174, 190; St Andrew's, Holborn, 103; St Martin-in-the-Fields, 18, 235; St Paul's Cathedral, 18, 45, 92–3, 108, 134, 176, 242; St Paul's, Covent Garden, 195; St Stephen, Walbrook, 134
- Clifford's Inn, London, 222
- Covent Garden, 156, 195, 219
- fire of 1666, 18, 72, 92, 101, 128, 141; reconstruction, 18–19, 128, 141
- glassmaking, 214–15, 216, 229; *see also* crown glass; Bear Garden glasshouse, 214–15; Ratcliff glassworks, 215, 216, 267
- Greenwich Hospital, 186
- Horse Guards, 195
- Lincoln's Inn Fields, 219
- Queen's House, Greenwich, 254
- Royal Hospital, Chelsea, 195
- royal palaces, 18, 93, 94; *see also* Hampton Court; Kensington Palace, 93, 141, 219; St James's, 18; Whitehall, 93, 219, 254
- Soho, 156
- Somerset House, 221, 253–4, 261
- Westminster Bridge, 165
- Westminster Hall, 81

Londonderry, 1st Marquis of, 185, 200
Longe, George, 211–12
Longleat, Wiltshire, 237
Lorraine (France), 212, 214
Lough Neagh, 114
Loughlinstown, Co. Dublin, 185
Loughrea barracks, Co. Galway, 50, 51, 54
Lucas, Charles, 22–3
Lucas, John, 153
Lynn, Norfolk, 210

McBlain family, 136
McCleery, Joseph, 38, 98
McCullagh, James, 239, 250, 251, 263
McDonnell, Joseph, 240
McGinnis, Owen, 28, 130, 131, 134, 200

McGrath, R. and Frost, A.C., 214, 215, 219, 222, 223, 229
McParland, Edward, 83
Magherafelt, Co. Londonderry, 197
Magill, John (Jack), 26, 40, 99, 217, 270
mahogany, *see* timber
Maine, Jonathan, 134
Mallow barracks, Co. Cork, 37, 51, 53
Malton, James
views of Dublin, *119, 154, 179, 220, 221, 222, 227, 227, 228, 230, 232, 232–3*
marble, 30, 134, 139, 164, 166, 176, 234, 235, 240, 262
- Millmount mills, *137*
- quarries, 133–4, *168*
Marlfield, Co. Tipperary, 169
Marplass, Richard, 95
Martin, Edward, 237
Martin, Robert, 136
Massy, Robert, 86
measurers' manuals, *see* architectural publications, manuals, etc.
medieval period, 252–3
- cage houses, 148
- carpentry, 81
- casement windows, 208
- glazing, 210
- guilds, 15, 20–1
- joinery, 86
- plastering, 234, 242
- roof framing, 66
- roof tiles, 193–4
- shopfronts, 232
- wall construction, 124, 140, 159, 161, 162
Mee, Isaac, 217
Meighan, William, 263–4
Meissonier, Juste Aurèle, 249
Memel (Lithuania), 104
Middlebrook, Thomas, 95
Midleton, Co. Cork, 167
Miles, Thomas, *The concise practical measurer*, 103, 108
Miller, Edward, 34
Millmount marble mills, Co. Kilkenny, *137*
Mills (mason), 44
Mills, Richard, 24, 129, 137, 153, 155, 156
Mitchell, James, 95
Molyneux, William, 35, 36
Moneymore, Co. Londonderry, 197

Montgomery and White (timber merchants), 114, 118
Montgomery, William, 101, 107
Montmartre, Paris, 238
Moore, Andrew, 197
Moosbrugger, Andreas and Peter, 242
Morel, Andreas, 242
Morland, Richard, 237
Morris, James, 28, 38
Morris, Robert, *Architectural remembrancer*, 26
Morrison, Richard, 58, 171
mortar, 124, 135, 151, 162, 163–6, 194, 200–1, 206, 234, 240
Morton (Martin), Robert, 136
Moss, Bridget, 101
Mosse, Bartholomew, 99, 235, 240, 272
Mount Ievers Court, Co. Clare, 127, 130, 140, 145, 156, 225
Mount Juliet, Co. Kilkenny, 169–70
Mount Kennedy, Co. Wicklow, 245
Mount Stewart, Co. Down, 136, 200
Mountcharles, Co. Donegal, 168
Mountjoy Fort, Co. Tyrone, 141, *142*
Mountmellick, Co. Laois, 114, 236
Mountrath, Co. Laois, 114
Mourne mountains, Co. Down, 167
Moxon, Joseph, *Mechanick exercises*, 28, 81, 87, 88, *89*, 90, 92, 98, 111, 112–13
Mulholland, Roger, 48, 84–5, 92
Murphy, William, 185
Murray, William, 171, 188, 243
Mussenden, Daniel, 105, 106, 107, 109, 117, 118, 121, 122, 200, 210
Myers, Christopher, 33, 45, 206
Myers, Graham, 187
Mylne, Robert, 83

Nary, Richard, 54
Navan barracks, Co. Meath, 24, 53, 120
Neal, Henry, 112
Nesbit (barrack master), 52, 54
Neve, Richard, *City and country purchaser*, 183, 186, 188, 190, 194, 195, 196, 197, 201, 210, 215, 216, 222
Nevill, Arthur Jones (surveyor general), 33, 35, 36, 39, 44, 48–53, 55, 83
New York, 59, 121
Newberry Hall, Co. Kildare, 158, 231
Newbridge House, Co. Dublin, 244–5
Newhall, Co. Clare, 158

Newry Canal, 36, 38
Newry, Co. Down, 122
Newtownards, Co. Down, 136, 185, 266
Newtownards Manor, Co. Down, 242
Nicholson, John, 202, 203
Nicholson, Peter, *Builder's dictionary*, 105
Nonsuch Palace, Epsom, 237
Nore River, 170
Nore Valley, 114
Normandy (France), 214
Northumbria, 81
Norway, 20, 103, 106, 108, 118, 120
Norwegian timber, 18, 20, 101, 103–6, 108, 109, 114, 117, 118, 120–2, 254
Nottinghamshire, 238

oak, 18, 20, 45, 93, 96, 98, 101, 106–8, 110, 113–17, 121, 122, 148, 197–8, 201–2, 236, 243, 254, 259, 261, 265; *see also* Irish oak
Oakfield, Co. Donegal, 46
O'Dwyer, Frederick, 226–7
Ogle, William and John, 122
Ó hEocha, Séamus, 16
Oppenord, Gilles-Marie, 249
Ord, William, 99
Ormonde, 1st Duke of (James Butler), 22, 31, 219, 221
Osborne, Patrick, 239, 244, 245, *246, 247*, 247–8
Osterley Park, Middlesex, 262
Owens, John, 98, 197
Oxford
    All Souls College, *67*, 68
    Sheldonian Theatre, *65*, 66, 67
Oxfordshire, 258, 259

Pain, William, 78, 85, 91–2, 115
    The builder's companion, 82
    The carpenter and joiner's repository, 91, *91*
    The practical house carpenter, *74*, 91–2, 105
paint, 11, 32, 253, 254, 257–65
Palace Anne, Ballineen, Co. Cork, 130, 140, 155–6
Palazzo Porto, Vicenza, *64*
Palladio, Andrea, 25, *64*, 66, 67, 163, 195, 225, 228, 268
    I Quattro Libri, 65, 66
panelling, 20, 86, 87, 88, 90, 93, 94, 95, 122, 253, 254, 265; *see also* wainscotting
pantiles, 30, 192, 193, 194–6, 199, 268–9

Pantin, Paris, 238
Parker, Mr, 52
Parsons, Sir Lawrence, 212
Parsonstown, *see* Birr, Co. Offaly
pattern books, *see* architectural publications, manuals, etc.
Pavier, Robert, 153
paviers, 22, 23, 36, 99
Pearce, Edward Lovett, 17, 34–5, 40, 68–9, 83, 150, 151, 156–8, 174, 176, 195, 206, 225–7, 228, 271
    Castletown, 195, 206, 268, 269
    Parliament House, 20, 26, 34, 35, 44, 46, 68, *68–9*, 81, 98–9, 101, 117, 135, 150, 171, 174, 176, 190, 225, 263–4, 266, 267, 268
Perceval, Sir John, 1st Earl of Egmont, 113, 139
Perceval, Sir Philip, 47
Pery, Edmund Sexton, 22
Phelan, Denis, 130
Pike family, 184
plaster of Paris (gypsum), 16, 32, 237, 238, 242, 244
Platten House, Co. Meath, 127, 130, 155
Plummer, Gilbert, 28
Pococke, Richard, 185, 198
Pomeranian baulk, 101, 108, 118, 120
Pool, Robert, 58
Pool, Robert and Cash, John, *Views of the most remarkable public buildings …* (1780), 85, *116*, *205*, 225, *226*, 227, 228
Pooley, Thomas, 256
Portarlington, Co. Laois, 212
Portland stone, 20, 34, 131, 132, 136, 166, 171, 173, 174–8, 180, 259, 261, 266, 267
Portsalon, Co. Donegal, 168
Portumna, Co. Galway, 51, 101, 114
Powell, Harry J., 219
Powerscourt, Co. Wicklow, 101, 124, 172
Pratt, Sir Roger, 254
Price, Francis, 59, 70, 72, 76, 78, 85, 87
    The British carpenter, 57, 60–1, 66, 68, 73, *73*, 115, 192, 195, 268
Price, Gabriel, 104
Priestley, Michael, 168
Proby, Thomas, 159
Purfield, Laurence, 51–2
Purfield, William, 40
purlins, 12, *62*, 66, *70*, *71*, 72, 73, 110, 115, 270

quarries, *160*, 166–8; *see also* granite; limestone; sandstone; slate
    Armagh, county, 172–3
    Ballyring, Co. Offaly, 197, 198
    Ballyvoy, Co. Antrim, 169
    Cork, county, 167; Bantry, 198; Kinsale, 31, 198, 203
    Down, county: Ards Peninsula, 198, 199, 200; Ballyhiney, 200; Ballywalter, 198–9, 203
    Dublin, county, 167; Milltown, 131; Palmerstown, 28, 131, 173
    Golden Hill, Co. Wicklow, 24, 28, 131, 172
    Killaloe, Co. Clare, 31, *31*, 198, 199, 200, 203
    Kingstown, Co. Galway, *168*
    Kinsale, Co. Cork, 31, 198, 203
    Leixlip, Co. Kildare, 173
    Limerick, county, 167
    Londonderry, county: Downhill, 198; Dungiven, 168–9, 179–80
    Moate, Co. Westmeath, 198, 199
    Portland, Dorset, 20, 28, 93, *178*
    Sheephouse, Co. Louth, 24, 173
    Valentia Island, Co. Kerry, 198, *199*
    Wales, 31, 114, 198, 269
queen-post trusses, *see* roof trusses
Quin Abbey, Co. Clare, 234
Quinn, Francis, 26, 27, 28, 34, 39, 94, 129, 130, 137, 150, 265

Ramsgate Harbour (England), 165
Raper, John, 218
Raphoe, Co. Donegal
    Bishop's Palace, 143
    cathedral, 161
Read, Isaac, 122
Reed, John, 188
Register House, Edinburgh, 262
Reilly, Richard, 50, 51, 52, 54
Rencher, George, 263
Reynolds, Michael, 250
Riverstown, Co. Cork, 239
Roberts (contractor), 52
Roberts, John, 161
Robinson, James, 95, 138, 176
Robinson, William (surveyor general), 33, 35, 36, 83, 95, 115, 123, 129, 140, 147, 149–50, 155, 255–6, 270, 271
    Dublin Castle, 115, 149, 219, 221

Marsh's Library, 269
Platten House, 155
Royal Hospital Kilmainham, 140–1, 147–50, 173–5, 184, 192, 219, 221, 268, 269
Roch, Andrew, 209
Rochfort, Robert, 95
Rock (glazing contractor), 210
Rocque, John, map of Dublin (1756), *146*, 147, *211*, 212
Rogerson, Sir John, 184
roof construction, 30, 115–16, 181, 182, 193
  copper, use of, 30, 190, 192
  framing, 20, 29, 58, 60–2, *62–3*, 66–70, *70–1*, *72*, 268, 269; see also roof trusses;
  lead, use of, 181, 184–90, 192–3, 195
  pitched roofs, 30, 66, 69, 195–6, 200, 206, 232, 268
  platform (flat) roofs, 30, 180, 184, 185, 188, 189, 190, 192
  shingled roofs, 193, 196–7, 198
  slated, 30, 181, 182, 193, 195–6, 197, 198–207; see also slate; slaters
roof tiles, 20, 30–1, 182, 193–6, 199; see also pantiles
roof trusses, 60, *65*, 66–8, *67*, *68–9*, 69–70, 115, *191*, 192, 195, 268
  king-post, 11, 20, 60, 66, 67–8, 70, 110, 268
  Palladian, 60, *64*, 66, 67–71, 268–9
  queen-post, 12, 60, 115
Roscommon, 42, 83, 121, 272
  barracks, 51
  charity school, 48, 55, 271
  courthouse/Sessions House, 48, 55, 199, 217, 271
Rose, Joseph, 244
Rosscarbery barracks, Co. Cork, 52
Rothery, Isaac, 270
Rothery, John, 156, 270
Roundwood House, Co. Laois, 170
Rowlett, John, 210, 216, 221, 222, 229
Royal Works (England), 18
Rudd, Benjamin, 24, 26, 80, 84, 85
Rudd family, 81, 85, 270, 271
Rudd, James, 26, 85
Rudd, John, 98
Rudd, Robert, 95
Rudd, Stephen, 85
Russborough House, Co. Wicklow, 172, 239
Russell, William, 86

Rutty, Dr John, 163, 164
St Gobain glasshouse (France), 223
Salmon, William, 81
sandstone, 132, 149, 161, 166–71, 174, 179–80, 266, 267
  quarries, 136, 168–9
Sandys, Francis, 58
sash windows, 28, 57, 86, 88, 90, 95, 96, 98, 106–7, 114, 115, 116, 122, 129, 214, 219, 221, 223–9, 254
  introduction and development, 20, 31–2, 93–4, 208, 216, 219, 221–9, 231, 266–7
sawyers, 22, 30, 60, 110–13, *111*, 111–12, 121, 139
Scalé, Bernard, map of Dublin (1773), 147
Scamozzi, 25
Scotland, 166, 170, 231
Scott, John, 112
Scriven, William, 95
sculptors, *29*, 30, 58, 134, 138, 139, 174, 235, 240, 249, 262
Seagrave, Thomas, 216
Semple, Edward, 32, 263
Semple family, 24
Semple, George, 25–6, 48, *61* (section), 70, 104, 106–8, 129, 151, 159, 161–3, 198–9, 201–2, 204, 206, 269, 271–2
  A treatise on building in water, *109*, 163
Semple, John, 28, 130
Settlement Commission, 143–4
Severens, Kenneth, 82
Shanahan, Michael, 30, 139, 168–9
Shannon Navigation, 36
Shannon River, 198, 199
Shee, Peter, 263
Sherriff, William, 23, 260
Shillelagh, Co. Wicklow, 101, 114, 117
shingles, 181, 193, 196–7, 198
shipbuilding, 113
Shire Hall, Hertfordshire, 261
shop windows, *232*, 232–3, *233*
Silcock, Thomas, 210
Silvermines, Co. Tipperary, 185
Simmons, Edward, 99
Simpson (stonecutter), 81
Sisson, John, 29, 92, 94, 95, 96, 97, 98, 99, 117, 122, 222, 257, 266
Sisson, Richard, 257
Skinner, Martin, 256
Slaney River, 117

slate, *182*, 193, 198–9, 200–3, 204, 206, 268, 269
   Liscannor slates, 200
   Malbay slates, 200
   prices, 198, 202
   quarries, 30–1, *31*, 114, 197, 198, *199*, 199–200, 202, 203, 269
   roofing material, as, 30, 181, 193, 195–6, 197, 198–207
   Welsh slates, 31, 198, 199, 200, 202, 203, 206
Sligo Harbour, 185
Smeaton, John, 166
Smirke, Robert, 56
Smith, Benjamin, 130
Smith Jeudwin, Thomas, 217, 229
Smith, Thomas, 200
smiths, 208–9
Smitz, Gaspar, 256
Smyth, Edward, 30, 137, 138, 176
Spencer, Nathaniel, 32, 256, 263
Spencer, Thomas, 255
Spike, George, 32, 256, 261, 263, 265
Sprengel, P.N., 238
Sproule family, 85, 270, 271
Sproule, John, 99
Sproule, Samuel, 43, 55, 84, 85, 100, 271
spruce, 103–4, 236, 254
Stapleton, Michael, 26, 235, 245, 251, 263
Stenton, Patrick, 23
Stephenstown House, Co. Louth, 152
Steuart, George, 103, 104–5, 122, 132, 179–80
Stewart, George, 99, 100, 118, 123
Stewart, Robert, later 1st Marquis of Londonderry, 185, 200
Stitt, William, 203, 258, 261
stone, 20, 27–8, 39, 127, 159–80, 163, 166–80, 171, 173, 174–80; *see also* granite; limestone; Portland stone; quarries; sandstone
stone carvers, 30, 134, 137–8, 139, 248; *see also* sculptors
Stone, George, Archbishop of Armagh, 49
Strickland, Walter, 255, 263
struts, 12, 60, 66, 67, *76*
stucco, 16, 55, 234–5, 236, 237–8, *239*, 239, 240, 242–5, *246*, 248, 249, *249*, 251; *see also* plaster of Paris
   costs, 247–8
Summer Grove, Co. Laois, 132

Summerhill, Co. Meath, 127, 150, 173, 225
surveyors general, 33, 35–6, 37, 83; *see also* barrack building programme
Sussex, 195
Swedish timber, 101, 105, 106, 108, 118
Switzerland, 235, 242
Synge, Edward, Bishop of Elphin, 117, 121, 197, 217, 242, 248
Syon House, Middlesex, 245

Tabary, James, 30
Tallow barracks, Co. Waterford, 37, 51, 53
Tassie, William, 136
Taylor, Erasmus, 210
technical manuals, *see* architectural publications, manuals, etc.
Thames Valley, 146, 156, 194
Thompson, Alexander, 187, 188
Thompson, F.M.L., 55–6
Thorpe, Charles, 26, 32, 55, 245, 251
tie-beams, 12, 66, 67, 68
tiles, *see* pantiles; roof tiles
timber; *see also* Norwegian timber; Swedish timber, Irish oak
   barrel and cask staves, 113–14
   baulk timber, 30, 66, 96, 101, 104, 107–11, 118, 120, 121
   cage structures. *see* cage houses
   fir, 101, 103, 104, 105, 107–8, 110, 114, 115–8, 254;
   hardwoods, 11, 20, 88, 103, 108, 113–14, 121–2; *see also* Irish oak; oak
   joists, *see* joists
   laths, *see* laths
   mahogany, 101, 108, 110, 112, 121
   mouldings, 87–8, 90, 92, 103, 244, 266
   panelling, *see* panelling
   prefabricated timber fittings, 95–6, 99–100
   prices, 105, 108, 109, 112, 117–18, 119–21
   sawing, 110–13
   shingles, *see* shingles
   softwoods, 12, 18, 101, 106, 108, 110, 254, 260
   spruce, 103–4, 236, 254
Tingham, Edmund, 86
Tomson, John, 257
Trim Castle, Co. Meath, 193
Trinity College Dublin, *see under* Dublin
Trondheim (Norway), 102, 104, 105, 106, 107, 108, 117, 121

trusses, *see* roof trusses
trussed partitions, 73, *75*
Tudenham, Co. Westmeath, 16, 71, 80, 127, 151, 173, 269
Tudor, Joseph, engravings, *97, 231*, 232
Tullamore barracks, Co. Offaly, 54, 221
Turner, Joseph, 86
Tyrone Collieries, 213
Tyrone House, Co. Galway, 16, 152, 173
Tyrrell, Maurice, 263–4

Ulster, 113, 167, 170, 179
    plantation towns, 20, 148, 196–7
    stonecutters, 136
Uppark, Sussex, 242

Vanbrugh, John, 35, 235
Vasari, Giorgio, 234–5, 240
Vierpyl, Simon, 136, 137, 138, 151, 173, 177
Vincent, Walter, 193
Vitruvius, 26, 85, 163, 234, 235, 238
Vizer, William, 208–9
Vorarlberg (Austria), 235

Wade, General George, 195, *204*, 206
wainscotters, 12, 86, 94; *see also* Guild of Joiners, Ceylers and Wainscotters
wainscotting, 88, 95, 96, 98, 99, 103, 108, 122, 253, 260, 265
Waldré, Vincent, 30, 33, 185
Wales, 166, 185, 198, 203; *see also* Welsh slates
Walker, William, 261
Wall family, 24, 32
Wall, John, 236, 248, 259, 263
Wall, Patrick, 236, 248, 263
Wall, William, 32, 209, 256, 263, 265
Ward family, 179
Wardstown House, Co. Donegal, 16, 152, 168
Ware, Isaac, 101, 163
Warwickshire, 24, 81, 237
Waterford, 20, 24, 72, 172, 203, 216
    barracks, 198
    Church of Ireland cathedral, 161, 173
Webb, John, 254
Wentworth, Thomas, 141
West, John, 251
West, Robert, 32, 43, 58, 100, 101, 229, 235, 238, 239, 240, 263

Westropp, M.S. Dudley, 211
Wharton, Robert, 184
Wheeler, George, 34, 40
Whinrey family, 266
Whinrey, John, 94, 129, 132, 135, 139
Whinrey, Nathaniel, 27, 81, 135
White, Caspar, 101, 114
Wide Street Commissioners (Dublin), 233, *233*
Wilkinson, George, *31*, 146, 166, *168*, 170, 198, *199*
Willes, Edward, Lord Chief Baron, 185
Wills family, 85, 270–1
Wills, Isaac, 29, 30, 34, 84, 96–7, 98, 104, 107, 115–16, 122
Wills, Michael, 26, 34, 82, 83, 84, 85, 270
    Drogheda schoolhouse, *63*
Wilson (contractor), 52, 54
Wilson, Hugh, 54
Wilson's Hospital, Co. Westmeath, 110
Wilton House, Wiltshire, 254
Wilton, Joseph, 262
Windele, J., 178–9
window glass, *see* crown glass; glass; glassmaking
Winslow Hall, Buckinghamshire, 94, 134
Wiseman, Thomas, 252
Wittkower, Rudolf, 81
Wood, Robert, *The ruins of Palmyra*, 85
Woodlands, Santry, Co. Dublin, 158
Woodstock, Co. Kilkenny, 169
Worth Library, *see* Dr Steevens's Hospital
Wotton's *Elements*, 85
Wren, Christopher, 18, 34, 43–5, 56, *65*, 66, 67, 92–4, 103, 107–8, 115, 134, 141, 163, 174, 195, 224, 242
Wyatt, James, 180, 206, 269
Wyattville, Jeffrey, 46

Yeomans, David T., 23, 58, 59, 66, 82
Yeomanstown House, Co. Kildare, 156
York
    Assembly Rooms, 195
    York Minster, 81
Youghal, Co. Cork, 169, 212, 237
    Uniacke House, 130, 140, 155

Zierikzee (Holland), 146
Zimmermann, Domenicus, 240

fig. 69.
fig. 70.
A
fig. 71.
A
fig. 72.
A
B
B
B
fig. 73.
fig. 74.
fig. 75.
A
A
fig. 77.
fig. 76.
fig. 67.
fig. 66.
fig. 78.
fig. 68.
fig. 85.
fig. 83.
fig. 79.
fig. 81.
fig. 87.
fig. 84.
fig. 80.
fig. 82.
fig. 86.
fig. 88.
B
A
fig. 93.
fig. 89.
fig. 95.
B
A
fig. 91.
B
A
fig. 90.
fig. 97.
fig. 94.
fig. 99.
fig. 98.
fig. 96.
fig. 92.
fig. 100.
fig. 104.
fig. 102.
fig. 108.
B
A
fig. 106.
fig. 110.
fig. 109.
fig. 107.
fig. 105.
fig. 103.
fig. 101.